Up from the Ashes: Nation Building at Muckleshoot

Bruce E. Johansen with Willard Bill, Sr.

Welcome.

Up from the Ashes: Nation Building at Muckleshoot
By Bruce E. Johansen with Willard Bill, Sr.
Copyright © 2014 by The Muckleshoot Indian Tribe

Published by
Seattle Publishing, Inc.
68 S Washington St.
Seattle, WA 98168
www.seattlepublishing.com

    All right reserved. No part of this publication may be reproduced, distributed, or transmitted in any form or by any means, including photocopying, recording, or other electronic or mechanical methods, without the prior written permission of the Muckleshoot Indian Tribe except in the case of brief quotations embodied in critical reviews and certain other noncommercial uses permitted by copyright law. For permission requests, contact the Muckleshoot Indian Tribe.

    Every effort has been made to trace copyright holders. If any unintended omissions have been made, the authors would be pleased to add appropriate acknowledgements in future printings.

Ordering Information:
Quantity sales. Special discounts are available on quantity purchases by corporations, associations, and others. For details, contact:
Joseph Martin, Assistant Tribal Operations Manager for Education
Muckleshoot Indian Tribe
39015 — 172nd Ave SE
Auburn, WA 98092

Cover and interior design by Amy Beardemphl, Seattle Publishing, Inc.
Production by Seattle Publishing, Inc.

Front cover: Muckleshoot canoe Eagle Spirit on Elliott Bay near Seattle, Washington, Summer 2014. Photo by John Loftus, Muckleshoot Monthly

First Edition
Library of Congress Control Number: 2014951092

ISBN 978-0-9857764-1-1
Printed in the United States of America by BookPrinters Network

All that remained after the Community Hall burned was this river-rock fireplace, kept up today as a reminder of a tough past, and the long road back.
Photo by John Loftus, Muckleshoot Monthly

Table of Contents

Muckleshoot History Timeline vii

Introduction xv

Acknowledgments xxv

Chapter 1 The Muckleshoot Ancestors' Natural World 1

Chapter 2 Treaty-Making: A Foreign Concept 35

Chapter 3 Stirrings of Revival 61

Chapter 4 The Right to Fish 101

Chapter 5 Protecting Natural Bounty 131

Chapter 6 "This Casino Represents Hope" 147

Chapter 7 Nation-Building at Street Level 161

Chapter 8 Canoe Journeys and Cultural Revival 201

Chapter 9 Education and Self-Determination 217

Chapter 10 Muckleshoot Language Revival: Learning **bəqəlšuɬucid** ... 243

Selected Bibliography 255

Index 267

Muckleshoot History Timeline

c. 8,000 BCE: First peoples, including Muckleshoot ancestors, migrated to present-day Western Washington after ice sheets receded.

c. 3,700 BCE: The Osceola mudflow, a mixture of mud, rock debris, and melted glacial water, spread over the Enumclaw Plateau, a relatively flat area into which the White River later carved a valley, merging with the Green River to form the Duwamish River a mile northeast of present-day downtown Auburn, covering most previous evidence of habitation.

To approximately 1770 CE: Muckleshoot ancestors and other peoples built settlements thousands of years before contact with European explorers. They hunted, fished, and gathered sustenance in a broad area extending north to the vicinity of Whidbey Island, south to Olympia, west to the Kitsap Peninsula, and east across the Cascades. Local cultures were complex, including technologies of wood construction, basketry, weaving, hunting and gathering, exploration, a trade economy, and art and design, as well as popular and elite sports, highly developed oral traditions, including songs and histories, religious practice, and healing arts.

Tens of thousands of people spoke Lushootseed's many dialects during the 1770s. The language that remains today is less complex than its historical form. As populations declined due to imported disease, immigrant pressure, elimination of speakers through educational assimilation, alcoholism, and other reasons, Native societies' linguistic memory was reduced, restricting the language's vocabulary and grammatical complexity. The roughly 20 dialects of Lushootseed in historic time have been reduced to about 12 today, some of which are endangered, as old speakers pass away.

1770s–1840s: European and European-American explorers visited the area for trade and exploration, beginning with early Spanish exploration in 1774. Trade began, followed by immigration. Initially, many Native peoples welcomed the immigrants, believing that the land could provide for everyone. Before a flood of immigration provoked conflict over land and resources, relations between the Muckleshoots' ancestors and a small number of new neighbors were mainly peaceful. Only later did the Muckleshoots' ancestors and other Native peoples realize that the newcomers were arriving in large enough numbers to take their land and resources.

Native peoples of the Northwest Coast soon learned to associate the arrival of ships with deadly, previously unknown diseases. The ships were disease vectors from Europe. Within a century, and by the time European-Americans had crossed the Continental Divide carrying many of the same maladies from the east and south, epidemics of smallpox, several venereal diseases, measles, tuberculosis, influenza, whooping cough, dysentery, cholera, and "fever and ague" (probably a strain of malaria) wracked the coastal peoples from the present-day Alaska Panhandle to Northern California. Smallpox swept through Northwest peoples in 1779-1783, 1802, 1836-1840, 1852-1853, and 1860-1867.

1850s: Increasing immigration produced pressure to sign treaties with the expanding United States. Railroads also required that the government procure peace with Native peoples (as well as a supply of land they could sell to immigrants). The Native peoples who were required to give up nearly all of their territories insisted on important rights in treaty-making: the right to live on a homeland near traditional sources of food, and access to their familiar forms of economic support — fish and shellfish, hunting and gathering, with water access. Such language was used in two treaties covering ancestral peoples who later would be called Muckleshoot: the **Treaty of Medicine Creek** (10 Stat. 1132, signed 1854; ratified 1855) and the **Treaty of Point Elliott** (12 Stat. 927, signed 1855; ratified 1859).

1855: The Point Elliott treaty included three peoples who later came to be known as Muckleshoot: "Skope-ah-mish," from the Coast Salish word "Skop," meaning "first big, then little," a reference to the sudden rises and falls of the Green River from storm runoff, making them "the people of the variable stream," "Smal-ka-mish" (or "Smulkamish") meaning "people at the head of White River," and "St-ka-mish," "people of the White River." All of these names are listed in the preamble to the Treaty of Point Elliott.

1855–1856: Treaty War: During the fall of 1855, the Green and White river peoples joined with the Yakamas, Nisquallys, and Klickitats, all of whom believed they had not been adequately consulted in the treaty negotiations, in a brief uprising in and near the area that later would comprise the Muckleshoot reservation. Arthur C. Ballard called this uprising a "treaty war," because it was caused by "the haste with which the treaties were forced upon the Indians and the inadequacy of the reservations." The war included a brief attack on a new town to the north called The Battle of Seattle.

1856, August 4: Fox Island Conference: After the Treaty War, Isaac Stevens was forced to reconcile, resulting in a conference at Fox Island at which the first reservation on Muckleshoot Prairie was created. The Indians at the conference understood that Stevens had promised to set aside all of the land between the White and the Green rivers as a reservation. However, an executive order issued in 1857 gave them only the military reservation formerly called Fort Muckleshoot. The reservation later was enlarged.

1858, February 19: A Nisqually man named Leschi, a major leader in the Treaty War, after relentless pursuit was arrested, quickly convicted of murder, and hanged, over the objections of many white immigrants as well as his Native allies.

1860s: "Muckleshoot" was adopted as a popular term for an amalgamation of the three treaty tribes listed in the Point Elliott Treaty and other peoples in the area, creating legal confusion over treaty rights that lasted for more than a century, until the Boldt decision defined fishing rights (1974).

1860–1900: Immigrant population increases: After the U.S. Civil War, the coasts of North America were linked by rail, with a terminus in Seattle, as immigration soared. Non-Indians west of the Cascades in Washington Territory, fewer than 5,000 people in 1860, swelled to about 25,000 in 1880. By 1900, the number of non-Native people in the area rose to more than 100,000. Native people comprised about half the population in 1860; as immigration increased, their populations fell, mainly due to disease and alcoholism. By about 1900, whites outnumbered Native peoples in the area by about 20 to 1. The first non-Indians took land on the Muckleshoot reservation in 1868. Of the original 3,500 reservation acres, by 1968, a century later, about two-thirds had passed out of Native ownership.

1878: St. George's Indian School was endowed by Katharine Drexel, an heiress from Philadelphia, who also founded the Catholic religious order that constructed it as the first educational institution in or near the small town of Milton, near Tacoma, which was first called Mill Town, after its main industry. The school was built mainly to educate Native children in reading, writing, and agriculture, but non-Indian children also attended until shortly after 1900.

1880: The Chemawa Indian Training School opened on February 25, 1880, in Salem, Oregon, enrolling Muckleshoots as well as other Native children from Washington and Oregon. Chemawa was the second oldest "Indian industrial school" in the United States in what became a nationwide system (the first, in Carlisle, Pennsylvania, Col. William Henry Pratt's flagship, had opened a year earlier).

1890: Fishing sites closed: Washington became a state in 1889, and within a year legislators closed six rivers, all of them Indian fishing grounds, to salmon fishing.

c. 1900s–1960s: Intensifying poverty: The Muckleshoot and other Native communities were caught in a trap: so poor that they could not qualify for bank or federal loans that might aid economic recovery. Rural poverty was particularly severe because of isolation. There was no bus service to the reservation, which was detrimental to anyone seeking employment. Lack of bus service limited job seekers without cars to a very small number of opportunities. Muckleshoots also had few operating automobiles during this period. Therefore, jobs that required regular commuting were beyond reach. The reservation itself offered very few jobs.

Wage labor in timber and agriculture was used in addition to traditional subsistence cycles, including travel to pick hops in the Yakima Valley, combined with berry harvests, as well as hunting, while visiting relatives. Many men were highly valued as loggers and workers at local timber companies. Women spun wool and knitted socks that were sold at Eddie Bauer in Seattle. People worked very hard to survive with little or no money during the 1930s Depression era, as some returned to hunting, trapping, and gathering in the mountains for sustenance.

1900, 1917: Non-Indian fishing increases. The number of commercial salmon canneries in the Puget Sound area, one in 1890, rose to 19 in 1900, and 45 in 1917.

1910: The Indian Shaker Church was legally recognized by Washington State.

1910: Anthropologist Arthur C. Ballard (1875–1962) started to record Muckleshoot history and myths. Ballard compiled the most detailed descriptions of Muckleshoot life, transcribing their stories with a fidelity that is treasured by many of today's Muckleshoots. Ballard began interviewing Muckleshoots about 1910 or 1911. His work on Salish myths began about 1916.

1916, February 4: In *State v. Towessnute* (89 Wash. 478), the Washington State Supreme Court held that treaty Indians fishing at usual and accustomed places off-reservation were "subject to state fishing regulations in the same manner as everyone else." The court rejected Native American fishing rights with this rationale: "The premise of Indian sovereignty we reject … The Indian was a child, and a dangerous child, to be both protected and restrained … Neither Rome nor sagacious Britain ever dealt more liberally with their subject races than we with these savage tribes, whom it is generally tempting and always easy to destroy and whom we have so often permitted to squander vast areas of fertile land before our eyes."

1914–1930s: Fishing harvest declines: During 1914, in Washington State, about 16 million fish (mainly salmon) were caught annually. By the 1920s the annual catch had declined to an annual average of 6 million. In the late 1930s, following construction of several large hydroelectric dams on the Columbia River and its tributaries, the annual catch had fallen as low as 3 million.

1933, January 1: Several Muckleshoots founded the Nesika Club, "a women's club with the view of improving home conditions, encouraging more social life, and organizing clubs for the younger people."

1934, April 21: The Community Hall opened, providing a nucleus for events and planning.

1958: The Muckleshoot Preschool started, enrolling about 30 children a year who met in an old Government Services Administration building owned by the Auburn School District with donations from local churches and volunteer teachers.

1960s: Fishing-rights protests intensified, receiving copious publicity as Indians fished with celebrities such as actor Marlon Brando and comedian Dick Gregory, actress Jane Fonda, and Buffy Sainte-Marie, a popular Cree folk singer. The protests came to be called "fish-ins," a conscious reference to the black sit-ins at southern lunch counters during the civil-rights movement. **Protests intensified in the fall of 1965**, after John Cochran, a Pierce County (Tacoma) state judge issued an injunction against Indians fishing in any way, or at any place, not approved by the state's fisheries bureaucracy. Muckleshoots Stanley Moses and several members of his family including Cecil Moses, Ronald Moses, and Alan Moses, were among several who purposely provoked state agents into arresting them so they could take their challenge to affirm treaty rights to federal court.

1965: Muckleshoot, with about 300 enrolled members, **received one of the first two federal Head Start grants** for Native Americans. (The Navajo, the largest Native nation in the United States, was the other funded program.)

Late 1960s: "The VISTAs" came to Muckleshoot. Members of Volunteers in Service to America (a domestic version of the Peace Corps) were prominent as community organizers during the late 1960s. Many older Muckleshoots long remembered them fondly by their first names — Pat, Mike, Bobby, and George, among others. One of several projects that "the VISTAs" hatched at Muckleshoot was a newspaper called the *Muckleshoot News*, later the *Muckleshoot Messenger*. They sought a Muckleshoot editor, and recruited Marie Starr, who was still well known as a member of the Tribal Council in 2013.

1970: Muckleshoot tribal (common) land ownership declined to about one-quarter of an acre. At about the same time, unemployment reached 80 percent during many winters.

1970, April 25: The Community Hall burned to the ground in a blaze so intense that firefighters had little recourse but to watch. Thirty-six years and four days after it had opened, and shortly after it had been refurbished, the fire burned the only building the tribe owned, on the Muckleshoots' only common land. Fire spared only the building's river-rock fireplace and chimney, which is still visible (and carefully tended) today.

1970, September 9. The "Fishing Wars" peaked during a fish-in on the Puyallup River near Tacoma, as a multiethnic camp of about a hundred fishing-rights supporters standing vigil for an array of treaty Indians on the river was torn apart by roughly 300 police in riot gear who arrested about 60 people. Four shots were fired at the police, who then dispersed the crowd with a volley of their own fire and a haze of tear gas. A week before police leveled the Puyallup camp, the Muckleshoot Tribal Council had voted its support. This confrontation contributed to the filing of *United States v. Washington*, which produced the Boldt ruling (1974), by prompting the U.S. Justice Department to make the case a priority.

1974, February 12: U.S. District Court George H. Boldt issued a landmark fishing-rights ruling in *U.S. v. Washington*. The Muckleshoot fishing fleet was revived. Upheld by higher courts, Judge Boldt's ruling affirmed the treaty fishing peoples' assertions of their rights, fundamentally and explicitly. Documented with the research of Barbara Lane, an anthropologist, Boldt used an 1828 edition of *Webster's American Dictionary* for his contemporary definition of "in common with," as entitling Native people to as much as half the salmon catch running through their traditional waters before the treaties had been signed.

1979, July 2: The U.S. Supreme Court upheld the Boldt ruling. The high court initially declined to review *U.S. v. Washington*, but the Washington State Supreme Court ruled that the state had no right nor duty to uphold Boldt's ruling. State Attorney General Slade Gorton took that decision as license to ignore it, setting up a confrontation that caused Boldt to enforce the ruling, beginning August 31, 1977, using the U.S. Coast Guard and federal marshals under the jurisdiction of his Federal District Court in Tacoma.

1984-2001: The Muckleshoots steadily built a new school system, beginning with the opening of the first classrooms (kindergarten through fourth grade) in 1984-1985 in the old Muckleshoot Community Center ("The Center"). Fifth grade was added in 1985-1986, and one additional grade each year, to twelfth in 1992-1993. The first high school students, Ginger Allen and Matt Allen, graduated in June 2001.

1985: The Muckleshoots' tribal roll included 725 members, compared to about 300 two decades earlier.

1985: The Bingo Hall opened. The Muckleshoots' first foray into gaming opened to a capacity crowd (people were waiting in line at the door), but netted only about $1 million a year during its first decade of operation, a trickle compared to the needs on the impoverished reservation.

1989: The first modern canoe rendezvous, "The Paddle to Seattle" was held during the Washington State Centennial celebration in July, 1989. Native American peoples decided to revive a distinctive mode of transport — long-distance journeys by canoe — along with an entire associated culture. Tribal canoe journeys in two decades became a summertime staple for Native peoples as well as thousands of non-Indian tourists in Washington, Oregon, and British Columbia, with some participants arriving from as far away as Florida (Seminoles) and New Zealand (Maoris).

1994 to 2000: Muckleshoot landholdings increased. In 1994, a year before the Muckleshoot Casino opened, the tribe owned 800 acres in common. By 2000, the Muckleshoot government had acquired 1,692 acres of the reservation's original six square miles, up from a quarter acre 35 years earlier.

1994: The Muckleshoots were among the first eight Native nations and tribes to receive funds in the federal Administration for Native Americans' new **Native Language Preservation Program,** $373,253 over three years from the Department of Health and Human Services Administration for Native Americans.

1994, December 20: Shellfishing harvest rights were legally supported. Federal District Court Judge Edward Rafeedie issued a decision supporting Native shellfishing rights that was upheld on appeal in January, 1998. On April 5, 1999, the United States Supreme Court refused to hear the case, and thus let it stand. Judge Rafeedie ruled strongly in favor of the treaty signatories in terms similar to those that Judge Boldt had used for salmon 20 years earlier. Judge Rafeedie determined that Native peoples had reserved rights to as much as half of the shellfish harvest in their "usual and accustomed places," in common with other citizens.

1995, April 28: The Muckleshoot Casino opened in a large tent. The casino's permanent home opened formally September 8, 1995, with a prayer dedicating it to a better life for Muckleshoot children. After the casino opened, the Muckleshoot Tribe became the second largest employer in Auburn (after Boeing), with 900 jobs, plus another 160 outside city limits. The casino was expanded as employment increased during the next several years. **Muckleshoot leaders and elders held a retreat to decide how to use anticipated gambling profits.** The design that came out of this meeting directed the money toward education, jobs, and services that had been so notably absent during more than a century of government colonialism. "I feel like I've waited all my life for this," said Muckleshoot chairwoman Virginia Cross. "We are not rich, but we are no longer starving. To me and all Muckleshoots, this Casino represents hope." From the beginning, between 20 and 25 percent of casino profits were invested in education. The tribe also pledged to put one-eighth (12.5 percent) of casino profits into housing.

1997: A 16-officer Muckleshoot police department began operations.

2000: U.S. Senator Slade Gorton, longtime opponent of Native American fishing (and other treaty rights) was defeated for re-election as the Muckleshoots combined resources with Native peoples across the United States, as well as many non-Indian allies. Maria Cantwell beat Gorton by 2,229 votes, a fraction of one percent. The First American Education Project coordinated a $100,000 television advertising campaign against Gorton. In 1994, when Gorton had last run for office, the Native tribes and nations in his home state had had little money or political clout. Roughly $2 to $3 million worth of Native American money went into the campaign against Gorton, about half a million dollars of which was contributed by the Muckleshoots. In 1998, the Muckleshoots gave $100,000 to 112 candidates in federal and state political races, of whom 104 were elected.

2000: Muckleshoots' housing: The tribal government was engaged in several programs to make sure everyone who wanted land suitable for housing could have it. For example, land that was not suitable for housing could be swapped for areas on which houses could be safely constructed. The Muckleshoot Constitution enables the Council to provide land for members. This definition includes families who own land that is not adequate for their needs.

2002: The Muckleshoot Seafood Company was established, selling smoked salmon in gift boxes. A *New York Times* food critic noticed the Muckleshoot salmon when it arrived in New York City during 2002 as a delicacy selling at $19.99 a pound. By 2004, sales of Muckleshoot seafood had reached $1 million a year.

2002: The Muckleshoots purchased 157 acres under Emerald Downs racetrack, the largest horseracing establishment in the Pacific Northwest, and part of the tribe's ancestral homeland.

2003: The new 52,000-square-foot Philip Starr Building, housing administrative offices, opened.

2003, June 14: The 20,000-seat White River Amphitheatre, the largest outdoor concert venue in western Washington, opened with the Seattle-area band Heart on stage.

2005, June: The new Health and Wellness Center, on which planning had begun in 1998 and construction in 2003, was opened and called "a Muckleshoot gem" by the *Seattle Times*. Proceeds from the casino largely funded the $19.3-million, 95,000-square-foot facility and its annual operating costs.

2006: The Muckleshoots hosted the Tribal Canoe Journey.

2009: A 113,000-square-foot Muckleshoot Tribal School (kindergarten through 12th grade) opened. The Muckleshoot Early Childhood Education Center — the Birth to Three Program, Head Start (ages three through five), and Muckleshoot Child Care Development Fund — was added in its own 20,000-square-foot building in October, 2010, completing seamless pathways so students can always see the next classroom, on a 37-acre campus.

2010: Muckleshoots' tribal roll contained 2,200 members, triple the number in 1985. The tribe also had created 3,500 jobs; when a national housing depression hit the United States in 2008, the Muckleshoot tribe bought much of the property put up for sale in its vicinity, supporting the housing market in the Auburn area.

2011, June 21: First earth turned for construction of new elders' facility east of the Health and Wellness Center, which replaced a small seniors' center in one of the oldest buildings on the Muckleshoot government campus. The new Elders' Center **was blessed May 23, 2012**; during the second week of June, staff and seniors moved into it from the old center.

2012, March 3: Revival of smokehouse spirituality at Muckleshoot was celebrated when construction began of a new longhouse. People had been using the sla-hal shed for ceremonies, which was cramped and had a cement floor. The new 16,000-square-foot building, which accommodates 500 people, has an earthen floor and log beams 30 inches in diameter, 18 feet above the floor, peaking at 33 feet. It also contains two large fireplaces, a dining hall, a kitchen, and an outside cooking area designed for cooking seafood and game.

2013: The Muckleshoots' largest single land purchase of 96,307 acres for $313 million, in three counties. Most of the land, 86,501 acres (for $282 million), is in the Cascades (Pierce and King counties) north of Mount Rainier National Park along State Route 410, The remaining 9,806 acres of forest land ($32 million) lies within Lewis County southeast of the park. The land, purchased from investment manager Hancock Natural Resource Group of Boston, has historical and economic value as a "working forest" to the Muckleshoots.

Introduction

Maggie Daniels Barr (seated); Peter Lee Daniels, the little war dancer; Robert Redthunder the older war dancer; Jeanette Morrison behind Maggie Daniels Barr.
Photo courtesy of Muckleshoot Preservation Program Archives

I want to take a time machine back to 1970 and tell people what has happened since, and watch their jaws drop. I want to tell them about the Internet. I want them to know that the Berlin Wall has fallen, the Soviet Union no longer exists, Nelson Mandela has served two terms as president of South Africa before passing away, salsa outsells catsup, and — I choose my words carefully because the tribe doesn't like to brag — the Muckleshoots are doing very well.

The work that follows describes the remarkable story of the Muckleshoots, a small Western Washington indigenous nation of about 2,200 people, which within two generations has developed from grinding impoverishment, down to its last quarter-acre of common land, to a developing nation that provides scholarships for its young people and new houses for its elders. Energized by legal recognition of its treaty fishing rights during the 1970s and gaming (first bingo, then a casino) during the 1980s and the 1990s, the Muckleshoots, with business acumen and generosity (but without the sometimes deadly factional violence that has afflicted some other American Indian peoples in similar situations) have become the second largest employer in southern King County (behind the Boeing Company), meanwhile providing services and employment to a growing population.

My longtime co-author Roberto Maestas, whose political orientation usually did not lead him to religious figures of speech, referred to all of this as "the miracle at Muckleshoot." The situation at Muckleshoot is a singularly powerful example of a renaissance that has been taking place throughout Indian Country. I was with Roberto during October of 2009, beginning a history of El Centro de la Raza, when he asked me: "Have you been to Muckleshoot recently?" No, I hadn't, I replied, not since my days as a young reporter for the *Seattle Times* during the early 1970s. Driving southeast along State Highway 164, through thick woods, I had recalled shacks needing paint, cars needing windshields, and shuttered fireworks stands out of season.

"You *must* see what *los Indios* have done," he said to me. And so we went, to witness a 40-year revival. Roberto had become an ally of the Muckleshoots during the fish-war days, when he led Latinos lending aid to fishing-rights protesters against state raids. His elder

Introduction

2012 Virginia Cross birthday party and family reunion, group portrait.
Photo by John Loftus, Muckleshoot Monthly

daughter, Amalia, an attorney with the tribe, is married to Muckleshoot John Daniels, Jr., with four children. On that November afternoon, as we watched a skirt of snow descend over majestic Mount Rainier, Roberto squired me around, making introductions. A few months later, Roberto, talking with Council Chairwoman Virginia Cross, heard from her that Willard Bill, Sr. had left a Muckleshoot history partially written when he passed away late in 2007. He said something along the lines of "I know someone who can write a book," and the rest — as was so often the case with *mi gran amigo* Roberto — is history.

Taking my imaginary time machine back to 1970, how would I explain to people then what has happened since? In the case of the Muckleshoots, who would have guessed that the path out of poverty would involve a judge appointed by a Republican president, a bingo hall, a casino, and a lot of spirit, mixed with a great deal of business sagacity?

A STRUGGLE AT EVERY STEP

During their first century of contact with non-Indian immigrants, the Muckleshoots were forced to struggle for every scrap — a name, a place to live, access to the fish that had been their ancestors' main source of sustenance for thousands of years, continuation of culture, including their own language, religion, and an education compatible with their needs, along with economic infrastructure in which to carry on a decent life.

Following Judge George H. Boldt's recognition of their treaty fishing rights in *United States v. Washington* (1974) the Muckleshoots expanded tribal services, established more communications with federal and state agencies, and developed a much improved fishing fleet. The "Boldt decision" provided for off-reservation fishing in usual and accustomed places that had been recognized by the treaties but denied by the state, on pain of arrest and confiscation of boats and fishing gear.

As they developed their fishing fleet, the Muckleshoots also opened gambling venues that provided investment capital for a business park and a 20,000-seat outdoor concert venue. "We are ready to shake off the chains of second-class citizenry and, for the first time in 150 years, take our destiny into our own hands," Virginia Cross told the *Seattle Times* in 1995, the year the casino opened (Westneat, 1995).

In 2004, *Seattle Times* columnist Danny Westneat recalled:

> Nine years ago I stood outside a tent in a muddy field here as tribal leaders described how gambling would shoot them to the moon. They predicted that out of the tent — a temporary casino — would flow a stream of money unlike anything the destitute tribe had ever seen. They also pledged that while some may see the business as seedy, all the winnings would be put to virtuous use — for economic development, health and education. I was skeptical. I figured the casino also would bring greed and corruption. I guessed the Muckleshoots were like any bureaucracy: grand plans, but soon infighting and inefficiency would bog them down. Was I ever wrong.
>
> That day in 1995, they promised the reservation a new water and sewer system. It was installed a year later. They pledged to spend casino cash on children. In 2003, they opened a 45,000-square-foot child-care center. They talked of health care. A $19.3 million [Heath and Wellness Center] is rising in the reservation's center. They said they would diversify beyond gambling. They've opened a mini-mall and a $30 million amphitheater, and even branded fresh-caught salmon for sale at Safeway. And they vowed they would control their educational destinies by building their own schools, including a college.
>
> Today, down an unmarked road between Auburn and Enumclaw, crews are completing the $2 million Muckleshoot Tribal College. It opens next week. Paid for with Casino profits, it has six classrooms and two computer labs (Westneat, 2004).

Left to right, Gov. Christine Gregoire, Tribal Council member Virginia Cross, LaVonna WhiteEagle Brown, and Michelle Obama. *Photo courtesy of Muckleshoot Indian Tribe*

In 1995, as the casino opened, Muckleshoot leaders and elders held a retreat to decide how to use the anticipated gambling windfall. "We've stuck to it ever since," chairman John Daniels Jr. said in 2004 (Westneat, 2004). The design that came out of this meeting directed the money toward education, jobs, and services that had been so notably absent during more than a century of government colonialism.

This is a book about how the Muckleshoots have been rebuilding a nation from the ground up. The Muckleshoots quickly turned casino profits into seed capital for other businesses, land purchases, and services. They decided to plow their money into businesses and services that provided employment, initially giving no one the "per capita" payments that often were used (and sometimes squandered) by other Native nations with large gaming revenues. The idea is to build infrastructure and put people to work.

The Muckleshoots retained a real estate agent who located all local sales listings, buying houses, condominiums, apartments, old farms, and so forth. While the rest of the United States was suffering from a surplus of properties for sale in 2010, "For Sale" signs were very difficult to find in areas near the Muckleshoots' reservation.

A REMARKABLE RECOVERY

Twenty-five years ago, life for most Muckleshoots was very difficult, lacking decent housing and health care. Today, if a Muckleshoot is an elder (age 60 or older), the MIT (Muckleshoot Indian Tribe) will build a 1,800- to 2,500-square-foot new house (on the elder's land or a lot purchased by the government, for those without land) and hand the new owner the keys — a gift for enduring the lean years. For homebuyers who are under 60, a mortgage is available at 1 percent, with a generous grant for a down payment and repairs as needed. The loan program is a reaction to a time during the 2000–2005 period, before the national housing collapse, when Native people in the area were sucked into private mortgages on double-wide trailers that ballooned to 27 to 29 percent.

Full-ride scholarships are available for anyone who wants to go to college. The Muckleshoots have constructed new buildings for a Native-run school system (kindergarten through community college), for the children of people who endured government boarding schools. On a reservation with no government health services, a new Health and Wellness Center combines medical and dental services with athletic facilities such as basketball courts and a swimming pool.

Martin "Bear" Starr, Louis Starr, and George "Rabbit" Starr on the White River. Note the cedar canoe.
Photo courtesy of George & Leona Starr

Some of the new money has gone into basic infrastructure — a water-treatment plant, for example. For many years, local water, mainly from wells, was not exactly toxic (someone with a strong stomach could drink it), but raunchy. The problems with the water were demonstrated by the fact that the first time the swimming pool at the Health and Wellness Center was filled, the water turned black.

Money also has gone into an addiction-recovery center. A youth drop-in center was designed by the young people, with a recording studio and theater. Many of the walls in the drop-in center have been left in rough form for murals to come. Elsewhere on the reservation, people started a community garden in 2009, and a new fire station opened in 2011. Trucks haul firewood for families who need it (many use wood-burning stoves for heating). The Muckleshoot government also has aided the renovation of the reservation's three churches (Shaker, Pentecostal, and Catholic), regarding them as necessary infrastructure.

The Muckleshoots have been funding cultural revival as well, a major example being their role in the annual Tribal Canoe Journey, which started as the "Paddle to Seattle" in 1989. By 2010 the midsummer event involved "pullers" from about 60 Native tribes and nations in Washington, Oregon, British Columbia, and the Alaska Panhandle, as well as guests from afar (Seminoles came from Florida in 2010, along with a delegation from New Zealand). Native peoples and tourists gathered in the thousands to greet the pullers when they made landfall. The canoe journeys have

Introduction

Walter Echo Hawk speaking at Muckleshoot, 2012.
Photo by John Loftus, Muckleshoot Monthly

become a conduit for recovery of indigenous languages, as well as ceremonial drumming, singing, and display of regalia.

Walter Echo-Hawk, a founder of the Native American Rights Fund (NARF), who first worked with the Muckleshoots as a young lawyer, said during a visit to the Muckleshoot schools in 2012 that "In my mind, for a smaller tribe ... I've always looked at Muckleshoot as a model for nation-building. I think all of Indian Country can look to this reservation as a model for tribal development and to our national tribal leaders that come from here: Leo LaClair, who is a pioneer in the tribal sovereignty movement, Indian activism, from the very birth of the modern era of federal Indian law. And folks like Mr. Hoagie King George, and the late Levi Hamilton, and others that are no longer here and, of course, Virginia Cross, who is a widely regarded and widely respected tribal leader" ("Famed," 2012, 1).

A HISTORY BEGUN BY WILLARD BILL, SR.

This history was begun by Muckleshoot elder Willard Eugene Bill, Sr. who used education to free himself from childhood poverty and alcohol addiction. "He broke out of a lot of cycles that a lot of our people still live with," said his son, Willard Bill, Jr. (Heffter, 2008). "He really provided a good role model," said the junior Bill (Rolph, 2008). Bill, who was among Washington State's best known Native educators, died in the midst of his work on this history at age 69, December 26, 2007, at Swedish Medical Center in Seattle, following a three-year struggle with the progressive muscle disease polymyositis (Heffter, 2008).

Bill was a faculty member in the School of Education at the University of Washington, where he also served in the Office of Minority Affairs and Diversity. He was a co-founder of the United Indians of All Tribes Foundation and the Washington State Native American Higher Education Consortium. Bill taught at Skagit Valley Community College as well as North Seattle Community College. He served as director of Indian Education and Equity

Willard Bill, Sr. (right) and Willard Bill, Jr. (left).
Photo by John Loftus, Muckleshoot Monthly

Introduction

Education for the State of Washington and was also an active proponent of the Muckleshoot Tribal College.

Born in 1938, Bill was raised in Puyallup, southwest of Tacoma. He told a story about his mother Iola Lobehan Bill. For a number of years, a solitary man showed up on the road in front of Iola's house. He would wait patiently. He didn't walk up to the door, but stood on the road and looked at the house. At first the kids could not understand what he was doing. They learned later that some men made a circuit every year, and that they remembered which people provided them with food. While the kids called the man a bum and a tramp, Iola prepared him a sumptuous sandwich, and asked her children to deliver it. Iola was always welcoming to people in need and where the children saw "bums" she saw individuals who did not have anything and could use some help. She would help them in a respectful manner. Her attitude toward the down-and-out persisted throughout her life.

Bill's son, Will Jr., told a story passed to him by George Starr, a longtime Shaker minister from Muckleshoot. "I've known your dad since he was a boy," Starr told Will Bill, Jr. with a chuckle as he describing a young Willard at eight or nine years of age. When all the families were out picking in the fields, you could always find him off under a tree somewhere, "reading a *National Geographic* or an encyclopedia," Starr said ("Dr. Willard," 2008, 2).

The senior Willard grew to more than six feet tall and lettered in football and track at Puyallup High School. Following graduation and a stint in the Army, he married Mary Ann Hall of Tacoma.

The senior Bill earned teaching credentials at Central Washington University, where he also played football. He then taught at Auburn Cascade Junior High School during the

Iola Lobehan Bill.
Photo courtesy of Muckleshoot Preservation Program Archives

next decade, while also coaching football and track, as he worked on a master's degree at Pacific Lutheran University. Bill then completed a PhD at the University of Washington.

During ensuing years, Bill taught at the University of Washington, served as an administrator at Skagit Valley Junior College, and worked for the state of Washington in the State Legislature and the Superintendent of Public Instruction's state office. Bill also served as a dean at North Seattle Community College. He was an educational activist and a board member for several groups, including service as president of Seattle's Daybreak Star Center's board of directors. Phil Lane, Jr., who worked with Bill at United Indians of All Tribes, described him as "a professional and a gentleman who devoted his life to Native education because he understood the need for a curriculum with a native perspective" (Heffter, 2008).

A rare muscle disease robbed Bill of his mobility, but he continued to work on his computer from the basement office of his home in

Muckleshoot Skopabsh royalty for 2012-2013: Left to right: Little Miss Skopabsh Leeschelle Rojero, Kiya Sandy Heddrick, Junior Miss Skopabsh Lauryn Courville, Miss Skopabsh LaShawna Starr, Little Warrior Troy WhiteEagle and Warrior John Starr Jr.
Photo by John Loftus, Muckleshoot Monthly

Seattle's Northgate neighborhood, researching and writing. He completed a draft of the history shortly before the holidays in December of 2007, just before his health took a turn for the worse. A few weeks later, a copy of that draft was buried with him at the White Lake Cemetery, following a traditional Native American wake and a memorial service, December 5, 2007, at the University Presbyterian Church in Seattle, where he was a member.

Bill was survived by his wife of 47 years, Mary Ann Bill. They had four children: Willard Bill, Jr., Julie Bill Wonderling, Denise Bill, and Jennifer Bill Youngman. Three of the four children entered professional education in the Seattle area; Julie became a business professional.

"His entire career, he was very dedicated to the tribe and his people," said Will Bill, Jr. "I think the American Indian existence is a constant struggle for civil rights" (Rolph, 2008). Bill himself stressed the importance of protecting tribal land and intellectual property, as well as the need for greater Native American political representation. "We've got a big job to do in training our young people to keep going. They will be the leaders who would continue to work on these issues for their community" (Rolph, 2008).

Will Bill, Jr., who lives on the Muckleshoot reservation with his three children (Justice, Freedom, and Sovereign) has followed in his father's footsteps, working in Native American education since he graduated from Washington State University, where he was president of the Native American Association. After graduation, Will joined in a three-month run to honor all living things, from Fairbanks, Alaska, to Santa Fe, New Mexico, running about 50 miles a day, sleeping on the ground and spending time with Native peoples in Canada and the United States along the way, learning about their histories and current issues.

Returning to Seattle, he worked for the Seattle Thunderbird House, focusing on healthy living for Native American teens. Will completed his master's degree and teaching credentials at Antioch University. In 2012, he was enrolled at Seattle University, completing principal and administrator credentials while acting as dean of students for the Muckleshoot Tribal High School. He has taught school in Seattle and at the Muckleshoot Tribal College. Will served as an administrator for the Indian Education Program in Seattle for four years with 1,500 Native American students. He has also been very active in the Muckleshoot

Introduction

Canoe Family as a skipper, puller, and co-captain ("Willard Bill, Jr.," 2005, 10).

Willard Bill, Sr.'s daughter Denise also followed in his footsteps, completing a PhD in education at the U.W. in 2012, after she had earned a BA in education and teaching credentials, a master's degree, and principal and administrator credentials. "Our parents really taught us as children that we were going to go to college, she recalled. "That was automatic — you didn't even think about stopping after high school" ("Denise Bill," 2012, 1).

The title of Denise's dissertation was "Native Educational Leadership in the Pacific Northwest." Her work included videotaped interviews with her father and several other Native American educators: Dr. Bill Demmert, Honorary Dr. Cecelia Smith-Carpenter, Denny Hurtado, Jim Egawa, Colleen Almouella, Virginia Cross, Romayne Watt and Patricia (Patsy) Whitefoot.

"My father was always wonderful to me," Denise recalled. "He was a really good listener. He was funny. He was very kind to me and my children, and he was always a role model to me of what a Native man should be" ("Denise Bill," 2012, 1). Denise also worked as program manager and college instructor at the Muckleshoot Tribal College.

Father Will and his children reflect the determined Muckleshoot revival that unfolds in the following pages.

"Five Generations" Elma Lozier holds her great-great-granddaughter Daniella Lopez in this five generation photograph. Standing behind her are Daniella's mom, Nora Jerry, grandma Lana James, and great-grandma Jeannie Moses.
Photo by John Loftus, Muckleshoot Monthly

REFERENCES

"Denise Bill Earns UW Doctorate Degree." *Muckleshoot Monthly*, June 2012, 1.

"Dr. Willard Bill Blazed a Trail for Others to Follow in the Field of Education." *Muckleshoot Monthly*, February 2008, 2.

"Famed Treaty Rights Attorney Walter Echo-Hawk Visits MIT." *Muckleshoot Monthly*, November 2012, p. 1.

Heffter, Emily. "Willard Eugene Bill Sr., 69, was Influential Indian Educator; Served on UW [University of Washington] Faculty." *Seattle Times*, January 2, 2010. [http://seattletimes.nwsource.com/cgi-bin/PrintStory.pl?document_id=2004103445&zsection_id=2003925728&slug=billobit02m&date=20080102]

Rolph, Amy. "Willard Bill, 1938-2007: Tribal Historian Never Stopped Teaching." *Seattle Post-Intelligencer*, January 3, 2008. [http://www.seattlepi.com/local/345986_obitbill04.html]

Westneat, Danny. "Muckleshoot Tribe Rises from Ashes of 1970 Fire." *Seattle Times*, July 26, 1995. [http://community.seattletimes.nwsource.com/archive/?date=19950726&slug=2133476]

Westneat, Danny. "Tribe Made Its Gamble Pay Off." *Seattle Times*, September 10, 2004. [http://community.seattletimes.nwsource.com/archive/?date=20040910&slug=danny10]

"Willard Bill Jr. Appointed as Seattle School Director of Indian Education." *Muckleshoot Monthly*, September 15, 2005, 10.

Acknowledgements

No book is a singular effort. In this case, assembling the history of a people required a great deal of work, aid, understanding, and criticism from many people, among them:

All the members of the Muckleshoot Tribal Council and Executive Committee for Education for inviting me in to learn, and share, a truly amazing history.

Joseph Martin, Rebecca Gallogly, Rachel Heaton, and Faline Marsette in the Education Department, throughout more than four years of research, writing, and production. Their efforts have been crucial, and their companionship rewarding.

John Daniels, Jr., Amalia Maestas-Daniels, and their two, then three, then four children, for lodging me in their home, where we watched the rising sun paint the sky red, orange, and yellow above the Mother of All Waters, quite a treat for a person who spends most of his life in the topographically challenged state of Nebraska. John also provided invaluable help with history and manuscript criticism.

Virgil Spencer for use of Willard Bill, Sr.'s papers.

Donna Hogerhuis, for many archival prints, as well as leads to printed material, innumerable copies, as well as good advice. The book would not have its depth of detail without her work.

John Loftus, for the entire Muckleshoot Monthly's press run (which were well used in this work), plus Muckleshoot annual reports and other publications. He worked overtime to prepare the majority of the color photos, but he supplied much more than images.

Laura Murphy, Muckleshoot archaeologist, for information on the *really* old days.

Grant Timentwa, for U.S. Census data and maps.

Eileen Richardson for reading the language-revival chapter.

Marie Starr, for her astounding memory for people and places in old photos.

Mary Ann Bill (Willard Bill, Sr.'s widow), for additions and corrections pertaining to her family.

Roberto Maestas, who, as in so many other important junctures of my life took me to Muckleshoot in 2010 and opened my eyes. A few months before he passed over, *mi gran amigo* Roberto midwifed this project with Virginia Cross.

My sister, Linda C. Edgar, and her husband, Bryan C. Edgar, for many days and nights of *pro bono* room and board in their Federal Way, Washington home during my visits.

Archivists at the University of Washington Libraries, Seattle's Museum of History and Industry, the White River Valley Historical Museum, and the Washington State Historical Society, for providing aid locating some of the archival images.

The production crew: Jay Stilwell, Claire Bonin, Amy Beardemphl, Jill Von Buskirk, and everyone else at Seattle Publishing, as well as the printers, part of a proud renaissance in American manufacturing.

Thanks to all — and many others not mentioned here — for making this book a reality.

—Bruce E. Johansen
June, 2014

Chapter 1

The Muckleshoot Ancestors' Natural World

Chapter 1

The Muckleshoot Ancestors' Natural World

Mount Tahoma (Rainier), over the White River.
Photo by John Loftus, Muckleshoot Monthly

For several thousand years preceding immigration to Western Washington by European-Americans, indigenous peoples lived there in a density higher than "nearly anywhere else in native North America north of Mexico" (Lane, 1973a, 1). This population density was centered on the watercourses of the region, and was dependent on the skillful harvesting and use of available food resources, several species of salmon being the most important. The dense forests, with a few exceptions, were usually light on game animals (Lane, 1973a, 3).

Rain-washed, with lush forests and prairies, the Muckleshoot ancestors' homeland occupied a plateau overlooking the Green River

Valley, as well as the entire Duwamish and Upper Puyallup river drainages, under the broad-shouldered, glacier-mantled visage of 14,400-foot Mount Tahoma, whose Coast Salish name was replaced late in the eighteenth century by that of an admiral in the British Navy, Peter Rainier. The immigrants anglicized the sacred mountain's name for a city, Tacoma. The Native name for Mt. Rainier, Tahoma (and several variations), means "nourishing mother," and "mother of waters." The mountain hosts several glacial fields that feed five rivers. Some Native legends also have it giving birth to surrounding mountains, its brood. Mt. Baker is called "Kulshan," and Mt. Hood is "Wyeast" (Mt. Tacoma, 1906, 95).

The naming of the mountain has long been a source of controversy. During the early 1890s, as the federal government set aside 700,000 acres for a national park, the Tacoma Academy of Sciences commissioned a study of its name by a local probate judge, James Wickersham, which favored use of "Tacoma" or "Tahoma." The report cited several newspapers (including the *Washington Post*) that took the same position (Wickersham, 1893).

Wickersham, also an ethnologist who collected a large number of South Puget Sound baskets, played an important role in extending legal protection to the Shaker Church in 1910 (Brotherton, 2008, 95). The report was presented in the company of several Native leaders, as well as members of the Academy. The study mentioned that Rear Admiral Rainier had never even visited America, much less Puget Sound, and never laid eyes on the mountain now bearing his name. Rainier had even fought with the British in the American Revolution. His only qualification seemed to have been that he was a friend of George Vancouver, who commanded the first British ship to visit the area, and whose crew sighted the mountain. Neither Vancouver nor his crew sought any contact with local Native people, and, according to Wickersham, had "the greatest contempt for them" (1893, 7).

The mountain demands respect not only for its size and beauty, but also because it is an active volcano that could, should the Earth's mantle crack, change life immeasurably for the three million people who now live in the Puget Sound region. At mention of "The Mountain," nearly everyone knows exactly which one you mean. The land itself is a geologic reminder of The Mountain's explosive past. The area is covered with mudflows (lahars). Ash layers from the eruption and from other volcanic events in the Cascades help date archaeological sites in the ground because eruption dates are known.

For thousands of years, ancestors of today's Muckleshoot people traveled and utilized the natural resources of a broad area extending north to the vicinity of Whidbey Island, south to Olympia, west to the Kitsap Peninsula, and east across the Cascades. Muckleshoot ancestors hunted, fished, and gathered while traveling widely throughout this area and beyond.

The land, and especially the rivers and sea, provided abundant resources, but that didn't mean life was easy. People could not obtain everything they needed in a stroll around their villages. Native peoples had to work to maintain their lives. "This was not a 'lotus land,' in which the native fishermen in a few hours' time could obtain a year's supply of food for his family," wrote anthropologist Barbara Lane (1973a, 11). Muckleshoot ancestral Salish culture is based on more than woodworking and fishing. It includes technologies of construction, basketry, weaving, hunting, gathering, exploration, trade economy, gaming and horse racing, art and design, as well as popular and elite sports and highly developed oral traditions, including songs and histories, teaching stories, religious practice, and healing arts.

The myth of a hyper-abundant homeland was sometimes promoted by the encroaching Anglo-American state in its efforts to restrict Muckleshoot ancestors' (and other Native peoples') claims to land and resources. People traveled to get what they wanted and needed, especially once horses came into use. The Muckleshoots and other Native peoples maintained broad networks of trading and family relations, east and west of the Cascades. Some Muckleshoot ancestors rode as far east as present-day Walla Walla, in what is now far southeastern Washington. People intermarried widely. After Native peoples came under the control of Washington State and the United States federal government, their movements often confounded category-minded government agents who wanted to build fences around specific groups of Native people who, drawn to opportunity, had ignored imposed boundaries.

Muckleshoot ancestors have sometimes been represented only as upriver hunters and "horse Indians," people not acquainted or skilled with saltwater navigation and technology, and not saltwater fishers. This is inaccurate. They had mastered both ways of life. Trails led to summer camp sites on the shore of Puget Sound that were used for fishing, clam harvesting, and other procurement activities.

FIRST ARRIVALS

The ancestors of those who would come to be known as Muckleshoots arrived in their present-day homeland roughly 10,000 years ago, following the recession of ice sheets that carved out Puget Sound and local lakes. About 5,700 years ago, the Osceola mudflow — a mixture of mud, rock debris, and melted glacial water — spread over the Enumclaw Plateau, creating a relatively flat area into which the White River carved a valley, merging with the Green River a mile northeast of present-day downtown Auburn.

The Osceola mudflow was one of the largest volcanic mudflows known to geologists, having occurred on the largest mound of glacial ice in the continental United States. Mount Tahoma (Rainier) erupts rarely. More often, it ejects materials that buries surrounding areas. The Osceola covered much of the area, and thus has limited the variety and number of artifacts available for archaeologists. Where mudflows were shallow or didn't reach higher elevations, artifacts as old as 8,000 years have been found. (One site near Enumclaw produced artifacts that may be older than 8,000 years, but as of 2012 these were in private hands.) The most often used date of Native antiquity in the South Puget Sound area is about 7,600 to 8,000 years ago (Smith, 2006).

The Osceola was one of many similar mudflows; geologists have estimated that roughly 60 debris flows have altered the landscape during the last 10,000 years. Seven debris flows large enough to reach Puget Sound have taken place during the last 6,000 years (Tyler, 2002, 2). Two small eruptions were noted during early Anglo-American immigration to the area in the nineteenth century, while the last eruption that added new rock to the mountain's summit took place between 1,200 and 2,100 years ago (Tyler, 2002, 3). The Osceola mudflow itself "was a vast landslide that removed much of the summit of Mt. Rainier, perhaps 2,000 feet of it, leaving a summit crater. Subsequent volcanic eruptions created the modern summit cone with the crater" (Tyler, 2002, 4).

Speculation that human presence in this area reaches about 20,000 years presently exceeds available evidence. While archaeology is a dynamic science which extends its time lines into the past as new artifacts are found, sometimes turning yesterday's speculations into tomorrow's record, climatic conditions make human presence 20,000 years ago very unlikely. Greg C. Burtchard, Mt. Rainier National Park Archaeologist, explained:

> There is no indication of human use of Mount Rainier at 20,000 years ago. At that time, the region was still in the grips of late Pleistocene ice, and Mount Rainier would have for all practical purposes been uninhabitable. There is good reason to believe, however, that vegetated habitats were established to at least 5,400 feet on the slopes of the mountain by about 11,500 years ago (radiocarbon dated wood from a joint Mount Rainier-MIT archaeological project at Buck Lake, unpublished). Earliest definitively established use of that site presently stands at about 8,500 years ago. Though less definitive, there is some indication for use at 9,500 years as well. As a result, I now typically refer to earliest known use as beginning between 9,500 and 8,500 years ago. (Personally, I believe that 9,500 will prove to be correct, but I am being conservative at present.) (Burtchard, 2011; Burtchard, 2009, 3-44)

Native American Encampment, Auburn, c. 1900.
Photo courtesy of White River Valley Historical Museum / 00466

NOURISHMENT FROM THE NATURAL WORLD

The coastal region west of the Cascades has a mild, marine climate, with rare episodes of extreme heat or cold. While the Cascades and the Olympic Peninsula (including its western and southern slopes) receive heavy rain and snowfall in the late fall, winter, and early spring, the plateau on which many Muckleshoots live is partially sheltered by the Olympics, limiting rainfall to about 40 inches a year.

While some ethnologists have argued that Northwest Coast Native peoples reached cultural complexity mainly without agriculture, this is not completely true. The Muckleshoots practiced organized food cultivation in wild areas that is sometimes called

Chapter 1

A hop harvest.
Photo courtesy of Muckleshoot Preservation Program Archives

"intensification of food production" and "food processing for storage." Muckleshoot ancestors grew several plants, including root crops. Basket materials also were cultivated, and periodic burning was practiced to improve habitat. The fires created park-like prairie landscapes that were attractive to European-American immigrants. Areas were burned for berries and animal forage.

Nature provided raw materials for clothing, shelter, and tools, upon which a highly developed culture based on the technologies of woodworking and fishing thrived. Muckleshoot ancestors' traditional life was (and remains) rich in artistry with roots in both ceremony and everyday life, including fine basketry and artistic woodcarvings, while developing a social structure with a nobility, middle class, and a few slaves. The class system was complex, but not as strictly structured as societies further north. Hierarchies of expertise and knowledge also existed.

In *Notes on the Ethnology of the Indians of Puget Sound*, Thomas Talbot Waterman provides detailed descriptions of Puget Sound Native peoples' lifeways and technologies,

Two masterpiece baskets.
Photo courtesy of Muckleshoot Preservation Program Archives

from weaving of baskets (which he found to be of very high quality), to blankets, which could be woven of dog and goat wool, as well as that of sheep. Woodworkers also fashioned spoons, dishes, roasting skewers, mauls, adzes, spears, cradle boards, and canoe paddles, among many other things.

Waterman was especially fascinated by a type of South Puget Sound berry picker that was found nowhere else, and showed "a considerable measure of ingenuity" (Waterman, 1973, 53). An elderberry picker was fashioned "by taking a short wide piece of cedar wood and splitting it down from one end, into thin strips. Cedar bark fiber is wound tightly around the other end to keep the whole together. The sections or splints are then separated by driving wedges in, so they spread apart like the fingers of the hand. Their points are then sharpened" (Waterman, 1973, 53). This tool worked as a rake that could be built in a few minutes, allowing a picker to whip the elderberry bush, detaching the berries, but not twigs or leaves. A mat was placed under the bush to collect the fruits, which were then poured into a basket. A second type of berry picker was used for blueberries, which grow on a small bush close to the ground. This one, often made of cow horn, had shorter "fingers" that curved inward, following the contour of the bush, allowing for a quick and very efficient harvest (Waterman, 1973, 54).

Before the arrival of European-Americans, the Muckleshoots' ancestors maintained at least seventeen villages related by a common culture, some as far north as Lake Washington and Lake Union in present-day Seattle, and others on the site of present-day downtown Auburn, as well as along the Green and White rivers. These were winter villages, as distinct from the traditional summer encampments. Many villages contained extended families that lived in permanent locations and moved to temporary camps, usually in late spring, summer, and early fall, for fishing, hunting, and berry gathering. Summer encampments were revisited annually. Families maintained favorite places to secure food and meet up with relatives at "the summer place."

George Starr, Jiggs Star, and Louis Starr, Berry picking at Corral Pass.
Photo courtesy of Muckleshoot Preservation Program Archives

Puget Sound Native peoples affixed names to many thousands of places and geographical features, including many that remained anonymous to the immigrants. Believing that all things were alive, and that all living things are sacred, Natives had specific references for objects such as prominent rocks, promontories, prairies, and locations along watercourses. They had names for locations that often described physical attributes of a place, such as a spot where a river narrowed, names of rapids for fishing, and locations of prairies for hunting game, names that translated as such references as Dirty Face Hill, Wild-Potato Place, Where They Slide Planks Down from the Hillside, or Little Place Where One Crosses Over, and so forth. The Muckleshoot language was descriptive enough to guide people to certain locations, much as a street address in a city or town served the immigrants.

The Native names for places tell stories. The story of one site on the Green River between Auburn and Soos Creek, on the north bank, was related by Waterman: "Old George (Sla'xEb) was fishing here a few years ago. [He] caught so many kinds and colors of fish that he became frightened and stopped. The place was regarded for a time as supernatural" (Waterman, 2004, 156).

Waterman described hundreds of place names, including these two examples:

> Stca'gwabats: "Where a trail goes over a point and down the other side," for an old river channel below the Crisp place. A water monster, it is said, used to come up at night and call in this slough. (Waterman, 2004, 157)

> SkqE'bEd: "Where the trail descends," for an old village site on a level flat at the mouth of a creek. Here, the trail from the Muckleshoot plateau came down to the river. (Waterman, 2004, 157)

A WATER-CENTRIC PROPERTY SYSTEM

The Northwest Coast, an area of steep mountains cut by many streams and rivers, provided many peoples with basic sustenance from the water. Territories of tribes and bands often centered on watercourses, usually rivers; boundaries were not well defined, and fell along the highlands between drainage basins (Smith, 1940, 197–211). While among Europeans, territory (terra = Latin for "earth") is usually thought of as space between borders, a solid land area, or "land base," Northwest Coast peoples usually conceived occupied space as including bodies of water — the open ocean, rivers, lakes, sounds, inlets — that provided sustenance.

The most important parts of this space were usually those bordering the water (Lane, 1980, 4). Even the notions of "indoor" and "outdoor" are water-oriented in the Muckleshoots' language. Hess (1979, 375) wrote that houses were traditionally built fronting on the watercourse, so to go outside was to face the water. Barbara Lane wrote (1980, 79) that "Puget [Sound] Salish … like other Northwest Coast languages, reflects the conceptual focus … on waterways as the … center of their world." Stewardship rights and duties over areas that produced food resources (such as clam beds, reef-net locations, cranberry bogs, or camas beds, for example) were inherited. Major villages were constructed where canoes could come ashore. Land transportation through forests and mountains followed an established network of trails.

Some of the earliest maps of Washington Territory illustrated a similar pattern, with river courses plotted into counties, often with local, Native names (Clallam, Skagit, Whatcom, et al.). Treaty commissioners also recognized this pattern by selecting chiefs with whom to negotiate from areas defined by river drainages. Among Native peoples, according to anthropologist Barbara Lane, people were acutely conscious of a home "'land'" in the center of a river drainage; boundaries were not strictly set nor important. The focus was on the source of resources, and that was in or near the water. "Water courses were almost never boundaries … Territory was defined from the center outward," she wrote (Lane, 1980, 6, 7).

This pattern has been followed on the Muckleshoot reservation to the present day, where the White River is the social center of the reservation:

> ... The fall fishery for silver salmon provides an occasion for community gatherings at the river. Fishermen wade in the shallow waters of the White River to stretch nets. ... Other fishermen wait in the river to gaff the fish which escape the nets. Women wait at the banks of the river for the fish which they then prepare and preserve for winter stores ... by smoking, canning, or freezing. Fish are provided to older people in the community who are no longer able to fish for themselves. Children are taken to the river on these occasions to learn Indian ways by observing their parents and by listening to advice and stories from the elders. (Lane, 1980, 63-64)

In pre-contact times, a group that occupied a specific river drainage asserted ownership rights in a collective way. Rights of use and possession were exercised, but no one had a right of disposal (to buy and sell parts of the land) as in European real-estate law. Longhouses that were occupied by a large number of related families were said to be "owned" by the eldest or highest-ranking man in a community.

No one had a right to buy, sell, or give away a longhouse, or any part of one. The right to a space in a longhouse could be inherited or acquired through marriage. Similarly, a fish weir was a product of community effort, and was owned by the people who built it. However, a senior man who had supervised the weir's construction was said to "own" it. That meant that he coordinated maintenance. Individuals could own stations on the weir from which they dipped nets, and could allow use by other people when they were not fishing. Waterways were community property (Lane, 1980, 19-20). Families migrated in summer to places where they traditionally harvested camas, berries, and other items, using fields and forests where use rights were held by kinship or marriage. These movements often seemed random to the immigrants, but they weren't, even when families used different areas in subsequent years.

As would be expected in a water-centered view of the world, bathing was important for spiritual reasons (to make oneself acceptable to the powers), as well as for health, cleanliness, physical strength, and stamina. (This also held true in other Native cultures, including many in the northeastern United States, where they taught European immigrants the value of a daily bath.) River bathing could be combined with a sweat bath on the shore. Cedar branches and sand were sometimes used for scouring while bathing. Men and women bathed separately. Sea lettuce was used as sunburn lotion, rose hips eaten to sweeten breath, and the bedstraw plant used as a type of perfume.

Haeberlin and Gunther (1930, 68-74) wrote that in Puget Sound Native peoples' cosmology, powers that were believed to be most beneficial to human beings were associated with bodies of water. Puget Sound peoples often sent their children out in stormy weather (when water was falling from the sky) in the belief that spirits came to the surface and were easier to acquire at that time (Lane, 1980, 81). Spirits also could be obtained by diving into deep water. According to the cosmology, other spirits lived in canoes far at sea.

The spiritual nature of bathing was related to guardian-spirit relationships, as well as a sense of personal rigor and self-control, a toughening of body and character "amounting at times to asceticism" (Elmendorf, 1960, 428). Thus, young children might be toughened by bathing in cold salt or fresh water, to the point of a winter dunk in a river through a break in thin ice. Except when ill, adults continued such immersions throughout life, just as canoe families in our time sometimes take morning baths in the cold waters of Puget Sound.

HUNTING, FISHING, AND GATHERING

While the first peoples of this area also hunted land animals, the salmon were the dominant food source, and a very regular one, with an annual migration cycle. Five types of salmon are caught, in order of their runs: spring (*yo'batc*), humpback (*ha'do'*), silver (*skwa'xits*), dog (*L!xwai'*), and steelhead (*skwa'wiu'l*). Spring salmon were most highly prized. Smelt, herring, flounder, cod, halibut, trout, rock cod, and skate, seal, sea lion, sea otter, porpoise, and whale were also caught in large numbers during ancestral times. As today, shellfish were important to the diet — mussels, clams, oysters, barnacles, and crabs. When the tide is out, local people long have said, the table is set. In ancestral times, if barnacles were harvested often enough, they became large and juicy, and often were preferable to oysters. However, barnacles had to be taken from areas with swiftly running tides. Those harvested in stagnant water could be toxic (Haeberlin and Gunther, 1930, 21).

Salmon swam in huge numbers from their headwater spawning areas, downriver and through an intricate array of saltwater inlets to the open ocean. After a period at sea, sometimes several years, the red-fleshed fish reversed direction and returned through the Strait of Juan de Fuca and Puget Sound to the exact spots on the same rivers and streams

Basket fishing traps, probably in Auburn, c. 1923. Photo taken by Arthur C. Ballard.
Photo courtesy of White River Historical Museum / 00439

A Muckleshoot Smokehouse. Photo taken by Arthur C. Ballard.
Photo courtesy of National Anthropological Archives, Smithsonian Institute via Muckleshoot Preservation Program Archives (Public record)

where they had been born, to breed. These destinations once were free of pollution, roadways, and hydroelectric dams. Since those early days, the Muckleshoots and other fishing peoples have harvested salmon with nets and spears, preserving them by smoking and drying. Like other Native peoples in the area, the Muckleshoot ancestors traded salmon in dried form several hundred miles inland. Fish oil, kept in waterproof bags, was used as a flavoring, much as olive oil is used in cooking today.

Muckleshoot ancestors hunted elk, deer, cougar, bear, ducks, geese, swans, pigeons, grouse, beaver, mountain goat, wolf, beaver, mountain lion, mink, land otter, and waterfowl into and east of the Cascade mountains, and up the slopes of Mount Tahoma. Green River people were known as hunters and tanners of skins. Mountain goats were difficult to capture; consequently their horns, so difficult to obtain, were treasured highly. Horns were steamed soft and then bent to make bowls. Beaver teeth were used to carve designs into them. Mountain goats were caught with netted snares set on the rocky ridges of the mountains' lower slopes. The goats' wool was made into burial robes. Nets hung inches above water in foggy weather were used to catch ducks. The ducks could not see the nets, and consequently became snared.

Hunting required an eye to the weather and a sense of ready opportunity. South Sound Salish hunters would wait for heavy snow in the mountains and foothills to drive deer to lower elevations, often to Puget Sound beaches, where they could be surrounded and killed. If a deer was spotted swimming to an island in the Sound, "several canoes might put out in pursuit, the men pounding the animals across the head with their paddles to

Digging clams.
Photo courtesy of Muckleshoot Preservation Program Archives

kill it" (Smith, 1940, 269). Strong social sanction prevented hunters from wasting meat. A lone traveler who had to kill a deer because no smaller game was available would feel compelled to stop and camp for several days to prepare the meat for the journey (rendering and drying it) so that nothing useful would be left behind (Smith, 1940, 272).

The old ways persisted into recent generations of elders. Iola Bill, mother of Willard Bill, Sr., recounted camping during summer months when her family gathered roots and picked huckleberries. Berries could be mashed into cakes and dried in the sun or with fireside heat. These round berry cakes, called *tuckams*, could be stored for months, even years. The family hiked into the mountains and made camp for about two weeks. First, they trampled the grass in a circle. Ferns were used as mattresses. Children placed blankets or tarps on the ground and stamped them down with their feet. They then dug a trench around the camp, so that if it rained, the water would not run into their sleeping area. The site was maintained with an eye to passing game.

Fishing, hunting, and gathering activities shaped Salish definitions of time and names for seasons. The Muckleshoots and other South Puget Sound Salish peoples identified phases of the moon that they associated with the lowest tides, so that they could migrate to the shoreline at the time when the shellfish harvest would be best (Ballard, 1950, 80).

Other natural signals were also watched closely. In old times, the dogwood was used as a signal to begin the clam harvest. When the dogwood's blooms were at their brightest, the clams were at their best. People then would camp on beaches to make the most of the harvest, using special digging sticks, then steaming the clams, which had been removed from their shells, on the spot. Clams were smoked on open fires, placed between layers of sword ferns, stamped until flat, then transported to villages in large baskets. The clams kept so well that they were considered a sign of wealth (Caster, 2005, 21, citing Noel, *Muckleshoot Indian History*, 1980, 29).

Lunar cycles were identified with various activities in a natural cycle; age was often reckoned in passages of cold seasons. A person might be said to be "nine winters old" (Ballard, 1950, 79). Late summer and early autumn was marked by the return of several species of salmon (jack salmon, humpback salmon, dog salmon, and silver salmon), each in its own time, as well as the renewal of greenery after the drought of summer. A time in late summer to early autumn is observed as "time to dry salmon" (Ballard, 1950, 82).

December and the rest of winter have contradictory names. It can be a time of hunger for people whose food stores run short, or a time of indoor celebration for those who have put food away — "gaiety, singing, dancing, feasting, and exchange of visits" (Ballard, 1950, 96). Either way, days are short and rainstorms frequent. Late January is the time that ducks freeze in the ice. The first signs of spring, often late in February on the modern calendar, were "when the frog talks." This period may be followed by tempestuous storms in March that make water travel difficult — the time to put paddles away. By April, the earth is said to be "pregnant," as plant life returns. In the salt water, the porpoise gives birth. Summer comes with the ripening of several varieties of berries — yellow salmon berries, red elderberries, blackberries, and the salal berry (Ballard, 1950, 82).

FISHING CEREMONY AND TECHNOLOGY

The ceremony of the First Salmon has been practiced since antiquity, and continues today. Each year the first salmon to return from the saltwater sea to the freshwater streams of its origin — a Spring Chinook — is ceremonially captured as an honored guest. Its flesh is cooked, then meticulously removed from its bones and shared by all members of the community. Later, the skeleton of the salmon is carried back to the river at the head of a torch-bearing, singing, dancing, and chanting procession. It is placed in the water facing upstream to tell its brother and sister salmon of the fine hospitality received from the Muckleshoot people, so the fish will return ("Overview," n.d.).

Villages were constructed to maximize food gathering, often built adjacent to rivers where residents launched fishing expeditions when salmon started swimming upstream. Salmon harvesting techniques (sun-drying, wind-drying, and smoking) were well developed, and preservation technologies allowed year-round domestic use as well as wide-ranging inland trade, which involved not only food, but many necessities and luxuries of life not available locally. Peoples west of the Cascades traded salmon, dried clams, camas and other goods for sheep's wool, porcupine quills, embroidery, grass that could be used to make thread, and other things. Sometimes dried salmon from the Yakima Valley was sold westward across the Cascades to people who preferred its taste to their own from Puget Sound (Lane, 1973a, 11).

Muckleshoot ancestors became adept at fishing in a variety of settings because their livelihood depended on it. Muckleshoot territory provided many opportunities to fish in both fresh and salt water, in the upper Puyallup, Carbon, Stuck, White, Green, Cedar and Black rivers. Tributaries of these rivers included Soos Creek, Burns Creek, and Newaukum Creek. Lake Washington also was used extensively. Saltwater fishing took place in Puget Sound. In Coast Salish country, water contamination was not permitted when a salmon run was imminent — no food scraps

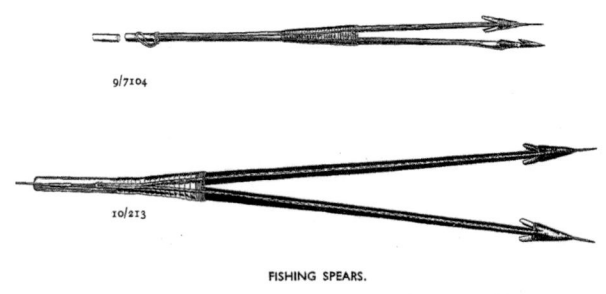

Drawings of fishing spears (with double points)
Photo courtesy of Waterman, T.T. Notes on the Ethnology of the Indians of Puget Sound. *Indian Notes and Monographs. Misc. Series No. 59. New York: Museum of the American Indian/Heye Foundation, 1973. Manuscript completed in 1921, but not published until 1973, plate XXXV. National Museum of the American Indian (Smithsonian): Public record.*

or other rubbish was allowed in a host river, canoes were not bailed out, and women in menstrual seclusion were not allowed to swim in the watercourse (Elmendorf, 1960, 62).

Spearfishing was common in both the Green and White rivers. A fisherman, standing in or near the water, watched for salmon or steelhead. Once a fish was spotted, he thrust a spear attached to a rope with maximum accuracy and speed. Spearfishing is much more demanding than using a net, and is practiced today as a sport. According to Ballard spearfishing was most effective in calm places where water pooled.

While spears were designed for fishing in river rapids where nets were useless, fish traps were designed to catch salmon early in their run upriver. Fishing devices were built and improved for thousands of years; fishing people used dip nets, set nets, and fish traps. Smaller nets were constructed for dipping out fish from traps. Bigger nets were used for dipping fish directly out of the water.

A salmon weir under construction. Photo taken by Arthur C. Ballard.
Photo courtesy of White River Historical Museum / 00139

One fish trap was called a "*Yidahd*," a grill-like structure that was placed atop narrow streams. Fishing people would scare fish downstream toward the trap, where the grill would "leave them floundering" (Ballard, 1951, 155). Ballard said he had never seen such a trap himself, but a Native person known to Ballard as Abb said one was used near the mouth of Neuwaukum Creek. He also said that white people had destroyed such traps.

The weir was called "*tsilósid*," and was used mainly from midsummer into autumn, for harvesting large fish, such as king salmon, silver salmon, and dog salmon (Ballard, 1951, 253-254). Weirs were constructed to block passage of fish in shallow areas of rivers, or to guide them into traps. The latticework was put up during fishing season and then taken down. Fishing nets and traps allowed capture of smaller fish than could be taken with spears. The fishing season began in the spring and continued through the fall, until people had enough to last the winter. If runs were sparse, they continued to fish into winter.

Arthur C. Ballard used interviews with several Muckleshoots to describe the construction and use of fish weirs with great precision (1957, 37-53), several decades after they were outlawed by state fish and game authorities during the 1890s. He noted that "in later years ... salmon weirs were set up at times and used surreptitiously" (Ballard, 1957, 37). These devices, also called "salmon traps," or "fish traps," used a tripod with legs of Douglas fir that imposed an obstacle in a stream or channel used by salmon migrating upstream, usually during the spring and fall runs.

The tripod's legs, roughly 30 feet in length, were lashed together with pliable cedar "withes." The tripod's legs were set in place by a team of fishermen, some swimming underwater, who communicated with each other as one man tapped on the tripod's legs with a stone (Ballard, 1957, 39). The weir was constructed with removable sections that allowed river-borne debris to be removed. The main working part of the weir was a net that formed the shape of a basket in the water, into which fish were guided, "loosely woven of cordages said to be from the bark of the pussy willow (*salix discolor*)" (Ballard, 1957, 39). After European-Americans arrived with trade goods, India hemp (imported from the United States east coast) was prized for its durability.

The weirs were so effective at harvesting fish that social pressure was brought to bear on families living downstream along the Green River to allow enough fish to escape so that their upstream neighbors could share the bounty. Ballard indicated that those who did not cooperate risked damage to their weirs inflicted by felled trees (Ballard, 1957, 44).

Other traps were also used, such as the "funnel snare," which was laid into riverbeds awaiting migrating steelhead. Ballard described one such snare that was about seven feet in length, "with a circular opening about eighteen inches in diameter at the entrance ... converging to a point at the lower end," woven of willow stems. Planks were placed at either side of the funnel to guide fish into it. A "grill" was used to catch steelhead and trout. The grill was about eight feet square, placed in a channel buttressed by dirt and gravel that led fish into a platform, where "they floundered about helplessly" (Ballard, 1957, 43).

Fishing was conducted primarily (but not solely) by men while women usually smoked, dried, and stored the catch. Once caught, fish were cooked quickly, usually on ironwood sticks set alongside or over an alderwood fire. Seawater or seaweed, with its salt content, served as a flavoring. Fish also were cleaned and then dried for several days, hung on racks in small smokehouses, where a continuous fire fed with sweet-smelling woods gave the cured fish a distinctive flavor that is still prized today. Shellfish also would be smoked, dried, and stored for trading. The cured fish were preserved through winter when fresh supplies were unavailable.

Upland hunting and gathering sites and river fishing weir sites close to winter villages were controlled by the local residents, although visitors would generally be permitted to use these resources. Marine fishing areas were freely shared among multiple groups. The marine fishery included an extensive shellfish harvest on the shores of Puget Sound, as well as trolling in saltwater for salmon, and the harvest of other species, such as porpoise. Hunting areas away from winter villages also often were communal. Marriages between people from different tribes led to sharing of resources. Saltwater fisheries and upland root and hunting grounds were shared, with exceptions at the river weir fisheries where intensive labor established priority of use.

The ancestors of the Muckleshoots and other fishing peoples also preserved the runs by keeping only the smaller fish so that the

Indian hop pickers in White River Valley.
Photo courtesy of University of Washington Libraries, Special Collection A. Curtis / 100441

larger ones could spawn upstream. This sort of rough genetic selection contributed to an increase, over time, in the size and weight of salmon, some of which could reach roughly 100 pounds. Even after contact, a 30-pound fish was not unusual. On one occasion, an elderly Louis Starr, who was born at Muckleshoot September 6, 1898, recalled having hooked a salmon that was so big it "literally pulled him out of his dugout canoe" (Tollefson, 1993, 13). Once non-Indians in fishing boats began to snatch the biggest fish at sea, before they returned to spawning streams, this system no longer worked.

With fish so large, and skills honed by years of practice, spearfishing was more efficient than it might seem to later generations accustomed to devices, such as nets, weirs, and fish wheels, that caught fish en masse. A traditional fishing spear usually was 14 to 16 feet long, with removable barbed harpoon points so that "a harpooned fish could be played and pulled ashore or into a canoe. ... once a fish was speared it was seldom lost" (Tollefson, 1993, 14). The harpoon's head was fastened to the shaft with a cord made of Indian hemp or dogbane, obtained in trade from peoples east of the Cascades, which was said to be more durable than rope. Nettles were used for nets, but this material was not as durable (nor as valuable) as hemp or dogbane.

PRODUCTS OF THE SOIL AND FORESTS

Muckleshoot soil is black, deep, and productive to this day. Muckleshoot ancestors maintained their prairies by regular burning

Chapter 1

to remove trees and create forage for elk, deer and horses, removing underbrush that inhibited hunting. Periodic burning also increased production of salmonberries, huckleberries, raspberries, soapberries, roots and other berries, as well as other plants that were used as medicine, such as camas, a medicinal perennial herb native to the Pacific Northwest.

Deer and elk jerky was dried in strips. Huckleberries were dried in the sun on mats, or in a firepit to keep bugs away. Camas also was baked in pits, then dried and sometimes pounded into powder for later use. Other prairie resources included skunk cabbage root, acorns, and hazelnuts. Cranberries were harvested from bogs dug by beavers; strawberries were gathered. Some European-American immigrants were surprised to find Native people growing relatively large crops of potatoes when they arrived. They may have reached the area from aboriginal people to the south, or from the Hudson's Bay Company.

Other vegetable roots or bulbs such as salmonberry sprouts, bitter roots, wapato, tiger lily, and fern were dug between early spring and late fall. During the summer and fall, berries such as red and blue elderberries, blackberries, salal berries, huckleberries, prairie berries, cranberries, wild strawberries, thimbleberries, and blackcaps were available. Huckleberry leaves were dried for tea.

The area has thick forests of fir and pine — Douglas fir, spruce, red cedar, yellow cedar, hemlock, and pine. Broadleaf trees mix at lower elevations, including maple, oak, dogwood, alder, aspen, birch, and madrona. Cedar is important in traditional Muckleshoot culture, providing longhouses, clothing, eating utensils, and canoes. Red cedar splits easily for planks. Soft yellow cedar and alder, which do not split easily, are better for bowls and dishes. Yew is flexible, and good for bows and spears.

The herbs of the forest shaped Muckleshoots' healing practices. Later, some of these practices were adopted by non-Indian naturopaths. For example, the bark of cascara trees, which grew throughout the Pacific Northwest, was used as a laxative. Muckleshoots and Puyallups harvested cascara, dried it in the sun, and sold it to pharmacies.

Marian W. Smith, who wrote the most complete ethnography of the region, described the use of herbs and other naturally provided substances to deal with physical ailments (1940, 90-99). Smith. In her preface to *The Puyallup-Nisqually*, Smith defined her work as

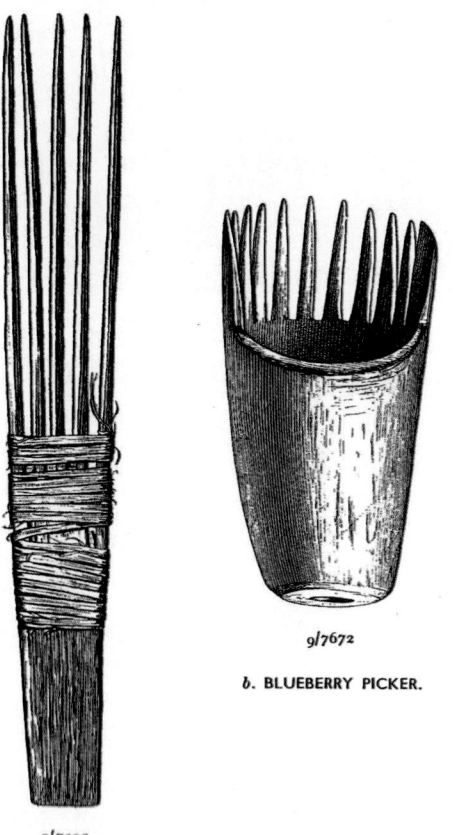

9/7672
b. BLUEBERRY PICKER.

9/7295
a. CEDAR WOOD BERRY PICKER.

Drawings of cedar wood berry picker and blueberry picker. *Photo courtesy of Waterman, T.T.* Notes on the Ethnology of the Indians of Puget Sound. *Indian Notes and Monographs. Misc. Series No. 59. New York: Museum of the American Indian/Heye Foundation, 1973. Manuscript completed in 1921, but not published until 1973, plate XXXIV. National Museum of the American Indian (Smithsonian): Public record.*

Muckleshoot tribal member Mary Dominick is seated on the ground working a sheep hide to remove the wool. c. 1900.
Photo courtesy of White River Valley Historical Museum / 00444

"applied to all Coast Salish of Southern Puget Sound" (1940, xi). The fieldwork was done in 1935 and 1936, with the cooperation of some well-known anthropologists, including Ruth Benedict, Franz Boas, Erna Gunther, and Arthur C. Ballard. The work was funded by the Columbia University Council for Research in the Social Sciences and the Columbia University Anthropology Department, and published in 1940 by the Columbia University Press.

Hundreds of such remedies were used by the South Sound Salish, according to Smith. A few included use of a willow bark poultice which, heated and applied to a wound, would stanch bleeding from a wound and cleanse it (90-91). A tea of wild cherry bark was used to treat internal injuries (91). Baked skunk cabbage root was heated and used to draw out infections and poisons. The tea of the salal berry was good for coughs, and nettlebark tea could blunt the symptoms of the common cold, as could tea brewed from cedar tips (91).

Ezra Meeker, an early European-American immigrant to the area, admired the Muckleshoot ancestors' food crops — dried camas and sunflower roots, he said, were very nutritious and quite tasty. He also wrote approvingly of a berry, "kinnikinnick," or Indian tobacco, that was dried, roasted, and smoked, mixed half-and-half with tobacco, "when it makes very fine smoking ... fragrant and very acceptable, [with an effect] like opium or ether. Some Indians I have seen using it would keel over in a trance." Kinnikinnick could also be eaten mixed with dried salmon eggs (Meeker, 1905, 174-175).

CLOTHING

Puget Sound Native clothing was designed to compensate for rain and moisture.

Capes were made from shredded cedar bark and nettle-cord twining. Clothing made from cattails was also efficient at shedding moisture. Cedar clothing was functional, acclimated to surroundings, and designed to clothe the wearer for many years. The bark was stripped into long sections and pounded soft.

Cindi Butler weaving.
Photo by John Loftus, Muckleshoot Monthly

Granddaughter of Muckleshoot Anne Jack wearing skirt and cape of cedar bark, effective in shedding rain, made of maple bark overlapped with bear grass. The Girl is Minnie Lobehan, sister of Iola Bill, 1910.
Photo courtesy of National Anthropological Archives, Smithsonian Institute / 79-4346

Cone-shaped hats with a narrow top and wide brim repelled rain and carried the water away from the head. Shirts and other garments were also made from pounded cedar. Bark was even used for diapers. The making of hats and other clothing from cedar bark has been revived in recent years, with a new wave of interest in canoe journeys.

Considerable work was required to weave a cedar cape, to make a blanket from the wool of a dog or a goat, or to tan hides. Old-man's-beard moss, which was disposable, was used for diapering babies. Variations on capes were used for fishing and hunting. Fishermen wore very little clothing; working in the water, clothing inhibited motion. Women wore capes for work or special occasions. Utilitarian moccasins were used for travel over rough rocks and terrain.

Wayne Suttles and Barbara Lane, prominent ethnologists in the region, wrote that during warm weather Coast Salish people wore minimal clothing; before Europeans arrived with their sense of shame at showing genitalia, men sometimes wore cedar-bark or animal hide breechcloths, or, knowing no shame of being ejected from the Garden of Eden, went naked in public (Suttles and Lane, 1990, 492). Women wore aprons or skirts of cedar bark. Animal fur was used for warmth, with mountain beaver fur for babies. Wool trade blankets had been available for decades by treaty times. For colder weather and ceremonial occasions, the skins of several animals were fashioned into robes for Puget Sound Salish peoples of both genders. According to an account in the *Handbook of North American Indians*, by Suttles and Lane, "Bear skins with the fur intact were made into robes. Skins of beavers, raccoons, mountain beavers, sea otters ... and even of birds were sewed together into robes." (Suttles and Lane, 1990, 491).

Lane's work was important in establishing the Muckleshoots' *bona fides* as a treaty tribe (see Chapter 4, "The Right to Fish"). Suttles, who edited the Northwest Coast volume of the Smithsonian's *Handbook of North American Indians*, was the first anthropology PhD from the University of Washington, earning the degree in 1952. He died at age 87, May 9, 2005. Suttles was widely respected by the Native people about whom he wrote, and was invited to potlatches from which all other whites had been excluded. He often served as an expert witness in court cases defending Native rights (Walker, 2005, n.p.).

Suttles and Lane wrote that animal and bird skins were used to make caps worn during winter. Coastal peoples usually held their hair in place with a headband of fur, wool or cedar bark. Hair was washed in a combination of plants to keep it healthy. Polished wooden combs about four inches wide with teeth two to three inches long were also used. Men and women wore dentalia and abalone shell earrings. Some people, usually the more affluent, also pierced the septa of their noses and inserted abalone ornaments (Suttles and Lane, 1990, 493).

A WORLD OF WOODWORKING

The Muckleshoots' ancestors became expert woodworkers, creating many functional items for the home, such as trays which were similar in design to a very small shovel-nose canoe; individual trays were about one foot long. Larger ones, three to four feet, were used to serve food during ceremonies. Wealthier people had polished, decorated bowls, some containing designs of shells or sea otter teeth on their edges. Yew, alder, or maple knots were used for making bowls that held fish oil. Spoons and wooden ladles used for serving food were also carved. Cedar, a very versatile straight-grained wood that has become relatively scarce and expensive today, was central to Muckleshoot traditional woodworking culture. Children were introduced to the characteristics of cedar because their futures depended on knowing its use.

Before contact with manufactured items imported by people of European descent, all Muckleshoot ancestors' tools were made by hand. Sharp-edged stones were used for scraping, cutting, and chipping. Rock, bone, or animal horns were used as wedges and adzes. Cedar bark made good twine and pine-tree pitch was used as a glue or sealer. Yew and vine maple were used for the tools that required durability. A variety of woods were used to make tool handles, wedges, bows, canoe paddles and eating utensils. Digging sticks pointed at one end to which a horn or antler was attached, also were created from many types of wood.

Cedar logs could be split with wood, stone, bone, or horn. Hammers of stone were used to drive wedges into wood. Adzes with stone blades and wooden handles wrapped in twine were made of wild cherry bark or cedar bark twine. Shells were sharpened and set in wooden handles for carving. Drills were fashioned with sharpened edges that included sharp pieces of stone attached to a stick. Wet sand, sandstone rocks and sand-coated string were used in carving and shaping stone, bone, and horn.

Chapter 1

Young Doctor carving a canoe at Neah Bay, July 27, 1914.
Photo courtesy of Museum of History & Industry, Seattle / SHS4781

THE CREATION OF CANOES

Canoes, which may be the oldest form of water transportation in the world, were central to Coast Salish cultures. Historically canoes were made for many reasons, including use in ceremonies, as gifts, and for warfare, transportation, trade, hunting and fishing. Puget Sound Native peoples have probably been using canoes in some form for at least about 8,000 years. Coast Salish canoes have ranged in size from 10 to 50 feet in length, the longest capable of carrying 8,000 to 10,000 pounds, 20 to 30 people plus cargo. Most canoes averaged 32 to 35 feet.

Seagoing canoes were built with "the lines of the hull ... designed with the idea of enabling the craft to ride waves without shipping [taking] water," wrote T. T. Waterman and Geraldine Coffin. "Every inch ... is carefully calculated to keep it 'dry.' No better craft for rough water, by the way, has ever been devised. The canoe rides the corners [waves breaking near a shoreline] better than the white man's boat. This was noted by Lewis and Clark more than a hundred years ago" (Waterman and Coffin, 1920, 11-12).

The Muckleshoot ancestors routinely used their canoes on rivers and throughout much of Puget Sound. A portage existed between Lake Washington and Shilshole or Salmon Bay (the present-day location of the Lake Washington Ship Canal and Ballard Locks). Historical references to the "passing-over place" actually meant the "little crossing-over place," a village site on Elliott Bay in the vicinity of the present King Street Station in downtown Seattle, once the site of a lagoon.

As with many maritime peoples around the world, seaborne transport framed culture, and invoked deep spiritual beliefs, in life and in death. Canoes were sometimes used as coffins on a journey to the spirit world. Some Native peoples burned important items of wealth after the death of an owner, including canoes. Some people were cremated in their canoes as a sign of respect. Non-Indians during the nineteenth century put increasing pressure on Native peoples to abandon such cultural practices because they were deemed pagan. The spiritual aspects of canoe culture have been described precisely by Will Sarvis (2003, 74-80). Will Sarvis' article in *The Journal of the West* also contributes a detailed bibliography of printed materials on Coast Salish canoe culture.

The master artistic achievement of traditional Muckleshoot woodworking was the construction, entirely by hand, of a red cedar or spruce canoe. Often canoe-makers specialized in the craft for their entire adult lives. Some families passed canoe-making skills through generations. Historically, canoe-makers were

"Evening on Puget Sound."
Photo courtesy of Edward Sheriff Curtis, 1913 (Public record)

invariably male. Today, some canoes are carved by women.

The canoe-maker possesses a special gift. The building of a canoe is a deeply spiritual undertaking from its very beginning. The carver is under the aegis of a guardian spirit acquired from an ancestor (or from a solitary vision quest). A canoe-maker must possess the proper *Tomanamus* (spirit) for the task. Philip Starr once told his son-in-law, Dave Siddle (who had married Louise Starr about 1917), that he was lacking the *Tomanamus* necessary to launch a canoe. When he launched it anyway, Starr said that a salmon would jump out of the water into his canoe. After a salmon did just that, Siddle thought twice when Starr gave him advice (Noel and Cross, 1980, 39).

A family might own several canoes for different purposes. They were used as automobiles are today, many people had them. Muckleshoot ancestors also had specialized craft for dolphin hunting, an elite sport requiring a pilot. Canoes were created in several shapes and sizes by function. War canoes, rare in Muckleshoot country, were large, ocean-going craft with lofty bows and sterns, and very sharply inclined sides for rough seas in the open ocean. A freight canoe was made to carry large loads, with a square bow that resembled an open mouth. A fishing or trolling canoe had a narrow hull suitable for accurate thrust of a harpoon.

The shovel-nose canoe was best used on rivers or quiet waters. This design had a hull with a forward scoop, like a shovel, which provided a place for a spearfisher to stand. According to Waterman and Coffin. "In spearing salmon in the streams … a spearman can ride on the extreme tip of the bow and strike fish almost under his feet, while a companion paddles" (Waterman and Coffin, 1920, 12). With little draft and no projection underwater, a shovel-nose canoe was ideal for shallow, confined waters, as well as waterways clogged with logs or other debris. They could be poled or paddled, and handled well in the swift-flowing waters common in the local rivers after heavy rains. They could hit logs or rocks and sustain little or no damage. A shovel-nose canoe could be hauled into and out of water easily, as well as around obstructions such as log jams (Lane, 1980, 53).

One-person canoes were also used for fishing. Children had small ones to allow them to practice (Noel and Cross, 1980, 41). These canoes have identical bows and sterns, and are well suited for sliding over sandbars. They may also be poled or pushed through streams. The ends of such a canoe were cut straight across, carved or built with platforms on which a man

Salish carver (left) and basket weaver.
Photo courtesy of Muckleshoot Preservation Program Archives

could stand to spear fish, looking straight into the water, while another paddled in the middle.

Canoes were carefully carved from cedar or spruce logs of the desired size. Once located, a log was dragged to a watercourse and floated downriver to a village, where it was split in half. Its center was then carved out. Mauls, wedges, adzes, and fire were used to hollow out the interior. Sometimes the center of the log was charred with fire and then gouged out; thus the term "dug-out canoe." Bark was stripped, and sometimes the wood's surface was charred and rubbed with fish oil to smooth it.

The canoe had to be curved to allow it to flow easily through water. Thickness of the canoe was critical and holes were drilled periodically to measure it. Later, these holes were filled. An effort was made to make the wood pliable by charring the inside and steaming the outside until the wood became easier to work. This is delicate work because a log will split if not carved carefully. Today most of the carving is done with power tools, but traditional hand tools are used for final shaping and smoothing.

Yew wood was placed between the sides of the canoe to make it wider in the middle and narrower at the ends. The yew wood was placed between the gunwales, like seats, so they kept the side bulging. The canoe then was allowed to dry in a curved shape. Cedar was used to fasten seats to the interior sides.

Eliza Sam with baskets. Photo taken by Arthur C. Ballard.
Photo courtesy of National Anthropological Archives, Smithsonian Institute via Muckleshoot Preservation Program Archives (Public record)

Canoe-makers used a combination oil paint by mixing red ochre with fish or seal oil. Modern paint is mixed with linseed oil. The exterior was charred to take off the roughness, which made the outside black. Sharkskin was used to polish the canoe and paddles.

BASKET-MAKING

Muckleshoot baskets were designed with function in mind; they were used for gathering food, cooking, storing and packing, tightly woven to retain or repel water. Like many other objects used in Muckleshoot daily life, the baskets also express a sense of high art. Basket-making required many months of advance planning. Baskets were primarily made in the winter months when women could sit for long periods of time surrounded by materials. Half the work of weaving baskets was preparing materials. Roots and limbs of young cedars were peeled and split into strands as wire. Coastal women used roots of the spruce tree. Work that required a coarser finish was accomplished by making strips the size of tape. They sometimes dried cattails and rushes. As with baskets, fishing nets also were woven by people who specialized in them. After contact, Indian hemp imported from the United States east coast was a prized material for nets.

Women made string that was used for containers, tying bundles and making mats. Nettle fiber made the best string. Nettles grow best in damp places. During autumn, women gathered large numbers of nettles with their four-sided stems. Stems were split into strips and hung up to dry. Outside fibers were pulled away from the soft, sponge-like center. Then they were laid on a mat, beaten, and combed over with a mussel shell or the rib bone of a bear. Fibers were also soaked to make them flexible.

When time for weaving arrived, the roots were taken down and soaked to make them easier to manipulate. Outer bark was removed by pulling the root through a split stick. The next shiny layer was removed, rolled, and saved for sewing material. Holes were punched with a bone awl. Decorative exterior material was added on top of the basket. Colored strips such as grass dyed yellow with Oregon grape root, or plain white grass, wild potato roots or black coil were woven with a passing stitch: before another stitch was added, the colored piece was bent forward to cover the last stitch and doubled backward on itself, so that the color showed, but the stitches did not.

MUCKLESHOOT SETTLEMENTS AND SOCIAL STRUCTURE

Muckleshoot ancestors usually lived in small groups, although some longhouses stood alone. The largest group settlement (their language contained no word for "village," but did refer to groups of houses) was Ilalko, which consisted of 16 or 17 longhouses. Other ancestral villages included Flea and Stkamish. The house, not the village, was a basic unit of social organization. Location was key — a site with access to water, convenient for storing canoes, in areas that provided fish (usually salmon) and shellfish. An average-sized longhouse contained four or five nuclear families, perhaps 20 to 30 people. The Muckleshoots did not erect totem poles outside their longhouses. Non-Indian immigrants realized the importance of longhouses, and sometimes burned them to force Muckleshoots and other Salish off land that they coveted.

The band (usually the extended family in a longhouse) was the basic kinship group. Unlike many eastern Native peoples, the Muckleshoots had no clans. The extended family organized the acquisition of food. People lived in

Minnie Lobehan, with baskets.
Scanned images from the Arthur Ballard Photograph Collection, Muckleshoot Preservation Program Archives. Original photographs can be found at the National Anthropological Archives, Smithsonian Institute (Public record).

longhouses and ate mainly off stored food in the winter, then moved to temporary camps close to fishing sites and other food sources in summer. Kin groups intermarried (sometimes over rather large distances, often east of the Cascades), forging alliances. Whites often associated the Muckleshoot ancestors with "Klickitats," a term often misused to describe Sahaptin speakers. The Muckleshoot ancestors and their neighbors were so mixed with others from the eastern side of the Cascades that Ballard called them a "two-language people," South Sound Salish and Klickitat, "a hybrid culture" (Watson, 1999, 35). Considerable mixing also included many downriver peoples from the Duwamish drainage.

A winter village had no "head chief" or "tribal council," a fact that confused Anglo-American treaty-makers who sought influential people (men, usually) with whom to negotiate. Leadership and authority was usually "task-oriented, with the appropriate specialist taking over leadership according to the occasion," such as a hunting party, a communal fish drive, a raiding party, or a ceremony

(Lane, 1973b, 8). This mix of authority took place within a society that was generally hierarchal, with an upper class, commoners, and a few slaves (Lane, 1973b, 8).

"There was practically no inherited social stratification," Marian Smith wrote in *The Puyallup-Nisqually* (1940, 34). Social stratification did exist, however, based on "status … achieved rather than ascribed (1940, 48). "Authority was invested in the men who were adept at certain important technical skills … hunters, harpooners, canoe makers, and gamblers" (p. 49). A skilled professional in such skills could become wealthy and influential. The ability to lead also was valued; in that field, as in others, according to Smith, influence was accumulated over time by a continuing records of achievements — "Influential men were those with established reputations" (Smith, 1940, 51).

GAMBLING, CHALLENGES, AND OTHER SPORTS

Gambling, sports, and other contests involving wits and physical strength were openly recognized as devices for management of interpersonal rivalries, or antagonisms between groups of people. A skillful gambler was recognized as a high-status professional among the South Sound Salish. This type of contest continues today in *sla-hal* games that draw many competitors, large audiences, and result in the awarding of sizable cash prizes.

Some contests came about as a result of challenges, *mano à mano*: disc gambling, weight pulling, harpoon throwing, and wrestling. Others were competitive contests among groups of people, such as *sla-hal*, tug-of-war, racing, a beaver-tooth game (played only by women), and others. "Shinny" was a little like modern-day American football, on a field with goals, but the two teams of eleven men each began play at right angles to the goals, facing each other, then used "shinny sticks" to advance a "ball," usually made of wood, "a wooden cylinder about three inches long" (Smith, 1940, 224) toward the goals. The game could get very rough, and was played only by men. Shinny sticks could be used to trip opponents as well as manipulate the ball across the field (Smith, 1940, 224). A "dancing game" involved repeated squats and jumps (it was an endurance contest, not a dance). Archery contests, swimming competitions, and sham battles also were staged. In a "laughing game," two people (often lovers) competed to see which one could hold a straight face until the other provoked laughter. Games were held for children and adults of both genders.

LONGHOUSES

Muckleshoot cedar longhouses were built to store food and to utilize space efficiently. A longhouse was home to as many as twelve families, each of which occupied a designated area. Shelves below the rafters were piled with smoked and dried fish, dried meat, roots and berries. Fish oil was saved and utilized as we use cream, butter, and salad dressing. Enough food was stored in each house so that a family could eat for several weeks, especially in winter, when fish did not run, and weather in the foothills and mountains was cool and wet (or even sometimes snowy), not suited for hunting and gathering. During summer months, families moved to different camps, living in temporary shelter where they gathered food for the winter. Food could be smoked, or baked outdoors in deep pits. It also could be boiled indoors in tightly woven waterproof baskets. Stones were heated over fires and dropped into water in the pots. Tongs of malleable green wood were used to carry the stones.

Muckleshoot longhouses, were built of cedar planks two to three feet wide and three to six inches thick. Some of the houses were of moderate size with one door at the end of the house, about 40 to 100 feet long and 20 feet wide. (One Coast Salish longhouse, the Suquamish Old Man House, was 528 feet long, and housed as many as a dozen families, but its size was unusual.) Houses, or parts of them, were passed on to members of extended families through inheritance. Longhouses are maintained today on several reservations around Puget Sound. Longhouses provided shelter for several families who worked as an economic unit. The large number of people allowed them to specialize (Smith, 1940, 33).

A central fire that usually burned at all times in the middle of the house was the primary source of cooking and heat. If more than one family lived in a house, several small cooking fires were used. Roof planks could be moved to let smoke out and admit sunshine. Cattail mats hung vertically to separate families' sections. Bed platforms usually were built into the sides of houses, with storage areas above the beds, dressed with cattail mats, "extra springy ... [made] especially for that purpose" (Waterman and Greiner, 1921, 37). Another mat, folded over, served as a pillow. Beds were positioned so that people could sleep with their sides facing the fire. Floors were made of dirt, which was compacted and swept to produce a hard surface.

Study of Native housing styles in the Puget Sound area has been complicated by the fact that the government's Indian Bureau destroyed all of them before 1920 (Waterman and Greiner, 1921, 9). Anthropologists, using photographs and the memories of living Native persons, have classified the old styles into several categories: some, built for the wealthiest people, had gabled roofs; others had "shed" roofs — though these were large, long-lasting structures, not sheds by present-day definition. A third type, according to Waterman and Greiner, writing in 1921 (9–10), "had a central roof, almost flat, with lean-to's added." These were usually built on a shoreline, facing the water, with long sides facing the beach (Waterman and Greiner, 1921, 18). These were general classifications and may not have been followed strictly by the Muckleshoot's ancestors, although Waterman and Greiner (8) indicate that they were using research supplied by Arthur C. Ballard, who worked with Muckleshoots intensively.

Some of these houses included equipment for drying and smoking salmon and other fish. "From the native standpoint," wrote Waterman and Greiner, "the center and soul of the house was a great rack for drying fish ... "

Cross-pieces were extended from one side of the house to the other, at the level of the lower eaves ... Poles were then laid lengthwise of the house, about 16 inches apart. Resting on these cross-pieces, salmon brought in by the fishermen were cut open and the backbones taken out. They were then skewered through their tails with a stick. The "stick" of fish was then laid across between two of the longitudinal poles, and the fish was left to cure in the smoke. (Waterman and Greiner, 1921, 38)

TRADING ROUTES

Some of the Muckleshoots' ancestors used a network of trails to traverse lands on the eastern side of Puget Sound, the Cascade mountains, and along rivers and saltwater bays. Many of today's highways and other roads follow old trade routes. Prior to highway construction between Auburn and Enumclaw, a trail connected the two towns. A Muckleshoot elder told a story to Willard Bill, Sr. indicating that "rapid transit" in those days consisted of a horse and a well-worn trail. Someone in Auburn owned a horse that was often borrowed by Muckleshoots to return home after shopping. The shopper would ride the horse several miles home, dismount with groceries, turn the horse around, and slap its rear end. The barebacked horse would then trot along the trail back to Auburn. The Hudson's Bay Company and Americans hired Indian canoe pullers to transport people and goods north and south along Puget Sound and the rivers before roads were built.

Intertribal trade was commonplace during the nineteenth century, before widespread non-Indian immigration. The ancestors of the Muckleshoot conducted commerce within a wide geographic area. Native parties traveled east and west over the Cascade mountains for trade and barter. Indigenous peoples of various nations often traded smoked seafood. Following contact with European-Americans, such exchanges continued, as salmon, other fish, oysters, and clams were sold to allow purchase of new technology, including metal items (such as cooking pots) and tools that aided in carving of canoes.

Oral history indicates that some of the Muckleshoots' forebears ranged as far east as Idaho and parts of the Rocky Mountains, trading dried fish for buffalo robes and meat. Possibly because their trade networks were so broad, the Muckleshoots' ancestors were among the first Coast Salish peoples to acquire horses, which came from the Spanish to the south and east before Anglo-American immigration reached their homelands. Some of their neighbors called them "Horse Indians" (Noel and Cross, 1980, 39). People living on the Green and Upper Puyallup Rivers probably acquired their first horses from neighbors and relatives among Yakama ancestors east of the Cascades.

Trails laced the dense forests of western Washington, developed for trade and other communication. In some areas, the ground was worn by years of foot traffic. Trails led to saltwater areas for harvesting clams, to berry fields and fishing streams. One trail led from Puget Sound to the Cowlitz River. Another traversed the Cascade mountains to the Yakima Valley. The trails helped maintain social relationships. Linkages between and within groups were facilitated by a number of cultural practices. Marriages cemented relationships between Muckleshoot ancestors' villages and people from other tribes and nations throughout what is now called western Washington. Similarly, marriages also created bonds between people from both sides of the Cascade mountains. Many people from the east side of the Cascades escaped its harsh climate by wintering on the west side of the mountains. All of this maintained alliances, as well as trading and family relationships.

Shell money of several types was used by the Coast Salish to facilitate trade. These items were subject to scarcity value. East of the Cascades, for example, discs of white clam shells about a centimeter in diameter (tc !au'wai) became more valuable. Discs were smoothed with rough stones and a hole was drilled in each bead so they could be used in strings. "Solax" was made from tubular beads traded from the north, usually "strung in pairs with a round bead between" (Haeberlin and Gunther, 1930, 29). Larger clam shells from the north had greater value because they were scarce. Some of the shells were worn in strings as adornment, or as ear ornaments by chiefs. Haeberlin and Gunther published a scale of purchasing power: so many Solax, for example, were generally worth one basket. A larger number might buy a small canoe. Tribes from the north who held slaves also converted their value into the various forms of shell money (Haeberlin and Gunther, 1930, 29).

SPIRITUAL ASPECTS

As with any culture that has evolved over thousands of years, the traditional spiritual beliefs of Puget Sound Salish peoples are complex, and not subject to complete description in a short survey. Religious and ceremonial practices are difficult to describe accurately in this limited context. They include healing, burial practices, and consideration of ancestors (naming), all of which remain important today.

Spirituality involves humans' relationship with nature. It is not "religion." We often do not have the words in English to describe these concepts. "Every individual characteristic and every cultural complex, except those related to sexual life, was understood and was thought to operate through power," Marian Smith wrote. "Adult life without power was inconceivable and childhood was viewed as a period of preparation for the reception of power" (1940, 56). Smith's *The Puyallup-Nisqually* includes a very detailed description of power's role in spirituality, as well as the ways in which individuals acquired a wide range of specific attributes that defined their relationship to the supernatural, as well as molding their personalities (56-75). One example (among hundreds) was a hunting power practiced by "a few individuals at Skokomish ... to jump out before a deer with a yell. The deer was so scared it fell dead" (1940, 81). Smith also describes "shaman curing" (75-90). The variety of spirits (called "powers" by Marian Smith) is very large; Haeberlin and Gunther (1930, 69-80) contains a summary of them, from those that bring good luck in hunting, fishing, and gathering clams, to those

Muckleshoot Smokehouse under construction, Mt. Tahoma (Rainier) in background.
Photo by John Loftus, Muckleshoot Monthly

that favor basket-making talents, leadership in war, or wealth and property. Other spirits brought happiness.

Wayne P. Suttles described the acquisition of "powers" or "spirits."

> To produce either food or wealth, a man had to have one of a number of special skills which, it was believed, were acquired and practiced with the aid of the supernatural. The important source of supernatural help was ... the vision, sought, especially during adolescence, by fasting and bathing in remote forest lakes or along lonely shores. During the vision the seeker encountered some animal — real or mythical — which conferred upon him a particular skill and became, in anthropological language, his "guardian spirit." The seeker also usually received a ... "spirit song," which came to him some winter later in life and made him sick. A shaman or ritualist recognized the sick person as ... a 'new dancer,'

and helped him to learn to control his song and to ... dance with it in a state of possession. Spirit songs also came unsought to persons suffering from grief. (Suttles, 1987, 204)

Smokehouse tradition retains these attributes, with each member having a spirit and portraying it through a costume, dance, and song. Haeberlin and Gunther (1930) describe two types of spirits: the *sklaletut*, "the spirit of the layman [that] brings luck in the acquisition of wealth and, through it, rank, or else ... makes war enterprises successful" (Haeberlin and Gunther, 1930, 67). The *x"áa'b* spirits aid shamans in finding cures. The idea of a deity styled as a human being (God, and various prophets) is European. Even the idea of a "Great Spirit" is a hybrid concept that introduces a human figure. Acquaintance with spirits is a highly personal matter, and only the person who knows them may describe their relationship. Spirits may be inherited in family lines. While spirits often are acquired by fasting, taking sweat baths, and enduring physical hardship at puberty, they also may appear later in life.

The sweat lodge was used for cleansing, a very important ritual in the smokehouse way. Stones were heated outside and brought into the sweat lodge to steam with water (fires were never built in a sweat house, or lodge). Cedar boughs also were used to rub the body (Noel, 1980, 43-44). Daily bathing, including the grooming of hair, is important because the spirit will not come to any soul housed in a dirty body (Caster, 2005, 55, citing Noel, 1980, 43-44).

The power of spiritual influence is believed to be related to rank and prominence in society, but lower-class persons, including slaves, may improve their status through acquisition of spirits. March and April, during stormy weather, is believed to be the time

Smokehouse under construction, October 2012.
Photo by John Loftus, Muckleshoot Monthly

when spirits are most likely to surface (Haeberlin and Gunther, 1930, 68). Some spirits may be acquired only by diving into deep water — which, in the Puget Sound area, involves enduring cold.

Each village usually included at least one old man who passed along stories with spiritual overtones, and attempted to heal the sick. There existed no formal office, and no shamanistic society. In this system of belief, the Sun is the father and the Moon the mother of all. The Changer was an important figure — not a god, but "an allegory of the human race itself, [at] some times benevolent, sometimes greedy, sometimes silly ... not all-powerful, and not all good" (Caster, 2005, 56). Wherever the Changer camped, life and the environment was transformed. Mountains appeared; pre-existing forms of life became the plants and animals we know today. Humans also appeared, transformed from another form known as First People. Usually beings accepted transformations brought by the Changer, but sometimes they were being punished. Salmon chose scales and a home in the water; wolves adopted fur and a habitat in the

Chapter 1

Donna Starr inspects the nearly completed Smokehouse, 2013.
Photo by John Loftus, Muckleshoot Monthly

forests. The oral history is not clear regarding whether human beings came about because of a deliberate action by the Changer, or by accident (Caster, 2005, 55–56, citing Underhill, 1944, 183–184).

Reality could take some inexplicable turns in this perceptual world. According to Marian Smith, in *The Puyallup-Nisqually*:

> One of the most distinctive ceremonial objects of Puget Sound is the heavy, ten-foot stick held upright and pounded against boards above the drummer's head. These drumming sticks sometimes became animate, the power of their owner "got into them." When animated, they might "dance alone," hold themselves upright in the air and continue beating without any human hands touching or close to them. (Smith, 1940, 113)

On some occasions, if an individual expressed skepticism about the stick's power, he would be asked to handle the stick during a drumming ceremony, whereupon, wrote Smith, "gradually the stick gained control and instead of being manipulated by the man, forced him to follow it" (Smith, 1940, 113). Some people reported to Smith that people had been dragged about, even out of a house and into a nearby river or bay. The stick was said to have maintained its power over the skeptic until its owner gave it a signal to desist. Typically, after a ceremony involving drumming and singing that involved the sticks, Smith's informants reported that they became inert.

March 3, 2012, revival of the smokehouse way at Muckleshoot received a boost when construction began with Tribal Council funding for a new longhouse. People had been using the sla-hal shed for ceremonies, but it was cramped and had a cement floor. The new 16,000-square-foot building has an earthen floor, and log beams 30 inches in diameter, 18 feet above the floor, peaking at 33 feet. It also contains two large fireplaces, a dining hall, a kitchen, and an outside cooking area designed for cooking seafood and game. The building accommodates 500 people ("Ground Is Blessed," 2012, 1, 10, 16). The smokehouse was nearing completion in mid-2013. An open house was held May 29, under the roof's newly erected beams.

REFERENCES

Ballard, Arthur C. "Calendric Terms of the Southern Puget Sound Salish." *Southwestern Journal of Anthropology* 6 (1950), 79-99.

Ballard, Arthur C. Testimony, Indian Claims Commission of the United States. *The Muckleshoot Tribe of Indians on Relation of Napolean Ross, Chairman of the General Council, Claimant, vs. The United States of America, Defendant*, Seattle, WA, November 26-28, 1951. 2 vols.

Ballard, Arthur C. "The Salmon Weir on Green River in Western Washington." *Davidson Journal of Anthropology* 3:1 (Summer 1957), 37-53. Copy in Muckleshoot Preservation Program Archives.

Brotherton, Barbara. "How Did It All Get There: Tracing the Path of Salish Art in Collections," in Brotherton, ed., *S'abadeb, the Gifts: Pacific Coast Salish Art and Artists*. Seattle: University of Washington Press, 2008, 68-139.

Burtchard, Greg C. "Holocene Subsistence and Settlement Patterns: Mount Rainier and the Montane Pacific Northwest." *Archaeology in Washington* 13 (2007), 3-44. [http://www.nps.gov/mora/historyculture/upload/AIW-Burtchard2007.pdf]

Burtchard, Greg C. Personal correspondence (email), September 12, 2011.

Burtchard, Greg C. Mount Rainier National Park. Archaeology. U.S. National Park Service. May 27, 2011. Accessed September 10, 2011. [http://www.nps.gov/mora/historyculture/archaeology.htm]

Caster, Dick. *Native American Presence in the Federal Way [Washington] Area*. Federal Way, WA: Historical Society of Federal Way, 2005. Copy in files of Muckleshoot Preservation Program Archives.

Elmendorf, William W. *The Structure of Twana* [Skokomish] *Culture*. Pullman, WA: Washington State University Press, 1960.

"Ground Is Blessed for New Muckleshoot Longhouse." *Muckleshoot Monthly*, March 15, 2012, 1, 10, 16.

Haeberlin, H. and Erna Gunther. *The Indians of Puget Sound*. University of Washington Publications in Anthropology 4 (1930), 1-84. Seattle: University of Washington Press.

Hess, Thom. "A Comparison of Marine and Riverine Orientation Vocabulary in Two Coast Salish Languages." *Anthropological Linguistics*. November 1979, 363-378.

Lane, Barbara. "Political and Economic Aspects of Indian-White Culture Contact in Western Washington in the Mid-Nineteenth Century." May 10, 1973. Typescript in Muckleshoot Preservation Program Archives. (1973a)

Lane, Barbara. "Anthropological Report on the Identity and Treaty Status of the Muckleshoot Indians." U.S. District Court, Tacoma, WA. Plaintiff's exhibit No. USA-270, *United States v. Washington*, admitted to the record August 24, 1973. (1973b)

Lane, Barbara. "The Muckleshoot Indians and the White River: A Report Prepared for the Muckleshoot Indian Tribe." September 1980. In Muckleshoot Preservation Program Archives.

Meeker, Ezra. *Pioneer Reminiscences of Puget Sound: The Tragedy of Leschi*. New York: Lowman & Hanford Stationery and Print. Co., 1905.

"Mt. Tacoma" in *Commemorative Celebration at Sequalitchew Lake, Pierce County, Washington, July 5, 1906*. Second Ed. Pierce County Historical Association, 33-34. Copy in files of Muckleshoot Preservation Program Archives, 93-95.

Noel, Patricia Slettvet and Virginia Cross. *Muckleshoot Indian History*, Auburn, WA: Auburn Public School District No. 408, 1980.

"Overview: The Muckleshoot Indian Tribe." Accessed January 3, 2010. [http://www.muckleshoot.nsn.us/about-us/overview.aspx]

Sarvis, Will. "Deeply Embedded: Canoes As an Enduring Manifestation of Spiritualism and Communalism Among the Coast Salish." *Journal of the West* 42:4 (Fall 2003), 74-80.

Smith, Allan H. *Takhoma: Ethnography of Mount Rainier National Park*. Pullman, WA: Washington State University Press, 2006.

Smith, Marian W. *The Puyallup-Nisqually*. (Columbia University Contributions in Anthropology, Volume 32.) New York: Columbia University Press, 1940.

Smith, Marian W. "The Coast Salish of Puget Sound." *American Anthropologist*, 43:2 (1941) [new series], 197-211.

Suttles, Wayne P. "Spirit Dancing and the Persistence of Native Culture Among the Coast Salish," in Suttles, ed., *Coast Salish Essays*. Vancouver, B.C.: Talonbooks and Seattle: University of Washington Press, 1987, 199-208.

Suttles, Wayne and Barbara Lane. "Southern Coast Salish," in Wayne Suttles, Ed. *Handbook of North American Indians: Northwest Coast*. Vol. 7. In William C. Sturtevant, General Ed. *Handbook of North American Indians*. Washington, D.C.: Smithsonian Institution, 1990, 485-502.

Tollefson, Kenneth D. "Remembering the Old Ways: Louis Starr's Reflections on Traditional Indian Subsistence Living." *Columbia: The Magazine of Northwest History*, 7:3 (Fall 1993), 13-16.

Tyler, Ron. "Mount Rainier, Volcano Hazards, and the Osceola Mudflow." Enumclaw Plateau Historical Society, March 2002. Copy in files of Muckleshoot Preservation Program Archives.

Underhill, Ruth. *Indians of the Pacific Northwest*. Washington, D.C.: Dept. of Interior/Bureau of Indian Affairs Branch of Education, 1944.

Walker, Richard. "Friend of Coast Salish People Dies." *Indian Country Today*, May 30, 2005, n.p.

Waterman, T. T. and Geraldine Coffin. *Types of Canoes on Puget Sound.* (Indian Notes and Monographs, Misc. Series No. 5.) New York: Museum of the American Indian, Heye Foundation, 1920.

Waterman, T. T. and Ruth Greiner. *Indian Houses of Puget Sound.* (Indian Notes and Monographs.) New York: Museum of the American Indian, 1921.

Waterman, T. T. *Notes on the Ethnology of the Indians of Puget Sound.* (Indian Notes and Monographs, Misc. Series No. 59.) New York: Museum of the American Indian/Heye Foundation, 1973.

Waterman, T. T. *Puget Sound Geography: Original Manuscript from T. T. Waterman. Ed. with Additional Material from Vi Hilbert, Jay Miller, and Zalmai Zahir.* Zahir Consulting Services, 2004. Copy in files of Muckleshoot Preservation Program Archives.

Watson, Kenneth G. (Greg). *Mythology of Southern Puget Sound: Legends Shared by Tribal Elders,* Reprint of the 1929 publication. Recorded, translated, and edited by Arthur C. Ballard. North Bend, WA: Snoqualmie Valley Historical Museum, 1999.

Wickersham, Hon. James. "Is It Mount Tacoma, or Rainier?" *Proceedings of the Tacoma Academy of Sciences.* Tacoma, WA: News Publishing Co., 1893. Copy in files of the Muckleshoot Preservation Program Archives.

Chapter 2

Treaty-Making: A Foreign Concept

Chapter 2

Treaty-Making: A Foreign Concept

Lobehan family, probably in Slaughter (Auburn), c. 1880.
Photo courtesy of White River Valley Historical Museum / 00429

European and European-American explorers began to visit the Pacific Northwest for trade and exploration late in the 1790s. Trade began to flourish, leading to immigration. Initially, many Native peoples in the Northwest welcomed the immigrants, believing that the land could provide for everyone. Before immigration provoked conflict over land and resources, relations between the Muckleshoots' ancestors and a small number of new neighbors were mainly peaceful. In 1906, the aged chief Slugamus Koquilton reflected the prevailing attitude among many Puget Sound Salish when whites began flooding into their lands during the mid-nineteenth century. He had witnessed the

Joe Bill walking alongside of a horse-drawn carriage containing his wife, Lucy, and their granddaughter, Lillian Paines. Muckleshoot tribal members. c. 1890.
Photo courtesy of White River Valley Historical Museum / 00443

influx as a young man. "We were glad to see the white people. ... The country did not belong to any nation, [it] just belonged to the Lord; it was for all the people" ("Talk," 1906, 33).

Only later did the Muckleshoots' ancestors and other Native peoples realize that the newcomers were arriving in large enough numbers to take their land and resources. The earliest conflicts between whites and Native people in the Puget Sound probably were related to the dispossession of Indian people from their village sites and the prairies on which they cultivated root crops.

EARLY EPIDEMICS AND POPULATION ESTIMATES

Imported diseases swept the area and crippled Native societies, wiping out families and communities *en masse*. The first epidemics arrived with explorers. By the 1850s, 90 percent of some Native communities had been wiped out by smallpox and other maladies. At the same time, the treaties forced the survivors to give up most of their land. According to Henry Dobyns' *Their Number Became Thinned*, smallpox swept through Northwest peoples in 1779-1783, 1802, 1836-1840, 1852-1853, and 1860-1867. Smallpox is cruel beyond imagining, with its swift spread, raging fevers, and large, festering, pus-oozing sores that ravage people's bodies before killing them. The disease devastated the Coast Salish peoples (and many others who, like them, had no immunity) long before sustained white immigration began about 1850.

Beginning with early Spanish explorations in 1774, the Native peoples of the Northwest Coast learned to associate the arrival of ships with deadly, previously unknown, diseases. The ships were disease vectors from Europe. Within a century, and by the time European-Americans had crossed the Continental Divide carrying many of the same maladies from the east and south, epidemics of smallpox, several venereal diseases, measles, tuberculosis, influenza, whooping cough, dysentery, cholera, and "fever and ague" (probably a strain of malaria) racked the coast from the present-day Alaska Panhandle to Northern California.

George Vancouver, captain of the Discovery, described a profound silence as he sailed the waters of the Pacific Northwest during June of 1792. The Puget Sound country seemed "nearly destitute of human beings. ... an awful silence" only rarely broken by a raven's cry, or the scream of an eagle. He did locate Native people, however, and had a lively trading encounter with some of them, who probably were Muckleshoot ancestors, after his ship anchored near Bainbridge Island.

Vancouver soon learned a major reason why the country seemed so empty of humanity. Sixty years before Anglo-American immigrants began to flood the area, smallpox had already ravaged it. Vancouver found several Native people near Hood Canal bearing the unmistakable signs of smallpox — pockmarked faces and missing eyes. "This deplorable disease is not only common, but it is ... very fatal among them, as its indelible marks are seen on many; and several had lost the sight of one eye" (Vancouver, 1798, 1:241). Longhouses were abandoned and prairies once tended were now overgrown with forest.

Depopulation by disease was not consistent. Some areas were devastated as others lost many fewer people. When Vancouver stopped at Bainbridge Island, a large number of canoes came over from Muckleshoot territory to greet him. The smallpox epidemic of 1853 largely missed the Muckleshoots' ancestors — but not entirely.

Evidence of death among Muckleshoot ancestors is scanty, but measles (1847–1848) and smallpox (1853 and other years) struck nearby, according to immigrants' records. Steilacoom (near Tacoma) and the Fort Nisqually area were hard hit by the measles epidemic. After it ended, dysentery and pneumonia claimed more lives. Fort Nisqually, as a trading hub, acted as a disease vector (Boyd, 1999, 155). In 1853, among some Indians in central and southern Puget Sound, "entire families have been cut off and whole villages depopulated," according to one witness (Boyd, 1999, 161).

Oral history accounts indicate that salmon in some areas suffered from running sores. The people realized the fish were very ill, but were dependent on them, so they caught and cured the fish, then put off eating them until they had nothing else, "and then began a terrible time of sickness and distress. A dreadful skin disease, loathsome to look upon, broke out upon all alike. None were spared. Men, women, and children sickened, took the disease, and died in agony by hundreds ... Camp after camp, village after village, was left desolate" (Boyd, 1999, 55). This epidemic may have taken place shortly after the first Spanish explorations; the informant said that the Squamish had partially recovered by the time "the first white men sailed up the [Fraser] River in their big boats" (Boyd, 1999, 55).

James Swan, an early ethnologist, wrote: "The ruins of their houses are still visible for miles along the shore (Boyd, 1999, 163). The Makahs refused vaccination, believing a rumor that it would sterilize their women and deliver their soon-to-be-emptied land to white immigrants. Within a few weeks, according to one observer, "hundreds of natives became victims to it; the beach for a distance of eight miles was literally strewn with [their] dead bodies ..." (Hancock, 1927, 182).

A major measles epidemic swept the Puget Sound area and much of the Northwest Coast in 1847 and 1848, often accompanied by dysentery and pneumonia. In many places the combination was deadly; one estimate said that 10 percent of Nisquallys died (Boyd, 1999, 159). Five years later, during 1852 and 1853, smallpox spread over the same areas, set off after a group of Indians boarded a wrecked merchant ship at the mouth of the Columbia River. The plague raced north, south, and inland, obliterating three-quarters of some coastal villages within two years.

NATIVE POPULATION ESTIMATES

Estimating the number of Native peoples in any one area at any one time was tricky business, so any "census" compiled by non-Indians in the early days was bound to be inaccurate. First, most census takers were outsiders who rarely counted everyone. Second, people moved with various harvests on a seasonal cycle, so the same people might have been counted more than once. Third, people moved from tribe to tribe, intermarrying, producing even more confusion. Fourth, many Native women departed reservations to marry white men, and were not counted.

The Muckleshoot population was given as 207 in 1881, in an enumeration used by the Indian Claims Commission in 1951. Another census about 1900 produced the lowest figure, 81. Arthur Ballard, however, in 1912, said of pre-contact peoples in the Green River area who came to be called Muckleshoot: "There were nearly a dozen villages, some containing hundreds of souls ... on streams convenient for trapping the ever-needed salmon. Their populations have faded and their names all but forgotten" (Noel, *Muckleshoot Indian History*, 91). A listing of Native peoples on the Green, White, and Duwamish rivers dated 1854 (including some Upper Puyallup people) listed 354 people (Caster, 2005, 18). George Gibbs, an ethnologist and lawyer who served on Isaac Stevens treaty commission, who had a major role in drafting the treaties, gave a figure for the same area as 850 (Gibbs, 1855, 34, 40-42). Gibbs made this and other estimates without visiting the area, so their accuracy has been questioned.

The ancestors of the Muckleshoots were more broadly dispersed than common references to Green River and White River Indians indicate, especially northward. Many Duwamish also identified as Muckleshoot, and ancestral Muckleshoot settlements have been found at least as far north as Lake Union in present-day Seattle. The watershed used for fishing by Muckleshoot ancestors reached much further north than that.

The immigrants who compiled the censuses found Muckleshoot names difficult to pronounce, so they gave them English names. In the early 1900s, records kept at Muckleshoot by the "farmer in charge" (an appointee of the Indian Bureau) dropped the Native names altogether. One such count in 1885 listed only 85 people.

ARRIVAL OF THE TREATY-MAKERS

Because of smallpox and other epidemic diseases, Native cultures' size and complexity had already been reduced by the time territorial governor Isaac Stevens arrived during the 1850s to negotiate a series of treaties. Stevens also was hired to lead one of the 1854 railroad surveys, having been promoted through the ranks of engineers of the United States coast and lands surveys. Murray Morgan, in *Skid Road: An Informal History of Seattle* (1952),

Chapter 2

characterized Stevens as "a diminutive, able, alert, vain West Pointer with a distinguished record in the Mexican War … who wore riding breeches and a red flannel shirt" (Morgan, 1952, 42-43). One of Stevens' biographers called him "The Little Napoleon" (Cook, 2000, 17-20).

The Donation Land Claims Act of 1850 attracted settlement of whites to Oregon Territory before lands were legally ceded by treaty, so a rush developed to negotiate land cessions. In addition, the gold rush in California at the same time created demand for fish and timber from Washington and Oregon. Some gold was also found in Eastern Washington and Alaska, accelerating in-migration.

Before the treaties were negotiated, a survey of Native peoples in Washington Territory was commissioned by Capt. George B. McClellan (later a famous Civil War general), commander of the Northern Pacific Railroad Exploration's Western Division. It was notable that an officer of the U.S. Army was so closely associated with railroad exploration. The entire operation very thoroughly linked government and corporations.

Isaac I. Stevens sitting.
Photo courtesy of Washington State Historical Society / C1950.67.3

McClellan commissioned George Gibbs (1815-1873), an artist and writer, and a graduate of Harvard University, to compile the report. Educated as an attorney, Gibbs had kept a journal of exploration in the Oregon Territory that was widely quoted in New York City newspapers during the late 1840s. He also collected minerals and birds, and quickly became a notable student of Native peoples and their languages. Gibbs drew maps for the railroads and became part of Isaac Stevens' treaty commission.

Gibbs' "Report … on the Indian Tribes of the Territory of Washington" laid the basis for the treaty negotiations. He was among the first to criticize ideas advanced by bureaucrats in the Indian Bureau who sought to concentrate all the Native peoples on one reservation in the name of administrative efficiency. "To remove the Indians altogether into any one district is impracticable," Gibbs wrote. "To throw the fishing tribes of the coast back upon the interior, even were the measure possible, would destroy them; nor is there any suitable region east of the Cascades where all of the tribes now living there could be concentrated and find food. They must, therefore, remain as they are …" (Gibbs, 1855, 28). Stevens' superiors directed him to negotiate treaties quickly to legalize the settlement rush provoked by the Donation Land Claims Act. Native peoples already were reacting negatively toward illegal in-migration.

Gibbs criticized the Donation Act as "the great primary source of evil" in relations with Native peoples, "contrary to established usage and natural right," by which the U.S. government "assumed to grant, absolutely, the land of the Indians without previous purchase from them." It followed, wrote Gibbs, "that as settlers poured in, the Indians were unceremoniously thrust from their homes and driven forth to shift for themselves" (Gibbs, 1855, 28). The Indians' distrust of the settlers and their government was natural, wrote Gibbs, given an act that was illegal even under its own law. Gibbs also severely criticized the Donation Act because it contained no provision to protect Indians' fishing rights, an oversight that "should be set at rest by law" (Gibbs, 1855, 29). Gibbs' insistence was written into the treaties and later became an important guarantee of Indians' rights to fishing and other sustenance rights late in the twentieth century.

THE IMPORTANCE OF TREATIES

The treaties that Stevens negotiated became the fundamental law that transferred millions of acres (as well as the resources on and under the land) from its earliest occupants to the United States of America, in exchange for supposedly secure rights to much smaller areas (reservations — so-called because they were legally reserved), as well as the right to fish and hunt, the Natives' main livelihood.

The Native peoples of Western Washington insisted on two important rights in treaty-making: the right to live on a homeland near traditional sources of sustenance, and the right to their familiar forms of economic support — fish and shellfish, hunting, and gathering, with water access. The treaty-makers generally did not understand that Native peoples used a system for allocating the taking of salmon among themselves. Spiritual observances such as the First Salmon ceremony were regarded by many whites as heathenism.

The treaties used two important phrases that federal court judge George Hugo Boldt would examine more than a hundred years later. The treaties reserved to the Native peoples "the right of taking fish, at all usual and accustomed grounds and stations ... in common with all citizens of the Territory" (Lane, 1977, 2). These words would long echo down the halls of history in the Pacific Northwest. Such language was used in two treaties covering ancestral peoples who would later be called Muckleshoot: the Treaty of Medicine Creek, 10 Stat. 1132 (signed 1854; ratified 1855) and the Treaty of Point Elliott, 12 Stat. 927 (signed 1855; ratified 1859), at Mukilteo, on Puget Sound north of Seattle, but south of Everett. Similar language was also contained in the Treaty of Point No Point, 12 Stat. 933 (1859); the Treaty with the Makahs (Treaty of Neah Bay, 12 Stat. 939, 1859), the Treaty with the Quinault (Treaty of Olympia), 12 Stat. 971 (1859), and the Treaty with the Yakamas, 12 Stat. 951 (1859).

In addition to preservation of fishing rights, the Medicine Creek Treaty also allowed "erecting [of] temporary houses for the purpose of curing, together with the privilege of hunting, gathering roots and berries, and pasturing their horses on open and unclaimed lands: *Provided, however*, That they shall not take shell fish from any beds staked or cultivated by citizens."

PROBLEMS WITH THE PROCESS

The Muckleshoot and other Native peoples did not ask for the treaties, which were negotiated to provide a basis within the legal system of the United States government to expand into the area, eventually laying the basis for Washington statehood in 1889. Treaties were a European concept, foreign to Native leaders. The ancestors of the Muckleshoot, who had lived in the area as long as 10,000 years, felt no need to prove their right to live on this land before a United States court of law. As Vine Deloria, Jr. was fond of quipping when asked what Indians called America before sustained European contact, it was "ours." They did not live by deeds.

Chief Seattle (or Sea'th'l).
Photo courtesy of Museum of History & Industry, Seattle / 1943.42.34127

Treaties were imposed on the Native peoples, who gave up most of their traditional lands, but retained rights to hunt and fish and (after some intense negotiation) portions of their homelands. Governor Stevens believed that he was pressed for time, so he was not particular about choosing leaders who actually represented the peoples whose lands were at stake in the treaties.

Stevens, following his orders, was eager to secure a right-of-way for a transcontinental railroad. A year before Stevens began negotiating treaties, in 1853, he conducted a land survey to pave the way across Washington Territory for that railroad. By negotiating the treaties, Stevens, in his own mind, was removing an impediment to civilization: European-American immigration spurred by the railroad would be facilitated by extinguishing Indian title to the land, concentrating tribes on reservations, and assimilating Native peoples who survived the immigrants' onslaught into their economy and culture. Stevens wanted to remove all of the Natives to a few areas, and leave all remaining land to the immigrants. Native peoples, attached to their homelands, as well as their fishing and hunting grounds, refused to accept this idea.

In addition to all of the other cultural inconsistencies of treaty-making, European-American definitions of land tenure were foreign to the Native people who were signing the treaties. No precedent existed in Native experiences of signing a document to extinguish title to a piece of land. Some of the Native "leaders" who "signed" the treaties probably did not realize that they were giving up land that their peoples had occupied for millennia.

It is not at all clear whether Chief Sea'th'l and the other treaty signers realized what the colonizers were asking of them, as Stevens' treaty negotiations east and west of the Cascades quickly acquired 64 million acres for the United States. The popular narrative features Chief Sea'th'l (anglicized as "Seattle"), who was well known to Stevens. Sea'th'l's mother was a White River Indian from one of the Duwamish bands ancestral to the Muckleshoot Tribe and his father was Suquamish. Sea'th'l was also closely related to Whatcom and other leaders of ancestral Muckleshoot villages.

Sea'th'l did not hurry to abandon his people's homeland on the city's present-day site. He stayed on the east side of Puget Sound as long as he could, under the protection of Arthur Denny and others; he withdrew to Suquamish when settlement pressures forced many Indians from their homes.

Some of the Duwamish migrated westward from Seattle across Puget Sound to a reservation with the Suquamish, following Sea'th'l's famous farewell speech. Fish runs were poor there; the people who remained behind said those who moved with the chief would go hungry. Others stayed at home, and some moved to the Muckleshoot Prairie.

Treaty-making also invoked several other fundamental misconceptions and impediments. While they had to deal with the official ideology that sought to turn Native peoples into farmers, some in the Stevens party also understood that if Indians continued to hunt and fish they could provide for themselves and reduce demands for government support. Reservation of fishing and hunting rights thus worked for both parties. Henry Webster, agent for the Makah, wrote to the Commissioner of Indian Affairs in 1865 that the best way to aid Indians would be to maintain their way of life, which was rooted in fishing.

The treaties were written in English, a language that almost none of the Native negotiators could read, placing them at a great disadvantage. The treaty proceedings were conducted in English and then translated into Chinook trading jargon, a common set of basic vocabulary used between white traders and various Indian peoples who did not share a common language. The jargon had a vocabulary of only about 500 words, lacking the abstract concepts necessary for a legal proceeding. Most people who were not traders did not understand Chinook.

Stevens employed staff who spoke Native languages, but he refused to address the Native treaty negotiators directly. What emerged from this linguistic gantlet was then translated into Native languages with various degrees of accuracy. George Gibbs represented the federal government with Stevens at the negotiations. They faced Natives who were often appointed by Stevens, and often had little influence with their peoples. The "treaty chiefs" — most of them had no other real credentials — enjoyed no legal assistance in any language. When Stevens proposed to appoint Leschi as a sub-chief, he tore the piece of paper to shreds and trampled it into the ground of the Medicine Creek council grounds.

Regardless of these problems, the treaty councils were recognized as important events by the Native peoples who were party to them. The Point Elliott Treaty was negotiated with 2,000 Indians in attendance. Over time, these imperfect and haphazard proceedings became the legal lockboxes of rights protecting the Muckleshoots and other Native peoples from oblivion. The Supreme Court has upheld the validity of the Puget Sound treaties at least seven times. Consequently, these treaties have become the Native peoples' guarantees of rights that remain vital to their livelihood and identity.

BECOMING MUCKLESHOOT

The tribes and bands that came to be called Muckleshoot were always an amalgamation, a mixture of peoples, mainly from southern Puget Sound, but sometimes from east of the Cascades. Arthur C. Ballard said that the people of the lower Green River were more likely to have mixed with the Duwamish, whereas those who raised their families on the upper Green River mixed more often with the Yakama and Klickitat. Having studied similarities in their myths and stories, Ballard traced roots northward into British Columbia and eastward to what he called "the prairies" (Ballard, 1951, 78).

As early as 1853, the word "Muckleshoot" was used to describe a prairie between the Green and White rivers. The term was not originally the name of a Native nation, but was acquired to describe the location occupied by three aboriginal peoples. According to T. T. Waterman, "Skope-ah-mish" was from the Coast Salish word "Skop," meaning "first big, then little," a reference to the sudden rises and falls of the Green River from storm runoff, making them "the people of the variable stream." "Smal-ka-mish" (or "Smulkamish") means "people at the head of White River," and "St-ka-mish" indicates "people of the White River." (Lane, 1973b, 30). In Coast Salish, the suffix "mish" means "people of."

All three of these names are listed in the preamble to the Treaty of Point Elliott. These names were identified by Barbara Lane for the legal case *United States v. Washington* (popularly called "the Boldt Decision"). In a manuscript filed with the case records (and in the National Anthropological Archives of the Smithsonian Institution, Washington, D.C., as manuscript number 2356), Gibbs estimated that the Smulkamish comprised about 50 people, at the head of the White River; the Stkamish about 30, on the lower White River; and the Skopeamish 50, at the head of the Green River.

Because the Muckleshoots were not recorded by that name in the Medicine Creek or Point Elliott treaties, the state of Washington challenged their fishing and other treaty rights. The state sued in an attempt to prove that the Muckleshoots were not covered by treaty provisions. Judge F. A. Walterskirchen of King County Superior Court in 1964 ruled that they were not a treaty tribe. Three years later, in the same court, Judge Lloyd Shorett ruled the opposite (American Friends, 1970, 108, 111).

Anthropological research also documented that the Muckleshoots were descended from ancestors covered by the treaties. According to Willard Bill, Sr.'s manuscript, research by Waterman between 1917 and 1920 and Ballard between 1920 and 1950 verifies names and tribal rolls that correlate with names identified from the nineteenth century. Villages were described with some accuracy, and historical tribal names are noted. Genealogical charts were entered as exhibits in *State v. Moses et al.*, No. 44836, Superior Court of the State of Washington for King County (1968).

By one account, the Muckleshoot called themselves "o'kelcul" (Caster, 2005, 18, citing Gibbs, 1855 and 1978). Ballard said that the term "Bucklelsooth-absh" was used among his informants for the people as a whole (Ballard, 1951, 81). Another root of "Muckleshoot" was relayed by anthropologist T. T. Waterman, as an anglicized version of "BE'kElcuL," meaning:

> Where a certain medicinal plant grows, for the third large prairie on this plateau. ... I never succeeded in identifying it. This word, transliterated as MUCKLESHOOT, has been used as the name of the reservation. Meany prints a statement, quoting Victor J. Farrar and C. L. Willis, that this term means "a river junction." This is certainly incorrect. There is a river nearby, called *Ila'lgo* ... where the Green River and the White River come together. (Waterman, 2001, 170-171)

Thom Hess wrote in *The Muckleshoot Language Book* (1952, 33-34) that the term "Muckleshoot" stems from a shortened form of "beqsedlSud," meaning "a nose," or promontory, a piece of land, from which one can see, between the White and Green rivers. "Beqsed" means "nose," and "*sud*" means "to see or look." However, in 1980 (and 1992) Virginia Cross and Patricia Noel noted in their curricular materials prepared for the Auburn schools (in a section that was unpaginated) that since the nineteenth century, "*lab*" has superseded "*sud*" to mean "look, or see." "Muckleshoot" also has been said to be a reference to the place where the White and Green rivers once met. Other reservation residents maintain that "Muckleshoot" is probably a reference to an abutment of land behind the present-day casino.

SUMMARY OF THE POINT ELLIOTT TREATY

The Point Elliott Treaty, signed January 22, 1855 and ratified by the U.S. Senate April 11, 1859, contained much more than the much-litigated phrases guaranteeing Indians the right to fish at their usual and accustomed places and stations (in Article V). The treaty was as notable for what it omitted as what it included. As described elsewhere, it listed at least three constituent tribes that became Muckleshoot.

The treaty, as ratified, included a description, in Article I, of land being ceded from the eastern side of Admiralty Inlet, midway between Commencement and Elliott Bays, eastward along the north edge of land previously ceded to the Nisqually, Puyallup and other Indians to the summit of the Cascade range, north to the 49th parallel, west to the middle of the Strait of Georgia to the Strait of Juan de Fuca, to Hood Canal and Vashon Island. Lands south of these had been ceded in the Medicine Creek Treaty. Article II contained legal descriptions of reservations.

Article III outlined a grant of land near Tulalip Bay to be used for an agricultural and industrial (boarding) school to be attended by the children of Indians living west of the Cascades, as well as an Indian agency. Article IV required Indians generally to move to their reservations within a year after the treaty was ratified. Article V protected fishing rights ("the right of taking fish at usual and accustomed grounds and stations ... in common with all citizens of the Territory ..." The same clause protected hunting and gathering rights, as well as places to erect temporary facilities for curing fish. Shellfish were not allowed to be taken from "any beds staked or cultivated by citizens" ("Treaty," 1855, 4).

Article VI outlined annuities, a total amount ($150,000), and a payment schedule. Article VII gave the U.S. government broad authority to remove Indians under the treaty from their assigned reservations, as the President of the United States might deem fit, as long as they were paid for improvement and expenses of removal. The same clause allowed removal to consolidate "friendly tribes and bands" ("Treaty," 1855, 5). Article VIII prohibited annuities from being used to pay debts of individuals. In Article IX, subscribing tribes promised to maintain friendly relations with the United States and not to commit "depredations on the property of [its] citizens."

Subscribing tribes also were prohibited from making war on other Indians, except in self-defense. In addition tribes were barred from sheltering fugitives from justice in the United States. Article X banned the importation and consumption of alcoholic beverages ("ardent spirits") on the reservations. Indians found guilty of importing or using liquor could forfeit their share of annuities.

Slavery was not pervasive, but enough of an issue to be forbidden by Article XI of the treaty. Sometimes it involved a tort system — a person's labor was provided as reparation for an offense. It did not usually involve lifetime ownership of "human capital."

In Article XII, Indians under the treaty agreed not to trade outside the United States, or allow foreign nationals to reside on reservations without permission of the superintendent or agent. Article XIII provided $15,000 for settlement costs on reservations, such as moving, fencing, or clearing of land. Article XIV repeated in more detail plans for an agricultural and industrial school. The last clause, Article XV, said that the treaty would come into legal force on the date of its ratification by the U.S. Senate and signing by the president.

THE "TREATY WAR"

Many Native peoples recall the treaties as unfair, imposed on them without consent, a very raw deal by Stevens and the immigrants he represented. Some of the colonists agreed. An article in the *Puget Sound Courier* at the time said that Stevens had robbed the Native people of their lands, fueling resentment and endangering the immigrants' lives (Archbold, October 28, 2005, A-14). Resistance to Stevens' hasty negotiation of several treaties developed east and west of Cascades.

During the fall of 1855, the Green and White river peoples joined with the Yakamas, Nisquallys, and Klickitat, all of whom believed they had not been adequately consulted in the treaty negotiations, in a brief uprising in and near the area that later would comprise the Muckleshoot reservation. Arthur C. Ballard called this uprising a "treaty war," because it was caused by "the haste with which the treaties were forced upon the Indians and the inadequacy of the reservations" ("The Treaty Sesquicentennial," 2005, 20). The Nisqually leader Leschi, working to unite Indians west of the Cascades against the white population, appeared in Olympia on October 22, 1855, and told the acting governor that war might come. Two days later, attacks began. The uprising was provoked by the Native Americans' realization of how much land was being taken from them by a rising tide of immigrants. By one account (cited and qualified by Kruger, 2011, 130) Leschi had been reluctant to go to war until warriors from bands that later came to be called Muckleshoot united with others led by chiefs Nelson and Kitsap to tell him how offended they were over the provisions of the Point Elliott Treaty.

Not all Muckleshoot ancestors participated in the war. Some upriver people took part, while most downriver did not. In the midst of antagonism, some areas were at peace. Duwamish, White River, and Green River ancestors were closely related although they took different positions in the war, for their people's survival.

Stevens already had appealed to his superiors for "1,000 stand of arms" to be housed at Fort Steilacoom, so that "settlers may protect themselves from Indian depredations" (Hunt and Kaylor, 1917, 145). With only 335 troops stationed in Washington and Oregon, Stevens felt very vulnerable. Many of the immigrants were nervous. S. L. Potter, homesteading Potter's Prairie along the White River, started a rumor that Indians had approached his cabin intent on killing him, but that he had escaped by hiding in a nearby tree. That rumor alone was enough to send several of Potter's neighbors fleeing to Seattle. None of their homes were burned, however, so the nervous immigrants returned.

BATTLES AND AMBUSHES

On October 28, 1855, Indian warriors descended upon settlements about a mile north of Auburn's future site, and killed nine people who lived there in three neighboring cabins

Chief Leschi.
Photo courtesy of Washington State Historical Society / 200

that were isolated from each other by thick woods. The dead comprised one-fifth of the immigrants in Pup Shulk Precinct; the name was a local Native term for "settlement on the prairie near a river" (Archbold, October 28, 200-5, A-1). The raiders may have been responding to provocation. Correspondence during the Treaty War indicated that U.S. forces tried to cripple the Indian resistance by blocking salmon runs, constructing weirs at the mouths of rivers, aiming to force resisting Indians into submission to avoid starvation (Lane, 1973a, 14).

The troubles began October 27, when Lt. James McAllister and a companion named Connell were killed by Indians as they were searching for Leschi near Enumclaw without success. Leschi and his brother Quiemuth had been spotted October 16 as they were sowing fall wheat on their farm near Steilacoom.

According to one account, "So quickly did the volunteers move that the two Indians were taken by surprise and barely escaped capture. Quiemuth left the plow in the furrow. Cattle and horses were running at large over the farm and some of these the soldiers appropriated for their own use" (Hunt and Kaylor, 1917, 148). Leschi and Quiemuth then joined a camp of Green and White river Native peoples who had allied with a group of Klickitats on the Green River.

Native warriors ambushed the troops who were searching for Leschi at a camp in a prairie on the Puyallup River, killing McAllister and Connell. The next day, October 28, Native warriors attacked farms on the White River, killing Harvey and Eliza Jones (as well as a hired hand on their farm), George and Mary King (and an infant), William and Elizabeth Brannan (and an infant), as well as Enos Cooper. Several children were orphaned. Many Indian assailants were also killed. Two more families (the Kirklands and Coxes) were driven from their homes. The settlement was burned to the ground. "Brannan's body, literally cut to pieces, was found in the house where he had made a brave fight" (Hunt and Kaylor, 1917, 149).

Harvey and Eliza Jones had a prosperous farm, with cows, hogs, and 2,500 fruit trees, at the time the insurgents attacked. Harvey Jones lay in bed that day, suffering from pleurisy, an inflammation of the lungs' lining that produces sharp pain. His body was found badly burned in the ashes of the Joneses' three-room cabin. Eliza was shot and then chopped with an axe as the hired man was shot in the back about 150 yards from the cabin. The children escaped, taking shelter in the woods. Later they were rescued by a Native man whom the immigrants called Indian Tom (Kruger, 2011, 134).

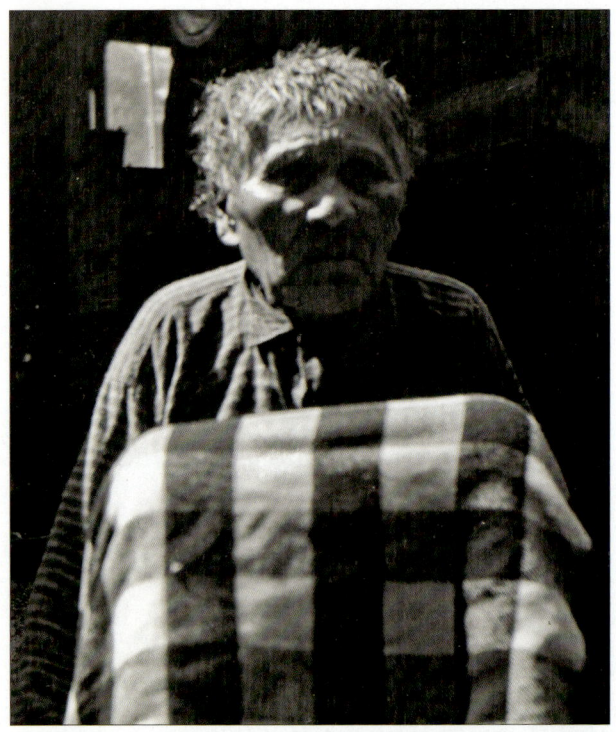

"Old Tom" or "Indian Tom" (Wiletchtid) of Muckleshoot c. 1905.
Photo courtesy of University of Washington Libraries, Special Collection. Edward S. Meany collection. In Muckleshoot Preservation Program Archives

Indian Tom's wife Elisa, probably in Auburn, c. 1914.
Photo courtesy of White River Valley Historical Museum / 00179

Indian Tom (also known as Wiletchtid, according to Arthur Ballard) was probably in his early thirties at the time of the Treaty War, when he saved the white children, transporting them more than 30 miles by canoe to Seattle, and turned them over to the authorities. He was a Catholic convert who was criticized by many Indians for being too friendly with the immigrants. Tom lived in Ilalko, the Muckleshoots' largest village, at the confluence of the Green and White rivers. Regardless of his friendliness toward "Bostons," Wiletchtid was well respected as a person who knew how to build a sturdy fish weir. He lived to between 90 and 100 years of age, dying February 7, 1914, having suffered inflammatory rheumatism and blindness. A stone marker later was placed over his grave in the Auburn Indian cemetery "in recognition of his deed" (Ballard, 1951, 267). The rescue was memorialized in Auburn's civic pageants for many years.

Louis (also called "Curley") Nelson, one of several men who carried the title "chief" at that time, led the attack. Nelson was said to have had a hot temper and a penchant for using his fists when irritated. He spoke English and had acted as a business facilitator between the Indians and the whites, using his canoe to transport money between the Green River Valley and Seattle. Nelson's Native name was Penah; his wife was Calaboo (Ballard, 1951, 262, 264). Nelson, who was born about 1810, was probably half Klickitat, illustrating, according to Ballard, that the "fusion of the Sehaptin, the eastern Washington people, and the Saltchuck (the salt water people) had been going on for a long time" (Ballard, 1951, 276-277).

Nelson had visited the Joneses' cabin two days before the attack. On his way out the door, Nelson told them: "It [will] not be very long until the Indian be gone and the white men have all the land around here" (Archbold, October 28, 2005). Years later Chief Nelson told a Native American interviewer that he had believed "It was to be a war of extermination and realizing that he would eventually be killed, [he] set out to kill and do all the damage he could" ("The Treaty Sesquicentennial," 2005, 20).

Harvey and Eliza didn't know what to make of the statement, until October 28, when "the Indians ... sprang from the ground with terrorizing war whoops ... [as] shots rang out and musket balls began tearing splinters from the [Joneses'] house" (Hunt and Kaylor, 1917, 149). After the massacre, Nelson befriended one of the orphaned children, George King. The child remained in the Indians' company until spring, when he was turned over to U.S. military authorities at Fort Steilacoom, to be sent east to join friends (Hunt and Kaylor, 1917, 150).

Moses (Ealachin) was also prominent in the Treaty War. His wife Julia was a sister of Philip Starr, whose father lived on or near Green River. His uncle resided with the Snoqualmie. One side of his family was Yakama, again illustrating how often people mixed. Moses' son Jim Moses served in World War I, and was married to a daughter of Jerry and Mary Dominick.

Chief Slugamus Koquilton also become known to the whites when he sheltered a five-year-old Anglo-American boy during the raid at White River. Slugamus tied the boy in a blanket and carried him on his back. Slugamus had been born at Brown's Point, across the bay from Tacoma, in 1816, and was about thirteen before he met a white man. Later he became a sailor and traveled to Alaska, the South Pacific, and England. He died December 8, 1909, at age 93.

After the raid on the White River, many of the white immigrants fled from the area to Seattle. Blockhouses were built nearby to shelter those who stayed. The next day, residents evacuated in wagons loaded with their household goods. As children drove sheep, hogs and geese, and men herded cattle. Another account described the exodus:

> Families were awakened and, hastily gathering their belongings, started for the towns and larger settlements. Men, women, and children, swearing, crying or praying, toiled along the way. Chicken coops and kitchen furniture; the women's clothing and the horses' harness piled together in the bottom of wagon beds were moved down the dark trails through the forest ... Cattle, sheep, horses and hogs, in many cases driven by the boys and the girls, took up the march. (Hunt and Kaylor, 1917, 150)

Ezra Meeker, one of the earlier European-American immigrants who lived in the area during the period, described the "White River Massacre" in detail (1905, 289-303). He placed blame for its provocation (and the rest of the Treaty War) directly on Stevens' haste and his ignorance of the Muckleshoot ancestors' needs in treaty negotiations (1905, 271-275). Given the faults of the treaties, Meeker wrote, "it was "small wonder that war followed. The great wonder is that a greater number did not enter the hostile camp" (1905, 275).

At a reunion of old pioneers, Meeker recalled that a minority of Indians took part in the Treaty War. Several whites spoke approvingly of the Indians' complaints, and were told two months before the uprising that they would not be harmed. For them, peace prevailed. Meeker recalled a mid-nineteenth century "Muckleshute" known as Mowich Man, "whom I have known for many years ... one of our neighbors [who] frequently passed our cabin with his canoe and people." "They were fine singers," wrote Meeker.

> His camp, or his canoe if traveling was always the center for song and merriment, but it is a curious fact that one seldom can get the Indian music by asking for it, but rather must wait for its spontaneous outburst. But Indian songs in those days came out from nearly every nook and corner and seemed to pervade nearly the whole country, so much that we often ... could hear the songs and accompanying stroke of the paddle long before our eyes would rest on the floating canoes. (Meeker, 1905, 129–130)

"I had lived among the Indians from childhood," George Dougherty told Meeker, "and in fact had learned to talk the Indian language before I could speak my mother tongue. At that time I believe there were twenty Indians to where there is one now" [It is unclear what date Dougherty is speaking of. Meeker's book was published in 1905, but much of the narrative is taken from the 1850s.] "Most of the Indians were friendly. Had it been otherwise they could have wiped out the white settlement completely, in spite of the military and volunteers" (Meeker, 1905, 172).

"Yes, and not left a grease spot of them," agreed another of the old pioneers, Mr. Rogers (Meeker, 1905, 172). "The Indians did not want to fight the whites, but were dissatisfied with their treatment by the government. They wanted their land back, and got it, too, after they whipped the whites ... If it had not been that a majority of the Indians were in favor of peace with the whites, they could have held this country for a number of years" (Meeker, 1905, 172). The Indians were being driven out of the fertile bottomlands, and into the woods, as whites took the better land. The Muckleshoots' ancestors and other signatories to the Medicine Creek and Point Elliott treaties needed access to fishing grounds, and prairie for the agriculture the government sought to teach them, as well as pasture for their horses.

Chief Nelson eluded capture after the Treaty War, but emerged from hiding swearing to forgo future violence. From 1870 to 1890, when he died, Nelson was a prominent leader of the Muckleshoots. In old age, Nelson was described as a man broken by the loss of all his children to tuberculosis. He lived in a house near the present-day intersection of Third and "R" streets Southeast in Auburn, adjacent to a Catholic mission that later was demolished. Nelson had made peace with Brannan, whose brother had been killed by the Indians. Brannan, said Ballard, had "done away with eight of the 12 Indians" who had killed the whites on White River, before a woman who later became his wife convinced him to stop his vendetta (Ballard, 1951, 280).

Realizing that retaliation by a large force of whites would follow the attack, a large number of Native people retreated upstream along the Green and White rivers. Leschi, regarding the attack as a tactical mistake, was furious at the warriors who had violated his strict orders to attack only combatants. After the raid at White River, wrote Meeker, "Indian testimony is abundantly in evidence that it was Leschi's master hand that stayed the havoc" (1905, 307).

The initial retaliatory strike was led by Lt. William Alloway Slaughter, a 28-year-old West Point graduate, who was "a dependable man, an energetic officer, a crack shot with a rifle" (Whale, 2010). On November 3, Slaughter led a militia of about 100 men, a combined force of regulars and volunteers, in skirmishes on the

Muckleshoot Prairie and along the White River. Their efforts were ineffective against the Indians' guerilla tactics. Slaughter's troops, having sustained several casualties, retreated to Ft. Steilacoom. Later in November they ventured out again, to blockhouses along the Stuck and Puyallup rivers.

On November 25, Slaughter's force made camp near the site where McAllister and Connell had been killed the previous October 27. Indians soon surrounded the camp, yelling and occasionally setting off volleys of rifle fire. A firefight followed in which Chief Kanasket and one soldier were killed. The Indians then broke off the fight, stealing about 40 of the Slaughter troops' horses as they melted into the woods.

On December 4, at the abandoned William Brannan homestead (now the site of Brannan Park), Lt. Slaughter allowed soldiers to build fires so they could dry out, sustain some warmth during a cold rain, and cook a meal. Lt. Slaughter surveyed the scene from an open doorway, against which the fire's light formed a perfect silhouette that allowed attackers to kill him instantly. Two corporals named Berry and Clarendon also were killed, along with four privates (Hunt and Kaylor, 1917, 152). Several other men were injured before the company scrambled to snuff its blazes and engage the attackers ("The Treaty Sesquicentennial," 2005, 20). The ambush of Slaughter and his compatriots was mourned in a resolution by the territorial assembly. All 30 of its members attended his funeral.

Lt. Slaughter later became a martyr in the same sense as George Armstrong Custer at the Little Big Horn, another casualty of poor battlefield judgment. A fort was erected on the Muckleshoot Prairie to house troops who were quelling the rebellion. In 1891, the new town about seven miles northwest of the fort

Lt. William Alloway Slaughter, with wife.
Photo courtesy of Muckleshoot Preservation Program Archives

originally took Slaughter's name in his honor, but later changed it to "Auburn," from the first line of a poem by the Englishman Oliver Goldsmith's, "The Deserted Village:" "Sweet Auburn! Loveliest village of the plain" ("City of Auburn," 2009).

Leschi, who was still being pursued as a fugitive by Army troops, sought peace after the eruption of violence, but not by surrendering. John Swan, who was supervising a reservation on Fox Island that housed Indians who had opted out of the war, was surprised January 5, 1856, by the arrival of six large canoes on a beach near his house. Leschi emerged from one of them, climbed the beach to Swan's house, and told him he had come to talk peace (Hunt and Kaylor, 1917, 152). Leschi and a group of about 30 to 40 Indians remained on Fox Island about 30 hours, talking with Swan, who had sent word of the visit to Fort Steilacoom. They

Brigadier General Isaac I. Stevens.
Photo courtesy of Washington State Historical Society / 2006.0.507

then departed, pulling their canoes through the Tacoma Narrows, into Commencement Bay, and up the Puyallup River. A month later, informal negotiations were renewed at the Indians' camp on the Green River.

Stevens returned from Blackfoot Country on January 19 and, perhaps unaware of Leschi's peace overtures, declared that enemy forces would "be prosecuted until the last hostile Indian is exterminated" (Hunt and Kaylor, 1917, 153). At about the same time, however, Stevens' public statement was contradicted by suggestions, perhaps advanced by Gibbs, Swan, and others, that the Indians had gone to war because they had been cheated in the Point Elliott Treaty.

THE "BATTLE OF SEATTLE"

Their peace overtures rebuffed by Stevens, the Indians (Yakama, Klickitat, Nisqually, Skopeamish and Smulkamish, under Chief Kamiakin) planned a campaign that included a brief attack on Seattle, then a village of about 100 people that had been founded only a few years earlier. Reacting to the killings at White River, citizens of Seattle built two large blockhouses of foot-square beams that could hold all the civilians in the village, hastily erected using lumber that had been destined for sale in San Francisco (Meeker, 1905, 351).

A Native war party approached Seattle on January 26, 1856, from the southeast along the long body of water that the immigrants had named Lake Washington. The insurgents came into the village near where Third Avenue and Marion Street now cross, advancing westward to Elliott Bay. The resistance was potent enough for the U.S. Navy to summon its only warship in the area, the 16-gun war sloop USS *Decatur*, which lobbed shells at the Indians onshore (Annual Report, 2000, iii). The Indians scattered eastward up the hill. Before they fled, the insurgents burned and looted a few buildings at the edge of town. The *Decatur* then lobbed shells at the houses that had been looted, blowing them to pieces. Leschi and the Yakama chief Owhi, who had led the intrusion, issued a defiant declaration that they would return (Hunt and Kaylor, 1917, 158). The whites lost two lives in the battle; the number of Indian dead was not tallied.

At about the same time, Gov. Stevens was reported by the *Olympia Pioneer and Democrat* (which Meeker characterized as the governor's mouthpiece) January 25, 1856 as delivering an address in the State House of Representatives "to an immense audience," and "deafening cheers," pledging that "The war shall be prosecuted until the last hostile

Painting of the Battle of Seattle by Emily Inez Denny, c. 1885.
Photo courtesy of Museum of History & Industry, Seattle / McCurdy Collection / 1995.921.2

Indian is exterminated." The *Journal of the House of Representatives of the Territorial Legislature* reported that Stevens had said: "I shall oppose any treaty with these hostile bands ... Nothing but death is a meet punishment for their perfidy. Their lives shall pay the forfeit" (Meeker, 1905, 342).

The next attack never came, as reinforcing troops arrived, closing in on the Native war bands from three directions. Indians who were friendly to the whites also were offered cash for severed heads — $80 each for a chief, $20 for a "brave," quite a bit of money in 1856. The bounty was offered to the Snoqualmies' turncoat chief Patkanim, who, it was said, "did not scruple to sacrifice his slaves when hostile enemies were not plentiful" (Hunt and Kaylor, 1917, 159). This was a time when a can of corn could be purchased for eight cents, a pound of raisins for seven cents, or a pound of roasted coffee for thirteen cents. A Smith & Wesson revolver cost about $13.00, a hammer 45 cents, and an 18-inch saw 99 cents. A steel kitchen range for coal or wood sold for $21.20 — the reward for a rank-and-file Indian's life.

The last major battle of the Treaty War west of the Cascades took place March 8, 1856 at Connell's Prairie, as about 250 fighting men flooded the area in pursuit of the Indians. An encounter took place that white soldiers' commanders told their superiors included a pitched battle that took about 30 Native lives. Roughly 150 Indians had attacked two companies of volunteer soldiers who were establishing a ferry crossing and blockhouse on the White River. The soldiers were said to have suffered no deaths and four wounded. At the end of the day, both sides withdrew. Or so the reports said.

The Indians' account of the day's events was much different, and Meeker said it was credible. Quoting the Puyallup Tyee Dick, Meeker wrote that the Indians had lost one man at most. The battle, according to Dick, was "hi-ue, he-he, hi-ue, he-he," "Lots and lots of fun ..."

> The Indians soon found that if any object was shown from under cover, the troops on the opposite side of the river would fire at it from various points, and so they began to push up hats and sticks until it came into sight, and bang, bang, bang would go the guns of the enemy, down would go the hat and another Indian reported killed. This thing went on until it became a standing joke and brought yells of delight from Indians all along the line. (Meeker, 1905, 314-315)

The real hostilities had ended by the spring of 1856, but Stevens had "'sown the wind,' and now reaped the whirlwind," according to Meeker, as volunteer militia spread out to enforce his order, interpreting the term "hostile" very loosely, killing Indians whom they found fishing or gathering wood, a total of 30 to 40 unprovoked killings, including many women and children (Meeker, 1905, 365, 367, 369). One of them was Quiemuth, called a "half brother" of Leschi in Meeker (1905, 139), who, in better times, had been a frequent guide and horseman for the whites.

A formidable number of the whites protested that Stevens was provoking murder of noncombatant Indians, and he reacted by declaring martial law against anyone who had "given aid and comfort to the enemy" (Meeker, 1905, 382). According to Stevens, the order allowed him to arrest and try anyone who opposed him (including several judges who refused to enforce the order) in front of a military tribunal (Meeker, 1905, 382). "Martial law must be enforced at all hazards in Pierce County," Stevens demanded (Meeker, 1905, 385). The order was extended to Thurston County.

Stevens was severely reprimanded on September 12, 1856, by Secretary of State William L. Marcy, speaking for President Franklin Pierce, after whom the county had been named. Stevens was also reprimanded on the floor of the U.S. Senate (Meeker, 1905, 400-02).

THE FOX ISLAND CONFERENCE

Facing stiff opposition from many white immigrants as well as Native peoples, Stevens was forced to reconcile, resulted in another conference, at Fox Island, on August 4, 1856, at which the first reservation on Muckleshoot Prairie was created. The Indians at the conference understood that Stevens had promised to set aside all of the land between the White and the Green rivers as a reservation. However, an executive order issued in 1857 gave them only the military reservation around Fort Muckleshoot.

Fox Island by that time was an internment camp for captive Nisquallys, Puyallups, and others, at which at least 100 Indians had recently died of tuberculosis and other diseases (Kluger, 2011, 180). At the Fox Island Conference, the Nisquallys and Puyallups also received enlarged reservations located on rivers that they had traditionally used for fishing and transportation.

After the Fox Island Conference, Stevens requested establishment of a Muckleshoot Indian Reservation through the Department of the Interior. On January 20, 1857, President Franklin Pierce approved the request. Later in 1857, the army withdrew from Fort Muckleshoot. On March 21, 1859, according to Willard Bill, Sr.'s research, Fort Muckleshoot was turned over to the Indian Department, and on July 1, 1860, Michael T. Simmons, a member of the Point Elliott treaty commission, Indian Agent for Washington Territory, recommended that the new Muckleshoot Reservation include all land from the military reserve to the junction of the White and Green rivers, within the jurisdiction of the Treaty of Point Elliott.

Yet another complication then arose. The new reservation was certified under the Medicine Creek Treaty, not Point Elliott. Why? Barbara Lane indicated that the Point Elliott Treaty had not been ratified at the time, so the Medicine Creek agreement was the only one available.

ENLARGING THE RESERVATION: 1856–1874

In the 1860s, a move was set afoot to designate more territory to tribes whose members were coming to be called Muckleshoot. Following the assignment of Fort Muckleshoot and surrounding lands at the Fox Island Conference, both the Native people and the federal government generally agreed that the land was not sufficient, mainly because it did not allow ready access to either the White or Green rivers, with their life-sustaining salmon runs. An effort was commenced during the late 1850s and 1860s to expand the reservation. Plans at the time called for the reservation to include all land lying between the Green and White rivers where they used to join in present-day downtown Auburn and eastward from there to the Muckleshoot Prairie.

In February 1868, the Commissioner of Indian Affairs recommended that all the land between the White and Green rivers in Townships 20 and 21 North, Range 5 East, be included in the reservation. The recommendation was forwarded to President Andrew Johnson. The measure died when Johnson was impeached. In 1873, the Indian Bureau backtracked on that recommendation, and substituted a much smaller one, of 3,367 acres, which was approved by executive order April 9, 1874. The government allowed the checkerboard pattern in violation of its own policies (that reservations be "compact," not checkerboarded) to achieve a solution between many competing interests (Lane, 1980, 38-48, 50-51).

By the early 1870s, when the expansion of the Muckleshoot Reservation was taken up again, railroad grants to the Northern Pacific Railroad Company had been made of all of the odd-numbered land sections in the vicinity of the Reservation. Thus, when the Muckleshoot Reservation was finally enlarged by executive order in 1874, it included only five even-numbered sections extending diagonally along the White River. A few years after the boundaries were

The Muckleshoot reservation was shaped by railroads' demand for land.
Photo courtesy of The Seattle Times

Railroad construction crew 1885.
Photo courtesy of Museum of History and Industry, Seattle / SHS5907

drawn, the reservation was surrounded by white farmers eager to extend their holdings. During the 1870s, railroads begin to build lines through the valley. The stage was set, in the century to come, for dispossession and impoverishment of the Muckleshoots.

TRIALS AND RETRIBUTIONS

Even as Stevens was forced to recognize Native discontent with the Point Elliott and Medicine Creek treaties at the Fox Island Conference in August, he was prosecuting several Native people who had expressed their discontent by taking up arms (of whom Leschi was the most prominent). Leschi was pursued relentlessly, arrested, quickly convicted of murder, and hanged February 19, 1858, a date postponed from January 22 because of a wave of protests. One of two attorneys who defended him, H. R. Crosby, was Bing Crosby's grandfather (Morgan, 1952, 51). Stevens' actions divided the immigrants — citizens, judges, and army officers. Many of the immigrants believed that Stevens was too aggressive. Many judges and juries found Indian defendants innocent because a state of war had existed, making their acts justifiable, not criminal.

Col. Silas Casey, commander of the U.S. Army's District of Puget Sound, refused to approve the hanging of Leschi at Fort Steilacoom, "denouncing the contemplated act in no unmeasured terms as murder" (Meeker, 1905). Casey was ordered to surrender Leschi to civilian authorities, who prepared to hang him on an existing scaffold a mile east of the fort.

Charles Grainger, the hangman who was assigned the duty of executing Leschi, performed his duty with severe misgivings:

> I felt that I was executing an innocent man. I had charge of Leschi for two weeks ... He was cool as could be — just like he was going to dinner. On the scaffold he thanked me for my kindness to him. He said again that he was not guilty; that Rabbeson had lied when he said he saw him in the swamp, and that he would meet him before his God, and he would tell there [that] he [had] lied. He said he was miles away when Moses [whom he was charged with murdering] was killed. (Hunt and Kaylor, 1917, 174)

Leschi, a solidly built man about five foot six, "with a very strong, square jaw and piercing dark-brown eyes" (Hunt and Kaylor, 1917, 174) ascended the hanging platform and looked up at the noose. He prayed for fifteen minutes. After the hanging, a small group of Native people placed Leschi's body in a plain wooden box and buried him in a secluded spot. Many years later, on July 4, 1895, the body was reburied near his Nisqually home, ushered there by a procession that was more than a mile long, "of carriages, buggies, wagons, people on horseback and people on foot," including many white people (Hunt and Kaylor, 1917, 175).

Reburial of Chief Leschi. Nisqually men named Bill Quiemuth, Luke, George Leschi & Yelm Jim, Washington, c.1899.
Photo courtesy of Washington State Historical Society / 1921.36.1

Ezra Meeker subtitled his book of pioneer memories "The Tragedy of Leschi," perhaps in the belief that no man was less qualified for a hangman's noose at the end of the Treaty War than the Nisqually who had met early immigrants in 1845 between the Columbia River and Puget Sound with a caravan of horses "loaded with food and presents" (Meeker, 1905, 215). This was the Leschi who was recalled by Lt. A. V. Kautz (later a general in the Union Army during the Civil War) as "characterized by greater intelligence and humanity than that of any of the other chiefs" (Meeker, 1905, 206). Leschi had instructed his men not to harm women or children, and not to plunder white homesteads. "On several occasions during the war he had individual white men in his power and his influence saved them from being killed by Kanasket," wrote Meeker — who added that he had been in that position himself (1905, 206).

Many of the early immigrants had become friends of Leschi. One of them, Owen Bush, told Meeker, "He had a benevolent countenance that unmistakably stamped him as a good man" (1905, 207). Leschi was rich and generous. Bush had learned Nisqually language and offered his services as an interpreter at the treaty councils, but Stevens turned him down, insisting that the proceedings be held in Chinook. "I couldn't raise a gun against those people who had always been so kind to us when we were so weak and needy," Bush told Meeker (1905, 208).

Not all the whites admired Leschi. Stevens was popular enough among the immigrants to have been elected as the territory's delegate to Congress in 1857 for a two-year term, by a vote of 986 to 149 (he had been appointed, not elected, as Washington Territory's governor). By 1861, however, he departed Washington Territory to take up arms as a brigadier general for the Union in the Civil War. On September 1, 1862, at age 44, Stevens was killed in action at the Battle of Chantilly in northern Virginia.

Many years later, during December 2004, a Historical Court of Inquiry and Justice granted Leschi a symbolic exoneration. Today parks, a Seattle neighborhood, and schools have been named after him.

REFERENCES

American Friends Service Committee. *Uncommon Controversy: Fishing Rights of the Muckleshoot, Puyallup, and Nisqually Indians.* Seattle: University of Washington Press, 1970.

Annual Report 2000. Auburn, WA: Muckleshoot Indian Tribe, 2000.

Archbold, Mike. "Auburn's History Shaped by Violence and Courage." *King County Journal*, October 28, 2005, A-1, A-15.

Bill, Willard, Sr. Unpublished Muckleshoot history files. 2005, unpaginated.

Boyd, Robert. *The Coming of the Spirit of Pestilence: Introduced Infectious Diseases and Population Decline Among Northwest Coast Indians, 1774-1874.* Seattle: University of Washington Press/Vancouver: University of British Columbia Press, 2000.

Caster, Dick. *Native American Presence in the Federal Way [Washington] Area.* Federal Way, WA: Historical Society of Federal Way, 2005. Copy in files of Muckleshoot Preservation Program Archives.

"City of Auburn, Washington. 2009-2010 Biennial Budget." Prepared by Department of Finance. February 23, 2009. Accessed December 10, 2010 [http://weblink.auburnwa.gov/External/ElectronicFile.aspx?docid=115737&dbid=0]

Cook, Sherburn F., Jr. "The Little Napoleon: The Short and Turbulent Career of Isaac Stevens." *Columbia* 14:4 (Winter 2000): 17-20.

Gibbs, George. *Indian Nomenclature of Localities in Washington and Oregon Territorie*s, 1853, National Anthropological Archives Manuscript 714.

Gibbs, George. *Report on the Indian Inhabitants of Washington Territory March 4, 1854.* Washington, D.C.: Smithsonian Institution, 1854. National Anthropological Archives Manuscript 2356.

Gibbs, George. *Indian Tribes of the Washington Territory,* in *United States War Department's Survey of Several Pacific Railroad Explorations.* Vol. 1. Washington, D.C.: War Dept., 1855. Reprint: Fairfield, WA: Ye Galleon Press, 1978.

Hancock, Samuel. *The Narrative of Samuel Hancock: 1845-1860.* New York: R. M. McBride and Co., 1927.

Harmon, Alexandra. I*ndians in the Making: Ethnic Relations and Indian Identities Around Puget Sound.* Berkeley and Los Angeles: University of California Press, 1998.

Hunt, Herbert and Floyd C. Kaylor. *Washington West of the Cascades.* Chicago: S. J. Clarke, 1917.

Kappler, Charles J., Comp. and Ed. *Indian Affairs: Laws and Treaties.* Washington, D.C. : G.P.O., 1904-1941. 5 v., volume 2.

Kluger, Richard. *The Bitter Waters of Medicine Creek: Western Washington's Indian Wars.* New York: Knopf, 2011.

Lane, Barbara. "Political and Economic Aspects of Indian-White Culture Contact in Western Washington in the Mid-Nineteenth Century." May 10, 1973. Typescript in Muckleshoot Preservation Program Archives. (1973a)

Lane, Barbara. "Anthropological Report on the Identity and Treaty Status of the Muckleshoot Indians." U.S. District Court, Tacoma, WA. Plaintiff's exhibit No. USA-270, *United States v. Washington*, admitted to the record August 24, 1973. (1973b)

Lane, Barbara. "Background of Treaty Making in Western Washington." *American Indian Journal* 3/4 (1977), 2-11.

Lane, Barbara. "The Muckleshoot Indians and the White River: A Report Prepared for the Muckleshoot Indian Tribe." September 1980. In Muckleshoot Preservation Program Archives.

Meeker, Ezra. *Pioneer Reminiscences of Puget Sound: The Tragedy of Leschi.* New York: Lowman & Hanford Stationery and Print. Co., 1905.

Morgan, Murray. *Skid Road: An Informal History of Seattle.* New York: Viking Press, 1952.

Noel, Patricia Slettvet and Virginia Cross. *Muckleshoot Indian History.* Auburn, WA.: Auburn School District No. 408, 1980.

"Talk by Chief Slugamus Koquilton" in *Commemorative Celebration at Sequalitchew Lake, Pierce County, Washington, July 5, 1906.* Second Ed. Pierce County Historical Association, 33-34. Copy in files of Muckleshoot Preservation Program Archives.

Thrush, Coll. *Native Seattle: Histories from the Crossing-Over Place.* Seattle: University of Washington Press, 2007.

"Treaty Between the United States, and the Dwamish [sic], Suquamish, and Other Allied and Subordinate Tribes of Indians in Washington Territory." January 22. 1855. Reproduced 1966 by the Shorey Bookstore, Seattle, WA.

"The Treaty Sesquicentennial: Treaty Wars, 150 Years Ago." *Muckleshoot Monthly*, October 15, 2005, 20. Reprinted from the *White River Journal*, newsletter of the White River Historical Museum.

Vancouver, George. *A Voyage of Discovery to the North Pacific and Around the World.* 3 vols. London: G. G. and J. Robinson, 1798.

Waterman, T. T. *Puget Sound Geography: Original Manuscript from T. T. Waterman. Ed. with Additional Material from Vi Hilbert, Jay Miller, and Zalmai Zahir.* Zahir Consulting Services, 2004. Copy in files of Muckleshoot Preservation Program Archives.

Whale, Robert. "Local Author Paul Nelson Tells of 'A Time Before Slaughter.'" *Auburn Reporter*, July 1, 2010. [http://www.pnwlocalnews.com/south_king/aub/community/97622364.html]

"White River Massacre Takes Lives of Nine Pioneers." *Kent News-Journal*, August 3, 1939, 7.

Chapter 3

Stirrings of Revival

Chapter 3

Stirrings of Revival

A century of social, political, and economic repression and poverty for the Muckleshoots and other Native peoples in the Pacific Northwest followed the signing of treaties with the invading United States. The flame of community never died, however, even in the worst of times. By 1970 Muckleshoot tribal (common) land ownership had declined to about one-quarter of an acre. The revival that followed took place against a stark background of decades during which the Muckleshoots suffered immensely. This era ended with the reassertion of treaty fishing rights in defiance of the state's armed force.

Covered wagons conveyed barely a trickle of immigrants to the Puget Sound basin during the 1850s, as regional treaties were negotiated and the "Treaty War" was fought. The alternative to the arduous cross-country wagon journey was a sea voyage around the southern tip of South America. Ten years later, after the U.S. Civil War, the continent was linked by rail, with a terminus in Seattle, and immigration soared. Non-Indians west of the Cascades in Washington Territory, fewer than 5,000 people in 1860, rose to about 25,000 in 1880. The U.S. Census listed 303 "citizens" (non-Indians) in King County as of 1860; by way of comparison, Arthur Denny, one of the founders of what he called the "little colony that developed into the city of Seattle" on Alki Point, described a Native population of more than 1,000 in that area (now West Seattle) in 1851 (Watson, 1999, ii).

Recurring waves of smallpox and other diseases, loss of land, alcoholism, malnutrition, and armed conflict were reducing Native American populations. By 1900, the number of non-Native people in the territory was more than 100,000. Native people comprised about half the population in 1860; by 1890, whites outnumbered them by about 20 to 1. Seattle, founded in the 1850s, contained barely 1,000 people in 1870, and almost 43,000 by 1890. Tacoma, founded in 1868, grew to 36,000 in 1890 (Harmon, 1968, 103–105). Between 1880 and 1890, the immigrant population of the Puget Sound region grew by 155,000 people, a 600 percent increase in ten years (Harmon, 1998, 132, 298n4). A census during 1870 listed 7,657 Indians west of the Cascades in Washington Territory (Marino, 1990, 172). By 1921, the Native population in the same area was listed in a federal government report as 5,003 (Marino, 1990, 176). Indian census numbers also were reduced as some Native people married whites and left reservations to qualify for homesteads.

THE MUCKLESHOOTS AS YEOMAN FARMERS

U.S. government policy often sought to turn Native people away from hunting, fishing, and gathering (all regarded as "uncivilized" means of support) and toward yeoman agrarianism, like that of Plains sodbusters, with the legendary half section and a mule. This policy also squared with the needs of the immigrating whites and the railroads to move the Indians off the large traditional range required for hunting and gathering. The Native peoples refused to relinquish fishing rights, although, if one believes the Indian Bureau's records and correspondence, they did not catch many fish. Policies were not consistent. Some government officials encouraged traditional Indian hunting and fishing in the short term to save

Lester George.
Photo courtesy of Virginia Cross and Patricia Slettvet Noel. Muckleshoot Today. Auburn, WA: Auburn School District no. 408, 1981.

money. Muckleshoots continued clamming, for example.

Internal politics sometimes divided people in the government. While some sought the white sodbuster's life for the surviving Indians, others wanted to abolish as many reservations as possible and consolidate population on a few tracts of land, regardless of people's homelands. Administrative efficiency usually was the cited rationale. As early as 1862, S. D. Howe, the agent at Tulalip told his superiors in Washington, D.C. that "keeping up of the [Muckleshoot] reservation is a useless expenditure of money" (Richards, 1991, 43).

This point of view didn't hold sway, however, and an "assistant farmer," John Webster, was assigned. He reported that the Muckleshoots were "anxious to put in crops," including oats and wheat (Richards, 1991, 43). For the next eight decades, the Indian Bureau, and later the Bureau of Indian Affairs (BIA), kept a detailed accounting of Muckleshoot crop production. In 1874, the reservation was expanded over the protests of some white farmers and the railroads, with the stated reason of providing enough land for all the roughly 160 Muckleshoots to develop their abilities as farmers. Two white immigrants protested that they already had the land under claim, but nothing came of it. However, the reservation's "expansion" in 1874 was really a contraction, compared to what had earlier been promised.

Slugamus Koquilton stands near trees, Lake Sequalitchew, Washington, April, 1906.
Photo courtesy of University of Washington Libraries, Special Collection / NA4192

By 1874, reports of Muckleshoot agricultural talents turned overwhelmingly positive, as agents reported to Washington that fishing, hunting, and gathering had been abandoned (no one knows how many fish were caught outside the agents' sight). The agents loved statistics; one might ask who was counting all those bushels. In 1887, the reports said they produced 4,350 bushels of oats, 5,400 bushels of potatoes, 227 tons of hay, plus smaller amounts of wheat, barley, and butter, all counted with inexplicable exactness.

The Muckleshoots also owned 63 head of cattle, 80 horses, 63 sheep, 45 hogs, and 300 chickens (Richards, 1991, 50). By 1892, the agent at Tulalip said that every last Muckleshoot was raising crops or laboring for others, "in civilized pursuits" (Richards, 1991, 50). The Indian commissioner asked the agent how many Muckleshoots were obtaining sustenance by "fishing, hunting, or root-gathering." The agent replied emphatically: "None" (Richards, 1991, 50) — a false response strongly influenced by agency policy that emphasized farming. A tribal census in 1890 listed the occupation of every single Muckleshoot as "farmer" (Richards, 1991, 50), another response skewed by agency policy.

Somehow, however, even the Indian Bureau records indicated that at least a few fish were being caught. A report in 1895 said that Muckleshoots had earned $75 from the sale of fish, but that number was outmatched by the $420 earned from knitting socks out of wool from reservation sheep, sold to whites in the cities for 50 cents a pair (Richards, 1991, 51).

To reinforce agrarian pursuits, in 1903, 3,357 acres were distributed in 39 allotments averaging 81.97 acres each. Reservation farmer Charles Reynolds reported that allotment "pleased" the Muckleshoots (Richards, 1991, 51). Competition from jobs off-reservation

Archie Lobehan.
Photo courtesy of Virginia Cross and Patricia Slettvet Noel. Muckleshoot Today. Auburn, WA: Auburn School District no. 408, 1981.

(logging and sawmills for men, maid services for women) was beginning to compete with farm work by 1907. Farming continued, however. In 1924, the Western Washington State Fair featured Muckleshoot produce. Dairy farming developed and a Carnation Milk plant opened in Kent. The Starr family was notable for its dairy, hay, grain, potatoes, and other vegetables. By 1926, three Muckleshoot families were conducting dairy business on a commercial scale. In 1937, the government tallied 18,480 pounds of potatoes, 240 pounds of onions, 2,400 pounds of cabbage, 1,840 pounds of red beets, 2,960 pounds of beans, 4,800 pounds of squash, including pumpkins, 8,600 pounds of carrots, 400 pounds of turnips, 1,600 pounds of peas, and 14,000 pounds of cucumbers harvested from Muckleshoot land (Richards, 1991, 54).

Chapter 3

Muckleshoot family with Slugamus Koquilton and William Lane near house, Muckleshoot Reservation, Washington, April, 1906.
Photo courtesy of University of Washington Libraries, Special Collection / NA4194

MUCKLESHOOTS EXTINCT? THEY WERE WRONG

When Chief Slugamus Koquilton, who had become known to the whites when he sheltered a five-year-old Anglo-American boy during the "Treaty War" of 1855 and 1856, died December 8, 1909 at age 93, the Seattle newspapers declared the Muckleshoots extinct. They were wrong. The Muckleshoots were few in number during the early twentieth century, but among them were some striking personalities, people who were determined to preserve language and culture. Most of the strongest leaders of this revival were women. Joining them was an amazingly foresighted witness to these stirrings of revival, Arthur C. Ballard, an early anthropologist. The road back was not an easy one. In 1960, the United States elected John F. Kennedy president. There was talk of sending men to the moon. The United States had acquired its fiftieth state, Hawaii. The Muckleshoot reservation acquired its first flush toilets on a sewer system (Noel and Cross, 1980, 73).

At the beginning of the twentieth century, the records of the Bureau of Indian Affairs occasionally hint that while the Muckleshoot tribe had no formal organization under a written constitution or bylaws, it clearly continued to exist as a political community. In 1903, for example, the Muckleshoot resident farmer informed Charles Buchanan, supervisor at the Tulalip Agency, that the Muckleshoots had organized no "tribal relations" nor raised up any chiefs in twenty years. The resident farmer, therefore, assumed authority to appoint a tribal court judge. Quickly, Buchanan received a petition of protest from George Nelson, whom the letter designated as "chief," with support of Joe Snohomish, Bob James, Justin Joseph, and Joe Billy, dated November 20, 1903, "in the name of all the Indians of this place," supporting the right "of all the Indians of Muckleshoot" to elect their own judges.

The letter was couched, however, in assimilationist language: "The Indians of Muckleshoot are now in path of a new law lighted on all sides so that they can see what is Just and So Be not wild any more but Civilized like the whites forever" (Harmon, 1998, 155, 309n71). In 1918, several men and women at Muckleshoot, reacting to conscription during World War I, wrote to the superintendent of the Cushman School rejecting the notion that their offspring were U.S. citizens (Harmon, 1998, 163-164, 312n12). The hand of the BIA laid very heavily on the Muckleshoot, and Indians generally, at this time, however. Muckleshoot Lyman Siddle was required, for example, to prove his competency to the BIA to receive $75 from his trust account to buy a piano (Harmon, 1998, 165, 312n18).

DISMANTLING THE MUCKLESHOOT RESERVATION

The first non-Indians took land on the Muckleshoot reservation in 1868. Of the original 3,500 reservation acres, by 1968, more than a century later, about two-thirds had passed out of Native ownership (American Friends, 1970, 56-57). Without land, poverty followed. Many people were forced into seasonal farm labor to sustain their families on or near land they once had owned. Fishing was seasonal, even when the state was not trying to shut it

George Nelson at Muckleshoot Reservation, Washington, 1905.
Photo courtesy of Universtiy of Washington Libraries, Special Collection / NA1219

down. People often struggled to catch enough fish to feed their families. In 1960, 270 Muckleshoots lived on the reservation. In 1975, the Muckleshoot tribal roll listed 640 members. Of 3,841 people living on the Muckleshoot reservation in the 1990 U.S. Census, 77 percent were non-Native.

Traditionally, Muckleshoot people hunted and fished on commonly held lands, based upon historic relations with neighboring Native peoples. They did not own individual pieces of land on the Anglo-American legal model. All of this changed with the passage of the Dawes (Allotment) Act of 1887, which allowed reservation land to be broken up into individual holdings. With the advent of individual ownership, landholders could sell their parcels. Desperate for cash, Native people frequently sold their allotted land to acquire money simply to stay alive. After a holding period of 25 years, if a Native property owner could demonstrate to the Bureau of Indian Affairs that he was competent, he was allowed to sell his parcel. At Muckleshoot, and across the United States, allotment provoked widespread land sales to non-Indians.

A cultural assault went hand-in-hand with enforced individual property rights. Indians also were told to give up living in extended families for the nuclear families for which allotment was modeled. Private land ownership was promoted over communal use. In Seattle at the turn of the century (1897 to 1917), a U.S. House of Representatives' committee's minority report drew attention to the real reason for the Dawes Act:

> The real aim of this bill is to get at the Indian lands and open them up to settlement. The provisions for the apparent benefit of the Indians are but the pretext to get at his lands and to occupy them. ... If this were done in the name of greed, it would be bad enough; but to do it in the name of humanity, and under the cloak of an ardent desire to promote the Indian's welfare by making him like ourselves, whether he will or not, is infinitely worse. (Fey and McNickle,1959, 73)

Allotment, pitched as a way to induct Native peoples into Anglo-American society, became a giant land agency that transferred real estate from Native to non-Native owners. Between 1887 and 1934, approximately 90 million acres were obtained from individual Indian ownership across the United States. Muckleshoot reservation lands were not actually allotted to individual families until after 1900, and then the lands were assigned to families under the provisions of the Treaty of Point Elliott, rather than the Dawes Act.

Later, allotment was stopped by the Indian Reorganization Act (IRA) of 1934, which also provided limited reservation government and established tribal rolls (membership rosters). A Muckleshoot Constitution was ratified under the IRA the same year it was enacted, and ratified by the Interior Department, as the IRA requires, in 1936. A tribal census also was compiled during the same year. The Muckleshoot constitution determined that the tribe would be governed by an elected tribal council of nine. This Council is subject, in turn, to a General Council, consisting of all members.

At Muckleshoot, loss of land continued until 1968, as land was taken, and water diverted, often blocking fish runs. In 1910, the Tacoma Water Department diverted water from the Green River as construction began on a dam. Puget Sound Power and Light also began diverting water from the White River to Lake Tapps. The next year, the White River was diverted to the Puyallup River to reduce flooding in Auburn. The Tacoma Water Department diversion dam on the Green River was completed in 1913. And, in 1916, the Black and Cedar rivers were diverted from the Duwamish into Lake Washington. In 1919, private levee construction was allowed along the entire length of the Green and Duwamish rivers, again to reduce flooding.

Indian agents often sought ways to combine operations within their bureaucracy, irrespective of Native homelands, survival requirements, or traditions. The Native people at whom these proposals were aimed repeatedly reminded them that a homeland had a purpose. In 1867, the Indian agent argued that the Muckleshoots' land should be sold and its 150 residents merged with the nearby Puyallups. In 1875, an Indian agent recommended abandoning the Muckleshoot reservation and sending its people to the Lummi, on the Canadian border, about a hundred miles away. The Muckleshoots refused to move.

Occasionally during the years when the land was slipping from the Muckleshoots' grasp, wild rumors flew about some huge payoff or another for lands taken. During 1957, reports spread in Seattle-area newspapers that the Muckleshoots were awaiting $3.5 million for 107,000 acres taken in 1859 under the Homestead Act. Their attorney, Frederick W. Post, was quoted as saying "That's what the Indians ought to get" (Johnson, 1957, n.p.). Post said that the land should have been valued at $10 an acre (its value in 1859). That would have been $1,070,000. Perhaps the $3.5 million figure included inflation, or interest, although the news accounts did not say so. Post said, "We've already been granted the judgment, but the amount wasn't stipulated. We received a favorable verdict from the Indian Claims Commission in August, 1955" (Johnson, 1957, n.p.).

The small type indicated that the $3.5 million so prominently trumpeted in the erroneous headline was a matter of speculation, not a legally binding figure. The $3.5 million would have been about $10,000 per Muckleshoot, enough to buy a small house in 1957. There is no indication that anyone actually received anything. One of the articles, in the August 4, 1957 *Seattle Post-Intelligencer Pictorial Review* ended by quoting an unnamed "aged Indian who sat on a low stump before a two-room cabin:" "They promise everything and give us nothing. They have taken our lands, our fishing rights, and our self-respect. We will get nothing" (Glover, 1957, 2).

Arthur C. Ballard, 1924.
Courtesy White River Valley Historical Museum / 01805C

The one land claims payment the Muckleshoots did receive, eleven years later, was much smaller — $68,689 for 101,620 acres taken in 1859 under the Point Elliott Treaty. That comes out to about 66 cents an acre. This provided $250 each to 253 Muckleshoots listed on the tribal roll in 1965, with the remainder going into the tribal general fund ("LBJ," 1968, n.p.).

ARTHUR C. BALLARD: A REMARKABLE WITNESS

The anthropologist Arthur C. Ballard described Muckleshoot people and culture during the first half of the twentieth century, under the heavy hand of foreign colonialism. While people were very poor, the flame of culture and cooperative enterprise never died. Dances and songs were performed, even as missionaries and government agents inveighed against them. Fishing continued, even as state game agents made it risky and sometimes dangerous. People survived. Ballard's work is maintained in the Muckleshoots' archives as one of few records of a time of trial, when the people were tested.

Ballard was (and in memory remains) deeply loved by many Muckleshoots. "What is not to love about a man with a broad and seeking intellect," asked Patricia Cosgrove, director of the White River Valley Museum, "who was by nature culturally inclusive; willing to be ridiculed by his neighbors for walking up the hill to befriend and learn from Indian people; capable of mastering the Muckleshoot language and pioneering a way of writing it; a man who (contrary to most anthropologists of his era and later), credited his Indian teachers by name and genealogy, reimbursed them for their time, and welcomed them into his home?" (Watson, 2007, 8).

Developing rapport with many of the elders in the area, Ballard compiled the most detailed descriptions of Muckleshoot life during the lean years. He recorded their stories with a fidelity that is treasured by many of today's Muckleshoots. Ballard's writing was skilled, and his descriptions precise enough to transport readers through time. Ballard maintained the sole surviving written record documenting Muckleshoot heritage, including many family lineages. They are like a time capsule ("Statue," 2003, 16).

With a passionate intensity, Ballard began collecting a vocabulary of the language at the age of 15 or 16, during the fall of 1891 or 1892. He began interviewing elders about 1910 or 1911. His work on Salish myths began about 1916. He seemed reluctant to call them Muckleshoots, regarding that as something of an after-the-fact invented name. Instead, Ballard used "Green River Indians," or the band names (such as Skopabish) used in the Point Elliott and Medicine Creek treaties, Quizzed at the Claims Commission hearings about the origins of the word "Muckleshoot," Ballard said he had heard local Native people pronounce it "Buckleshooth" (Ballard, 1951, 21–22, 71).

Ballard's parents, Dr. Levi Ward Ballard, a physician, and his wife, Mary Ballard, migrated from New England to the Pacific Northwest during 1857, in the first wave of Anglo-American immigration, leaving poor farming land for a region where, they had been told, the soil was rich and the climate salubrious. They traveled by sea to the Isthmus of Panama before the Ship Canal was built, then rode a train that was so slow that people could hop off and pick flowers. The sea voyage continued on the Pacific side, to Oregon, where they spent seven years. In 1866, the family arrived in Washington Territory by covered wagon.

Born in 1875, Arthur Condict Ballard was a brother of Capt. William Rankin Ballard, a steamboat skipper whose name was affixed to the Seattle neighborhood of Ballard. The Ballards were among the founders of the town that came to be called Auburn. They established a homestead along the banks of the White River, building a post office and store on a wagon road that later became Auburn Avenue. "Old Nelson," the Muckleshoot who had led the Treaty War uprising in 1855 and 1856, then made peace with the immigrants, and cleared the first few acres of the property (Watson, 1999, vi).

Born on the homestead, Ballard survived a diphtheria outbreak that ravaged the area and claimed one of his older brothers. One of Arthur's earliest memories was of neighboring Native people gathering outside the family home to sing a mourning song in sympathy. His parents knew many of them; they harvested local crops and worked as maids. At the age of two, Arthur himself became very ill. Betsy Whatcom, a Native woman, volunteered to nurse him. According to a later account in the *Seattle Times Sunday Magazine*, Whatcom stationed herself at his cradle rocked it when he stirred, and materially assisted in nursing him back to health (Widrig, 1952, 5).

Ballard worked in his parents' local post office, as a city clerk, and as secretary-treasurer in the Azurite Gold Company, a family mining business. Beginning in 1901, Ballard also taught at the Klickitat Academy in nearby Goldendale, a school maintained by the Presbyterian church. He married Jane Casselman, a Canadian schoolteacher from Ontario, in 1906. Six years later, Arthur's parents donated land for a Carnegie library in Auburn a few feet from their home. Jane also served on Auburn's school board. Arthur grew up playing a rosewood piano owned by his mother (Watson, 2007, 8).

A self-taught, avid reader, Ballard by his teenage years was reading such books as Prescott's *Conquest of Mexico and Peru*, and "a local history that my father had subscribed to that had a chapter on the mythology and culture of the Yakama Indians" (Ballard, 1951, 3-4). Ballard graduated from the University of Washington with a major in Latin during 1899, at a time when Auburn was "largely ... board walks, frame shacks, [and] wagon-rutted muddy roads" ("Death Claims," 1962, n.p.). At the time, the University of Washington had no curriculum in anthropology (then called "ethnology"). He also attended classes at Whitworth College when its campus was in Tacoma, and in Sumner, a town north of there ("A. C. Ballard," 1962, n.p.). (Today Whitworth University is located in Spokane.) In 1912, the *Argus*, an Auburn newspaper, published articles by Ballard based on some of his early research.

By 1911, Ballard had begun to interview elders in southern Puget Sound and record place names in the Muckleshoot language,

"Dr. Jack," (with pipe).
Photo courtesy of Museum of History & Industry, Seattle; Dam Brothers Collection 1992.9.2

which he learned with Muckleshoot interpreters as he interviewed several elders and leaders. The informant best known to the immigrants was called "Big John" (Sukwa'lasxt). He was born about 1840, and was a teenager when the European-Americans moved to the area in large numbers, started farms, built homes, and laid claim to the land. He was known as a fisherman of great physical strength who used a large weir trap on the Green River. Big John explained to Ballard the origins of his people and Muckleshoot language words for animal and place names, family genealogies, and accounts of historical events from a Muckleshoot point of view, leaving a valuable record. Many of the stories and legends of Puget Sound indigenous peoples would have been lost if Arthur Ballard had not met Big John and other Muckleshoot elders.

Ballard was highly skilled as a linguist. In addition to English and Latin, he was fluent in Spanish, German, the experimental universal language Esperanto, and several Coast Salish dialects (as well as some Native languages from east of the Cascades) (Watson, 1999, vii).

All his life, Ballard was questioned because he lacked what some anthropologists regarded as proper academic credentials. He was ashamed of his interest in Native studies until he heard a lecture on the Suquamish in 1909 by a Professor Harrington, who, he said, "encouraged me" (Ballard, 1951, 4). Later, Ballard attended lectures by Prof. Thomas Talbot Waterman of the University of California, who in coming years would work with him and make use of his work on the Puget Sound Salish. Ballard's lack of formal ethnological credentials did not bother Waterman, a nationally esteemed anthropologist who based large parts of his *Notes on the Ethnology of the Indians of Puget Sound* on Ballard's observations. Archivists at the Royal Anthropological Society in London did not require a degree in the field to store Ballard's ethnographic and linguistic field notes there (Watson, 1999, viii).

Waterman's *Notes* were compiled between 1918 and 1921, while he consulted in anthropology at the University of Washington, but were not published until 1973, by the Museum of the American Indian (Heye Foundation) in New York City. Waterman said that "a good deal of the field work [for this volume] was done in company with Mr. Arthur C. Ballard of Auburn, who previously, on his own initiative, recorded a very considerable body of

Big John (Sukwa'lasxt).
Photo courtesy of White River Valley Historical Museum / 00438

information concerning Indian life around Puget Sound. Mr. Ballard may be regarded as the leading authority on the Indians of the state of Washington. His acquaintance with them and with their mode of life has extended over a long period and is extremely intimate" (Waterman, 1973, vii). Waterman added that "Certain information obtained by Mr. Ballard is embodied in the present paper, which to that extent is a joint enterprise" (Watson, 1999, vii).

During the 1930s, Ballard helped to raise funds for the Muckleshoots' community center, which was built as a public works project. The opening of the center was hosted by the Nesika Club, a public service organization in the Muckleshoot community known for its presentations of traditional Native American songs and dances at public gatherings (Watson, 2007, 8). His wife, Jane M. Ballard, died in 1939.

During November 1951, and again in 1954 and 1955, Ballard was called as an expert witness before the Indian Claims Commission regarding the identity, continuity, and traditional territory of the Muckleshoot people. For three days, Ballard, then more than 75 years of age, provided more than 500 pages of testimony (as well as additional maps, documents, photographs and other evidence) describing the territory occupied by Muckleshoot ancestors ("Death Claims," 1962, n.p.).

Even in 1951, after decades of work, Ballard was questioned extensively by the government's attorneys about his academic qualifications. Ballard had no academic position and worked among Native people without salary. He was listed as a "field research assistant" in anthropology in later years at the UW, but never paid. He spent several hundred dollars, a significant amount at that time, supporting his Indian work. Recognizing standards of Native reciprocity and hospitality, as well as

John Halcum also known as John Newhauken, John Kiyawit, or Little John, April 1921. Kodak picture taken by A. C. Ballard. *Photo courtesy of National Anthropological Archives, Smithsonian Institute, Ballard Collection. (Public record) via Muckleshoot Preservation Program Archives*

genuine need, much of the money bought food for the people Ballard interviewed, whom he also paid for their time (Watson, 1999, viii).

Greg Watson wrote that he "located villages, traced genealogies, explained traditional technology and beliefs, and in general spoke for friends and colleagues long since passed away, whose wisdom he had kept safe into his own old age." A tribal roll (census) of Muckleshoots was compiled in 1881 that contained both Native and English names. In the

Chapter 3

Group at house of Jerry Dominick on the Muckleshoot Reservation, December 17, 1917. Photo by Arthur Ballard. From left to right: 1. Mrs. John Seattle (Skíeídpam); 2. Daniel James also called James Daniels (pa loítubda and other Indian names); 3. Betsy Whatcom (Siveítsida) half sister to Tom Wiletchtid; 4. Mary Dominick daughter of Big John (is the only one of this group living in Jan. 1952); 5. Samson (Siyuíl) born about 1840 at the village forks on Green/White River; 6. Charlie Sotiakum (Sotaíyakeb) reported to have been a longshoremen in San Fransisco in mid-1850s and present at the signing of the Treaties; 7. Joseph Bill (leílkaibAíl); 8. Bob James (kwikaíyebxed), in doorway, Shaker leader; 9. Big John (Sukwa'lasxt) born about 1830 present at the Treaty signing; 10. Nancy Big John (Tkwiyaítdubelut) 11. Little John or John Halcum, John Newhauken (Kíiyaíiut). His father (Da whal kin) was a shaman, wife was daughter of Christine, Muckleshoot; 12. John Seattle (Sodiída), distant relative of Chief Seattle.
Photo courtesy of National Anthropological Archives, Smithsonian Institute, Arthur Ballard Collection (Public record)

1951 Claims Commission hearings, attorneys questioned Arthur Ballard about nearly all of them in detail.

The United States was using the Claims Commission in an attempt to dismiss a claim for compensation on grounds that the Muckleshoots were "not a tribe, band, or other identifiable group of American Indians as required by the Indian Claims Commission Act" (Ballard, 1951, 2). Ballard, wrote Watson, "helped build a persuasive body of evidence that the culture that signed the treaties nearly a century before had not died, but was alive and remembered things given up and promises made" (Watson, 2007, 8). Ballard was always an advocate of Muckleshoot nationhood. Near the end of three days of extensive interviews, Ballard was asked his opinion of the government's assertion that the Muckleshoots "are not identifiable as a tribe of Indians." "I'd say that contention is invalid," he replied

(Ballard, 1951, 342). He traced an organized tribal council to the late 1860s, with Whatcom as chief (344).

After he died in mid-November 1962 at the age of 85, much of Ballard's work long remained closed in museum collections or in the hands of families. In 2005, however, Dr. Charles Ballard, grandson of Arthur, signed an agreement to share papers, photos and artifacts that the elder Ballard had compiled. At the time of his death, Ballard also was completing a book manuscript entitled *Listen, My Nephew: Myth, Tradition and History on Southern Puget Sound*, an account of Washington State Native peoples told from their viewpoints. The book was finished, but never published. The papers shared by Charles Ballard provided the Muckleshoots the first access to that manuscript, along with many other unique items of value to Muckleshoot historians. "Dr. Charles Ballard has earned our deep appreciation for being a

Dr. Charles Ballard shakes hands with Tribal Chairman John Daniels Jr. after signing a long-awaited agreement to share papers, photos and artifacts of great cultural and historic importance with the tribe from Dr. Ballard's grandfather, Arthur C. Ballard (1876-1962).
Photo by John Loftus, Muckleshoot Monthly

friend to the tribe, just as his grandfather was," the *Muckleshoot Monthly* commented ("Cultural Treasures," 2005, 2).

BALLARD DESCRIBES THE MUCKLESHOOT WORLD THROUGH MYTHS AND STORIES

Ballard published two collections of Southern Salish "myths" and "tales" through a series with the University of Washington Press in 1927 and 1929. The shorter collection, *Some Tales of the Southern Puget Sound Salish*, drew on interviews of several Native people, two of whom were Big John (born 1835 or earlier) and Jack Smohalla, who were identified as "from Green River and Suise Creek." Big John had a Duwamish mother, and Smohalla was part Klickitat (Ballard, 1927, Preface, n.p.). The others were Puyallup, Klickitat, Duwamish, Snoqualmie (Snuqualmi), and Nisqually.

The longer collection ("Myths") compiled stories from many more people; those who were Muckleshoot (or lived on or near the Green and White rivers) were identified by the name of the river, and included the following: Sampson, born about 1840 (and his parents), August James, born about 1890 (and his mother); Mary Jerry (Mrs. Jerry Dominick) and her mother; Big John (and his father and mother); Jack Smohalla (as well as his father, mother, and son Jonah Jack, born April 1872); Annie Jack, born about 1875; Stuck Jack; Ann Jack, born about 1835 (with her father, mother, and two maternal uncles), and Charles Sotiakum, born 1830 or earlier (Ballard, 1929, 35-41). The birthdates used here are derived from a corrected list compiled by Ballard 20 years after the original publication (Ballard, 1949, n.p.).

Ballard noted that because intermarriage was common throughout South Puget Sound many ancestries were mixed, and stories were similar. The 1927 volume contains as many as seven versions of the same stories. People included Puyallup, Klickitat, Duwamish, Snoqualmie (Snuqualmi), Nisqually, and Yakama, with many intertribal relations.

Many of the stories are fanciful, such as "The Magic Salmon," which takes place "in the neighborhood of Spirit Lake ... In that stream [where] the Tyee [chief] Salmon used to spawn." Three brothers came upon the stream while hunting. Hungry, they decided to catch some salmon. The youngest brother decided not to take part.

> However, the elder brothers caught some salmon, which they skinned, cooked, and ate ... The elder brothers were very thirsty. They thought they should drink, [but] the youngest warned them against doing so. They drank copiously. The eldest brother dove and swam. When he appeared again he had become a merman. The next oldest brother did the same. (Ballard, 1927, 73)

Many of the stories mete out moralistic justice or defy notions of European-American physics. The tales are full of shape-shifting, as just about everything in nature assumes (or sometimes loses) human attributes. Moon, "The Transformer," ranges the countryside doling out just deserts, or protecting prerogatives. The Deer, caught whittling a weapon with his fingers to attack Moon, loses them and becomes a threat to no one, and meat for humanity. An ogress who tempts people off a road and kills them is transformed into a rock. Passersby can tell which rock was the ogress because it menstruates blood. The storyteller was precise enough to tell Ballard that five such rocks exist.

Another story describes a gigantic skunk capable of killing people with the product of its scent gland, until Transformer scaled down its size and potency to the merely obnoxious skunk of today. In some of these stories, rocks may double back on people who throw them, depending upon their inclinations. Everything is alive, and changing, as lines drawn in European-American perceptions of reality (such as the border between animate and inanimate) shift, fade, and re-form.

Kill the wrong garter snake and its brethren may organize and attack (Ballard, 1929, 85–87). Girls marry sea beings and disappear beneath the waves. A man, his face dusty from gathering firewood, refuses to wash it until, badgered by relatives, he surrenders. His act of washing, at river's edge, provokes a rainstorm and a massive flood that kills everyone except him; he becomes a bird and takes flight on the rain-bearing southwest wind (Ballard, 129, 49).

Many of the myths are evocative of weather conditions in and near the Puget Sound region. "North Wind and Storm Wind" is a meteorological parable for the battle between a cold, dry continental air mass that during some winters forces its way southward from the interior of British Columbia, along the Fraser River and into Puget Sound ("North Wind"), encountering wet, mild storms ("Storm Wind") moving west to east off the Pacific Ocean. Anyone who has lived in the area for a length of time has experienced this weather pattern, which produces several days of cold, clear weather followed by a wild, stormy regime that may begin as heavy snow and end with heavy rain.

The story, related by Big John and Ann Jack to Ballard (in two of seven versions), involves an old lady and her people, the Rain Wind people, in conflict with the Cold Wind people. The Rain Wind people are killed by the Cold Wind people, except for one old woman and a few survivors, who are taken as slaves. One surviving boy, Storm Wind, is raised as an orphan by Mountain Beaver Woman. In the meantime, "Cold Wind held the land under his power. All the land was covered with ice and snow. He stretched a fish-weir of ice across the Duwamish River. No fish could get up the river past this trap. Further up the valley the people starved. They could get no fish to eat. The land was desolate" (Watson, 1999, 56).

In the meantime, the boy Storm Wind is growing up, and learning how his people have suffered at the hands of the Cold Wind. Storm Wind acquires a bow, growing bigger all the time, and visits a mountaintop mat house, where the old lady — his grandmother — is making baskets. They decide to fill all of her many baskets with rain to swamp the Cold Wind people and break the ice that blocks the river. "If Cold Wind had not been chased away," Big John told Ballard, "we should all be cold and hungry all the time. As it is, we have a little ice and snow, but not for long" (Watson, 1999, 57). A version of this story told to Ballard by Ann Jack features a battle for the hand of a young woman between North Wind, who is cold and brings no food, and Chinook Wind, "who brings gifts of food" (Watson, 1999, 59).

The stories are full of mayhem and murder, of ogresses eating babies' flesh, and the Transformer (Xode), like a lone, very busy cop on the beat, coming up behind it all and doling out shape-shifting justice. One such tale, "Transformer and the Mountain," may be an allegory for a land studded with active volcanoes. Ballard recorded, from Puyallup Tom Milroy: "T'qbId [the mountain] was a woman in the ancient time. She was bad; she ate people … She killed one, two, three. The Transformer approached The Mountain and told her to vomit. The mountain belched, and out came the bones of Indians." Trying to restrain the Mountain with ropes, Xode was drawn inside her, finding Bear and other animals. Xode then set a fire and "melted all the fat from her body … Now she is dead … Xode pronounced judgment upon her. 'Well, in the future you shall be harmless rock. You shall not eat people. People will walk upon you and you shall not eat them'" (Watson, 1999, 121).

On September 21, 2003, a life-sized bronze sculpture of Big John (Sukwa'lasxt) by Reynaldo Rivera of Albuquerque, commissioned by the Muckleshoot Tribe, was installed at the White River Valley Museum at a ceremony attended by some of Ballard's many descendents. The sculpture depicts the Muckleshoot leader, who was elderly when Ballard was a young man, "standing, pausing during a story, while Arthur Ballard sits nearby, notepad and pen in hand, ready to continue taking notes" ("Statue," 2003, 16).

THE SHAKERS

The Pacific Northwest produced the Shakers (not to be confused with the sect of the same name founded in England in the 18th century), a unique religion that anthropologist Wayne P. Suttles described as "a blend of Christian and Native religion …" (1987, 203). They remain very important among the Muckleshoots and on other Northwest Coast reservations today. The Shakers believe that their faith "was a new instrument provided by God to Indian people in their time of great need" (Amoss, 1990, 633).

The Shakers grew out of the trials and tribulations of John Slocum (Squ-sacht-un). He lived in the Mud Bay region just south of present-day Olympia. Slocum could have claimed high status among Indians in Puget Sound because of his lineage. He was also the boss of a logging operation. He expended great energy on gambling, horse racing, and alcohol, until his apparent death at age 40, in 1882.

Slocum had a near-death experience, he later described a glimpse of the hereafter. Slocum said he was met by angels who told him he had lived a terrible life gambling, swearing and drinking. They said, "You've been a pretty bad Indian" who had paid inadequate attention to his traditional culture (Finley, n.d.). Other versions of this account said that he met Big Father, who told him to return to life and build a church, pray, and depart from a lifetime of sin.

Slocum is said to have arisen from the dead very suddenly, sitting up and surprising several friends in a manner that provoked them to call the experience a resurrection, like that of a very well-known Christian prophet. Slocum, however, did Jesus Christ one better. He died again a year later (some say he had been tempted to gamble) and was brought back to life with a "shake" that became a signature ritual for the church.

In addition to inveighing against smoking, drinking, and gambling, the early Shakers avoided shamans. Upon Slocum's relapse, however, some of his relatives were so desperate that they called upon a traditional healer. Hearing the invitation, Slocum's wife Mary

Muckleshoot Shaker Church, new and old, from the air.
Photo by John Loftus, Muckleshoot Monthly

whose faith in his vision was strong, left the house in protest. As she wept and prayed she was overcome by an uncontrollable shaking. Still shaking, she re-entered the house and prayed over her husband. Her ministrations restored him and her shaking was hailed as the medicine God had promised. (Amoss, 1990, 633)

Mary also prayed, sang, danced, and brushed evil from John's body, all of which became elements of the Shaker healing ritual. The number of Shakers then began to grow quickly, northward to Vancouver Island, southward to Northern California, and eastward to the Yakama nation, east of the Cascades. (The mother church is in Mud Bay, Washington, between Olympia and Shelton.) In 1892, five years before Slocum died, the church was legally constituted. In 1913, the Muckleshoot Shaker Church was dedicated.

In the Shaker faith, Natives combined traditional Native beliefs with charismatic healing. The "shake" combined American Indian shamanistic healing practices with the signs and symbols of Christian spirituality. Writing in the *Handbook of North American Indians*, Pamela T. Amoss said that "The stronger the trance manifestations that accompany the involuntary trembling, the stronger the contact with divine power" (1990, 636). In 1900 Charles Rakestraw, who worked at the Chehalis Reservation Indian School, quoted Slocum:

When people are sick we pray to God to cure them. We pray that He [remove] the evil and leave the good. When our body and heart feel warm, we do good and sing songs. We learn good while we pray — Voice says "Do good." We learn to help ourselves when sick [rather than receiving help from Indian doctors] — for help to cure him. We learn something once in a while to cure him. If we don't care to help him we generally lose him. (Rakestraw, 1900, 704)

When the Shakers first organized, neither the U.S. government's agents nor the missionaries of Anglo-American religions liked what they saw. On June 14, 1905, Neah Bay Agency Superintendent Edwin Minor told Shakers on the Quileute reservation that their meetings would be restricted to two hours on Wednesdays and three hours on Sundays. He said that no children should attend during evening services, that church windows could not be closed, and that only one of the Shakers' trademark bells could be rung at a time. Agency police were instructed to arrest anyone who violated these rules (Watson, 1999, v). The Shakers ignored Minor's edict (Marino, 1990, 174). Charles Buchanan, the Indian agent in charge at Muckleshoot in 1914 submitted to his superiors a report entitled "The So-Called Shaker Indians of the Northwest." On page 21, he called the Shakers "altogether pagen" [sic], a thinly veiled reprise of old ways that the government had made illegal, "under the guise of quasi-Christianity" (Sneddon, 1960, 26). Buchanan wrote that Shakerism was a cross of Catholicism or Protestantism with barbarism (Sneddon, 1960, 31).

During their orgies and frenzies they jump, sing, leap, dance, beat the air or their bodies ... every available muscle in the body in a state of rapid tonic and clonic spasm ... This performance profoundly appeals to Indian imagination and nature and is considered overwhelming evidence of supernatural influences and powers. (Sneddon, 1960, 26)

Helen Clark of the Presbyterian Women's Board of Home Missions at Neah Bay, on the northwest Washington coast, writing in *Home Mission Monthly* (28:4), February 1914, said that Shakerism was being used by Indians as an antidote for drunkenness, because giving up alcohol was (and remains) a central tenant of the Shaker way of life (Sneddon, 1960, 27).

The Shakers invoke a hypnotic trance-like state during their rituals to go "out of this world" (Sneddon, 1960, 1). Some Shakers believe they have the power to locate a lost soul and restore it to an "errant person"; the removal of illness by moving hands around a person's body while in a "shake" is called "brushing" (Sneddon, 1960, 7). The Shakers, given the ways of their founder before he was revived, place a heavy emphasis on redemption and forgiveness. Some have been called by the spirit to give up alcohol or other errant behavior several times. Others have fallen out of the church, become physically ill, and returned to health through a "shake."

Annie Jack, a Muckleshoot and a lifelong resident of the reservation who practiced the Shaker religion during the middle of the twentieth century, performed healings by placing an ill person on a chair. She then conducted a "shake." First, she constructed an altar in her house with candles and a Christian cross. She then made the sign of the cross and burned candles. Jack's hands began to shake as she brushed them over the ill person. Jack did not touch the person, but used her "power" to extract the illness. She and other Shakers specialize in the ringing of bells (three to ten inches in diameter) during the service, which may continue many hours or even days. Jack was noted for her power to use the Shaker Church for healing and was often called upon by many Muckleshoot people.

Bernice White, chair of the Muckleshoot Shaker Church Council, its governing body, journeyed with her mother and a friend about 1957 to visit a sister in Toppenish (in the Yakima Valley) whose two-month-old infant had pneumonia and was bleeding internally. The white doctors had given her up as dying. White and the others "shaked" and prayed for three days. After that, the baby regained health. At the time that Sneddon wrote his report almost three years later, the child remained healthy (Sneddon, 1960, 9).

White herself during the summer of 1959 had a falling out with another member of the church, so she left it. Soon afterwards, she became very lame with severe arthritis, "so badly she could hardly walk" (Sneddon, 1960, 9). After six months of pain, White decided to return to the church, requiring assistance because of her hobbled ankles. Church members "shook" over White for several nights, as she improved. Within four weeks, her arthritis had disappeared (Sneddon, 1960, 9-10).

According to Sneddon's report, which reflects many practices still used today, most shakings took place on Saturday nights, followed on Sunday by a relatively tranquil church service with a sermon, singing, and bell ringing. Most of the congregants wore casual clothes, with many men in white T-shirts. One shaking witnessed by Sneddon began with a sumptuous feast (salmon cooked three ways, deer meat, potatoes, and salad, among other things). Five chairs were then arrayed in the middle of the room for the people to be cured by the coming shake, and they were seated. The feast was followed by a walk around the table three times, as everyone gave thanks with prayer, singing, and ringing of bells. The leader then turned toward the prayer table, and rang a bell in each hand. Candles were used in services because their flame is said to heal and cleanse. Members stood in a line, faced the wall, chanted a hymn, and stamped their feet. As sound and motion rise in intensity, people "get the power" (Amoss, 1990, 638). Sneddon continued:

> For the next seven hours without a stop they stamped their feet, rang bells, and sang. The bell ringers stood around the periphery while the balance of the Shakers worked in the interior. The workers gesticulated and stamped the floor in their own style. ... As the evening progressed, the fervor increased ... it seemed they were in an hypnotic state. The bells and singing became louder and the stamping became harder. Gradually the men became very wet from perspiration. The entire church vibrated in rhythm with the stamping. (Sneddon, 1960, 14-16)

The Shakers have debated whether to use the Bible. Slocum never used it (he could not read), but some Shakers introduced it into their services later (the Muckleshoot Shaker Church does not use it). Some Shakers read it at home, but regard church as the realm of the spirit, without mediation from the printed word. Alexander Williams, the Muckleshoots' Shaker minister in 1960, was quoted by Sneddon as saying: "The written word kills the spirit. No contact can be made if everyone is concentrating on a book" (Sneddon, 1960, 28). The debate over use of the Bible became so bitter that at one point, during 1945, it prompted a superior

Nesika Club group photo, 1930s. Copy in Muckleshoot Preservation Program Archives
Photo courtesy of National Anthropological Archives, Smithsonian Institute, Arthur Ballard Collection (Public record)

court in Snohomish County to split the local Shaker church into two congregations, a separation that continued into the 1980s (Amoss, 1990, 636).

Things are done in threes. For example, a funeral service may be planned to end at a church by noon so that everyone will exit the cemetery by 3:00 P.M. Shakers believe that they must always be ready to travel to aid anyone who is sick and needs their aid, in or outside the church. In recent years, aid has been provided to people wishing to break addictions to illegal drugs as well as tobacco and alcohol. Aid is provided without payment (if money is offered, Shakers refuse it). All they ask is the host's best hospitality. While Shakerism affirms life after death, "the overwhelming emphasis," according to Amoss, "is on living this life well" (1990, 638).

THE NESIKA CLUB, AND A COMMUNITY CENTER

On January 1, 1933, several Muckleshoots founded the Nesika Club, "a women's club with the view of improving home conditions, encouraging more social life, and organizing clubs for the younger people" (McIlveen, 1933, 3). The word "Nesika" was taken because it means "Ours" in Chinook jargon. The club's members also set a goal of raising funds for a community center, mainly by performing Native songs and dances for white people, "depicting the former life of their [Muckleshoot] people," including love songs and "the mountain song" (McIlveen, 1933, 3). The club dressed in a mixture of family heirlooms and Plains-style feathered headdresses. Gladys McIlveen, a social worker on the reservation, wrote that the women worked for days beading dresses, the beads for which they bought for a few pennies at the Goodwill or Salvation Army. ... They went miles looking for feathers for headdresses which the men helped them make. [People at Muckleshoot wore feathers because they were culturally related to Plateau people east of the Cascade mountains.] They spent hours with the old people being taught the old dances, songs, and customs. There was a great revival of interest in everything that pertained to the life of their ancestors. (McIlveen, 1937, 7)

Many whites in Auburn lent aid; a high school typing class created programs, and the high school's band provided music. The Auburn *Globe-Republican* published advance stories of the upcoming event. KOMO Radio in Seattle announced it, and Dr. Erna Gunther, a well-known anthropologist at the University of Washington, summoned her friends and colleagues. Arthur Ballard helped as well. The night before the program, however, one of the older women told the young girls that their dancing was poor, and so, their feelings hurt, they decided to quit. After a meeting, however, the situation was reconciled, and the show went on.

McIlveen described the event on Friday afternoon, February 24, 1933, at the Auburn American Legion Hall, giving credit to an account in the *Globe-Republican*. Walls of the hall were lined with booths in which artisans, young and old, wove baskets, and beaded bags "in the form of animals, birds, and flowers" (McIlveen, 1937, 8). Others wove cattail mats, spun sheep's wool, and knitted it into socks and sweater jackets. Another booth contained a display of patchwork quilts, embroidery, and crochet work. A model of a salmon weir, built by Jerry Dominick, was also on display.

Matilda Siddle called the audience to its seats with a welcoming address, and then

Farming at Muckleshoot was encouraged by the Works Progress Administration (WPA) during the 1930s.
Photo courtesy of White River Valley Historical Museum / 00435

Morris Lobehan, president of the Tribal Council, gave an historical talk, Professor Gunther commented on the revival of Native arts and crafts, followed by song, dance, and a Native wedding ceremony, described by the *Globe-Republican* as featuring "the plume of eagle feathers, some dentalium shells ... the bark of cedar, the Indians' sacred wood, the songs of girls, matrons, and men ... mingled in harmony and the rhythm of dancing feet portraying the emotions of love, mourning, and joy — dance of the magic wands, dance of the magic boards, girl's dance, wolf dance of the Yakama, love song, dance of the homesick bride" (McIlveen, 1937, 8-9).

The event cleared $41, a purse that rose to about $140 with seven other performances over a year in neighboring towns and cities, including Seattle (at Helen Bush School), over several months, but not nearly enough to build a community hall. In the spring of 1934, however, the federal government allocated funds though the Tulalip Indian Agency. The funds came with a short deadline, and the community hall was built by white workers in a flourish. The Muckleshoots felt as if they had been left in the dust. They had been hoping to build it themselves (McIlveen, 1937, 12). The Community Hall opened April 21, 1934, and provided a nucleus for events and planning.

One such project was a community garden funded by the Works Progress Administration that spurred the Muckleshoots to raise crops "equal or better in some cases than their white neighbors" (McIlveen, 1937, 12). They canned 3,000 quarts of peas, beans, and carrots, and an additional 250 gallons of pickles. An article in the Indian Bureau's magazine *Indians at Work* said the women who did the canning labored from early morning until after midnight "with a spirit never before seen among the people" (McIlveen, 1937, 12).

Morris Lobehan wrote to Edward F. Teague, WPA supervisor of their garden project, July 15, 1936 that it had been undertaken because "winter was being faced with dread." The state had precluded hunting and fishing, most of their best agricultural lands had been taken by whites, and unemployment levels had risen during the Great Depression. The farming and the ensuing canning marathon was necessary to avoid hunger and the stigma of applying for welfare ("relief"). The small tools, tractor, and plow provided by the WPA had been put to good use. Teague wrote to his boss, Fred G. Guenther, in the WPA Division of Operations, in Seattle, in an undated letter that despite a late start (April 26, several weeks after most farms in the area had planted their crops) and soil that had laid fallow for many years, the Muckleshoots' harvest was equal to that of their neighbors (Teague, n.d., 2).

"There should be some way for the Government to help the Red Man get the necessary equipment and stock so that he may be self-supporting on his own land," Lobehan wrote to Teague. "We have proven that we can farm as well as any other people. Now, is it necessary that we continue as relief clients? No, not if we are given a chance, and if we are not we will be forced to continue on relief and live from day to day. Should we be kept in this state? The answer is proven in the negative" (Lobehan, 1936, 2). As they set about farming, the Muckleshoots implemented the IRA by passing a constitution and bylaws April 4, 1936, by a vote of 46 to 2. The Secretary of Interior approved the election May 13 of the same year.

The Nesika Club drew about 400 people, white and Native, to the Community Hall during April 1939 for a celebration of the building's five-year anniversary. The *Seattle Times* ran a full page of photographs in its April 30 editions. The dancing included a mixture of local traditions ("Miss Eva King George leading other girls through intricacies of the bird and paddle dances"), along with some Plains transplants, such as "Chief Stepping Fast" and "Sunset Eagle" in a "Bison Dance."

In 1939, George P. LaVatta, an inspector from the Bureau of Indian Affairs, described the community hall as "a very fine building [with] a large room for community gatherings [and] two additional rooms ... one a community kitchen [and] the other a sewing room ... [and] a meeting place for committees and of the Council ... The women's organization is proud of this hall, and they keep the building immaculate" (LaVatta, 1939, 2).

THE ELEMENTS OF POVERTY

Muckleshoot and other Native communities were caught in a trap: so poor that they could not qualify for bank or federal loans that might aid economic recovery. Rural poverty was particularly severe because of isolation from basic services. There was no bus service to the reservation, which was detrimental to everyone seeking employment. Lack of bus service limited job seekers without cars to a very small number of opportunities. Muckleshoots also had few operating automobiles during the hardest days. Therefore, jobs that required regular commuting were beyond reach. The reservation itself offered few jobs.

Wage labor in timber and agriculture was used in addition to traditional subsistence cycles, including trips to pick hops in the Yakima Valley, combined with berry harvests, as well as hunting, while visiting relatives. Many men were highly valued as loggers at local timber companies. Women spun wool and knitted socks that were sold at Eddie Bauer in Seattle. People worked very hard to survive with little or no money during the Depression era, as some returned to hunting, trapping and gathering in the mountains for sustenance.

Basic services were unavailable to most Muckleshoots on the reservation during the 1960s, including running water, decent housing, basic medical care, dentists, law enforcement, and sewage. Even in the quite recent past (before the Muckleshoots built their own Health & Wellness Center) it was very difficult to get medical care for someone in an emergency on the reservation, even to find a working vehicle and gas to transport a person. Many babies were delivered at home. Infants were weighed on the scales at the smoke shop. Under the traditional "trust" relationship with the Bureau of Indian Affairs, the Muckleshoots during the 1960s were not making much headway in developing decent living conditions. Reservation population had declined throughout the decades preceding the 1960s, with no incentives that would bring Muckleshoots home to contribute to economic solutions. Poverty bred upon itself, as businesses refused to locate on the reservation.

While paternalistic government policies did little to improve conditions for the Muckleshoots, some governmental initiatives during the 1960s did begin to spark economic development. The New Frontier and Great Society programs under Presidents John Kennedy and Lyndon Johnson, notably the Office of Economic Opportunity (OEO), granted funds directly to poor communities for the first time. The OEO aided small business start-ups, and seeded the idea that poor communities could improve their economic conditions.

In the meantime, some Muckleshoots worked as loggers, and others took jobs in agriculture, picking fruit and vegetables. Others took part in a government relocation program to large cities such as Seattle, Los Angeles, and

San Jose, California, which taught vocational skills. The federal government believed that if Indians were trained in cities, they would choose to live there permanently, one more way to depopulate reservations and transfer their land and resources to other people. Some Muckleshoot took advantage of this plan to upgrade their skills, but most never intended to spend the remainder of their lives in cities.

Physical illness was rampant at Muckleshoot during the century of repression. Smallpox, sexually transmitted disease, tuberculosis, respiratory illness, and a variety of other maladies sharply reduced all Native populations. The Cushman Hospital of the Indian Health Service, in Tacoma, had many tuberculosis patients, many of whom died there. Several were buried in the hospital graveyard.

Even as the state made survival by fishing as difficult as possible (and people worked very hard to survive), the federal government was receiving studies that blamed Indian unemployment on their own shiftlessness. In 1956, a Stanford University study offered a peculiar opinion, much at variance with copious evidence: Muckleshoots, it said, "are generally unwilling to work, show little responsibility, and apparently prefer to subsist on welfare. ... The local employment agency is reluctant to recommend Indians for jobs other than common labor for fear that employers will discontinue use of the service." Muckleshoot Annie Garrison laid the blame on white prejudice, saying that Indian children were dropping out of school after non-Indians taunted them (Harmon, 1998, 221-222).

The Tacoma *News-Tribune* in 1968 published a detailed report describing conditions at Muckleshoot. One five-room house contained 24 people, who used kerosene lamps for lighting. The Bureau of Indian Affairs had installed a few bare light bulbs and wiring, but the local electric utility was demanding $350 (about $1,200 in 2014 dollars) to run a line from a power pole 500 feet away. An Auburn water line ran directly in front of the same house, but people inside had no access. They used a car and bottles to obtain their water from a spring on the Green River two miles away. Another large family "has lived in a tent in the forest, without water or sanitary facilities, since their house burned last September," eight months previously (Jeffords, 1968, A-1).

Employment was scarce in 1968, with a winter unemployment rate reaching 80 percent some years, except for seasonal logging and occasional fishing by 15 to 30 Muckleshoots who were willing to risk arrest and loss of their boats and gear to the state. Nearly 100 percent of the Muckleshoots living on the reservation had incomes below the federal poverty line. More than 90 percent of housing was dilapidated. Not a single reservation home had hot water. Many had no running water at all (Jeffords, 1968, A-15, A-16).

REVIVAL DURING THE 1960S

The 1960s are remembered as a time of extreme poverty at Muckleshoot, a time when several people shared one car to go grocery shopping. Photos from that era are rare today because of the many house fires. People used wood stoves and stuffed the eaves with newspapers as cheap insulation. Homes became firetraps. About 1970, some people at Muckleshoot said their houses had no running water, except for the rain that fell through holes in the roof. The Unitarian Church, the State Highway Department, the Bureau of Indian Affairs, and the Tribal Council found a way to address the Muckleshoots' housing shortage in a small way: homes that were displaced by new highways were moved to the reservation intact and installed on new foundations. At the time, the tribe said that 90 percent of the 60 homes on the reservation could be condemned under federal standards. The unemployment rate was 60 to 80 percent, depending on the season (Rupert, n.d., A-1). In 1971, the Muckleshoots took aim at the housing issue with a Housing Authority. The new authority set out to find funds for repair of old homes, and construction of new ones ("Indians to Form," 1971).

"THE VISTAS" COME TO MUCKLESHOOT

The Muckleshoots made extensive use of VISTA (Volunteers in Service to America, a domestic version of the Peace Corps) during the late 1960s. Many older Muckleshoots remember volunteers fondly by their first names — Pat, Mike, Bobby, and George, among others. One of several projects that "the VISTAs" hatched at Muckleshoot was a newspaper, called the *Muckleshoot News* for its first two editions (May and June, 1967). The 10- to 12-page, legal-sized mimeographed newspaper was very low-budget. The 250 copies of the second edition cost $10.97 to produce, including $6.92 for paper, and $2.40 for postage (the paper was mailed with a 4-cent stamp), 62 cents for stencils, 52 cents for correction fluid, and 41 cents for staples.

The second issue headlined the graduation of five Muckleshoots from local high schools (four from Auburn, one from Enumclaw), who were treated to a dinner in the Shaker Church's mess hall on Sunday, June 11. This was the Muckleshoots' largest graduating class to date. Sonny Bargala planned to attend Green River College in the fall to study political science after a summer working in the woods. Marlene Cross planned to spend her summer working with Head Start in Auburn, before moving to Dallas, Texas, to attend Dallas Vocational School to train on IBM machines or as a dental assistant. Liz James was seeking work in the summer to finance her studies at Green River Community College; Vernon Hungary also planned a fall at Green River CC, on a Bureau of Indian Affairs scholarship. Brenda Starr had a BIA grant for beauty school in Tacoma, but also hoped to attend Green River CC.

The paper needled the Bureau of Indian Affairs for seeking money to add 459 people to its payroll while telling Congress that Native American mothers were having too many babies, seeking contraceptives to stem the growth in Native population. More bureaucrats, fewer Indians, it implied. Locally, child care was described at the Muckleshoot Indian Preschool Cooperative, where children were learning how to take turns, share, and play together, as well as enjoy field trips to see cattle at the stockyards, picnic, visit a pumpkin farm, a fish hatchery, the Auburn fire department, and a pet shop. Shots were recommended at the Well-Baby Clinic.

The newspaper described many self-help initiatives on the reservation. For example, the VISTAs organized a food-buying club so that Muckleshoots could save money on groceries by buying in bulk. Willard Bill, Sr. was described as using his many connections at the State Employment Agency in Auburn to place people in jobs. The VISTAs were organizing trips to the Auburn YMCA so that young people could use its swimming pool (cost: 15 cents). A BIA agent described a program called "mutual help housing" by which participants would learn skills necessary to help build their own homes. There was no indication that any homes had actually been built that way at Muckleshoot.

During the spring of 1967, five Muckleshoots (Marie Starr, Norma Eyle, Bernice White, Florence Miller, and Virginia Brown) flew to Salt Lake City for training in an anti-poverty

Community Action Program (CAP) organizing to design on-the-job training in carpentry, plumbing, welding, as nurses' aides, and secretarial work. Fifty people attended a council meeting in the Community Hall to hear their report on May 15, 1967, where "suggestions from the floor stressed the need for housing repairs, the building of new homes, water for many houses, education for the young and old, job training, recreation, and repairs and improving the [Community] Hall" ("Tribal Meeting," 1967, 10). The *Muckleshoot News* listed a CAP Advisory Board with 32 members.

Other Muckleshoots organized trips to local newspapers to learn how to produce their own. The *Muckleshoot News* summoned supporters of Cecil and Robert Moses to "the Seattle Courthouse" (the short story in the paper didn't say which one) for a "fishing trial." Bernice White, a former Tribal Council member, was appointed to the state Committee on Indian Affairs. "Bring some of your problems to her," enjoined the newspaper ("More News," 1967, 5). The newspaper also described an Indian death rate from traffic accidents that was five times the state average. "Unless we become more careful," the account said, "we'll terminate ourselves before the White man gets a chance" ("Did You Know?" May 1967, 7).

By its third issue, in July 1967, the newspaper had a new name, the *Muckleshoot Messenger*, provided by Mary Williams. The lead story was a sweep by the Muckleshoot baseball team of a July Fourth tournament in La Conner. The paper also found itself almost $14 in debt, having spent its reserve of $4 and then some on five reams of paper. Despite food sales at a dance that raised $8, the newspaper said it would be charging $2 a year henceforth for off-reservation subscriptions.

The newspaper also carried results of a survey conducted in June 1967 by "the VISTAs"

Bernice White was the great-grandmother to three sets of twins, who are pictured here with their mothers. Front row: Donald Jerry Jr., Leetah Jerry, Zach John and Ryan John (Michael John's boys); Middle row: Lisa James, Bernice White, Millie (Bubbles) White; Back row: James Daniels, Sean Daniels and Connie Daniels.
Photo by John Loftus, Muckleshoot Monthly

(they were always referred to in the newspaper without names, in the plural), which had reached 80 percent of residents, with the remainder "not at home when the VISTAs went around." The survey found 372 people on the reservation (the account did not say whether this total included non-Native people, or those who were not at home). Of the 372 people in 59 houses, the average number per household was 6.3, and the average number of rooms in each house was 4.5. The average household income in homes with at least one person employed regularly (seasonal work was included) was $4,072 a year. Nearly 60 percent of the families earned less than $3,000 a year. More than 75 percent of men were employed seasonally, most of them in farming, logging, or construction. Curiously, fishing was not listed as an occupation in the questionnaire. The survey also asked people what kinds of repairs they needed on their homes, to which several responded: "foundation work, paint, flooring, roofing, walls, doors, chimneys, windows, garbage disposal, toilets, bathtubs, hot water, and electricity" ("CAP Survey," 1967, 6). Otherwise, the July edition contained a potpourri of daily life at Muckleshoot. Ten American Friends Service Committee volunteers had finished clearing the upper cemetery, filling a ditch outside the Well-Baby Clinic, and sanding the floor of the Community Hall.

At about the same time, Willard Bill, Sr. announced from his post at the State Employment Office in Auburn that applications were being taken for nurses' training. A dance was held at the Community Hall, 10 P.M. to 2 A.M., July 22, a Saturday night, with music by the Saints. Admission was $1. The paper, responding to instruction in the Muckleshoots' language, decided to print a word or two in each edition. The first was *[w]hooud*, meaning "firewood," with a note: "the '[w]h' is a blowing sound." This was another small spark in what would soon become a roaring flame of revival stoked by fishing-rights activism.

RESERVATION LIFE DURING THE LATE 1960S

The *Messenger*'s September 1967 issue carried a report by Dossie Miller (Wynne) of a meeting with King County sheriffs and Enumclaw police chief Brydon about reservation policing problems, including unwelcome visits by "outsiders who belong to other reservations trying to take over the reservation … juvenile delinquency [and] car thefts, shootings, and fights," many provoked, according to the report, by alcoholism (Miller, 1967, 2). The same edition carried a letter by Marie Starr describing a dance staged by the Muckleshoot Cooperative Preschool mothers to raise $275 to $300 for a "Language Master" machine (something like a large tape recorder) that would help teach children language skills. The dance, over

Muckleshoot Messenger logo.
Photo courtesy of White River Valley Historical Museum

the Labor Day weekend, ended in a drunken brawl during which gunshots rang out. "When I say [people had] too much to drink I'm not saying they were drunk," Starr wrote. "but that they had just enough to drink to want to fight" (Starr, September 1967, 3).

The event, which raised $175, was the preschool mothers' last fund-raising dance. Fund-raising attention turned to a flea market. Local people took out stalls and sold whatever they had, sharing proceeds 75/25 percent with the preschool. Some people sold handmade dolls, cradleboards, beadwork, totem poles, and baskets. The flea market, held at Camelot Elementary School November 11, 1967, raised more funds for the Language Master. Money was still being collected in February 1968. In the meantime, the program's federal grant (about $24,000 for a school year) had arrived six months after the period for which it was meant to provide money. The previous year, the funds had been almost eight months late. Pinching pennies, the preschool stayed open.

The *Messenger* was rich in local anecdotes that gave it a homey air. It described how Willard Bill, Sr. recruited more than 50 people through an employment program at the Auburn State Employment Office called New Careers to train as forest rangers, teacher aides, and health care assistants. Also in September 1967, John Belindo, Washington State director for the National Congress of American Indians, told the *Messenger* that the NCAI was protesting an ABC-TV series called "Custer." Legal counsel for the NCAI was petitioning the Federal Communications Commission for equal time under the Fairness Doctrine. The September issue also carried a complete reprint of the Medicine Creek Treaty of 1854 (15). Several reports described trips by the Head Start teachers to Salt Lake City for training in the Montessori method and other curricular matters. In 1968, the eight members of Muckleshoot Girl Scout Troop No. 236 sold 220 boxes of cookies at $1 each, for which they were rewarded with a dinner and an award presented in Seattle.

During the late 1960s, the *Messenger* described how the Auburn Public Schools employed a Muckleshoot "home visitor" part time (usually five hours a week), who inquired about school-related problems (mainly truancy) with families. Willard Bill, Sr. held the job until October 9, 1967, when Marie Starr filled it. "I think it is time to find out why so many of our children are dropping out of school," she wrote in the *Messenger* (Starr, "Home," 1967, 3).

The *Muckleshoot Messenger* often carried national news. One brief item (August 1967, 3) noted that a copy of Edmund Wilson's *Apologies to the Iroquois* was available at the Muckleshoot VISTA Library, "at Mike and Joan's house" (October 1967, 8) and that it "will really make you angry" with its description on the inundation of the Senecas' Cornplanter Tract by the Kinzua Dam. The same issue, on page 15, carried a poem on the Kinzua controversy, along with (on the same page) a brief report on Iroquois activities to reclaim wampum belts from the State of New York. The

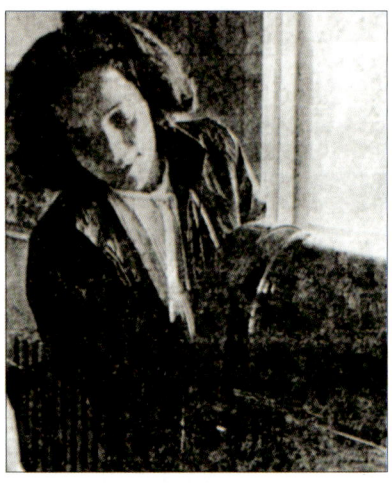

Marie Starr over mimeograph machine, producing the *Muckleshoot Messenger*. Edd Jeffords. "Muckleshoot Messenger Closes Communication Gap." Tacoma *News-Tribune*, no date, p. C-6. Photo courtesy of Tacoma News-Tribune

link to the Iroquois was probably VISTA volunteers Mike and Joan (a couple; their last name was Weisbrot), who were from Flushing, New York. During this time, the *Messenger* carried artwork and sharply political commentary involving Iroquois wampum belts by Mohawk culture bearers Ray Fadden and his son John Kahionhes Fadden. Contacted more than 40 years later, John Fadden recognized the work (Fadden, 2011).

Mike and Joan aimed to find a Muckleshoot editor for the *Messenger* and, by early in 1968, Marie Starr took the job. Starr would go on to serve on the Tribal Council in 1972. She later worked 14 years as director for the Muckleshoot Youth Home. She also spent six years as a caseworker for the Puyallup Tribe before returning to the Muckleshoots when she ran for Council again. Throughout her many terms of service on the Council, she held the Chair and Vice Chair positions for several years. On January 16, 2011, she was once again elected to Tribal Council, with priorities on education and employment. By this time, she had been married for 49 years, and enjoyed playing bingo and shopping with her children and grandchildren.

When the Weisbrots departed Muckleshoot in February 1968, they were remembered fondly. Joan said that she had shared food, stories, and friendship. "I think I've laughed more and cried more and learned more this year than any other year of my life," she wrote in the *Messenger* (February 1968, 14). Mike added: "I'll miss the mountains, the rivers, and the woods, but most of all I'll miss the kids" (February 1968, 14). A month

Chapter 3

"Muckleshoot girls in Pow-Wow clothing". Back row: Delrina Courville, Sandra Lovie, Steve Baker, Pauline Baker, Angela Williams. Front row: Flora Pacheco, Katie Moses, Sherann Courville, Josie Courville, Sonja Moses.
Photo courtesy of White River Valley Historical Museum / 02554

later, two new VISTAs (Robert and George) arrived from Philadelphia. By April, the *Messenger* commented, "They already feel at home" ("New VISTAs," 1968, 1).

On November 7, 1967, Tribal Council members Bertha McJoe, Eva Jerry, Aletha White, Elvin Hamilton, and Elaine Baker reluctantly agreed to accept $50,000 compensation from the federal government for lands taken when the reservation was established. Attorney Frederick Post said that "all appeals have been unsuccessful, and that the tribe had no choice but to accept the settlement" ("Tribal Meeting," 1967, 1). The Council decided to keep the payment to use for land acquisition, housing, small business development, and other purposes. Per capita payments would have amounted to less than $200 per person and, said a report in the *Messenger*, "would have been spent quickly" ("Tribal Meeting," 1967, 1). At the same meeting, the council authorized attorney Fred Paul to sue the state of Washington for $10 million for loss of fishing rights.

During that period, political jockeying in the U.S. House of Representatives was threatening funding for the Office of Economic Opportunity, part of President Lyndon Johnson's "war on poverty." An alliance of Southern Republicans and conservative Democrats united to accuse the programs of rampant waste. The funding included many of the social programs that were beginning to energize political action among the Muckleshoots, including VISTA, Head Start, Community Action, Legal Services, and Neighborhood Youth Corps. The 4,000 VISTA volunteers' stipends were cut off for a time. The *Messenger* noted that two VISTA volunteers in St. Albans, Vermont, had accepted shelter in the Franklin County Jail when their money ran out. The Senate approved funding, and the programs continued, but many at Muckleshoot were shaken. This was more evidence that, in the long run, self-sufficiency was the best route.

Dossie Miller, tribal chairwoman, in the June 1968 *Messenger* called for "MAN POWER Now!" to build a fence around the tribal cemetery, with a locked gate, so that vandals would have a harder time using the headstones for target practice. She estimated that (with donated labor) the fence would cost $1,132 for wire, fence posts, cement, and the use of a small bulldozer. The editors of the *Messenger* added a note to Miller's article that said: "If you want your people to rest in a whiteman's garbage dump, keep talking, because before Dossie Miller took on the job, kids were going over and target practicing at the headstones and teenagers [were] parking and dumping beer bottles and people even dumped garbage there. ... She has the courage to do what should have been done years ago ..." ("Cemetery," 1968, 8).

Also in June 1968, the *Messenger* for the first time carried paid local advertising from the Hillside Lanes Bowling Alley, Wilbur photo studio, Kettman's Shoe Store, Brandt's Western Shop, Jim's Chevron Service, Tennant's Book Shop, Shoeland, Hillside Roller Rink, Cubby's Drive-in, Cavanaugh Hardware, Cash Auto Parts, and Art's Hiway Super Market. Another half-page display showed the famous actress Raquel Welch in a pair of Foster Grant sunglasses, with several models of the eyewear arrayed below her at $1 to $3 a pair, but with no indication of where they could be purchased.

Activism manifested itself in other ways. The city of Auburn, for example, was planning to build a four-lane road under an existing bridge in the R Street Southeast area (no cross street was provided). The project was stalled because two Muckleshoot women, Eva Jerry and Elvina Cross, refused to sell their land. They contended that a four-lane road would threaten children in the area. When the city threatened to exercise eminent domain to force the sale, the two women deeded the land to the Muckleshoot Tribe, giving it immunity from eminent domain.

The *Muckleshoot Messenger* described a new dental clinic that was open five days a week, 8:30 A.M. to 4:30 P.M., with dentists and

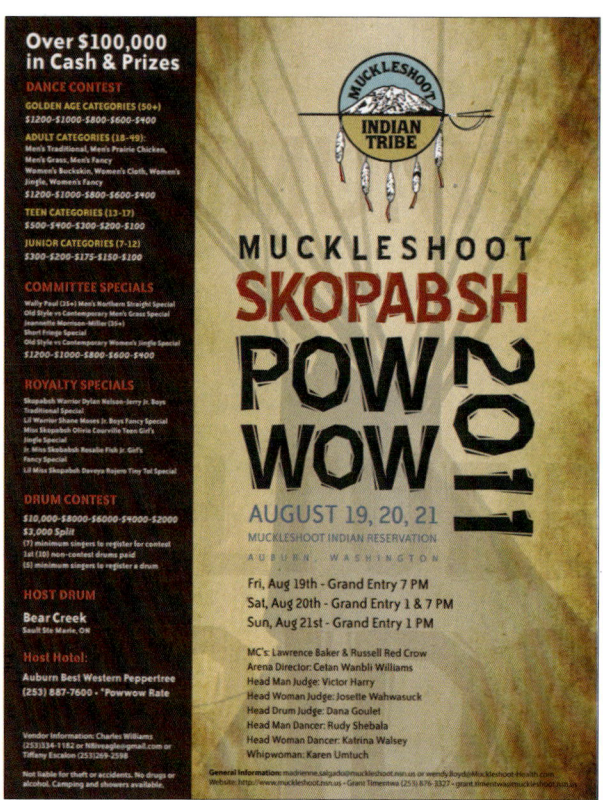

Color flyer, 2011 Skopabsh Pow Wow.
Photo courtesy of Muckleshoot Indian Tribe

aides capable of providing fillings, crowns, bridges, dentures, extractions, corrective oral surgery, and interceptive orthodontics. The article, signed by Michael G. Logelin, DDS, also said that the Indian Health Service Hospital in Rapid City, South Dakota, might be used for laboratory work at no charge (Logelin, 1976, 4).

The *Muckleshoot Messenger* in April 1976 carried a committee report by Shirley Sneatlum for one of the first Skopabsh Days (which started in 1975), to include a war-dance contest (the budget contained a hoped-for $3,000 in prize money), stick games, kids' sports, salmon barbecue, arts and crafts, and a raffle for Pendleton blankets and other items. The name was chosen after "one of the bands or villages on [the] Green River before there was a reservation" (Sneatlum, 1976, 3). To this day, Skopabsh Days attracts several thousand people, Indians and others, to Muckleshoot each August in a three-day event of Native arts and crafts, traditional clothing, and regional Native cooking, as well as stick games, music, and dancing.

Among all of the stirrings of revival at Muckleshoot, the most propitious was the assertion of fishing rights, against the armed force of state game officials, under treaties

Women smoking salmon on an open rack. Probably c. 1950. This picture was chosen by the National Museum of the American Indian, Smithsonian Institution, to help illustrate a recipe for cedar-planked, fire-roasted salmon in NMAI's *Mitsitam Cafe Cookbook*. Left to right: Alice Williams, Laura Siddle, one unidentified woman, Genevieve Siddle John Luke, Bena Barr Williams, Annie Garrison, and Irene Siddle.
Photo courtesy of Museum of History & Industry, Seattle / Seattle P-I Collection PI23907

Stirrings of Revival

Front page banner headline, Auburn *Globe-News*, Wednesday, April 29, 1970. *Muckleshoot Preservation Program Archives.*

that now were more than a century old. Beginning in an organized way during the 1960s, and culminating in the 1970s, the Muckleshoots joined other Western Washington fishing peoples in re-establishing their right to fish, and to claim an economic base that would catapult them out of poverty.

THE COMMUNITY HALL BURNS

On the evening of April 25, 1970, a Saturday, the Community Hall burned to the ground in flames so intense that firefighters had little recourse but to watch. Thirty-six years and four days after it had opened, and shortly after it had been refurbished, the fire burned the only building the tribe owned, on the Muckleshoots' only common land. Fire spared only the building's river-rock fireplace.

Two fire units from Auburn Fire District 46 responded to a call at 6:26 P.M. The cause of the fire was listed as unknown, but witnesses said that it probably started from two electric heaters that had been left running in the building's front room. The Community Hall, which contained a small branch of the King County Library and a King County Health Department clinic as well as meeting space for the Tribal Council, was not insured. It had been remodeled the previous summer with new wiring, fluorescent lighting, new restroom fixtures and upgraded heaters ("Fire Destroys," 1970, 1).

Children playing in the backyard of Marie Starr's home said they saw flames in the building within 45 minutes after a meeting had ended there. The hall had been vandalized several times during previous months as the Muckleshoots had tried without success to get a King County sheriff's office patrol assigned to the area ("Fire Destroys," 1970, 1). The old community center's charred chimney has become something of an icon, a reminder of how hard life at Muckleshoot has been. Eligibility for many programs is determined by residence within a 30-mile radius of the chimney. Upon these ashes a remarkable revival would be built, beginning with assertion of the right to fish.

Chapter 3

The brick chimney remaining from fire at the Community Hall.
Photo by John Loftus, Muckleshoot Monthly

LOUIS "DOC" STARR: TRADITIONS AND MEMORIES

Louis "Doc" Starr, who knew how to carve bone fishing spears, died in 1991 at the age of 92 of pneumonia at St. Francis Community Hospital in Federal Way. He "not only knew how to carve and bind them with pitch and twine, but also knew the trick of balancing on a narrow wooden canoe, and hurling the spear at salmon like their Muckleshoot ancestors. He knew because when he was young he was groomed to be chief. ... He remembered being carried on the shoulders of fishermen and being taught what you might call philosophy — the old ways of belief" (Leovy, 1991).

In addition to being a skilled traditional fisherman, Starr was an avid cooker and canner of salmon. He could also carve a canoe out of a burned-out log; he provided one for the Washington State Centennial in 1989. Starr also knew traditional herb medicine. He could, for example, distill a tea from ferns to ease arthritis. Also, in the early 1990s, he was one of only a handful of people who were fluent in the Muckleshoots' language.

Louis "Doc" Starr.
Photo courtesy of Duane Hamamura

Friends said, according to one account, that "He had an inner strength he always preserved. He always carried himself with the utmost dignity" (Leovy, 1991). He was the last Muckleshoot to be raised up as a leader in the traditional system, in which certain women (one of his aunts, in this case) held "spiritual gift of naming chiefs." He was named at his birth in 1898 (Leovy, 1991). Starr raised ten children; he was survived by 31 grandchildren, 33 great-grandchildren, and eight great-great-grandchildren. Sonny Bargala, a Muckleshoot commercial fisherman, described Starr as having possessed a keen ironic sense, "but he never seemed bitter about the changes he'd witnessed or the disappearance of his tribal ways, Bargala said. 'He was very much a realist. To him, things just happened. I guess he found that bitterness would eat away at you. He tried to spend his energy on other meaningful things'" (Leovy, 1991).

Funeral services for Starr were held at the Muckleshoot Shaker Church, of which he was a member. He was survived by five daughters: Florence Wynne of Wellpinit, Stevens County; Brenda Sheldon of Enumclaw; Lillian Smith of Warm Springs, Oregon; Lorraine Starr of Shelton, and Janice Starr of Marysville; two sons: Marvin Starr of Auburn and Les Adams of Maple Valley; and a sister, Elsie Simmons of Oakville, Grays Harbor County.

JULIA JOHN SIDDLE'S STRUGGLE TO SURVIVE

The life of Julia John Siddle provides a personal narrative of the struggles that Muckleshoots and their related neighbors underwent to survive during the leanest years. Today Siddle is known as one of the area's foremost basket weavers. Anthropologist Erna Gunther collected her baskets and showed some of them at San Francisco's Golden Gate International Exposition in 1939. One of her baskets was presented as a gift to President Franklin D. Roosevelt, and today others reside in the collections of the Burke Museum at the University of Washington. In her own time, weaving was one of many ways Siddle used to support her family as a widowed (and therefore single) mother.

Born into an aristocratic Duwamish family during 1866 near the Black River on the site that became Renton, Julia John Siddle was raised by Cheshiahud, who also was known as Lake Union John (Marr, 2008, 208). She met with Arthur C. Ballard and was cited in his writings. Julia was expert in the use of medicinal herbs, using them to treat illnesses. She was also a well-known midwife. Picking hops, she met Lyman Siddle, marrying him in 1883. They later moved to the Snoqualmie Indian community along the southeastern shore of Lake Sammamish, and had six children (David, Lena, Laura, Hogan, Clara, and William). Siddle worked as a U.S. marshal on the railroads. The Siddles saved money while Lyman was working, and bought land near Tukwila during the middle 1880s.

In 1910, the Siddles joined the Muckleshoot Tribe and received an allotment of 138.75 acres, including a tract of timber land on both sides of the White River about four miles southeast of Auburn. In addition to his work on the railroad, Siddle cut cottonwood into cords for sale in Seattle, dug holes, and practiced "water-witching" — the location of sites for productive wells. The family also caught and smoked salmon and raised some of their food in a large garden. Members of the Siddle family, like many others, camped in the woods in summer to pick berries. Many family members also worked as farmhands. Julia John continued to work as a midwife as well, and as a basket-maker of uncommon talent. Large, intricate baskets didn't sell often, however.

Lyman died in 1918, after which Julia John was forced to feed her family by her wits in tough times. She took children to the woods to gather cedar roots that would be soaked, separated, and dried as strands for baskets. Members of the family traveled with her to Seattle to acquire wool and fish heads. The wool was spun into yarn and knitted into socks for sale. The fish heads were boiled with bitter herbs into soup. At times, Julia John and other Muckleshoots also ate hatchery salmon that had been cast off after they had been stripped of their eggs or sperm ("Julia John," n.d., 4). During the 1930s, times became even tougher. Eight to ten family members often lived with Julia John as she became a grandmother. Traveling Shakers also often lodged in the house. She was widely mourned upon her death in 1952.

FLORENCE (DOSSIE) MILLER/WYNNE: WE ARE A SOVEREIGN NATION

Florence (Dossie) Wynne was born October 19, 1929, the fourth oldest of thirteen children, to Mabel Barr-Starr and Louis (Poshnikai) Starr, Sr. in Auburn, Washington. The nickname "Dossie" was given to her by a brother, Lawrence, as a mispronunciation of "Florence." She received an Indian name, "Sly-a-Chod," "woman leader," from her paternal great-great-grandmother. The name was prescient, for she was one of several women leaders who provided inspiration to the Muckleshoots as they emerged from a desperate time.

Florence "Dossie'" Starr Wynne demonstrating the use of a traditional fishing spear, as sister-in-law Marie Starr looks on.
Photo by John Loftus, Muckleshoot Monthly

Dossie's family includes leaders on both sides — Barr and Starr. She was a daughter of Louie Starr and a granddaughter of Philip Starr. Her uncle Earnie Barr was a leader among the Snoqualmies. Many people recalled Dossie on the Tribal Council during the fish wars as a font of energy, "a real go-getter who never let [us] down," who told people who asked "Can we do that?" with "Sure, we can. We're a sovereign nation!" She organized legal talent with nearly no money — a useful talent when the council had next to nothing.

She served on the Muckleshoot Tribal Council during the late 1960s and 1970s, as chairwoman for a time, when the Muckleshoots had so little money that she sometimes took expenses from her own pocket for travel to represent the tribe. Dossie also organized many bake sales. She and her father contributed to research that supported the Boldt fishing-rights decision. They also were active in the Indian rights movement during the 1970s, working with the American Indian Movement and Survival of American Indians Association not only in fishing rights but also in the occupation of Fort Lawton in 1970 that created the Daybreak Star Cultural Center. She also knew how to fish, hunt, and gather a wide variety of Native foods, such as camas, bitter roots, service berries, huckleberries, salmon berries, and blackberries, as well as many types of seafood and shellfish.

Dossie was a master herbalist, having learned from her father and grandmother how to identify, pick, and prepare the medicinal plants that may be used to make traditional Indian remedies for stomach problems, spider bites, cuts, fevers, rashes, and other maladies. She was known throughout Indian Country as a medicine woman.

Arnold Alexie, elder brother of the renowned Native author Sherman Alexie, called upon her knowledge after he was bitten and seriously injured by a brown recluse spider. At first, "the bite wasn't that painful," Alexie said. "However, it did begin to swell and look like the form of an egg over-easy with a huge yolk" (Alexie, 2012, 3). A doctor told him the bite could be fatal. "He then showed me pictures of other people who had been bitten and the horrible scars it had left," said Alexie. Medicine was prescribed, but the bite continued to get worse.

Dossie then heard about Alexie's bite. She also had been bitten by a brown recluse, said Alexie.

> ... and she knew exactly what to do. She brought me two gallons of liquid with the instructions to drink one and soak the bite area in the other. After three or four gallons of this liquid magic ... The bite had cleared up and left no scar whatsoever. ... The doctor was amazed, and after taking a blood sample declared that I had a clean bill of health. He then asked me what I did. I told him, and he asked if he could have a sample of this liquid. I told him that it would be impossible because it was Indian medicine, and it would be kept that way. (Alexie, 2012, 3)

Dossie and her husband Jim Wynne took in many people, children and adults, who needed a place to stay — some for a short time, some for much longer. Anyone who asked for help was always welcome at the Morning Starr Wynne Ranch on the Spokane Indian Reservation in Wellpinit, Washington.

Both were deeply rooted in their Shaker faith. They took part in pilgrimages and songfests in Wellpinit and Muckleshoot. They also traveled to Canada, Montana, Idaho, Oregon, and throughout Washington for Shaker events. She instilled a strong faith in her children, grandchildren and those who came to live with them. Dossie also was an expert cook, drug and alcohol counselor, culture teacher, tribal elder and friend.

Shortly after she passed over on January 27, 2012, at age 82, Sonny Bargala recalled Dossie as "an authentic true woman warrior, just as all her brothers were real warriors. My fondest memory of Aunt Dossie is her love for the people, and the sacrifices she made of time and energy on our behalf. She demonstrated her love by serving our people as chairwoman of the Muckleshoot Indian Tribal Council during a very difficult time of change in our recent past" (Bargala, 2012, 3). A memorial and headstone blessing was held for Dossie Wynne May 12, 2012 at the Wellpinit Long House, followed by a memorial dinner and give-away.

REFERENCES

"A.C. Ballard, Authority on Indians, Dies." *Seattle Times*, May 13, 1962, n.p.

Alexie, Arnold. "Florence 'Dossie' Wynne: Once Bitten, Twice Shy." *Muckleshoot Monthly*, February 2012, 3.

American Friends Service Committee. *Uncommon Controversy: Fishing Rights of the Muckleshoot, Puyallup, and Nisqually Indians.* Seattle: University of Washington Press, 1970.

Amoss, Pamela T. "The Indian Shaker Church," in Wayne Suttles Ed. *Handbook of North American Indians: Northwest Coast.* Vol. 7. In William C. Sturtevant, General Ed. *Handbook of North American Indians.* Washington, D.C.: Smithsonian Institution, 1990, 633-639.

Bargala, Sonny. "The Passing of a Great Leader." *Muckleshoot Monthly*, February 2012, 3.

Ballard, Arthur C. "Some Tales of the Southern Puget Sound Salish." *University of Washington Publications in Anthropology* 2:3 (December 1927), 35-41; 57-81. Seattle: University of Washington Press, 1927.

Ballard, Arthur C. "Mythology of Southern Puget Sound." *University of Washington Publications in Anthropology* 3:2 (December 1929), 31-150.

Ballard, Arthur C. "Notes on Data Concerning Informants in Mythology of Southern Puget Sound, Vol. 3, No. 2, *University of Washington Publications in Anthropology*." May, 1949, 167. Manuscript copy in Muckleshoot Preservation Program Archives.

Ballard, Arthur C. Testimony, Indian Claims Commission of the United States. *The Muckleshoot Tribe of Indians on Relation of Napolean Ross, Chairman of the General Council, Claimant, vs. The United States of America, Defendant,* Seattle, WA, November 26-28, 1951. 2 vols. (1 to p. 256; 2: 257-466).

"CAP Survey." *Muckleshoot Messenger*, 1:3 (July 1967), 6.

"Cultural Treasures Come Home to Muckleshoot." *Muckleshoot Monthly*, November 15, 2005.

"A Dance Festival Without a Single Jitterbug." *Seattle Times*, April 30, 1939. n. p.

"Death Claims Arthur Ballard, Son of Prominent Auburn Pioneer Family." *Auburn Globe-News*, November 1962, n.p.

"Did You Know?", *Muckleshoot News*, 1:1 (May 1967), 7.

Fadden, John Kahionhes. Personal correspondence, January 28, 2011.

Fey, Harold E., and D'Arcy McNickle. *Indians and Other Americans.* New York: Harper & Bros., 1959.

Finley, Werdna. "As My Sun Now Sets." Typescript in possession of the Finley family, n.d.

"Fire Destroys Muckleshoot Indian Hall." *Auburn Globe-News*, April 29, 1970, 1.

Glover, H. J. "White Man, Red Making Amends: Muckleshoot Indians Await $3.5 Million Windfall from Uncle Sam." *Seattle Post-Intelligencer Pictorial Review*, August 4, 1957, 2.

Harmon, Alexandra. *Indians in the Making: Ethnic Relations and Indian Identities around Puget Sound.* Berkeley and Los Angeles: University of California Press, 1998.

"Indians to Form Own Housing Authority." *Auburn Globe-News*, February 12, 1971, 1.

Jeffords, Edd. "White Man's Poverty Trap Holds Muckleshoot Indians in Misery." Tacoma *News-Tribune*, May 5, 1968, A-1, A-15, A-16.

Jeffords, Edd. "Muckleshoots Hold All the Cards So Street in Auburn Still Unbuilt, Paleface Outfoxed." Tacoma *News-Tribune*, June 4, 1970, C-7.

Johnson, Robert. "Muckleshoots May Get $3,500,000 for Land 'Taken.' *Auburn Globe-News*, Thursday, May 23, 1957, n.p.

"Julia John Siddle: Family History." Draft manuscript in Muckleshoot Preservation Program Archives, n.d.

Lane, Barbara. "Memorandum: On Usual and Accustomed Fishing Places." Photocopy of manuscript in Muckleshoot Preservation Program Archives, n.d.

LaVatta, George P. To Commissioner of Indian Affairs, Washington, D.C. [regarding visit to Muckleshoot reservation, November 24, 1939.] December 13, 1939. Typescript in Muckleshoot Preservation Program Archives.

"LBJ Gets Muckleshoot Land Payment Measure." *Auburn Globe*, September 18, 1968, n.p.

Leovy, Jill. "Louis 'Doc' Starr, 92, Chosen Chief and Master of Ancient Tribal Arts." *Seattle Times*, July 3, 1991. [http://community.seattletimes.nwsource.com/archive/?date=19910703&slug=1292515]

"Levi Hamilton: Tribal Chairman of the Muckleshoots, Embodiment of Hope." *Auburn News-Journal*, May 4, 1975, 5.

Lobehan, Morris, to Edward F. Teague, July 15, 1936. Copy in files of the Muckleshoot Preservation Program Archives.

Logelin, Michael G., DDS. "Muckleshoot Dental Clinic Opens." *Muckleshoot Messenger*, April 1976, 4.

Marino, Cesare. "History of Western Washington Since 1846," in Suttles, Wayne. Ed. *Handbook of North American Indians: Northwest Coast.* Vol. 7. In William C. Sturtevant, General Ed. Handbook of North American Indians. Washington, D.C.: Smithsonian Institution, 1990, 169-179.

Marr, Carolyn J. "Objects of Function and Beauty: Basketry of the Southern Coast Salish." In Barbara Brotherton, ed. *S'abadeb, the Gifts: Pacific Coast Salish Art and Artists.* Seattle: University of Washington Press, 2008, 198-225.

McIlveen, Gladys. "Community Organization on the Muckleshoot Indian Reservation." Social Work 254a, Dr. Clara Kaiser, July 16, 1937. Institution not specified. Student paper, photocopy in Muckleshoot Preservation Program Archives.

McIlveen, Gladys. "The Annual Report of the Muckleshoot Reservation: December 1, 1932-November 30, 1933." Mimeograph in Muckleshoot Preservation Department Archives.

Miller, Dossie. "Law Enforcement Meeting." *Muckleshoot Messenger*, September 1967, 2.

Miller, Dossie. "Cemetery." *Muckleshoot Messenger*, June 1968, 8.

"More News." *Muckleshoot News*, May 1967, 5.

Moses, Stanley. Interview at Muckleshoot. August 17, 2011.

"New VISTAs Arrive." *Muckleshoot Messenger*, March/April 1968, 1.

Noel, Patricia Slettvet and Virginia Cross. *Muckleshoot Indian History*, Auburn, WA: Auburn Public School District No. 408, 1980.

Rakestraw, Charles D. "The Shaker Indians of Puget Sound." *Southern Workman* 29 (December 1900), 704.

Richards, Kent D. "Agrarianism, United States Indian Policy, and the Muckleshoot Indian Reservation." In William L. Lang, ed. *Centennial West: Essays on the Northern Tier States*. Seattle: University of Washington Press, 1991, 39-58.

Rupert, Ray. "Houses Find a Home on Reservation." *Seattle Times*, n.d., A-1.

Sneatlum, Shirley. "Skopabsh Committee Report." *Muckleshoot Messenger*, April 1976.

Sneddon, James O. "Out of This World: A Study of the Indian Shakers at the Muckleshoot Reservation." Anthropology 210, November 1960. No school indicated; probably University of Washington. Copy in files of Muckleshoot Preservation Program Archives.

Starr, Marie. "Home Visitor." *Muckleshoot Messenger*, October 1967, 3.

Starr, Marie. Letter to the *Muckleshoot Messenger*, September 1967, 3.

"Statue of Muckleshoot Elder Big John to Be Unveiled September 21 at Auburn Museum." *Muckleshoot Monthly*, September 5, 2003, 16.

Stein, Alan J. "The Echo of Distant Drums: Large Tribal Gathering Held at Juanita in 1933." 2007. Bellevue College typescript in Muckleshoot Preservation Program Archives.

Suttles, Wayne P. "Spirit Dancing and the Persistence of Native Culture Among the Coast Salish," in Suttles, ed., *Coast Salish Essays*. Vancouver, B.C.: Talonbooks and Seattle: University of Washington Press, 1987, 199-208.

Teague, Edward F. to Fred G. Guenther, no date. Copy in files of the Muckleshoot Preservation Program Archives.

"Tribal Meeting." *Muckleshoot Messenger*, November 1967, 1.

"Tribal Meeting Held." *Muckleshoot News*, May 1967, 10.

Waterman, T. T. *Notes on the Ethnology of the Indians of Puget Sound*. (Indian Notes and Monographs. Misc. Series No. 59.) New York: Museum of the American Indian/Heye Foundation, 1973.

Watson, Kenneth G. (Greg). *Mythology of Southern Puget Sound: Legends Shared by Tribal Elders*, Reprint of the 1929 Publication. Recorded, Translated, and Edited by Arthur C. Ballard. North Bend, WA: Snoqualmie Valley Historical Museum, 1999.

Watson, Greg. "Arthur C. Ballard: A Good Neighbor to the Muckleshoot People." White River Valley Museum in *Muckleshoot Monthly*, October 12, 2007, 8.

Widrig, Charlotte. "Auburn's Collector of Indian Myths." *Seattle Times Sunday Magazine*, September 21, 1952, 5.

Chapter 4

The Right to Fish

Chapter 4

The Right to Fish

To Northwest Native American peoples, the salmon was as central to economic life as the buffalo on the plains; 80 to 90 percent of the protein in the Native people's diet came from fish and shellfish. The salmon was more than food; it was the center of a way of life. Among the catch were Chinook, coho, sockeye, chum, pink salmon, and steelhead. These fish also were smoked and dried for storage and trade. Fishing methods included nets, weirs, funnel snares, grills, set nets, and spears.

From the first, the immigrants were astonished by the abundance of salmon. Lewis and Clark noted "great quants. [quantities] of salmon" when they passed along the Columbia River during 1805. In 1854, George Suckley, who was describing the land for a railroad survey, wrote that salmon were "one of the striking wonders of the region ... These fish ... astonish by number, and confuse with variety" (Suckley, 1854, n.p.). In 1855, salmon sold in Seattle for ten cents a pound, half the price of pork, at a time when a dozen eggs or a gallon of whiskey sold for a dollar (Meeker, 1905, 452). In 1850, a "good axman" (an experienced timber cutter) earned $5 a day, which was regarded as a living wage (Meeker, 1905, 538). Approaching "Whidby's Island" by sea in 1855, Ezra Meeker witnessed "[A] mass of fish moving in the water ... [with] no end to the school as far as the eye could reach ... The air was literally filled with fish ..." (Meeker, 1905, 69).

The Muckleshoots and other Coast Salish peoples developed several ingenious ways of catching salmon. One involved saltwater trolling. A four-to-five inch herring was tied to a hook on a line weighted with a small rock, and

Muckleshoot Indian Tribe Treaty Drainage Area (reaches from north of Edmonds, east of Bellevue into the Cascade foothills along the Cedar, Green, and White rivers, south to the glacier field of Mt. Rainier, southwest to Tacoma).
Photo courtesy of U.S. v. Washington court documents (Public record)

dragged behind a canoe. Location was important; once the salmon reached fresh water, they ignored the bait (Suckley, 1860, 311). Another device, the weir, was so effective at corralling entire runs on rivers that they had to be partially closed, allowing fish to continue upriver to spawn. Weirs were declared illegal by Washington State late in the nineteenth century, in part because they disrupted navigation. Use of weirs continued, however, as Muckleshoots asserted their reserved treaty rights, according to accounts taken by Arthur Ballard.

Muckleshoot fishermen also used funnel snares, as well as nets made of grasses that grew in the area to harvest some of the fish runs that the European-American immigrants found so astonishing.

Washington became a territory of the United States on March 2, 1853, with no consent from the Indians who occupied most of the land. Isaac Stevens was appointed governor and superintendent of Indian affairs for the territory. As governor, Stevens wished to build the economic base of the territory; this required the attraction of a proposed transcontinental railroad, which in turn required peace with the Indians, as well as the cession of millions of acres of land. Stevens worked with remarkable speed; in 1854 and 1855 alone, he negotiated five treaties with Indian peoples west of the Cascades. By signing the treaties, the Indians ceded to the United States 2,240,000 acres of land, an immense sacrifice. They refused, however, to give up their right to fish, their lifeline. The treaties were very specific: they retained the right to fish "at all usual and accustomed grounds and stations," "in common" with the immigrants.

COMPETITION FOR SALMON

The immigrants very quickly came to appreciate the economic value of salmon. A newspaper account in the *Columbian* (of Olympia), January 15, 1853 mentioned that dried salmon had been shipped to China. Some of this salmon may have been caught by Indians and sold to whites. During the decade before the treaties were negotiated, Native catches of salmon increased in large part due to demand by the immigrants, as well as Indian use of the fish to earn cash for purchase of new items such as calico, flour, and molasses (Lane, 1973, 13). Within a generation after the treaties had been signed, the industrial revolution hit salmon. It became a marketable commodity across a broad area with construction of the transcontinental railroad in the late nineteenth century (later, refrigeration made the fish even more portable). Vacuum canning became available in 1866, seven years before the railroad linked the Pacific Northwest's fisheries to the rest of the world.

Washington became a state in 1889, and within a year legislators closed six rivers, all of them Indian fishing grounds, to salmon fishing. The state then methodically banned net fishing (the main way Indians acquired salmon at the time) on all rivers except the Columbia, all in the name of conservation. As it would be through the "fish wars" of the 1960s and early 1970s, "conservation" was being used as a rationale to keep the Indian fishing people out of rivers outside of the tiny slivers of land set aside as reservations. In the meantime, the number of commercial and sport fishermen exploded. The number of commercial salmon canneries in the Puget Sound area was one in 1890, 19 in 1900, and 45 in 1917 (Marino, 1990, 175).

As early as 1916, Muckleshoots wrote to the Commissioner of Indian Affairs seeking protection from state efforts to erode their treaty fishing rights. A committee including

Dennis Anderson, Jr. fishing at sunset on Puget Sound.
Photo by John Loftus, Muckleshoot Monthly

Bob James, John Newhauken, Frank Ross, Joe Hill, George Jack, and Walter Davis wrote May 15, 1916 that "State authorities have forbidden our spearing salmon in the Green River and threatened us with arrest and imprisonment if we were apprehended in taking fish in this manner" (James et al., 1916, 1). They invoked Article III of the Medicine Creek Treaty as protection for their right to fish. Fish had been marketed by Muckleshoot ancestors and other fishing peoples from first contact with the immigrants. People in Seattle were supplied from the town's early days; salted salmon also were shipped to San Francisco well before 1900.

The state of Washington's courts regularly upheld restrictions on Indian fishing; Washington State courts agreed with the state fish and game bureaucracy's assertion that the treaty phrase "in common with" meant "no different from other citizens" (Ziontz, 2009, 85). An example was *State v. Towessnute* (February 4, 1916) (89 Wash. 478), in which the State Supreme Court "held that treaty Indians fishing at usual and accustomed places off-reservation were subject to state fishing regulations in the same manner as everyone else" (Lane, 1980, 97). As a result, the Muckleshoots found themselves restricted mainly to fishing on the portions of the White River that ran through their reservation. The state, given its preference, prohibited the Muckleshoots and other Native peoples from fishing in most of the rivers that emptied into Puget Sound during closed seasons (Lane, 1980, 96). The State Supreme Court rejected Native fishing rights in *State v. Towessnute*, with this rationale:

> The premise of Indian sovereignty we reject. ... The Indian was a child, and a dangerous child, to be both protected and restrained. ... Neither Rome nor sagacious Britain ever dealt more liberally with their subject races than we with these savage tribes, whom it is generally tempting and always easy to destroy and whom we have so often permitted to squander vast areas of fertile land before our eyes. (Wilkinson, 2000, 53)

Muckleshoots and other Native fishing people sustained themselves with small nets and boats, while non-Indians employed fish wheels that pulled fish out of the water at exceedingly high rates 24 hours a day, seven days a week. A single fish wheel harvested 20,000 to 50,000 fish a day. These wheels were primarily located on the Oregon side of the Columbia River, and were outlawed in Oregon in 1927 and in Washington during 1935.

As the state resisted Indians' rights to fish off reservations, their land base was shrinking. The Muckleshoot reservation, in particular, made no geographic sense to anyone but a railroad agent (and nearby farmers), with its series of disconnected squares. It is a great design for a railroad plot, but as a location of several hundred people related by kin and culture, requiring sustenance from rivers and forests, it demonstrated the intellectual limitations of federal bureaucrats. The map-making system shared something with the methods of colonizers across North America who took out pencils and drew arbitrary lines without consideration of cultural factors or importance of hunting and fishing areas in the case of Muckleshoot. So it was with the right to fish — and survive — for the Muckleshoots and other Native peoples of Western Washington. They would regain the right, but not without taking risks that defined the lives of several generations.

As the population grew in and around Seattle, the fishing environment changed. Barbara Lane, an anthropologist who supplied

Barbara Lane.
Photo by John Loftus, Muckleshoot Monthly

historical research for the United States on Native fishing practices and sites, as well as the mid-nineteenth century treaties, found that human alteration of the landscape had obliterated many of the Muckleshoots' "usual and accustomed" fishing places. Al Ziontz, whose law firm aided the Indian case in *United States v. Washington*, said later that Barbara Lane was "The most important member of the plaintiff's team" (2009, 97).

The construction of a ship canal between Lake Washington and Puget Sound (which opened in 1916) lowered the lake's level by nine feet, wiping the Black River (once thickly settled with fishing villages) off the map. Parts of Lake Washington that had covered much of present-day Renton vanished. Coal mining that began as the treaties were being signed also altered the landscape. Within a decade, ships laden with coal were leaving harbors along Puget Sound bound for San Francisco, which was supplying coal miners on what had been Muckleshoot territory (Lane, 1972, 10-15).

By the early 20th century, the "usual and accustomed places" for fishing lay mainly outside reservation boundaries, even as state fish and game agents insisted that the Natives had no right to fish there. This was no trivial matter. The state's assertion forced Indians to fish on the sly, at night, and face arrest, as well as confiscation of their boats, nets, and other fishing gear.

FISH RUNS DECLINE WITH IMMIGRATION

As the state pressured Native people to restrict their fishing to reservations, the total number of fish available to everyone was falling as well. In 1914, in Washington State, about 16 million fish were caught annually. By the 1920s annual catches had declined to an annual average of 6 million. In the late 1930s, following construction of several large hydroelectric dams on the Columbia River and its tributaries, the annual catch had fallen as low as 3 million. By the 1970s, with more aggressive conservation measures in place, including construction of fish ladders at most major dams, the annual catch rose to 4 to 6 million ("Physical Yield," 1977, 89).

Native fishing people resisted state restriction on their fishing rights as early as 1897, when a commercial fishing company interfered with the Lummis' harvest at a favored spot at Point Roberts and Lummi Island, off their reservation. Judge C. H. Hanford ruled against the Lummis in *United States, et al. v. Alaska Packers Association* (C. C. Wash 79F 152). The Lummis appealed, and the case reached the U.S. Supreme Court, which dismissed it in 1899 (Marino, 1990, 175). At the same time, Washington State's attorney general, Patrick Henry Winston, asserted that "No Indian treaty interferes with the right of the state to protect the game or fish of any kind" (Woods, 2005, 415).

In *United States v. Winans* (1905), the U.S. Supreme Court upheld treaty provisions that allowed Indians to fish at usual and accustomed places (even if the land had come under private ownership) in a case involving a white-owned fish wheel at a location traditionally used by the Yakama. The court put forth "the reserved-rights doctrine" which stated that Indians reserved rights to themselves and granted certain rights to others. This doctrine has become important across the United States in many treaty-rights cases. The rights were not conveyed, as the whites argued, from the state to the Native peoples. The state routinely ignored such federal rulings in blatant disregard of the federal supremacy clause of the U.S. Constitution. Even while it upheld treaty rights, however, the Court in *Winans* also affirmed the state's right to circumscribe treaty fishing: "Nor does it [treaty language] restrain the State unreasonably, if at all, in the regulation of the right" (*U.S. v. Winans* 198 U.S. 371 at 384).

The Muckleshoots and others long resisted the state's assumed monopoly on regulation of fishing. In the early 1940s, a Yakama Indian fishing off reservation was convicted of lacking a state license. The Washington State Supreme Court upheld his conviction. Upon review, the United States Supreme Court reversed the state court. The Supreme Court determined that the requirement did not apply to treaty Indians fishing off-reservation. However, the court also said that Indians fishing under treaty were subject to state law (*Tulee v. Washington*, 1941). The U.S. Supreme Court upheld Tulee's right to fish without a dip net license, but also said that the state could regulate off-reservation fishing by members of treaty tribes if it was "necessary for the conservation of fish" (Woods, 2005, 419; *Tulee v. Washington* 315 U.S. 681). "Conservation" thus became a rationale of state regulation for decades to come.

In 1951, in *Makah Indian Tribe v. Schoettler* (192 F.2d 224), the Ninth Circuit Court of Appeals reacted to the state's loose use of the conservation rationale to prevent Indians from fishing. The Makah, who used the Hoko River in an area where state law allowed only hook-and-line gear, said that coho would not take a hook, so the Indians were effectively prevented from exercising treaty fishing rights. The state used conservation as a rationale for the regulation; the circuit court agreed with the tribe that conservation was not at issue, reversing a district court ruling (Woods, 2005, 420). The court held that the state must prove that regulation is "necessary for the conservation of fish" (Makah, 1951, 224).

In 1954 and 1957, a county court and the Washington State Supreme Court dismissed charges of gillnetting in violation of state law against two Puyallups, Robert Satiacum and James Young, who had fished with a net in Tacoma during a state closure, in *State of Washington v. Satiacum*. 314 P.2d 400, "ruling that the state had not proven the closure necessary for conservation" (Woods, 2005, 420). Six years later, the State Supreme Court upheld the state's right to "periodically" close fishing in certain areas for conservation. The same year, the state closed Indian fishing in Southern Puget Sound, provoking a wave of fishing-rights protests (Marino, 1990, 176).

FISHING-RIGHTS PROTESTS ESCALATE

By the 1950s and early 1960s, Native peoples who had signed the Medicine Creek Treaty, and others, were having a difficult time harvesting enough fish to survive. As

Native American student demonstration against Bureau of Indian Affairs, Seattle, 1971.
Photo courtesy of Museum of History & Industry, Seattle / Seattle P-I Collection 1986.5.53853.1

fish runs declined, state enforcement efforts of its arbitrary policies became more brutal. By the early 1960s, state fisheries police were conducting wholesale arrests of Indians, confiscating their boats and nets.

The Muckleshoot, like other small tribes in Western Washington, had few resources to resist state authorities' restrictions on fishing rights jurisdiction that was enforced with armed force sanctioned by state courts. From 1924 through the 1960s, the Muckleshoots had limited funds to fight for their fishing rights. Most lawyers had little interest in taking complicated cases for small, impoverished tribes such as the Muckleshoot, Nisqually, and Puyallup.

The increasing intensity of fishing-rights protests during the 1960s was a matter of survival — emphasized when the fishing people banded together in a group that they named The Survival of American Indians Association. These protests took part within a general context of ferment on civil rights issues, against the control of the Bureau of Indian Affairs. The Puyallups drew copious publicity as they fished in their local river with celebrities such as actor Marlon Brando and comedian Dick Gregory. Other well-known people attended, such as actress Jane Fonda, Buffy Sainte-Marie (a popular folk singer who is Cree), Richard White, who was becoming one of academia's best known historians, and Elisabeth Furse, then employed by the American Friends in Seattle, who later became a member of Congress and a judge from Oregon.

Everywhere in the fishing controversy activists found the fingerprints of Hank Adams, "tireless, fiery, chain-smoking, lights-out brilliant, and soul-deep loyal to a sacred undertaking" (Wilkinson, 2000, 44). He enticed Charles Kuralt, a famous correspondent for CBS News, to cover the "fish-ins" at Frank's Landing. Adams also played a major role in writing, and raising funds to publish, the American Friends' report *Uncommon Controversy*, which provided a sober, scholarly analysis of treaty fishing rights.

Adams, having attended an organizational meeting of National Indian Youth Council in 1963, came to know its firebrand leader, the Ponca Clyde Warrior, and, through him, met Marlon Brando, "a rebel *with* a cause," who within a year was taking part in Puget Sound "fish-ins" (Smith, 2012, 21). Adams' use of Brando was calculated to bring attention from mainstream media to the fishing-rights struggle, and it worked.

Adams was also at the head of a column of Native students who, in 1966, visited University of Washington law professor Ralph Johnson in his office and asked him to teach an undergraduate course in Native American law. Johnson had no experience in the area at the time, but he acquired it. Along the way, in 1972, Johnson published a seminal law-journal article that influenced the course of fishing rights litigation before the U.S. Supreme Court (Johnson, 1972). Johnson taught the course until he died in 1999 (Wilkinson, 2000, 46).

The protests came to be called "fish-ins," a conscious reference to the black sit-ins at southern lunch counters during the civil rights movement. Reuben Wright, Sr., a Puyallup tribal councilman, was arrested and jailed in Pierce County. Other Puyallups and a Nisqually also were arrested. Bob Satiacum drew attention to the fishing struggle and took part in many demonstrations on the Puyallup River. Satiacum sent a letter to President Lyndon Johnson that said in part: "Bands of Indians arming. Open warfare with Washington State Department of Fish and Game certain over fishing rights guaranteed by Medicine Creek Treaty of 1854, signed by U.S. Presidents Pierce and Grant. Presidential action needed immediately to avoid bloodshed. Signed Chief Satiacum, Puyallup Indian Reservation" (Johnson, 1965). As people fished by night, they "loaded bright, freshly cleaned Nisqually salmon into a plain white truck bound for sale in San Francisco's Union Square, properly launched into the dark with a Frank's Landing send-off of muffled laughter and *sotto voce* whispers of "go get 'em!" and "You're doing the Great Spirit's work!" (Wilkinson, 2000, 42).

On March 3, 1964, the National Youth Council summoned Native peoples from across the United States to join fishing people in Western Washington for a rally on the grounds of the State Capitol in Olympia. In *Red Power Rising* (2011), Bradley Shreve wrote that 1,500 to 5,000 people gathered, making the demonstration "the largest intertribal protest ever assembled" (130). Charles Wilkinson, in *Messages from Frank's Landing*, put the figure at 2,000 (2000:44). Makahs performed traditional dances on the steps of the Capitol and at the governor's residence. A set of demands was issued to state government that amounted to allowing fishing unhindered in "usual and accustomed places" as set out in the treaties.

A Native group (and Brando) met with governor Albert Rosellini for several hours, after which the governor spoke to the demonstrators. While Rosellini congratulated them for exercising their rights, however, he refused to back off of the state's insistence that it would set the rules. Siding with white sportfishing groups, Rosellini characterized Indian fishing as a threat to conservation of the species, at a time when Native catch accounted for no more than 6 percent of the total (Shreve, 2011, 130–132, 136). Fishing rights publicity was not limited to the summoning of celebrities. Activists erected a tipi on the lawn of the city-county building in Tacoma, and sent smoke signals from the roof of Tacoma's Winthrop Hotel. At one point, an attempt to "liberate" the battleship USS *Missouri* from a dock at the Bremerton Navy Yard (west across Puget Sound from Seattle) was foiled by military police ("Court Move," 1968, n.p.).

Treaty Trek passing community center, 1966.
Photo courtesy of Larry Dion / The Seattle Times

Fishing protests began in an organized fashion a year and a half after Survival of the American Indian Association (SAIA) organized, in the fall of 1965, after John Cochran, a Pierce County (Tacoma) state judge issued an injunction against Indian fishing in any way, or at any place, not approved by the state's fisheries bureaucracy. On October 7, state game wardens in a large powerboat rammed a canoe occupied by Billy Frank, Jr. and Al Bridges as they were tending nets on the Nisqually River. Two days later, state wardens cornered two teenage Native fishermen on a log jam in the same river. More Indians converged on the scene and cornered the agents, who then called for reinforcements. Soon a large group of people were engaged in a full-scale riot. "Some cars were busted up, as well as some people," according to one report (McCloud and Casey, 1968, 30). Thurston County sheriff Clarence van Allen, who was respected by the Indians, talked everyone into desisting. The police withdrew and no one was arrested.

The SAIA held a fish-in on the Nisqually River at Frank's Landing on October 13, 1965, involving about 30 Native people, many of them women and children, to protest the state's raids. More than 100 state wardens and other police waded into the protest as soon as the first net was set from a canoe containing six Indians, a family dog, and three newspaper reporters. Following shouts of "Get the sons of bitches," three large power boats rammed the Indians' craft (McCloud and Casey, 1968, 32). The Native people then turned on riot police in the underbrush along the river and "began pelting the State's forces with anything they could lay their hands on" (McCloud and Casey, 1968, 32). Eight were arrested. Evan Roberts, Jr., a physician who observed the event for the American Friends Service Committee, filed a report alleging that some of the wardens had been drinking. Another observer said that the wardens "were like animals that smelled blood" (McCloud and Casey, 1968, 35). The melee was copiously covered on radio and television, as well as in local newspapers.

The fishing-rights battle's early "fish-ins" drew large crowds — and some rather garish newspaper headlines. "Indians Make Warlike Moves Against State" blared the *Auburn Citizen's* front page in inch-high type September 1, 1965. On May 13, 1966 about 70 Native people and non-Indian college students marched 13 miles in support of treaty fishing rights from the Muckleshoot Community Hall, through Auburn, to District Justice Court in Federal Way. The march was coordinated by Muckleshoot fishing-rights activist Leo LaClair. Yakama, Walla Walla, Tulalip, Nisqually, Umatilla, Klallam, Arapaho, Makah, and Cree people took part, as well as Muckleshoots. The marchers carried copies of the Treaty of Point Elliott as a way of stating that federal law trumped state attempts to control Native fishing rights. A copy of the treaty was presented to Judge Robert Stead at the district court ("Muckleshoot Treaty," 1966, 1).

Eight young Native people trekked the entire 13 miles. The march was undertaken in support of four Muckleshoots (Cecil and Robert Moses, Sherman Dominick, and Larry Maurice), charged with illegal fishing in the Green River. Midway through the trek, marchers paused for lunch in Auburn's Les Gove Park, and to hear speakers, some of whom included Muckleshoot Bernice White, Nisqually Janet McCloud, and Alvin Ziontz of the American Civil Liberties Union (ACLU), which was providing legal support for the four defendants in the fishing case ("Indian Treaty," 1966, 1).

As the Muckleshoots fished in defiance of the state, so did the Nisquallys, from Frank's Landing, with a nucleus of activists that included the Frank family, Sid Mills (a Yakama), and others. As a young man, Billy Frank, Jr. established himself as an Indian activist, fishing for salmon and steelhead on the Nisqually River in defiance of state authorities, but with the support of century-old treaties. In later years Frank became a leader and negotiator who

Sherman Dominick, 1970.
Photo courtesy of Museum of History & Industry, Seattle / Josef Scaylea Collection 1994.20.240

strove to ensure that tribal treaty fishing rights were upheld. Frank was first arrested for fishing at age 14, in 1945, on a cold night in December, a few days before Christmas. After that, he was arrested by police and game wardens about 50 more times during the fishing-rights battles that stretched from the 1940s to the early 1970s.

Frank recalled that his cedar canoe was rammed and capsized by an aluminum boat filled with state game and fish officers in riot gear. "They got real serious about this," he said." And this was the time of Selma; there was a lot of unrest in the nation. Congress had funded some big law-enforcement programs and they got all kinds of training and riot gear — shields, helmets. And they got fancy new boats. These guys had a budget. This was a war" (D'Ambrosio, 2009, 162). A shovel-nose canoe that the state had seized from Frank in 1964 was returned by the state on Frank's birthday in 1980. Years later, a flood carried it down the Nisqually, but a niece of his found the craft downriver. It was returned, and hung from the ceiling of the We He Lut Indian School at Frank's Landing. Johnny Bob, a friend, had carved the canoe for Frank about 1950 in exchange for 15 salmon.

After Frank died suddenly May 4, 2014, at age 83, the state of Washington that so many times had seized his fish and boat, and shredded his nets lowered its flags to half-staff in his honor. More than 6,000 people, including Gov. Jay Inslee, gathered at a memorial service six days later.

A MULTIETHNIC COALITION

To defend their fishing rights, the Muckleshoots and other Puget Sound Native peoples called upon non-Indian allies, most notably the multiethnic coalition forming in Seattle around such issues as the Indian occupation of Fort Lawton and the birth of El Centro de la Raza. Seattle was unusual for its alliances across racial lines; at the same time that defense of fishing rights reached fever pitch, Latinos, Asians, Black, and white allies were asserting economic rights and identity in the urban area. They aided each other.

El Centro had nurtured Native American ties since its beginnings. It grew up with the fishing-rights battles. El Centro's principal

Gilbert (Hoagie) King George (right) and others, fishing with spears. Probably late 1960s or early 1970s.
Photo courtesy of Muckleshoot Preservation Program Archives

Fishing on the White River during the "Fish Wars," late 1960s or early 1970s.
Photo courtesy of Muckleshoot Preservation Program Archives

founder, Roberto Maestas, was married to Estela Ortega in an Indian ceremony at El Centro, after which they spent their honeymoon at Wounded Knee during the winter of 1973 as the American Indian Movement's activists took the site of the 1890 massacre for 71 days. The occupants of the old school on Beacon Hill were fortified in October of 1972 by several hundred pounds of salmon from Native people in the Nisqually delta, taken in danger of life and limb from assault by state game and fish agents (Martinez, 2004). After the Nisquallys brought the cache of salmon, a ceremony was performed to bless it. Then they said: "You're going to need this fish. It's going to be a long haul. Count on us for whatever we can do" (Martinez, 2004, Tape 7).

The inter-ethnic alliance put bodies on the line, with the sit-in being the most familiar tactic. In the case of the fishing-rights battles, non-Indians lined the shore as Native people took to their boats with nets, forming a human chain between those who were fishing and the state game and fishing agents who were determined to prevent activity that the Indians (later supported by federal law) insisted was legal under the treaties.

The fish-ins assumed a familiar pattern:

> The game wardens — a dozen to almost fifty — would descend the banks in a stone-faced scramble toward a few [Indian] men in a canoe or skiff unloading salmon from a gillnet. Usually the [Indians] would give passive resistance — dead weight — and five officers or more would drag the men up the rugged banks toward the waiting vehicles.

Fishing on the White River in recent times.
Photo by John Loftus, Muckleshoot Monthly

The dragging often got rough, with much pushing and shoving, many arms twisted way up the back, and numerous cold-cock punches. The billy clubs made their thuds. Sometimes the Indian men struck back. Sometimes Indian people on the banks threw stones and sticks at the intruders. The stench of tear gas hung in the air. (Wilkinson, 2000, 38)

Following the holidays, on January 29, 1966, Indians and their allies held a rally at Frank's Landing on a cold, rainswept evening, meeting around a huge bonfire, which was used to light a life-size effigy of Governor Dan Evans. By February 6, Dick Gregory, a famous black comedian with a sharply political sense of humor, had arrived. He stayed for several weeks, going to jail with his wife Lillian, who was greeted at the Thurston County Jail in Olympia by Indian marchers carrying flowers for her. The marchers then stopped at the governor's mansion to protest Evans' opposition to the treaties (McCloud and Casey, 1968, 40). Gregory fished several times during the spring of 1966, was arrested, convicted, and served 40 days of a 90-day sentence in the Thurston County Jail (American Friends, 1970, 108–111). Marlon Brando hoisted a net, but was not arrested. Brando had also been arrested for fishing illegally on the Puyallup River in 1964, but was released on a technicality and not tried.

Gregory, age 35 in 1968, ramped up the publicity value of his protest by losing 20 pounds on a hunger strike during the six weeks he was imprisoned. He was released July 17, 1968. Gregory also used the media platform created by his imprisonment and hunger strike to denounce U.S. intervention in Vietnam. He was still in the area soon thereafter, when two fish-ins were held back-to-back, one on the Nisqually River, and the other, organized by the Muckleshoots, on the Green River. The Muckleshoot fish-in was the larger of the two, drawing about 300 people — fishing on the river, with many more, Indian and not, onshore.

Witnesses recalled:

> When the large force of game wardens descended on the Green River fish-in and started to rough up a young Indian girl, the assembled Indians ... stoned them — men, cars, and everything in sight. The wardens left the scene and made on-the-spot arrests. ... Later four Indians who had gone fishing were arrested. (McCloud and Casey, 1968, 41)

THE SITUATION AT MUCKLESHOOT

Muckleshoot fishermen exercised their right to catch fish for survival and to provide a traditional diet to their families. Muckleshoot fishermen, warriors defending treaty fishing during the twentieth century, faced some problems. To begin, salmon returning to spawning areas from the Pacific Ocean, the Strait of Juan de Fuca, and Puget Sound were subject to earlier harvest by many others — international, sports, Native and other fishing people — before they reached Muckleshoot territory. Dams also reduced fish runs.

As it arrested Muckleshoots for fishing before the Boldt decision, the state used every available rationale, all of which were proved false in subsequent court rulings: the reservation was a "grant," and therefore not legal; the treaties didn't apply to the Muckleshoots; the arrested fishing people were not really Muckleshoots (although they were enrolled); they were using gear that had not been invented when the treaties were signed; their fishing would destroy the fishery, although it amounted to a minuscule percentage of the total catch.

If they fished off-reservation, Muckleshoots were harassed, arrested, and prosecuted by the state of Washington. The state restricted river activity to hook-and-line sports fishing: net fishing and trolling were usually permitted in marine waters such as Elliott Bay. Without purchasing power, however, most Native fishing people could not obtain modern fishing gear, so they had to rely on set nets, dip nets, and spearfishing in the rivers. None of these methods provided enough fish to support family subsistence or ceremonial needs. LeRoy Courville, a Muckleshoot Tribal Council member and a Vietnam war veteran, recalled that he relied on fishing to feed his family. His fishing gear was minimal, but not unusual. He and another person shared a small boat with a four-horsepower motor that required an hour to reach their fishing areas.

Fishing was important for day-to-day survival. By the mid-twentieth century, many Muckleshoot were unemployed, and basic life was very difficult. Fishing often was the only way to put food on the table and care for elders. Muckleshoot fishermen knew that they needed to fish in a broader area to feed their families. State regulations, always arbitrary, were also economically devastating to the Muckleshoots. The context of poverty and restrictive state legal harassment blocked Muckleshoot sovereignty and forced fishermen to fight for their fishing rights to survive.

The state also exploited confusion over the various terms used to identify ancestral Muckleshoots. During September 1963, state game wardens arrested 13 Muckleshoots who had placed nets across the Green River. Judge F. A. Walterskirchen found that, as members of the Skopeahmish band, they were not signatories to the Point Elliott Treaty. The judge did not realize that the Skopeahmish were, indeed, one of three bands that did sign the treaty who later had come to be called Muckleshoot. That fact would be introduced to the legal system a decade later by Barbara Lane, an expert witness on the Boldt case.

MOSES VERSUS THE STATE OF WASHINGTON

Hints of legal respect for treaties did pop up in state courts, but they were rare. In January 1961, for example, James Starr, Louis Starr, Jr., both Muckleshoots, and Leonard Wayne, a Puyallup who had grown up at Muckleshoot, set gill nets in the Green River. They returned the next morning and hauled in one coho. As soon as they touched it, seven state game wardens sprung from surrounding bushes, revolvers drawn, and arrested them for using gill nets and fishing outside of the state-defined season. All three were held in King County jail for two weeks on $250 bail each. Twenty-two months later, in November 1962, King County Superior Court Judge James W. Hodson in *Washington State vs. Moses* found that the Muckleshoots had been fishing legally, exercising their treaty rights (Josephy, 1982, 177). Hodson upheld the state's right to close fishing for conservation reasons, however.

Stanley Moses and several members of his family (Cecil Moses, Ronald Moses, and Alan Moses among them), began fishing during the early 1960s, purposely provoking state agents into arresting them so they could take the challenge to affirm treaty rights to federal

Fishing boats on Elliott Bay, Seattle skyline in the background.
Photo by John Loftus, Muckleshoot Monthly

court. In 1963, they were arrested and taken to court along with Nisqually and Puyallup fishing people in a case that reached the U.S. Supreme Court and became known popularly as "Puyallup I," in which the Court affirmed the state's authority to regulate Indian treaty fishing to the extent reasonable and necessary for conservation and remanded for a determination by the state courts whether the prohibition on net fishing in rivers met that standard.

As the Supreme Court ruled in Puyallup I, the Southern Christian Leadership Conference (SCLC) was convening its Poor Peoples' March blocks away on the National Mall, camped in Resurrection City. The day after the ruling, May 28, 1968, about 300 people — Indians, blacks, Latinos, and others — marched from Resurrection City to the front steps of the Supreme Court in protest. Hank Adams was photographed with SCLC leader Ralph Abernathy (Martin Luther King, Jr.'s principal assistant until King was fatally shot April 4, 1968), Chicano leader Corky Gonzalez, and others (Smith, 2012, 30).

The Washington State Supreme Court found that fishing regulation was "reasonably necessary for the preservation of the state's fisheries on that river" (Moses 79 Washington 2d at 115, 483 P. 2d at 838). The fishing-rights protests that preceded the Boldt decision started the revival at Muckleshoot, Stanley Moses said. "It gave us a sense of what a treaty really meant" (Moses, 2011). "We were trying to get arrested to set a precedent," Moses said later (Moses, 2011). Reviewing the case [*Moses v. Washington* 389 U.S. 428 (1967)], the U.S. Supreme Court denied *certiorari* (calling up the record), for lack of jurisdiction, without further explanation.

Barbara Lane, providing research for the court in *Washington State v. Robert Moses, et al.* during the late 1960s, used the knowledge of Louis Starr, Bill Garrison, and John Hungary to provide detailed information about fisheries in the Green River-White River region. This research convinced a state judge, Lloyd Shorett of the State Superior Court, that Isaac Stevens reported to his superiors that he had treated with the Indians in the Green River-White River region. The federal courts didn't make this connection fully until Judge Boldt's ruling in *U.S. v. Washington* half a decade later. Lane also used unpublished work by T. T. Waterman, housed at the Smithsonian Institution, to make these connections. Waterman recorded place names, including village sites and fishing places ("Making the Case," 2012, 12). The anthropologist Wayne Suttles had alerted Lane to Waterman's work. On January 10, 1968, Judge Shorett ruled that the Muckleshoots were descended from the Skopeahmish, who were party to the Treaty of Point Elliott, and thus a treaty tribe.

As the latest Moses case made its way through the court system, Muckleshoots had continued to fish. In a later case, also titled *State of Washington v. Moses*, on July 3, 1966, four Muckleshoots were arrested for catching eight steelhead trout, regarded as game fish under Washington state law, with gill nets near the Neely Bridge on the Green River. They were convicted of fishing with gill nets for a game fish, a violation of state law. Judge Shorett ruled that "Use of gillnets in the upper reaches of rivers is destructive of the runs since gillnets tend to eliminate certain segments of the runs of salmon and steelhead and, in addition, injure and frighten many fish which are not caught" (Brown, 1968, n.p.). The conviction was upheld on appeal through the state courts (American Friends, 1970, 99-105). Robert Moses, Cecil Moses, Sherman Dominick, and Larry V. Maurice were sentenced to six years in prison, but the time was suspended.

In August 1967, the Muckleshoot Tribal Council passed a resolution urging the Interior Department to take over management of the Green River fishery from the state of Washington. "We expect only blind determination from [the state] to extinguish our rights to our beloved salmon, no matter what, in any way [it] can," said the resolution, which made up most of the *Muckleshoot Messenger's* front page ("Resolution," 1967, 1). The resolution pointed out that the state was encouraging commercial and sport fishermen to harvest salmon at sea before they returned to rivers that ran through Muckleshoot fishing grounds.

PRECURSORS TO THE BOLDT RULING

A precursor to the Boldt decision was handed down in an Oregon federal court during 1969, in *United States v. Oregon* (*Sohappy v. Smith* 302 F. Supp. 899 [D. Oregon 1969]). The United States sued on behalf of Robert Sohappy and several Indian tribes after allegations that Oregon state law violated treaty rights on the Columbia River. Complaints alleged that state regulations denied Indians an adequate catch at their traditional (usual and accustomed) sites upriver, while favoring non-Indians downstream. The state contended that Indians were not entitled to separate recognition or protection. Federal District Judge Robert C. Belloni rejected the state's case, holding that state regulation of Indian fishing must be 1) necessary for the conservation of the fish; 2) that regulation "must not discriminate against the Indians" and that 3) regulation must meet appropriate standards (Johnson, 1972, 227-228).

Belloni said that the treaties required Oregon's fisheries management to pass a "fair and equitable share" test, allowing Indians to catch enough fish to fulfill treaty requirements (Woods, 2005, 426). Unlike Judge Boldt five years later, Belloni did not put a percentage on the phrase. Later, however, he adopted Boldt's fifty-fifty rule (Woods, 2005, 431). Belloni's ruling also applied to a small portion of the Columbia River, while Boldt's governed fishing in Puget Sound, as well as much of the Strait of Juan de Fuca and state coastal waters.

Six years before the Boldt ruling, on May 27, 1968, in "Puyallup I," the U.S. Supreme Court upheld Washington State regulation of Indian fishing in the case brought by the Nisquallys and Puyallups. In a unanimous opinion written by Justice William O. Douglas, the court held that the state could regulate Indian fishing so long as it was reasonable and necessary for conservation, met appropriate standards, and did not discriminate. The decision in 1968 also said that the state could not restrict where Indians fished, since treaties allowed them to use "all usual and accustomed places." The decision settled little; the state continued to arrest Indians and confiscate their gear, and the Indians continued to defy state enforcement.

The fishing-rights case also was evolving in the federal courts. Following Puyallup I, Puyallup II (1973) illustrated how the law was changing. The majority opinion in both cases was written by William O. Douglas, who had been raised in Eastern Washington. In 1968, he had found that the state could legally regulate off-reservation fishing if such regulation was "reasonable and necessary" to achieve "conservation" of the species. The state, of course, argued that it had been doing just that. In 1973, however, in a case regarding the state's ability to close the fishery for steelhead (which it defined as a game fish that Indians were not allowed to harvest), Douglas said that the state's system was not necessary for conservation.

Alison Bridges being painfully shackled during the September 9, 1970 raid on a fishing encampment.
Photo courtesy of University of Washington Libraries, Special Collection / Delores Varela Phillips /1210.8N6

SHOTS AND ARRESTS

The ground-level fishing wars peaked September 9, 1970 during a fish-in on the Puyallup River near Tacoma, as a multiethnic camp of about a hundred fishing-rights supporters standing vigil for an array of treaty Indians on the river was torn apart by about 300 police in riot gear who arrested about 60 people. Four shots were fired at the police, who then dispersed the crowd with a volley of their own fire and a haze of tear gas. A week before police leveled the Puyallup camp and arrested 60 people, the Muckleshoot Tribal Council had voted its support (Smith, 1970, 39). This confrontation contributed to the filing of *United States v. Washington*, which produced the Boldt ruling. The growing scale of the conflict over fishing rights prompted federal attorneys to make it a priority.

The camp, which had been maintained all summer, was bulldozed by the state as Muckleshoot, Nisqually, Puyallup, and other fishing people were driven off the water by the state's armed fish-and-game police. Indian boats were seized and nets cut. By the time it was over, occupants of the camp had burned a railroad trestle in anger as most of them were removed in handcuffs. One activist, Alison Bridges, was dragged away by her hair as photographers recorded what became an iconic moment.

Some of the roughly 300 people in the camp documented the arrests on videotape and provided the fishing people with food, shelter, moral support, and bail money (Mapes, 2010). All charges stemming from the arrests were later dropped, as judges found that drawing the state's ire by camping on a river was not a crime. A contemporary account said that "Fifty-five adults and five juveniles were arrested in an encampment that had been established one mile north of Tacoma where Highway 99 crossed the Puyallup River. Police seized firearms and knives and fishing nets, but there were no injuries. Two days later, Tacoma Police Chief Lyle Smith ordered the encampment bulldozed" (Shots Fired, 1970, A-1; Wilma, 2000). The fish-in was deemed illegal by the state after Indians fished outside of its three-day-a-week limit. The Indians said that the treaties allowed them to fish at their "usual and accustomed places" without time limits. (Carson, 1970, B-10; Puyallup, 1970, A-4).

A LANDMARK FEDERAL FISHING DECISION

At first, the Native fishermen were not impressed by Tacoma Federal District Court

Judge George Hugo Boldt. He had been appointed by President Dwight Eisenhower, with no notable background in American Indian law. A native of Montana, Boldt was also a sport fisherman. Alvin Ziontz wrote in his memoir *A Lawyer in Indian Country* (2009, 95) that Hank Adams became so worried about how the case was being conducted by the Justice Department that he flew to Washington, D.C., and pressed officials to start over.

Adams' argument did not involve expected bias on Judge Boldt's part, however, but criticized preparation of the case by U.S. attorneys, whom he said had failed to consult adequately with the tribes they were supposed to represent, having paid too much attention to sheer numbers of fish, and too little to the historical and cultural context of the case. Adams said that the Muckleshoots in particular had been denied harvest of several million salmon over 50 years from traditional grounds in the Green and White River system, a history that the attorneys on the case should recognize (Wilkins, 2011, 31). "We need protection from [U.S. Attorneys] George Dysart and Stan Pitkin!" Adams wrote to Interior Secretary Rogers Morton on March 2, 1971 (Wilkins, 2011, 30).

Another letter complaining of inadequate consultation was sent by Adams, Ramona Bennett, and Billy Frank, Jr. to Attorney General Elliot Richardson on August 14, 1973, as the case was going to trial. "The different tribes were invited and encouraged to independently enter the case as interveners — while attempts to intervene were vigorously, and successfully, resisted by the United States," the letter said (Wilkins, 2011, 67). Regardless of the protests, Billy Frank, Jr. said later, regarding Judge Boldt's conduct from the bench: "He listened to us. He listened very carefully" (Tizon, 1999).

Judge Boldt's decision marked an evolution in federal law regarding Native American fishing rights, aided by an important article published in the *Washington Law Review* in 1972 by University of Washington law professor Ralph W. Johnson. At about the same time Justice William O. Douglas' wife, Cathy, also a lawyer, had visited Frank's Landing at the behest of Hank Adams. She studied the case and became convinced that the Indians were correct.

Johnson wrote that Indians had been asserting their rights to fish according to the treaties ever since they were signed. In 1896 (*Ward v. Race Horse*), 1905 (*United States v. Winans*), 1942 (*Tulee v. Washington*), and 1968 (*Puyallup Tribe v. Department of Game*), the U.S. Supreme Court fundamentally accepted the state's position that the law allowed its regulation of Native fishing for conservation of the resource. Johnson argued that the Court had been recycling its own original legal error and that "No valid basis for the existence for such state power can be found" (Johnson, 1972, 208).

Treaties, as the "supreme law of the land" under the U.S. Constitution, wrote Johnson, cannot allow unilateral regulation "unless the treaty so provides or unless Congress so legislates" (Johnson, 1972, 208). Neither had occurred. "Therefore," Johnson wrote, "the Supreme Court should clearly hold that the states have no power to regulate Indian off-reservation fishing unless and until Congress expressly delegates the power to do so" (Johnson, 1972, 208).

Boldt's decision followed the legal evolution of previous Supreme Court rulings that any state regulation of treaty Indian fishing must be reasonable and necessary for conservation, and must not discriminate against treaty Indian fishing. Upheld by higher courts, Judge Boldt's ruling affirmed the treaty fishing peoples' decades-long assertions of their

A model salmon weir was built by Jerry Dominick in Everett.
Photo courtesy of White River Valley Historical Museum / 00441

rights, fundamentally and explicitly. Documented with the research of Barbara Lane, Boldt used an 1828 edition of *Webster's American Dictionary* for his contemporary definition of "in common with," as entitling Native people to as much as half the salmon catch running through their *traditional* waters, *before* the treaties had been signed. Legally, "stations" were defined as fixed, specific locations such as weirs or platforms. "Grounds" were defined as larger areas that could contain several "stations."

The Boldt decision challenged the allocation of legal power in an ambit much broader than fishing alone. The treaties could no longer be dismissed by the state or subject solely to its own definition by police power. Native peoples became equal in the eyes of the law. The ruling also contained several other endorsements of sovereignty that were not specific to fishing, holding that the state could not discriminate against Native peoples, and that the intent of Congress was to enhance Native self-government.

THE MUCKLESHOOTS AS A TREATY TRIBE

Work by Barbara Lane as part of *U.S. v. Washington* established the Muckleshoots, once and for all, as a treaty tribe. Lane, a 1953 PhD in anthropology at the University of Washington, was (at various times) a professor of anthropology there, as well as at the University of Hawaii, the University of Pittsburgh, the University of British Columbia, and the University of Victoria (B.C.). She had done field work with Pacific Northwest peoples, as well as in the New Hebrides Islands and parts of India before, as a private consultant, she was called upon as an expert witness in *State v. Moses* (79 Wash. 2d 104), as well as *United States v. Washington*.

During the litigation that led to Judge Boldt's ruling in 1974, the Muckleshoots faced some extraordinary complications. The name "Muckleshoot" was not applied to an Indian tribe in the 1850s, when the treaties were negotiated. Originally it was the name of a prairie on a site near present-day Auburn. This fact was cited often by the state in its assertions that the Muckleshoot lacked treaty status. The name "Muckleshoot" appears in the historical record as a reference to a group of people first in 1864, when John Montgomery referred to his common-law wife as "an Indian woman of the Muckleshute tribe" (Lane, 1973, 8). The Commissioner of Indian Affairs' first such reference was in 1868; in 1870, a report of the same office reference a "Muckleshoot Tribe" (Lane, 1973, iii). The constituent peoples included Smal-ka-mish meaning "the head of White River," Skope-ah-mish ("Green River") and St-ka-mish ("White River"). The Skope-ah-mish, Stakamish, and Smulkamish had been named in the preamble to the treaty; Judge George Boldt in 1974 ruled that Stevens used Chief Sea'th'l's signature to imply consent by all the people of the Duwamish drainage, including the Muckleshoots' ancestors.

Lane was able to establish "without doubt" that many residents of the Muckleshoot reservation were direct descendants of the three tribes represented at the Point Elliott treaty council (Lane, 1973, 10). She referred the Court in the Boldt case to genealogical charts entered as exhibits in *State v. Moses et al.*, No. 44836, Superior Court of the State of Washington [1968]. (Lane, 1973, 10).

The contending parties spent three years preparing the case before Judge Boldt. The trial itself took several weeks. Testifying during trial of *U.S. v. Washington*, Muckleshoot Bernice White expressed what many Indian people felt: "Washington State, at the time of the treaty ... was a territory. The treaty was made with the understanding that we retained this right [to fish]. So we don't have to come to the state. The state has to come to us. It is our right, and it is our rivers and our [Puget] Sound." She told the court that living in poverty, on welfare, was not a choice that Muckleshoots and other Native people preferred:

> Many of the people in my tribe are on welfare. It is something that you don't like, but if you have a large family [and] you are not working, you have to accept this. You are always looked down upon and your children are not dressed right, you're not eating right ... and you are more or less degraded by being on welfare. But there is no other choice for our people; they lack education and there is no employment. We have no natural resource. The only thing we can look towards is the fish. (Transcript, 1974, 3146-81)

On November 13, 2013, a short street in Seattle's Duwamish industrial area was dedicated as "Elder Bernice White Place." "It might not look like much from the street that runs past it — West Marginal Way," commented the *Muckleshoot Monthly*. "It's mostly under the West Seattle Bridge in an area riddled with railroad tracks and industrial structures. But in many ways, it's the perfect place to honor Bernice White, and all others who risked their necks and worked for nothing to win back the Muckleshoot Tribe's freedom to fish." During the late stages of the "fishing wars," as Judge George Boldt's ruling was being implemented, this was a site of a "fishing shack," described as "a hub of activity for Native fishermen exercising their treaty rights on the Duwamish River ... and life on the River was tense. Tribal fishers were subjected to many challenges as they openly exercised their Treaty rights for the first time, from net theft to gunfire" ("Bernice White Park," 2013, 1).

Muckleshoot Louis Starr told Judge Boldt's court that the fishing landscape had changed since treaty times: "The rivers themselves have changed ... as the people ... make the pipes bigger, drain the rivers. We can no longer fish in the Green River or the Cedar River and up above the White River where they used to fish is drained dry now. We are left there with nothing ... and as for fishing, we have to beg around to get a chance to fish" (Transcript, 1974, 3182-90).

In his memoir *A Lawyer in Indian Country*, Alvin Ziontz, who attended the trial, wrote that the testimony of Native people "had a powerful impact on Judge Boldt" (2009, 114). In his closing statement, he said that this kind of case should have been brought 50 years earlier to avoid decades of suffering and bitterness. A true solution would take time, Boldt said, but "I am hopeful that all will come together as citizens, acting like brethren in that wonderful relationship" (Ziontz, 2009, 122). After another contentious decade, these words proved to be prescient.

Chapter 4

THE LIMITS OF THE BOLDT DECISION

United States v. Washington was limited to anadromous fish (salmon), which are born in fresh water, migrate to the ocean, then return to their birthplaces to spawn. Allocation of shellfish, herring, and other non-anadromous species was left for later adjudication. The Boldt decision defined its applicable territory as the watersheds of Puget Sound and the Olympic Peninsula north of Grays Harbor, and adjacent offshore waters. The case includes hatchery-bred fish. Boldt used more than 200 pages to interpret the wording of the treaties in an opinion which some legal scholars believe is the most carefully researched, thoroughly analyzed ever handed down in a Native fishing-rights case.

In summary, Judge Boldt's ruling found that:

1. Treaties reserved to Indian tribes fishing rights that are distinct from those of other citizens;
2. Off-reservation Indian fishing rights extended to every place each tribe customarily fished;
3. Indians had reserved rights to a fair share — 50 percent — of the harvestable fish exclusive of on-reservation catches and of fish taken for subsistence and ceremonial purposes;
4. The state may regulate Indian off-reservation fishing only to the extent necessary for conservation, but not in ways limiting treaty rights to state-preferred times and fishing methods;
5. The state classification of steelhead as a "game" fish restricted Indian fishing rights and violated the treaties; and
6. Fourteen treaty tribes, plus three more upon federal approval, were entitled to share in the decision (Marino, 1990, 176-177).

The Washington State Department of Game had argued that no special right existed for Indian fishing but that Indians needed a special allocation, which it would determine according to the state's definition of conservation requirements and the demands of sport and non-Native commercial fishers. The state of Washington also asserted that Native fishing people were obliged to abide by state laws, which restricted fishing to reservation boundaries contained in treaties. Judge Boldt denied all of this. As of 1974, the court estimated that within the jurisdiction of the case 794 Native fishing people were active, compared to 6,600 non-Indian commercial fishers and 283,650 sport fishers.

Seizure of fishing gear and other property was held to be illegal under Boldt, as the state also was prohibited from limiting the types of technology that Native fishing people may use. Some opponents of Native fishing rights had argued that they should be limited to the technologies that were in use when the treaties were signed. They applied no such technological limits to non-Indian sport or commercial fishing activities.

Judge Boldt placed Native fishing rights in a broader social, economic, and legal context:

> The treaty-secured rights to resort to the usual and accustomed places to fish were a part of larger rights possessed by the treating Indians, upon the exercise of which there was not a shadow of impediment, and which were not much less necessary to their existence than the atmosphere they breathed. The treaty was not a grant of rights to the treating Indians, but a grant of rights from them, and a reservation of those not granted. In the Stevens treaties, such reservations were not of particular parcels of land, and could not be ex-

pressed in deeds, as dealings between private individuals. The reservations were in large areas of territory, and the negotiations were with the tribes. The treaties reserved rights, however, to every individual Indian, as though described therein. There was an exclusive right of fishing reserved within certain boundaries. There was a right outside of those boundaries reserved for exercise "in common with citizens of the Territory." (*U.S. v. Washington*, 1974, 80)

BACKLASH TO THE BOLDT DECISION

State officials and the fishermen whose interests they represented were furious at Boldt. Among Washington state officials during the middle and late 1970s a backlash to Indian rights formed, which would become the nucleus for a nationwide non-Indian campaign to abrogate the treaties. Washington State Attorney General (later U.S. senator) Slade Gorton called Indians "supercitizens" with "special rights," and proposed that constitutional equilibrium be reestablished not by open state violation of the treaties (Boldt had outlawed that), but by purchasing the Indians' fishing rights. The tribes, which had been listening to offers of money for Indian resources for a century, flatly refused Gorton's offer. To them, the selling of fishing rights would have been tantamount to termination — collective cultural suicide.

A flurry of appeals by non-Indian fishing interests followed the Boldt decision. The non-Indians had been stunned that Boldt, widely known as a conservative, had issued such a pro-Indian ruling. They felt betrayed, and shaken that the law had been found to side with what the Muckleshoots and other treaty peoples had been telling them.

The Ninth Circuit Court of Appeals upheld Boldt's ruling in 1975. Among the salient points of its ruling were:

- Treaty language secured the right of taking fish at usual and accustomed places; Indians are entitled to a share of the catch, not merely what they can get in competition with the general population.
- "In common with" was defined so that treaty and non-treaty fishermen were entitled to an equal share of yearly harvest.
- The fishing agreement with Canada and the United States for an equal share of their fishery did not preempt treaty-fishing rights.
- The decision made it clear that federal law is supreme to state law and that the state could be directed to adhere to federal law even if state law prohibited that action.
- The decision by the federal court did not violate the equal protection clause of the U.S. Constitution because American Indian tribes have semi-sovereign status that is constitutionally recognized.

The U.S. Supreme Court initially declined to review the case. The Washington State Supreme Court then ruled that the state had no right nor duty to uphold Boldt's ruling, and Slade Gorton took that decision as license to ignore it, setting up a confrontation that caused Boldt to enforce the ruling, beginning August 31, 1977, using the U.S. Coast Guard and federal marshals under the jurisdiction of the Federal District Court in Tacoma.

State officials and the fishermen whose interests they represented directed their fury at Boldt. Rumors circulated about the sanity of the 75-year-old judge. It was said that he had taken bribes of free fish and had an Indian mistress, neither of which was true. Judge Boldt was hung in effigy by angry non-Indian fishermen. The removal of effigies from courthouse grounds in Western Washington became a routine ritual for U.S. Marshals. White sport fishers formed "convoys" with their boats and rammed Coast Guard vessels that had been dispatched to enforce the court's orders. One Coast Guardsman was shot.

Alvin Ziontz later wrote that "It was Gorton who led the state's legal campaign against the Indians and whose failure to support enforcement of the Boldt decision led to the complete breakdown of law enforcement on state waters" (Ziontz, 2009, 128). Fishing people and managers who did not accede to Boldt's orders could have faced federal criminal citations for contempt of court (Woods, 2005, 432).

With the state's new challenge to the Boldt Decision in *Washington v. Washington State Commercial Passenger Fishing Vessel Association* [443 U.S. 658 (1979)] the U.S. Supreme Court agreed to rule on the conflict. It largely affirmed Boldt's ruling in a 6-3 decision issued July 2, 1979. When the Supreme Court addressed the scope of state regulation approved by its previous decisions in this case, it found state regulatory authority limited to that essential for conservation. In this decision, the Supreme Court noted (in footnote 36) that its decision to render a final judgment had been partly based on Washington State's attempts to evade the rulings of lower courts:

> The state's extraordinary machinations in resisting the 1974 decree have forced the District Court to take over a large share of management of the state's fishery in order to enforce its decrees. Except for some desegregation cases … the District Court has faced the most concerted official and private efforts to frustrate a decree of a federal court witnessed in this century.

BARBARA LANE RETURNS TO MUCKLESHOOT

In 2006, Barbara Lane returned to Muckleshoot. She had come to review manuscripts and artifacts recently received in the Arthur C. Ballard Collection, anticipating a quiet day in the archives. Since Lane had an appointment, the tribe planned an honoring for her long service, but it was a surprise to her. A blanket was wrapped around her shoulders and she was given a tour. Lane's first visit to the Muckleshoot reservation had been in 1949, when most people obtained drinking water from hand pumps and no one had electricity or flush toilets.

"People were very poor," Lane said. "There was high unemployment, and at that time the tribe wasn't recognized as a treaty tribe. Things were very bleak, except that there were some very talented women who were active in tribal politics and running things on the reservation, doing good works — Annie Garrison, Ollie Hungary and her husband, and Lizzie McGillivray, and others …" ("Muckleshoot Honors," 2006).

The *Muckleshoot Monthly* reported:

> It's been more than a half-century since she first visited the Muckleshoot Reservation, and more than 30 years since the landmark Boldt case. During that time, British Columbia anthropologist Barbara Lane may have lost some of the spring in her step — she uses a cane now — but she still has a sparkle in her eye, a keen and curious mind, and a deep love for Native people ("Muckleshoot Honors," 2006, 1).

"Those who remembered the role she played 'back in the day' lined up, eager to show her the phenomenal progress that Muckleshoot has experienced over the past decade," the *Monthly* reported. "And so, instead of spending her time quietly in an archival vault, she found herself being treated like visiting royalty as she marveled at all the wonders that are now reality at Muckleshoot." ("Muckleshoot Honors," 2006, 1)

When Lane passed on December 31, 2013, the *Muckleshoot Monthly* summarized the importance of her work: "The Northwest might be a very different world today if it wasn't for Barbara Lane. As the U.S. government's expert witness on behalf of treaty tribes in *U.S. v. Washington* ... her keen intellect, tough-mindedness, and impeccable research turned the tide in what became their greatest legal victory ever" ("Treaty Rights," 2014).

The fishing ruling had ignited a revolution in the lives of the Muckleshoots and other treaty tribes, the results of which astonished her, as she watched the revival of a nation. A quarter century after the fact, Vine Deloria, Jr. said that Lane had "demonstrated skills bordering on pure genius" (Deloria, 1997, 215). Lane and, until his death, her late husband, Robert Lane, continued to work on a variety of projects with the Muckleshoots following her testimony in *United States v. Washington.*

She returned to the reservation during 2012 to take part in planning, and commented that "These new developments are testimony to the perseverance and vision of the present Muckleshoot Tribe — its administrators, members, and employees. Present accomplishments have deep roots going back through generations of Muckleshoot leaders — prominent persons and ordinary family members who fought to preserve and protect traditional territory and resources, treaty rights, and traditional culture. [and who] sought to remain self-supporting and to live in peace with their neighbors. Recognition of the important role of these ancestors is reflected in the historic pictures adorning the walls of the public buildings and in the names bestowed on the buildings" ("Making the Case," 2012, 1).

REMEMBERING BERNICE WHITE

One of the Muckleshoots' most celebrated former leaders, she was tribal chair during the fish wars and personally presented her statement of the tribe's needs to President John F. Kennedy, who told her that hers was the best he had received. It was the proudest moment of her life. With much publicity, the City of Seattle in 2012 named a new salmon enhancement / park site under the West Seattle Bridge, as well as the street that leads to it, "Tribal Elder Bernice White Place." She has many prominent descendants, including two grandsons on the Tribal Council. The current Miss Skopabsh (who is the tribal princess) is also a granddaughter.

— *John Loftus*

Sign designed and placed by the City of Seattle at the Bernice White park site under the West Seattle swing bridge.
Photo by John Loftus, Muckleshoot Monthly

LEO LACLAIR'S FISHING-RIGHTS ACTIVISM

Leo LaClair, a tall Muckleshoot, actively participated in the fishing struggles of the 1960s and 1970s. LaClair graduated from the University of Washington Law School and became a national Native-rights leader who advised that Muckleshoots join the fishing-rights case that became the Boldt decision.

LaClair graduated from Auburn High School with a grade point average of nearly 3.8 during his senior year. He then attended Central Washington State College in Ellensburg, graduating four years later with an education degree, one of the first Muckleshoot people to obtain a college education. LaClair's father died at the age of 34, so Leo and his siblings were raised by their mother.

According to Willard Bill, Sr.'s research, LaClair early developed a goal-oriented personality and paid his own tuition at a time when the Bureau of Indian Affairs was not providing higher education funds. He graduated from college at a time when the BIA was actively encouraging Native peoples to terminate their reservations. LaClair met Robert (Bob) Johnson, a reporter with the Auburn *Citizen*, who published many articles about Muckleshoot reservation life. Johnson became an advocate for Muckleshoot people. LaClair applied to a pre-law program at the University of New Mexico and attended a summer seminar. He was accepted into the UCLA Law School, spending a year there before transferring to the University of Washington, where he worked with Prof. Ralph Johnson, a well-known advocate of Native fishing rights in Washington State.

LaClair also met Chuck McEvers, who was affiliated with the Seattle office of the American Friends Service Committee. McEvers had printed the Medicine Creek and Point Elliott Treaties for students. Study of the treaties turned LaClair into a fishing-rights activist. LaClair also met Bruce Wilkie, a Makah who had graduated from the University of Puget Sound in Tacoma, who became president of the National Council of American Indians (NCAI). All of them helped to organize the National Indian Youth Council (NIYC), a source of Native activism during the 1960s and 1970s.

Pearl Warren, the first director of the Seattle Indian Center, also mentored LaClair. She helped to provide social services to many Native people who had relocated to Seattle for employment and training during a time when the BIA was moving Native people off reservations to terminate land base and collective identity. She represented the American Indian Women's Service League, which started in a storefront on Seattle's First Avenue, and later moved to a former church building on Boren Avenue. When Warren enlisted LaClair to address Native issues in Washington D.C. he met Washington senators Warren Magnuson and Henry Jackson.

Leo J. LaClair, Boldt 40 celebration, February 2014.
Photo by John Loftus, Muckleshoot Monthly

LaClair used his knowledge of Indian law to promote the idea of fishing off-reservation that correlated with rights granted in the treaties of Medicine Creek and Point Elliott, contrary to the state's legal position. He and others formed a Fish Commission that operates to this day at Muckleshoot. Cecile Moses worked with LaClair to advocate off-reservation fishing rights.

LaClair's activism extended beyond fishing rights. He was a member of the Committee of One Hundred (with 14 other Native Americans) who were planning Martin Luther King, Jr.'s Poor People's Campaign, which was developing a massive march on Washington, D.C. by people of all races at the time King was assassinated, April 4, 1968. The Poor People's Campaign advocated an Economic Bill of Rights to end job discrimination and guarantee employment to all people of working age. Plans for the campaign continued after King's assassination.

The fifteen Native Americans drafted a letter to Secretary of Interior Stewart Udall pointing out that under government's paternalistic wardship, American Indians had become the most impoverished group in the United States. The letter said that paternalism was like a virus, and the Interior Department was its host. Several Native people were spurred by this statement to picket (and, for a brief time, occupy) the Bureau of Indian Affairs headquarters in Washington, D.C., provoking several arrests, four years before a much larger (and better known) occupation of the same offices at the conclusion of the Trail of Broken Treaties in 1972 (Shreve, 2011, 175).

STANLEY MOSES: DEFENDING FISHING RIGHTS

Stanley Moses Jr.
Photo by John Loftus, Muckleshoot Monthly

A *skookum* young man when the Muckleshoot Fisheries Commission selected him to be arrested in order to get a case into court and argue for their treaty rights, his arrest, along with others, ultimately led to the Boldt Decision. When Cecil Moses, the tribe's leader and chief strategist in the fishing wars died, Stan was chosen as his uncle's successor, and was soon elected to the Tribal Council as well. Over the decades that followed, under Stan's leadership, treaty rights once dismissed by outside entities became an immutable fact of life in the Puget Sound area. A soft-spoken and cordial man, he was tough as nails when his people's rights were at stake. Restoring salmon runs in the most urbanized area of the state was a monumental challenge, but one that was met. Stanley Moses Landing, the tribe's fishing terminal under the 1st Avenue Bridge on the Duwamish River, was a favorite project of his and is named in his honor.

— *John Loftus*

REFERENCES

American Friends Service Committee. *Uncommon Controversy: Fishing Rights of the Muckleshoot, Puyallup, and Nisqually Indians.* Seattle: University of Washington Press, 1970.

"Bernice White Park on Duwamish Is Dedicated." *Muckleshoot Monthly*, December 20, 2013, 1, 2.

Brown, Bruce. *Mountain in the Clouds: A Search for the Wild Salmon.* New York: Simon & Schuster, 1982. [http://www.astonisher.com/archives/mitc/mitc_ch1.html]

Brown, Larry. "4 Indians Convicted on Fishing Charge." *Seattle Times*, January 11, 1968, n.p.

Carson, Jerry. "Indians Face Court Battle over Puyallup Fishing," *Seattle Times*, September 10, 1970, B-10.

"Court Move Could End Fishing Dispute." Tacoma *News-Tribune*, March 18, 1968, n.p.

D'Ambrosio, Antonino. *A Heartbeat and a Guitar: Johnny Cash and the Making of Bitter Tears.* New York: Nation Books, 2009.

"Indian Treaty Trek Linked to Trial of 4 Muckleshoots." *Auburn Citizen*, May 18, 1966, 1.

James, Bob, John Newhauken, Frank Ross, Joe Hill, George Jack, and Walter Davis. Letter to Commissioner of Indian Affairs, May 15, 1916, in Patricia Slettvet Noel and Virginia Cross, *Muckleshoot Indian History*. Auburn, WA: Auburn Public School District No. 408, 1980, 101.

Johnson, Ralph W. "The States Versus Indian Off-Reservation Fishing: A United States Supreme Court Error." *Washington Law Review* 47:2 (1972), 207-236.

Johnson, Robert. [untitled]. *Auburn Citizen*. September 1, 1965. Vol. 4, No. 34. Auburn, Washington, n.p.

Josephy, Alvin M., Jr. *Now That the Buffalo's Gone: A Study of Today's American Indians*. New York: Knopf, 1982.

Lane, Barbara. "Anthropological Report on the Traditional Fisheries of the Muckleshoot Indians." October 6, 1972. Typescript in Muckleshoot Preservation Program Archives.

Lane, Barbara. "Anthological Report on the Identity and Treaty Status of the Muckleshoot Indians." U.S. District Court, Tacoma, WA Plaintiff's exhibit No. USA-270, *United States v. Washington*, admitted to the record August 24, 1973.

Lane, Barbara. "The Muckleshoot Indians and the White River: A Report Prepared for the Muckleshoot Indian Tribe." September 1980. In Muckleshoot Preservation Program Archives.

Makah Indian Tribe v. Schoettler 192 F. 2d 224 at 226 (9th Circuit) (1951).

"Making the Case for Muckleshoot Treaty Rights." *Muckleshoot Monthly*, July 2012, 12.

Mapes, Lynda V. "Fish-Camp Raid Etched in State History." *Seattle Times*, September 6, 2010. [http://seattletimes.com/html/localnews/2012827306_fishwar07m.html]

Marino, Cesare. "History of Western Washington Since 1846," in Suttles, Wayne. Ed. *Handbook of North American Indians: Northwest Coast*. Vol. 7. In William C. Sturtevant, General Ed. *Handbook of North American Indians*. Washington, D.C.: Smithsonian Institution, 1990, 169-179.

Martinez, Regino. "Roberto Maestas Interviews: The History of El Centro de la Raza. Seattle, WA. 2004. Transcribed by Kristina Cook, 2010.

McCloud, Janet and Robert Casey. *The Last Indian War*. Seattle: Seattle Group Bulletins, No. 29 and 30, 1968. Mimeographed. In El Centro de la Raza archives.

Meeker, Ezra. *Pioneer Reminiscences of Puget Sound: The Tragedy of Leschi*. New York: Lowman & Hanford Stationery and Print. Co., 1905.

Moses, Stanley. Interview at Muckleshoot, August 16, 2011.

"Muckleshoot Honors Barbara Lane; B.C. Anthropologist's Expert Testimony Helped Persuade Judge Boldt to Rule in Favor of Tribal Treaty Rights." *Muckleshoot Monthly*, April 15, 2006, 1, 2, 11.

"Muckleshoot Treaty Trek Is Historic Indian Event: LaClair," *Auburn Globe-News*, May 18, 1966, 1, 11.

Norton, Dee. "Federal Suit Attacks Indian-Fishing Laws," *Seattle Times*, September 19, 1970, A-4.

"Physical Yield of Washington State Salmon Fisheries, 1989-1974, " in Russel L. Barsh, *The Washington Fishing Rights Controversy: An Economic Critique*. Monograph Series, University of Washington Graduate School of Business Administration, 1977.

"Puyallup River Indian Camp Destroyed by Bulldozers," *Seattle Times*, September 11, 1970, E-7.

Puyallup Tribe v. [Washington State] *Department of Game* 391 U.S. 392 (1968).

"Resolution," *Muckleshoot Messenger*, August 1967, 1.

Shreve, Bradley. *Red Power Rising: The National Indian Youth Council and the Origins of Native Activism*. Norman: University of Oklahoma Press, 2011.

"Shots Fired, 60 Arrested in Indian-Fishing Showdown," *Seattle Times*, September 9, 1970, A-1.

Smith, Sherry L. *Hippies, Indians, and the Fight for Red Power*. New York: Oxford University Press, 2012.

State [of Washington] *v. Tulee* 7 Wash. 2d 124, 109 P.2d 280 (1941) (en banc).

State of Washington v. Satiacum 314 P.2d 400.

<u>State of Washington v. Moses</u> 1963-1967, citations:
County:
No. 609180 (King Co. Super. Ct, filed Nov. 4, 1963.
Washington Supreme Court:
State v. Moses 70 Wash 2d 282, 286, 422 P.2d 775, 778.
U.S. Supreme Court:
Cert. denied 389 U.S. 428 (1967).

Suckley, G, "Report Upon the Fisheries Collected on the Survey: Report Upon the Salmonidae." *In Reports of the Explorations ... 1854. The Pacific Railroad Report.* Washington, D.C.: Thomas H. Ford, 1860.

Tizon, Alex. "The Boldt Decision: 25 Years – The Fish Tale That Changed History." *Seattle Times*, February 7, 1999. [http://community.seattletimes.nwsource.com/archive/?date=19990207&slug=2943039]

Transcript of Proceedings, *U.S. v. Washington* 384 F. Supp. 312 (Western District of Washington, 1974). Civ. No. 9213.

"Treaty Rights Champion Barbara Lane Passes On." *Muckleshoot Monthly*, February 15, 2014, 1.

Tulee v. Washington 315 U.S. 681, 685 (1942).

U.S. Commission on Civil Rights. "Fishing in Western Washington – A Treaty Right, a Clash of Cultures." 61-100 in *Indian Tribes, a Continuing Quest for Survival: A Report of the United States Commission on Civil Rights.* Washington: U.S. Government Printing Office, 1981.

United States v. Washington 384 F. Supp. 312 (1974).

United States v. Winans 198 U.S. 371 (1905).

Ward v. Race Horse 163 U.S. 504 (1896).

Washington v. Washington State Commercial Passenger Fishing Vessel Association 443 U.S. 658 (1979).

Wilkins, David E., ed. *The Hank Adams Reader: An Exemplary Native American Activist and the Unleashing of Indigenous Sovereignty.* Golden, CO: Fulcrum, 2011.

Wilkinson, Charles. *Messages from Frank's Landing: A Story of Salmon, Treaties, and the American Way.* Seattle: University of Washington Press, 2000.

Wilma, David. "Tacoma Police Arrest 60 Persons at a Fish-In on September 9, 1970." HistoryLink. August 25, 2000. Accessed January 2, 2010. [http://historylink.org/index.cfm?DisplayPage=output.cfm&file_id=2625]

Woods, Fronda. "Who's in Charge of Fishing?" *Oregon Historical Quarterly* 106:3 (Fall 2005), 412-441.

Ziontz, Alvin J. *A Lawyer in Indian Country: A Memoir.* Seattle: University of Washington Press, 2009.

Chapter 5

Protecting Natural Bounty

Chapter 5

Protecting Natural Bounty

Elson "Beeb" Moses holds a large Chinook salmon.
Photo by John Loftus, Muckleshoot Monthly

Following the Boldt decision, Native people could quit demonstrating for the right to fish and spend their time actually fishing. Other businesses also began. In 1978, the Muckleshoots' smoke shop opened. A tribal administration building was completed in 1979. By 1984, the Muckleshoots had 20 gillnetters with 117 fishers. The same year a new smoke shop opened on the Auburn/Enumclaw Highway. During the 1980s, the tribe purchased the Keta Creek Hatchery.

The Muckleshoot Fish Commission, initially formed before the Boldt decision, assumed an important role in managing resources in cooperation with other bodies, allocating fishing dates and times to prevent overfishing. The commission sets rules for commercial sales, personal use and ceremonial fisheries, co-managing with the State of Washington's Department of Fisheries. The commission also negotiates conflicts that arise on rivers and streams, and plays a role in regulating fisheries on Lake Sammamish, Lake Washington, Elliott Bay, the Duwamish River, White River, Green River and the Lake Washington Ship Canal, all usual and accustomed Muckleshoot fishing areas. Additionally, they are accountable for the Keta Creek and White River hatcheries. By about 2005, the Muckleshoots were raising 1.5 million fish a year.

Once money was available, the Muckleshoot adopted high-technology methods such as hydroacoustics to count juvenile sockeye in Lake Washington. Adult Chinook in Elliott Bay and Chinook, coho, and chum in Green River have been counted using the same methods. A GPS database has been used since 2003 to track placement of each Muckleshoot's fishing net.

The Muckleshoot also host a fishing derby three times a year at the Keta Creek Hatchery, where many people catch trophy-sized fish.

The hatchery fishery has been replacing natural runs, as the spread of urbanization across the Muckleshoot homeland damages the fishing landscape that Native people had used for thousands of years. A freeway and other roads paved over many farms, burying some of the richest land in the United States under streets, parking lots, strip malls, and suburban housing developments. Most salmon never even reached this polluted, urban gauntlet because they were caught at sea by Canadian, Alaskan, and other non-Indian fishing operators long before they could return to their upstream spawning grounds.

After the threat of arrest by state fish and game agents was removed, fishing could be dangerous, even deadly. On October 20, 1986, Levi Hamilton, one of the Muckleshoots' best-known leaders, was crushed to death when his body was caught in a gill net as it spooled onto a six-foot-wide disk on the back of his boat. Hamilton had been tribal chairman, as well as longtime pastor (1966–1984) of the Muckleshoot Full Gospel Church. Seattle Police found the 51-year-old Hamilton under several layers of tightly wound net, suffocated, his ribs shattered, near the north end of Lake Washington, adjacent to Wolfe Bay. He had been fishing alone (Clements, 1986, A-2).

MUCKLESHOOT SEAFOOD PRODUCTS

Muckleshoot Seafood Products (MSP) was established to help fisherman market their catch by purchasing salmon directly from tribal members at a fair and equitable price. Before the company was organized, market prices swung wildly for small fishermen, making investment in boats and equipment risky. The company also negotiates retail sale. For example, it reached an agreement with the Safeway Corporation, the largest grocer in the Puget Sound area, for purchase of Muckleshoot seafood, principally salmon, providing a large, stable market. Effective management and marketing enabled the tribe's fishing fleet to grow from about 50 to about 80 boats. Muckleshoot salmon got a nod from a food critic at the *New York Times*, who wrote in 2002 that "Fairway Markets sell it for $14.99 a pound;

On the road with Muckleshoot Seafood Products.
Photo by John Loftus, Muckleshoot Monthly

Citarella has it for $19.99 a pound. Rosedale has steaks for $15 a pound, fillets for $20 a pound" (Fabricant, 2002).

John Halliday, former marketing and sales manager for Muckleshoot Seafood Products, said that the idea of Muckleshoot-marketed salmon was first raised in 1973. It became real in 1996 when revenue from the Casino (see chapter 6) provided capital. The MSP started in 2002, selling Muckleshoot smoked salmon in gift boxes. Sales of Muckleshoot seafood reached $1 million a year in 2004. The company also developed new products, such as several varieties of fish sticks, as well as smaller, frozen or breaded fish sold in boxes. Soon, Muckleshoot fish were being sold not only to Safeway, but to other food stores, such as the Northwest regional retailer Fred Meyer, several locations on the U.S. East Coast, and

Chapter 5

Unloading salmon at the dock.
Photo by John Loftus, Muckleshoot Monthly

in Europe. By 2004, the Muckleshoots' seafood firm had purchased one million pounds of fish and paid Muckleshoot fishermen more than $600,000 a year. By 2011, that figure was more than $1 million. The Muckleshoot Casino's restaurants also serve fresh salmon, and fish from a Muckleshoot smokehouse is being sold widely in such venues as the Seattle-Tacoma Airport.

THE RISE AND FALL OF THE SOCKEYE SALMON

The number of salmon returning to their home streams can vary wildly season to season, complicating the lives of both fishing people and regulators. One type of fish (sockeye, for example) may nearly vanish, while others, such as king and coho, flourish. An example was provided after the year 2000 by the rise and fall of the sockeye runs.

An excellent run of sockeye returned to Lake Washington during the summer of 2000, allowing the first harvest season there in four years. By 2008, however, the number of sockeye returning through Seattle's Ballard Locks was the lowest on record. No one could totally explain the decline, which was also affecting sockeye runs throughout the region, although warming waters seemed to be a factor.

On July 2, 2000, the *South [King] County Journal* saluted the Muckleshoots' role in restoring the sockeye:

> Without the Muckleshoot Tribe there would be no sockeye fishery this year. In the early-to-mid 1990s the Washington Department of Fish and Wildlife literally abandoned the sockeye as a viable fishery. The Muckleshoots have stepped in, using their own financial resources and a considerable amount of their time, to address many of the problems that have plagued the Cedar River sockeye. The work the tribes have done on water flow levels and hatching of sockeye eggs, coupled with a healthy 1998 out-migration of sockeye smolt may mean another strong sockeye return next year. Maybe we will see the end of this cycle of a fishery only every four years. ("MIT Gets Cheers," 2000, 1).

At that time, an estimated 500,000 sockeye were expected to return to the rivers and streams flowing into Lake Washington at a rate of 10,000 to 18,000 a day. At least 350,000 sockeye must survive to keep the run at healthy levels and allow a harvest. A run above that number is split evenly between Native and sport fishers. The run is closely monitored by state and Native biologists at the Ballard Locks, which contains fish ladder between the salt water of Puget Sound and the fresh water of Lake Washington.

The year 2004 was successful for fishing, with a record run and harvest of coho salmon from the Green River of more than 120,000 fish caught, 50,000 more than the previous

Native shellfishery in the Duwamish watershed of Puget Sound is conducted in an industrial context.
Photo courtesy of Patrick Robinson / West Seattle Herald

best year. The Muckleshoots' total catch from all areas exceeded 185,000 (Annual Report, 2005, 38). After the record year in 2004, however, the total catch plummeted to 76,000 in 2005, then rose again to more than 165,000 in 2006 (Annual Report, 2006, 31).

In 2004, however, about 200,000 Lake Washington sockeye, about half of the run, failed to return to spawning grounds. In 2005, fewer than 100,000 sockeye returned from the ocean out of a run previously estimated at 398,000 fish. "We should be getting 10,000, 20,000 fish a day, and we're getting 1,000 to 2,000," said Mike Mahovlich, a Muckleshoot fish biologist. "We've lost 90 percent of our fish in the marine area" ("No Sockeye," 2005, 4). Mahovlich could tell something was wrong with the runs in 2004 when he found salmon carcasses floating belly-up in the Ballard Locks, between Lake Washington and Puget Sound. Dying salmon lay gasping on rocks. Biologists worried that climate change could create long-term damage to the fishery.

After the Muckleshoots had been hailed a few years earlier for their role in saving the sockeye runs, in 2005 no catch at all was allowed when warm water devastated the sockeye run in Lake Washington. The Muckleshoots even went without their subsistence catch of about a thousand sockeye for ceremonial events and needy tribal members. A return of 100,000 fish was the lowest ocean survival rate ever recorded for Lake Washington sockeye, said Jim Ames, sockeye program manager for the Washington State Fish and Wildlife Department. "The best theory we have right now is that these fish entered very warm temperatures, which pushes their food supply out of the normal migration pattern. This also brings in a lot of warm water predators, such as mackerel and tuna, that prey on these weaker, smaller fish — the salmon," said Mahovlich ("No Sockeye," 2005, 4). A 2004 study by University of Washington and King County scientists found that average summer water temperatures had risen sharply. Ship-canal water rose to 68 degrees F. by June 21, two weeks earlier than ever recorded. On July 18, the temperature reached 71.6 degrees. For salmon, water above 68 degrees creates dangerous stress, making them more vulnerable to disease. At 77 degrees F, salmon die.

Poor sockeye runs continued through 2007, as the Muckleshoots were again unable to harvest even a minimal number for ceremonies and the needy. Other species (Chinook, coho, chum) recovered from time to time. Only 254 sockeye found their way into the nets of the designated fishers, amounting to only a little over one-fourth of the target number. MIT Fisheries biologists attributed this to the overall weakness of several sockeye runs and, not wishing to further weaken the run by taking more fish, elected not to go after the other 750 fish. Muckleshoot Seafood Products reported favorable runs of Chinook and king salmon.

During August of 2011, the humpback salmon, which return every two years, flooded Puget Sound in huge numbers — six million from Seattle south to Olympia, coursing up every available stream and river, despite dams, pollution, their reduction to a remnant run, and the fact that most other species of salmon were doing poorly. Why were the runs of "humpies" doubling and tripling every year or two, "multiplying like crazy"? Stanley Moses, who had served as Chair of Muckleshoot Fisheries Commission for many years, said that no one in the vast assemblage of experts who tend the fishery knew (Moses, 2011).

THE SALMON HOMECOMING

The Native tradition of receiving the first salmon of the season with ceremony has been extended society-wide in the Pacific Northwest. The Salmon Homecoming has an office in Muckleshoot tribal government, supervised by Walter Pacheco, which is charged with "plan[ning] and organiz[ing] the Salmon Homecoming Celebration for the benefit of the salmon, the environment, and the way of life. This is an opportunity to educate the community at large about the cultural values of the salmon and the pivotal role the tribe and everyday people play in the preservation of the quality of life. The Coast Salish people were the stewards of the resources and the culture we practice promotes these efforts" (Annual Report, 2007, 14).

The Salmon Homecoming has reached far beyond the reservation to become part of the fabric of life in Seattle and King County, especially among environmentally conscious people. The intent of the celebration is to provide a forum for these groups to educate each other and the general public on the importance of the salmon as an indicator species and the environment needed to support the salmon, according to the Muckleshoots' *2007 Annual Report*. "The tribes play a pivotal role in the connection they have with the salmon as a cultural resource and its spiritual values …" (14).

TREATY RIGHTS AND SHELLFISH

The allocation of shellfish — clams, oysters, and others — remained controversial after *U.S. v. Washington State* adjudicated salmon. Access to shellfish was complicated by their stationary location on shorelines in a state where homeowners (unlike most other places) hold title to beach property and consider shellfish in these areas to be their property. Article III of the Treaty of Medicine

Salish Bounty Co-curator Elizabeth Swanaset holds clams collected on a Puget Sound beach. The clams were then smoked and preserved for winter use.
Photo courtesy of Warren King George, 2011

Creek treats shellfish differently from salmon: "[The] ... right of taking fish, at all usual and accustomed grounds and stations, is further secured ... Provided, however, that they shall not take shellfish from any beds staked or cultivated by citizens." Puget Sound Native peoples had gathered shellfish since antiquity in waterfront locations where homes owned by non-Indians were subsequently constructed. The federal court did not settle the issue, but said:

> In order to be entitled to exercise off-reservation treaty fishing rights to non-anadromous fish and shellfish, any tribe party to this case shall, prior to any attempt to exercise such rights, present *prima facie* evidence and arguments supporting its claim to treaty entitlements to such non-anadromous fish and shellfish upon which the court may make a preliminary determination as to the tribe's entitlement of such species, pending final determination of tribal treaty-right entitlement to non-anadromous fish and shellfish ... [459 F. Supp. 1020, 1037 (1978)]

State v. Courville preceded the filing of the shellfish proceeding in *United States v. Washington*. The defendants put forth evidence to establish that Saltwater State Park was a traditional Muckleshoot shellfish harvesting area and argued that they were exercising their treaty right to harvest shellfish. Barbara Lane and tribal members Louis Starr and Bernice White testified on the issue in the State District Court. On the basis of that testimony, the District Court found that Saltwater State Park was a usual and accustomed shellfish harvesting area of the Muckleshoot Tribe, that the defendants were exercising their treaty right to harvest shellfish, and dismissed the charges.

However, the state appealed to the Superior Court, which reversed, holding that individual Indians could not mount a treaty defense to state fishing violations unless their rights had been first definitively determined in *United States v. Washington*. On appeal to the Washington Court of Appeals, the three Muckleshoot defendants prevailed and the court held that the treaties were self-executing. During the argument before the Court of Appeals, one of the judges asked the attorney arguing for the state whether he thought that the Indians who signed the treaties would have believed that they needed to seek permission from the territorial courts before exercising their treaty rights. The attorney did not have a good answer.

Following the Boldt decision, an attempt was made at co-management between treaty signatories and Washington State to share shellfish, but negotiations failed. In 1989, the treaty tribes filed suit seeking restoration of their rights to harvest.

Testimony was gathered during a three-week period by Federal District Court Judge Edward Rafeedie from Native representatives, fish biologists, homeowners, other members of the general public, growers, and state employees. Each group provided information to the court regarding shellfish propagation, as well as treaty-based reserved rights of Indians harvesting mullusks and crustaceans. Shellfish are a vital part of the Muckleshoot diet, according to testimony at the trial. While winter villages often were sited upriver, near good spots for building fish weirs and traps, summer camps might be located near the beaches and good harvesting locations. Native elders described how they were taught to gather shellfish by their parents and grandparents.

The state of Washington argued that shellfish were not "fish" under the treaty, that all private lands should be considered staked or cultivated under the treaty provision excluding Indian harvest from such lands, and that tribes were not entitled to harvest shellfish from sub-tidal areas not readily accessible to them at treaty times. In addition, the state argued that treaties allowed Native peoples to harvest only those areas that they had used before the treaties were signed. Growers argued that areas they maintained should be excluded from treaty provisions as private property, even if they were within the traditional harvesting ranges of Native peoples.

Judge Rafeedie presented his decision December 20, 1994. It was upheld on appeal in January 1998. On April 5, 1999, the United States Supreme Court refused to hear the case, and thus let it stand. Rafeedie ruled strongly in favor of the treaty signatories in terms similar to those that Judge Boldt had used 20 years earlier. Judge Rafeedie determined that Native peoples had reserved rights to as much as half of the shellfish harvest in their "usual and accustomed places," in common with other citizens. All of the state's arguments were rejected by the District Court and on appeal by the Ninth Circuit.

As Boldt had ruled, Judge Rafeedie stated that a treaty is not a grant of rights *to* the signatories, but a grant of rights *from* them to the United States. He found that treaty signatories had been promised a permanent right to gather shellfish, stating that the right was promised as a sacred entitlement, one that the United States had a moral obligation to protect. The court, he said, may not rewrite the treaties nor interpret them in a way contrary to settled law simply to avoid or minimize hardship to the public or to the interveners (private-property owners).

Judge Rafeedie ruled that treaty rights regarding salmon and shellfish were different in one respect: the nature of individual property rights on shorelines, referring to owners of beachfront property that contained shellfish. The decision required that Native harvesters set times and conditions, and notify property owners of places and times that they would use the shorelines. Harvesters were allowed to cross private property unless there was safe access over water, by boat or other means. Harvesting was restricted to five days a year on any beach with less than 200 feet of shoreline.

A MUCKLESHOOT SHELLFISHERY ON VASHON ISLAND

Following Rafeedie's ruling, the Muckleshoot continued to develop a shellfish program, addressing the effects of water pollution from industrial waste, commercial ship discharge, septic-tank seepage, and runoff from fertilizer and animal waste. Muckleshoots historically had used locations such as present-day Saltwater State Park, Redondo Beach, and Adelaide Beach, all sites that by late in the twentieth century could not be used for harvesting because of pollution. Finding its traditional sources polluted, the Muckleshoot sought to buy seaside property on which shellfish could be cultivated and harvested. With shellfish biologist Andy Dalton and realtor Ken Lewis leading the search, they found land for sale on the east side of Vashon Island for $2 million that contained a good beach, upland property, and undisturbed acreage.

Stanley Moses and LeRoy Courville from the Muckleshoot Council and Phil Hamilton from the Fish Commission were impressed with the land, according to Willard Bill, Sr.'s research. Purchase was authorized by the Muckleshoot Council, after which the Muckleshoot Fisheries Division spent three years acquiring required federal, state and county development permits. The purchase also required compliance with roughly 40 conservation measures in the Endangered Species Act, mainly regarding protection of Chinook salmon and bald eagles on the property.

Once the land was purchased, the Muckleshoots created a shellfish harvesting site on their tidal flats that elders said would be culturally relevant, healthy, and sustainable. Gilbert (Hoagie) King George, who was involved in much of the development, helped plant shellfish in a manner much like a farmer, preparing the shoreline, according to Willard Bill, Sr.'s account. The Muckleshoots received a permit to enhance the area in 2000, using principles similar to those of fish hatcheries. King George, tribal chairman while Boldt was being implemented, had been a fishing-rights activist during the pre-Boldt years. He had been a logger, fisherman, and barber, and was tribal chairman during a time when Muckleshoot was making some major decisions regarding development. As a young man, he danced with youth groups for a variety of audiences where people contributed money, but he stopped dancing because he felt that he was compromising the culture by accepting payment. He then became one of the tribe's foremost cultural preservationists (LaBranche, 1984).

Twenty acres were later added to the site, totaling a half mile of shoreline from which little neck clams, mussels, geoduck clams, and Pacific oysters may be harvested for family subsistence and ceremonies, but not for commercial sale. Foot-long hard plastic tubes are used to plant geoducks in the beach, protecting them from predators. The geoducks take four to six years to mature as they dig into the beach. Oysters were planted in mesh cages for two years to protect them from crabs, starfish, and other predators. A shrimp farm has been discussed.

The Muckleshoots were reconstructing at least part of the marine environment that had sustained their ancestors, even as Puget Sound's urban area closed in around them. Maintaining a shellfishery in southern Puget Sound is complicated not only by urban pollution but also by the rising acidity of the water.

Many Muckleshoots use the tribe's shellfishery on Vashon Island. The *Muckleshoot Monthly* regularly publishes tide tables (to schedule clam digging when the tide is out) and warnings describing which beaches along Puget Sound are polluted or threatened by red tide, rendering clams and other shellfish hazardous. A telephone hotline (1-800-FISH NOW) is also provided. When conditions are good, the newspaper may say "There are lots of butter clams and some steamers, horse clams and cockles at the beach [on Vashon Island]" ("Things," 2008, 19).

Chapter 5

BUILDING AN ELK HERD CAN BE A TRYING BUSINESS

Treaty rights involve land animals (hunting rights) as well as fishing. The Muckleshoots for many years have tracked elk migrations near their homeland in the foothills of Mount Tahoma (Rainier) to increase the size and maintain the health of herds. Hunting of elk is strictly regulated to maintain herd size. For example, the shooting of cows (female elk) is usually forbidden. By 2000, the number of elk counted by helicopter surveys in the Green and White river watershed had declined to about 200 (a low of 170 in 2001), from roughly 800 during the 1980s and early 1990s. Human hunting of elk in the area stopped in 1996, but cougars continued to take a toll.

The herd increased 50 percent between 2001 and 2002, mainly by moving elk from other areas, some by trailer, others, immobilized with tranquilizers, by helicopter. They were fitted with numbered ear tags and radio collars. A tooth was pulled from each elk to determine age, and blood tested to established whether females were pregnant. The animals were also tested for several diseases and parasites. Measurements of fat and muscle were taken to assess body condition, and several shots were administered. In 2002, Muckleshoot wildlife staff anticipated that habitat improvements and cougar hunting would help the herd recover to at least 350 animals and ultimately 500. All hunting of elk was banned during 2002 to help the recovery.

The Muckleshoots, working with the Washington Department of Fish and Wildlife, as well as volunteers from Eyes in the Woods, KBH Archers, and the Rocky Mountain Elk Foundation, moved 82 Roosevelt elk into the Green River watershed during March 2002, from the Chehalis River, Mox Chehalis, McCleary, and Centralia steam plant areas. During the next year, 28 of these elk died — nine from cougar attacks, three from road-kill, three shot legally by state hunters, and the rest from malnutrition or causes related to having been moved.

Despite radio tracking, several elk disappeared. Of the 48 known to have been alive a year earlier, only 15 remained in the Green River watershed. Many of the animals simply wandered away, having no idea that the humans' goal was to build a herd in one area. One venturesome elk was found feeding near Ellensburg, east of the Cascade mountains. In March of 2003, the elk population in the Green River watershed remained near its low, at 150 animals ("Green River Elk," 2003, 8). Wildlife managers were learning that building an elk herd could be a trying business.

The *Muckleshoot Monthly* carries regular reports of efforts to trace elk with radio collars and maintain herd sizes, as well as warnings against shooting females. Each household is usually allowed a hunting quota of one male elk per year. During hard winters, the Muckleshoot feed the elk alfalfa — during the notably tough winter of 2008 (six weeks in February and March), 66 tons were trucked into the upper White River area. "The goal," said the tribe's 2009 annual report, "was to reduce

Deshawn Ross-Jansen's first deer.
Photo courtesy of Dwayne Ross, Jr.

Protecting Natural Bounty

The Wildlife Program staff are involved in intensive research studies using helicopters that involving radio-collared elk, cougar, and deer in the White and Green River watersheds.
Photo courtesy of Muckleshoot Monthly

over-winter mortality and help cows produce healthy calves in the spring" (24). While wildlife officers generally do not approve of feeding wildlife (which may spread disease, cause the animals to become dependent on human-provided food, and encourage their reproduction beyond the carrying capacity of the land), exceptions are made when severe weather may cause them to starve.

The Muckleshoots also carry out regular surveys of mountain goat populations south of Interstate 90 into the foothills of Mt. Tahoma (Rainier), at the boundary of the national park. The information is shared with other Indian tribes and the state, and was being used in 2008 to make a case that hunting of the goats should be banned in the south Point Elliott Treaty area due to low populations (Annual Report, 2009, 25).

THE HUCKLEBERRY MOUNTAIN LAND EXCHANGE

The U.S. Forest Service has long arranged swaps of old-growth timberlands in national forests for well-lumbered land with timber companies such as Weyerhaeuser. The Muckleshoots (as well as the Pilchuck Audubon Society, and the Huckleberry Mountain Protection Society), challenged one such swap, agreed to March 28, 1997, involving about 30,000 acres spread over five counties, from Weyerhaeuser, for 4,362 of Forest Service land, which came to be known as "the Huckleberry Land Exchange," in an area near Enumclaw, where the Muckleshoots have hunted and gathered since antiquity. The land is located in the Green River watershed in the Mt. Baker-Snoqualmie National Forest.

Weyerhaeuser had acquired the land about 1900 for $6 an acre in a checker-board pattern from the Northern Pacific Railroad's

Elk around Crystal Village are "tame," unlike most elk, which ran when approached after a snowstorm.
Photo courtesy of Mike Middleton and Dave Vales

Muckleshoot Public Works lent a hand transporting and offloading hay for elk after a major snowstorm. Each bundle weighs 2,000 pounds on a pallet.
Photo courtesy of Mike Middleton and Dave Vales

Hunting Committee Vice-Chairman Frank "Hoppy" Jerry restrains an elk calf for radio-marking to study calf elk mortality rates and causes in the Green River watershed.
Photo courtesy of Muckleshoot Monthly

land grant. The legal challenge to the land exchange asserted that most of the land Weyerhaeuser had offered was logged over or too high in ele-vation to grow trees.

In addition to its need for new logging resources, Mack L. Hogans, senior vice president, corporate affairs for Weyerhaeuser, said the land exchange would benefit the public. "The exchange provides an opportunity for improved public land management by eliminating the awkward checkerboard pattern along Interstate 90, allows public access to prime recreational areas, and adds thousands of scenic acres and several mountain lakes to lands owned by the public," Hogans wrote in the *Seattle Times*. He continued:

Katherine Arquette examines her cougar. She was the first to sign up for the Hunting and Culture Program's list of people wishing to receive cougar parts. Her opportunity came on Thursday, July 27, 2000, when hounds brought down this big male. After a long chase, Leeroy Courville, Jr. killed the cornered cat with a clean shot to the head.
Photo by John Loftus, Muckleshoot Monthly

> Portions of the land are already recreational jewels, including the 2,000 acres Weyerhaeuser donated to the Alpine Lakes Wilderness area. Most importantly, the exchange ensures that future generations will continue to have access to these lands. This is why the exchange earned the support not only of the Sierra Club, but also the Alpine Lakes Protection Society, The Mountaineers, North Cascades Conservation Council and the Washington Environmental Council. (Hogans, 1998)

Federal District Court Judge William Dwyer ruled late in 1997 that the exchange was legal, and in the public interest (as required by law). The Forest Service and Weyerhaeuser exchanged deeds quickly, and logging commenced before an appeal was heard.

The appeal, contended that the Forest Service had violated the National Environmental Policy Act (NEPA), 42 U.S.C. § 4332, and the National Historic Preservation Act (NHPA, 16 U.S.C. § 470-470w. The Ninth Circuit Court of Appeals reversed the lower court's decision May 19, 1999, saying that the Forest Service had violated environmental laws, that the exchange needed more study, and that logging there should stop while the case was under review.

The Circuit Court held that the Forest Service did not adequately consider the historical significance of some features (such as the Divide Trail) in the exchange area (*Muckleshoot v. Forest Service*, 1999, at paragraph 16). "The Indian ancestors to the present Muckleshoot Tribe included people from villages on the Green and White Rivers that form part of the drainage for Huckleberry Mountain," the Circuit Court's opinion stated. "The Tribe alleges that for thousands of years, the ancestors of present tribal members used Huckleberry Mountain for cultural, religious, and resource purposes — uses that continue to the present day. The Forest Service lands exchanged to Weyerhaeuser were part of the Tribe's ancestral grounds" (*Muckleshoot v. Forest Service*, 1999, at paragraph 13).

Additional NHPA provisions apply to Indian tribes, the Circuit Court ruled. "Properties of traditional religious and cultural importance to an Indian tribe ... may be determined to be eligible for inclusion in the National

Register ... In carrying out its responsibilities under Section 106, a Federal Agency shall consult with any Indian Tribe ..." (*Muckleshoot v. Forest Service*, 1999, at paragraph 16).

The ruling continued:

> The Tribe's claims under NHPA can be divided into three categories. The Tribe first contends that the Forest Service failed to consult adequately with it regarding the identification of traditional cultural properties. The Tribe also contends that the Forest Service inadequately mitigated the harmful impact of the exchange on sites of cultural significance. Finally, the Tribe argues that the Forest Service violated NHPA by failing to nominate certain sites to the National Register. We conclude that the Forest Service has not satisfied NHPA's mitigation requirements. (*Muckleshoot v. Forest Service*, 1999, at paragraph 20)

The Circuit Court also found that the Forest Service's environmental impact statement had failed to consider the impact of logging on the Green River watershed, and lacked scope and consideration of alternatives in several other areas (*Muckleshoot v. Forest Service*, 1999, at paragraphs 51, 61-71, 81). The court concluded that "in this case, the Forest Service failed to take the necessary hard look at the environmental impacts of the exchange and similarly failed to consider adequate alternatives to the proposed exchange" (*Muckleshoot v. Forest Service*, 1999, at paragraph 84).

The ruling was not a total defeat for the Forest Service and Weyerhaeuser, however. Like professors flunking a student's sloppy term paper, the judges wrote: "We REVERSE and REMAND to the district court with directions that it remand to the Forest Service for further proceedings consistent with this opinion" (*Muckleshoot v. Forest Service*, 1999, at paragraph 90).

During November 2001, the Forest Service agreed to pay $6 million to buy back 17 percent of the land involved in the exchange, having provoked a sharp congressional debate over the ways that the Forest Service exchanges land with private companies. The settlement allowed Weyerhaeuser to retain 3,600 acres of the timberland it had sought. The federal government kept the 30,000 acres that the company had proposed to trade. The 717 acres that Weyerhaeuser did not keep contain parts of the Huckleberry Mountain Divide Trail, which the Muckleshoots cited in their lawsuit as culturally significant, as well as lands with 200-year-old trees. The Forest Service also agreed to manage almost 11,000 acres along the Green Water drainage as winter elk habitat (Welch, 2001).

Janine Blaeloch, with the Western Land Exchange Project, said: "I'm sorry it's going through, but I know it has had a substantial effect on Forest Service policies. I don't think the Huckleberry exchange is something they would propose again. Companies now know they can't freely make trades without people paying attention anymore" (Welch, 2001). The controversy sparked an investigation by the General Accounting Office which revealed, said Blaeloch, that "the Forest Service and the Bureau of Land Management had given away millions of dollars a year by swapping lands for less-valuable property — sometimes illegally, and sometimes based on sloppy or bogus land appraisals" (Welch, 2001). The Huckleberry Mountain case was cited in the report. According to an investigation by the *Seattle Times* in 1998, "Private landowners acquired federal land for thousands of dollars, only to sell it to a third party for millions" (Welch, 2001).

Chapter 5

CULTURAL REVIVAL: MONITORING OF REMAINS

The Muckleshoots maintain a cultural monitoring office that inspects development projects on and near the reservation, as well as throughout King County, northern Pierce County, and the Cascade mountain range to identify artifacts. Projects may range from highways, housing developments, and logging sites to cell-phone towers. If the development is on federally owned land (including national parks and national forests) such inspection is legally required. Otherwise, it is a matter of cultural sensitivity.

Very few sites in the Puget Sound region actually produce artifacts, as the area's moist climate does not allow long-term preservation of bone or other organic materials. However, burial sites are sometimes uncovered during site excavations. In 2002, for example, Muckleshoot cultural monitors reported that one such locations had been uncovered in Seattle's Alki Beach (along Puget Sound), when "a homeowner unintentionally uncovered a burial when they were rebuilding their bulkhead alongside their basement wall. Carefully, the dirt that was disturbed was sifted to collect the remains and they were re-interred into their original resting place and sealed with cement. ... Gilbert King George conducted a special ceremony" ("2003 Program Update," 2003).

Cultural monitoring sometimes goes far afield. On one occasion, the bones of a Muckleshoot were found in a New York museum, and plans were made to repatriate and properly bury them in the new White Lake Cemetery under the provisions of the Native American Graves Protection and Repatriation Act (NAGPRA) (Annual Report, 2003, 14).

REFERENCES

2003 Program Update; Muckleshoot Tribal Administration. Auburn, WA: Muckleshoot Indian Tribe, 2003.

Annual Report: Muckleshoot Tribal Council, January 20, 2003. Auburn, WA: Muckleshoot Indian Tribe, 2003.

Annual Report for 2006: Muckleshoot Tribal Council. Auburn, WA: Muckleshoot Indian Tribe, 2006.

Annual Report for 2007: Muckleshoot Indian Tribe. Auburn, WA: Muckleshoot Indian Tribe, 2007.

Annual Report, 2009: Muckleshoot Indian Tribe. Auburn, WA: Muckleshoot Indian Tribe, January 19, 2009.

Annual Report, Muckleshoot Tribal Council, Prepared for the Annual Meeting of the Muckleshoot General Council, January 17, 2005. Auburn, WA: Muckleshoot Indian Tribe, 2005.

Annual Report to the Muckleshoot Community. Auburn, WA: Muckleshoot Indian Tribe, January 26, 1995.

"Biologists Probe Fate of Last Year's Sockeye Run; Half of Run Failed to Reach Spawning Grounds Due to Freshwater Mortality Fishing Prospects Grow Dimmer." *Seattle Times* in *Muckleshoot Monthly,* July 15, 2005, 4.

Clements, Barbara. "Muckleshoot Leader Dies in Boat Accident." *Valley Daily News,* October 22, 1986, A-2.

Fabricant, Florence. "Food Stuff: A High Roller Gets a Break from a Casino." *New York Times,* August 14, 2002. [http://www.nytimes.com/2002/08/14/dining/food-stuff-a-high-roller-gets-a-break-from-a-casino.html]

"Green River Elk Augmentation – One Year Later." *Muckleshoot Monthly,* March 15, 2003, 8.

Hogans, Mack L. "Huckleberry Exchange Was in the Public Interest." *Seattle Times.* October 7, 1998. [http://community.seattletimes.nwsource.com/archive/?date=19981007&slug=2776188]

LaBranche, Janet. [untitled] *New Journal Globe News,* March 14, 1984, D-1.

"MIT Gets 'Cheers' from the *South County Journal.*" *Muckleshoot Monthly,* July 2000, 1.

Moses, Stanley. Interview at Muckleshoot, August 16, 2011.

Muckleshoot Indian Tribe v. U.S. Forest Service and Weyerhaeuser Co, 177 F.3d 800 (1999) 99 Cal. Daily Op. Serv. 3724, 1999 Daily Journal D.A.R. 4767. Order of Ninth Circuit Court of Appeals, March 10, 1999. [http://ftp.resource.org/courts.gov/c/F3/177/177.F3d.800.98-35231.98-35043.html]

"No Sockeye Season This Year." *Muckleshoot Monthly,* July 15, 2005, 4.

"Things You Should Know About Clam Digging." *Muckleshoot Monthly,* May 15, 2008, 19.

"Tribe Goes Fishing." *Muckleshoot Monthly,* July 15, 2000, 1, 12.

"Tribe Makes History with First Muckleshoot-Brand Sockeye." *Muckleshoot Monthly,* July 15, 2004, 2.

Vales, David. "Hunting Update: Status of Elk Herds." *Muckleshoot Monthly,* November 2000, 16.

Welch, Craig. "U.S. to Buy Back Part of Huckleberry Mountain." *Seattle Times,* November 20, 2001. [http://community.seattletimes.nwsource.com/archive/?date=20011121&slug=huckleberry21m]

Chapter 6

"This Casino Represents Hope"

Chapter 6

"This Casino Represents Hope"

By the 1980s, Muckleshoot leaders decided that their overriding priority was finding a way to alleviate grinding poverty. Thus, a decision was made to take up gambling. Gilbert King George, tribal chairman and cultural leader during the 1980s, said: "My people have no other alternative but to support economic development. ... It will be a great challenge to lead my people out of poverty" (LaBranche, 1984, D-1). Fishing runs were declining due to urbanization and the fact that the Muckleshoots got their shot at the salmon only after many other fishing people had had a chance to catch fish that were migrating to their spawning grounds from the open ocean.

The same urbanization that had destroyed many of the salmon runs (and saddened many Muckleshoots) also brought a financial boost: gaming drew players from the large and growing non-Indian urban population of Puget Sound. Income from the casino enabled the purchase of land, creation of businesses, and a wide array of social services. The Muckleshoots saw it coming, and made a plan, which is still unfolding.

The 3,500 acres remaining within the Muckleshoots' jurisdiction became more valuable with the spread of suburbs between Seattle and Tacoma. What became even more valuable was location near an interstate highway in the midst of an urban area of more than two million people, vibrant with cultural energy and technological innovation by Microsoft and other companies. The Muckleshoot Casino, the closest such venue to Seattle itself, quickly became one of the most profitable in the United States.

Gambling per se is not new to the Muckleshoots. The scale of the games, and the purposeful use of the revenues to rebuild their nation is an innovation, however. The Muckleshoots are not moralistic about gambling, and generally resented attempts by nineteenth-century missionaries to ban their sla-hal (stick game) social gaming as sinful. The games sometimes grew so large that they redistributed wealth, another problem for the missionaries. Sla-hal is described by today's participants as a social event: "We sing, drum, shake rattles, and use hand motions. We laugh, mimic, tease, and just all-out have a great time. Sla-hal has been around for a long time, and is for people to get together and have fun. We visit with relatives and friends we haven't seen for a long time. It's a gathering time to share laughter, love, stories, and fun" ("Sla-hal," 2010).

In the sla-hal game, one team tries to guess the location of unmarked bones hidden by

Playing the traditional Sla-hal game, 1957.
Photo courtesy of Muckleshoot Preservation Program Archives (Franklin Lozier)

their opponents. The searching team would be heckled by their opponents with songs of praise (for themselves) and shame (for the guessing team). An equal purse was bet by both teams. In times past, games often matched teams from different tribes or villages. Money has long been wagered on the sla-hal games, which could last several hours and sometimes even days. In 2004, 61 teams vied for $15,000 in prize money at Muckleshoot sla-hal games. In 2011, the Muckleshoots' 20th annual Easter Stickgame tournament during late April drew 103 teams (some from as far away as South Dakota) and awarded $75,000 in prizes, including $30,000 to the winning team led by Beth Montoya of Swinomish, WA. An elders' game also drew 50 participants. The oldest was Wally Selam of Toppenish, WA, age 83 (Sneatlum, 2011, 18).

Modern commercial gaming has an assigned role at Muckleshoot, no more, no less. Matt Conner wrote in *Indian Gaming Business*, a publication of the National Indian Gaming Association:

> While business programs often support cultural activities, the tribe does not expect casino or bingo hall patrons to come away from their gaming experience with a deep-seated knowledge of Muckleshoot history and culture. "The tribe has used, and will continue to use, the resources from its gaming operations to support, directly and indirectly, many cultural and traditional activities," said John Daniels [chairman of the tribal council]. "However, the tribe operates its gaming facilities as a business, not a cultural facility, with all proceeds going to support the tribal government. Through the tribal government, support for cultural and traditional activities is maintained. While some neighbors expressed concern prior to each facility's opening, skeptics have become believers that the tribe would exceed its promise to be a good and responsible neighbor." (Conner, 2002, 12)

AN EXPERIMENT WITH BINGO

As soon as the Muckleshoots proposed to improve their lives with a large-scale bingo hall (or other businesses), some of their non-Indian neighbors complained that their rural lifestyle would be compromised, even though the areas in which development was proposed had become suburbs of Seattle and Tacoma already flush with retail stores on several strip malls. The pattern began in September of

Iola Lobehan Bill at the Muckleshoot Bingo Hall.
Photo by John Loftus, Muckleshoot Monthly

1984, when more than 70 people lined up to tell the Auburn City Council that the new facility, with parking for as many as 700 motor vehicles, would draw too much traffic and overload sewers. Many objected to the fact that an Indian reservation's sovereign legal status barred the City Council from banning Muckleshoot businesses. The Muckleshoots planned to comply with city zoning codes and widen nearby streets anyway. The hall would maintain a security force and sell no liquor. A $1.7 million annual payroll would add to the local economy as well, and the tribe would contribute to city fire and police budgets, because it is not taxed (Rommel, 1984, 1). Debates over the casino (opened in 1995) and the White River Amphitheatre (opened in 2003) shared many of the same elements.

Work on bingo hall construction was stopped by protests from Concerned Citizens for Safety (CCS) demanding an environmental impact statement. The CCS wanted to know impact on traffic circulation, sewer capacity, police protection and other services. Judge Donald S. Voorhees of the U.S. District Court lifted a stay on construction of the facility, ruling that Concerned Citizens for Safety had overstated its case.

The Muckleshoots, with only 725 members in 1985 (a membership that would triple in 25 years), opened their first bingo hall under contract with the Seminoles of Florida, who had been the first Native nation to plunge into large-scale gaming with their own establishment during the late 1970s. The Seminoles drove a hard bargain for the 1,450-seat Bingo Hall: the Muckleshoots were required to repay a $2.3 million construction loan at the prime interest rate, and pay the Seminoles 44 percent of the profits for 10 years, until 1995. Tony Herrera, business manager for the Muckleshoots, said that "Sure we'd like [the Seminoles] to get less of a percentage, but they are providing a lot, too. We didn't have the expertise or money to build the bingo hall" (Richey, 1985, 1).

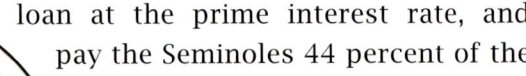

Muckleshoot Bingo opened in 1985. *Photo courtesy of Muckleshoot Indian Tribe*

The hall generally netted the Muckleshoots about $1 million a year during its first ten years of operation, a trickle compared to the needs on the impoverished reservation. The Muckleshoots' first foray into gaming opened to a capacity crowd (people were waiting in line at the door), but the bingo hall initially failed to turn a profit under Seminole management, so the Muckleshoots contracted for a time with British America Bingo, which guaranteed a minimum monthly income. Later, the Muckleshoots assumed full control. The hall celebrated its 25th anniversary in 2010, by which time 37 percent of its employees were Native (18 percent Muckleshoot). The bingo hall by that time had been expanded to 65,000 square feet with both electronic and paper bingo, pull tabs, and a bar with a billiards room, a gift shop, a players club, and dining facilities (McMaster, 2010, 1, 2).

Muckleshoot General Manager Randy Williams, anticipating the opening of the new casino in 1995, wrote: "The tribe is reaching a goal barely conceived when I first started working for the tribe in 1976: economic self-sufficiency. I am proud, as is our entire staff, to be part of this advance by the Muckleshoot Indian Tribe into this new and exciting era. We anticipate that in two to three years any tribal member who desires employment can have it,

"This Casino Represent Hope"

(Top) The Muckleshoot Bingo Hall. (Bottom) A busy day at the Muckleshoot Bingo Hall, with caller Carlene Moses.
Photos by John Loftus, Muckleshoot Monthly

Chapter 6

and ... everyone will have an opportunity to have safe and affordable housing in the near future" (Annual Report, 1995, n.p.).

The Muckleshoot government's annual report for the year 1994, issued January 26, 1995, was nearly giddy with anticipation for the future. "The tribe is on the fast track to a brighter future. Strap yourself in because it's going to be an exciting and dizzying ride" (Annual Report, 1995, n.p.).

A PLAN TO ESCAPE POVERTY

Early in the 1990s, the Muckleshoot government purchased twenty-five acres within reservation boundaries for a casino adjacent to the bingo hall. Soon thereafter, in 1993, Washington Governor Mike Lowry signed the compact with the Muckleshoots that is required by a federal law (the Indian Gaming Regulatory Act of 1988), which initially covered only table games. Slot machines, video poker, and other games were added later.

By 1993, public support for gaming as a form of Native economic development was increasing. A *Seattle Post-Intelligencer* editorial said that the problems of unemployment, alcoholism, poverty, poor health, poor education "... are among reasons that tribes need economic development" (August 1, 1993, E-2). The article pointed out that gaming was not a sure thing, but poverty among American Indians had created a need to try something to develop their communities that was suited to their large measure of sovereignty: "To argue that Indians, having shown they can be spectacularly successful at a home-grown

The Muckleshoot Casino first opened in a tent.
Photo courtesy of Muckleshoot Preservation Program Archives (Photo by Chris Roberts)

enterprise given the chance, now have to be protected from their own success is just more of the same tired old paternalism. It has no place in relations between Indians and non-Indians at this late date in our history" (August 1, 1993, E-2).

Even as the state of Washington signed a gambling compact with the Muckleshoots, some of its agencies resisted it. Parts of the state bureaucracy dug in against Indian gaming much as fisheries and game agencies had, in an earlier time, resisted Indian fishing rights. This time, state bureaucrats appointed themselves as guardians of citizens' morals, contending that they were serving the public good by regulating or eliminating Indian gaming. Since the state was conducting its own lottery and licensing bets on horse racing, morals probably meant less than potential competition for gambling dollars. When the state inveighed against the "evils of gaming," it feared a threat to its own disintegrating gaming monopoly.

Bob Roegner, Auburn's mayor, was less than enthusiastic about the casino when it was being planned in 1992, as the Muckleshoots negotiated a gambling compact with the state of Washington. Roegner, who was usually very pro-development in other contexts, complained about potential impact on traffic and said that such a large new business would stretch police and fire services in Auburn ("Auburn Mayor," 1992).

The Muckleshoots signed the gaming compact with mixed feelings, described in a contemporary newspaper account: "This compact does not represent the best interests of our

Lines formed as the Muckleshoot Casino opened.
Photo courtesy of Washington State Historical Society, photo 2003.75.19

tribe. It limits our sovereign rights; We're not accepting this agreement because we believe it's wise, which we do not, but because we are desperate. We simply can not afford further delays and expenses of litigation" (*Valley Daily News*, 1993, n.p.).

The casino opened April 28, 1995, in a large tent that was replaced by a mainframe building four months later. "I feel like I've waited all my life for this," said chairwoman Virginia Cross, of the Muckleshoot Tribe. "We are not rich, but we are no longer starving" (Wallace, 1995, B-1). "To me and all Muckleshoots," Cross said, "this casino represents hope" (Archbold, *Valley Daily News*, n.d., A-12). Cross added that "Unlike some tribes, who have seen a lot of their casino revenues scatter to the winds, every dollar generated by this casino will go to provide a better future for all Muckleshoots" (Archbold, *Valley Daily News*, n.d., A-12). The tent, which operated through the spring and summer of 1995, became so crowded that the gaming floor developed a human gridlock. On weekends, many people waited as long as an hour to get in the door.

Harold Moses recited a prayer in which he blessed the venture. "You can walk down through this bingo hall here and you see many smiles from people you don't know. They raise their hand at you with a good heart. That is the way it should be. We should all be that way to one another. It doesn't make any difference what color we are, what race we are. Just get along in life together. That is the only way we are going to get along in this world. Let's walk hand in hand," Moses said. (Archbold, *Valley Daily News*, n.d., A-12.)

Construction used funding from Capital Gaming, which received a percentage of the revenue. Within a few weeks after the casino moved out of its tent, it was the busiest gaming facility in the state of Washington. In December 1998, the Muckleshoot Tribe bought out Capital Gaming's share after it forgot to renew a state gambling license.

PUTTING CASINO MONEY TO WORK

Upon the opening of its casino, the Muckleshoot Tribe instantly became the second largest employer in Auburn, with 900 jobs, plus another 160 outside city limits. The largest employer, the Boeing Company, had 7,827 workers, and number three, Supervalu Holdings (a grocery-store chain) had 818 employees (Archbold, January 8, 1996, A-7).

Within six months of its opening, the casino was bearing financial fruit: Muckleshoot employment rose by 150 jobs (in a tribe that at the time enrolled 1,400 members). The casino at the beginning was grossing about $2.75 million a month before operating expenses (in 15 years that figure would be roughly estimated at $30 million a month). Before the casino's opening, income from the bingo hall and smoke shop had been averaging about $1.5 million a year ("Casino a Big Winner," 1995, n.p.; "Muckleshoot Tribe's Revenues," 1996, n.p.).

With the casino in its first year of operation netting about $18 million, Gregg Paisley, the Muckleshoots' director of economic development, met with John Daniels, Jr., Virginia Cross, and others to create a plan, "to build," as the *Seattle Daily Journal of Commerce* phrased it, "a personalized, multi-tiered approach to improve the lives of tribal members" ("Casino a Big Winner," 1995, n.p.). "It would really offer a lot of people a chance to get to work. ... We're improving things for our children and our children's children. We're thinking generations ahead," Cross explained. Cross set the tone when she said that the Muckleshoots had begun to "close out a long chapter of financial dependence and move into a proud and prosperous period of true self-determination" (Archbold, 1997, A-7). "Our people have a tendency to never leave," even when there are opportunities elsewhere, Cross said. "This is where the reservation is and this is where my family is." "We are creating a situation where people can stay here on their homelands and create a wonderful life," said Paisley ("Casino a Big Winner," 1995, n.p.; "Opponents," 1999).

From the beginning, the windfall was invested in education. The idea was to produce spin-off businesses and career-track jobs in several fields, not just gambling, and to improve conditions on the reservation. "I didn't want to create all these workaday jobs," said Paisley. "I wanted to create career-track jobs. What's the use of doing that if you don't have people trained for it?" ("Casino a Big Winner," 1995, n.p.) By 1996, the Muckleshoots were setting up a fund to finance their young people's higher education at the colleges of their choice. The council members started planning for a child-care center.

By 1997, a 16-officer Muckleshoot police department had begun operating, plans were underway for an amphitheater seating more than 20,000 people, and a 65-unit housing project was rising. The tribe had pledged to put one-eighth (12.5 percent) of casino profits into housing. That represented $2.2 million (a figure that has risen substantially since), compared to the $60,000 per year that it had been receiving for housing from the federal government ("Tribal Leaders," 1996, n.p.). A new tribal administration building (the Philip Starr Building) was under construction, and fishing, hunting, and wildlife programs were being enhanced with more than $1 million a year. The Muckleshoots also were diversifying into businesses other than gambling, such as seafood processing and sales, horse racing, and resorts. Shortly after the casino opened, the Muckleshoots began returning up to 2 percent of profits to the city of Auburn, the state patrol, and local fire departments to cover costs of police, fire, court and other services, an average of $300,000 to $500,000 each three months.

After seven years, the initial $10 million that the Muckleshoots' spent on the casino had proved to be a very good investment. It grew in several steps. In 2000, the casino, which began in the 13,000 square-foot tent (63,000 square feet in its first permanent building) expanded to more than 145,000 square feet (3.3 acres) with a $20 million renovation. A new restaurant was added with a family theme and seating capacity of 490 people. In 2009, 46,662 more square feet were added, connecting two existing buildings, adding a family buffet, sweet shop, and gift shop, plus gambling venues (Annual Report, 2009, 49). By 2010, the rambling edifice was more than a third of a mile long. Employment rose from 400 in 1995 to 1,200 in 2001 and 1,800 in 2005, and 2,100 a year later.

On August 31, 2006, the Muckleshoots opened a non-smoking adjunct to its main casino, the first such facility in Washington state (state indoor smoking prohibitions do not apply on reservations), 42,000 square feet 80 feet from the existing casino. The two casinos totaled 257,000 square feet. ("New Muckleshoot," 2006, 1).

In 2010, the casino was described by *Seattle Times* reporter Tom Scanlon as an "apparently exponentially expanding funhouse ... [with] splashes of neon and blasts of adrenaline. While it's a long, long way to Vegas, the Muckleshoot has certainly brought some Nevada flash to Auburn and its neighbors" (Scanlon, 2010).

> After sundown, [on State Highway 164] you hit a stretch of quiet, unlit country road, you turn a bend and then — wham — there it is: an explosion of electricity lighting up the southeast Auburn night. A giant video screen amid the neon shows people winning and

Finishing touches on the Casino.

One of several Casino expansions goes up.

An aerial view of the Muckleshoot Casino in 2005, with the Bingo Hall in the foreground and the White Lake Cemetery visible in the background.
Photos by John Loftus, Muckleshoot Monthly

having assorted great fun. It then turns to screaming text: "MUCKLESHOOT CASINO THE BIGGEST AND BEST IN THE NORTHWEST." ... If you come by here once a year or so, you'll be amazed at the growth — it seems like one of those sci-fi creatures that gets exposed to radiation and keeps mutating ever larger. (Scanlon, 2010)

The main floor of the casino never closes. The 200,000-square-foot "entertainment center" that Scanlon described has become as well known for its no-cover-charge entertainment and excellent dining options as its gambling. Scanlon, in fact, advised his readers to bypass the slot machines and craps tables and head for the restaurants and night club: "A cynic might say this place has more suckers than a lollipop factory. If you leave with a light wallet, you can take heart in knowing that millions of dollars of the casino's winnings go to good causes, such as new Muckleshoot schools and a medical center" (Scanlon, 2010).

The Club Galaxy, a retro bar with "an elevated, deep stage for bands, huge video screens and a wide, seductively lit dance floor — jamming, on most weekend nights" where

> Ring-less [i.e., unmarried] women come dressed to impress, in cocktail dresses and tight outfits. Many of the men are disco-ed up as well, with a few sharp suits ... [looking] like a reunion of the class of '73 ... Club Galaxy is something of a rarity in this corner of our youth-dominated, MTV-generation galaxy — a club where forty-, fifty- and even sixty-somethings can cocktail it up, dance, socialize and hear "the good stuff." (Scanlon, 2010)

Games include Blackjack, Progressive Blackjack, Caribbean Stud, Craps, Baccarat, Midi Bac-

Muckleshoot Casino chip.
Photo courtesy of Muckleshoot Indian Tribe

carat, Roulette, Fortune Pai Gow Poker, Spanish 21, and Three Card Poker, plus about 3,500 machine games. The casino has five eating establishments, including an eclectic (Chinese/Vietnamese/American plus fry bread and salmon) restaurant which serves a crab and steak plate (a high-roller's dish for those who have gotten lucky or believe they soon will that some gamblers call surf & turf). The crab legs (Alaskan king crab) are the size of billy clubs, dwarfing a 12-ounce New York steak, and go for $75.95.

HELPING NEIGHBORS

Each gaming tribe, through its compact with the state of Washington, is legally required to pay an annual 2 percent community contribution tax. As revenues rolled in from the casino, the Muckleshoots began to share with local governments. The casino has enabled the Muckleshoot Nation to contribute an average of $1 million to about 150 charities a year. They have also established a record of direct assistance to government agencies and charitable organizations. Community groups have been encouraged to apply for funds to meet local needs. A committee determines recipients and makes allocations; the Muckleshoots publish these in local newspapers.

In September 1995 the tribe provided funds to Auburn Food Bank, Auburn St. Vincent de Paul, the Auburn School District lunch program, Kent-based Domestic Abuse Women's Network, Kiwanis, Auburn Junior Football, Catholic Community Services, and Auburn Chamber of Commerce. (Archbold, n.d.).

In November 1996, Virginia Cross presented a $482,544 check to Mayor Chuck Booth of Auburn for nine months' worth of police, fire, and medic services provided to the casino by the city. The Washington State Patrol received $10,000 and King County Fire District 46 $37,000. Children's Home Society $6,500; Auburn Youth Services $10,000, and Foundation for Enumclaw $10,000.

The Tribe, recalling Christmas baskets sent by its congregation during leaner years, helped a local Adventist church replace one of its dormitories that burned down in winter.

In 2007, the Muckleshoots donated $100,000 to the Native American Rights Fund, which had helped them with early legal battles. "I thought they did so much for us when we had absolutely nothing for the tribe," Cross said. "I thought we should do something for them" ("Native Legal," 2007). In 2009 the Muckleshoots gave more than $4.1 million worth of Muckleshoot Charity and Community Impact Funds. The Charity Fund helped more than 200 nonprofit organizations, churches, and schools in Washington state, from school supplies and curricula to medical research, health care, and disaster assistance, as well as cultural and arts programs, environmental projects, and human services. Similar levels of giving continued in subsequent years.

A typical $5,000 grant was awarded early in 2011 to the St. Vincent de Paul Society of Seattle/King County. The grant was used to prevent hunger and evictions facing impoverished neighbors by staffing a community-information line that received 52,150 calls during 2010, 58 percent more than 2008. St. Vincent de Paul Society also distributed 1.6 million free meals a year in King County. "The Muckleshoot Indian Tribe's grant is a great boost for us. We will be able to help more people struggling from devastating unemployment or the affects of poverty. In addition, their support will encourage others groups to join St. Vincent de Paul in our mission to prevent eviction, hunger, utility shut-offs and more," said Andre de Klaver, executive director of the St. Vincent de Paul Society of Seattle/King County ("Muckleshoot Tribe," 2011, n.p.).

DEALING WITH GAMBLING ADDICTION

Gambling revenues totaled more than $1.3 billion in Washington state by 2003, roughly double the revenues of five years earlier, as abuse rose as well, "damaging thousands of lives and adding about $78 million a year to the state's social costs" (Skolnik, 2004, B-1). Regarding gambling addiction, casinos in the state rely on customers to recognize the problem. For those who do, the casino will grant requests for a "self-bar" or "self-exclusion," that is not permanent. If customers ask to return, they have to wait only a week. At the larger Indian casinos, including Muckleshoot and Tulalip, self-exclusions are permanent. Customers face a possible trespassing arrest if they return.

"I think it's great," said Gary Hanson with the Washington State Council on Problem Gambling. "I think it demonstrates what we've seen — that the Muckleshoots have been in the forefront of the issue." In a letter to

Muckleshoot Casino slots.
Photo courtesy of Muckleshoot Indian Tribe

Washington Governor Gary Locke, Muckleshoot Indian Tribal Council Chairman John Daniels, Jr. said that the Muckleshoots are "stepping up to address the urgent and immediate funding problem faced today by contributing $350,000 to support problem gambling treatment and training programs" (Skolnik, 2004, B-1).

They were donating to a $500,000 program started by the state of Washington's Division of Alcohol and Substance Abuse within the state Department of Social and Health Services to help with similar problems associated with the State Lottery's Mega Millions. The program was a success, but the state's appropriation had run out during June of 2003. In January 2009, the Muckleshoots added $500,000 more to provide aid to programs that deal with smoking cessation as well as gambling addiction. "We are proud to partner with charitable organizations and government agencies who provide invaluable services to the people of Washington," said Chairwoman Charlotte Williams. "We thank them for their important work and reaffirm our commitment to helping our neighbors and building communities" ("Muckleshoots Invest," 2009).

"The Muckleshoots have now taken the leadership advantage on this issue and made a commitment not only to their tribal community but the community at large," said Jennifer McCausland, a citizen-activist who was raising funds for the program. "My hope is that this is just the beginning. Now, all other gaming tribes, the commercial industry and state government will contribute," she said (Skolnik, 2004, B-1).

SLOT MACHINES ON EVERY CORNER?

During 2004, the Muckleshoots joined with a broad coalition to defeat State Initiative 892, which would have expanded gambling, most notably slot machines, to non-Indian card rooms, for-profit mini-casinos, bowling alleys, and restaurants. The Muckleshoots estimated that passage of I892 could have cut their gaming revenues in half devastating their income base and programs (Annual Report, 2005, 2, 22). The initiative lost by a decisive margin, more than 20 percentage points.

The Muckleshoots and other Washington Native peoples called on alliances with church congregations, schools, civic groups, and peoples of color, defining the issue as an expansion of gambling, while supporters of I892 used the appeal of extra tax revenue that would enable a property-tax cut. The Muckleshoots also bought television time for four anti-892 ads that made a case that having lightly regulated slot machines would degrade neighborhoods. In one of them, children peered out a window of a school at ranks of people playing the slots. The ads did not air in the Portland, Oregon media market (which includes the Vancouver area), the only part of the state where I892 passed.

TAX THE CASINOS?

By the time the Muckleshoot Casino opened in 1995, proposals were already circulating in the U.S. Congress to levy taxes on Indian gaming profits; one would have taken 34 percent. Profits of smoke shops were also on the legislative radar, advanced by politicians seeking non-Indian votes in the name of "leveling the playing field" for all businesses, as if Native peoples had been playing on any kind of level field for the previous century or more (Westneat and Simon, 1995).

"There is a pattern here," Ron Allen, chairman of the Jamestown S'Klallam tribe on Hood Canal, west of Seattle, said in 1995. "First, the legal power and stature of tribal governments has grown dramatically. And with casinos, we're starting to develop an economy

Muckleshoot Casino craps table.
Photo courtesy of Muckleshoot Indian Tribe

that's raising some eyebrows. So they want to tax us before we even get off the ground" (Westneat and Simon, 1995). Native Americans were called upon again to haul out the copious case law from the U.S. Supreme Court from the 1830s onward that defines them legally as governments with sovereign powers rather than taxable corporations. As soon as the financial rudiments of nationhood were at hand, the United States federal government and constituent states were talking about moving the legal goalposts.

"Why are they singling out Indian tribes?" asked Eddie Palmanteer, Jr., a councilman and business leader with the Colville Tribe in Eastern Washington. "The state government is more heavily into the gambling business than we are [through its lottery], but there's no proposal to tax them" (Westneat and Simon, 1995).

Even so, the nature of Native American reservation sovereignty in the United States remains ill-defined. The U.S. Congress assumes its right to abrogate treaties without Native consent through a doctrine called "plenary power." At this point, the relationship becomes colonial, Great White Father to wards of the government. Earning their own money and taking charge of their own affairs, Native nations test that relationship.

Ralph Johnson of the University of Washington Law School noted that economic development on reservations was the main rationale of a 1988 federal law that recognized the rights of Native Americans to establish and operate casinos and other gaming establishments, such as bingo halls. The idea was to reduce dependence on federal money. In that sense, the Muckleshoots are doing exactly what the law expected. "Imposing the tax defeats (Congress') own purpose of making tribes self-sufficient," Johnson said (Westneat and Simon, 1995).

PROPOSALS TO TAX GAMBLING — AGAIN

With the Washington State budget $2 billion in the red late in 2011, Republicans who opposed other taxes favored expanding slot-machine gaming from Indian reservations to the state as a whole, and taxing the proceeds. The Republicans argued that allowing slot machines statewide would bring in $160 to $200 million per year in state revenue (Governor Chris Gregoire questioned those estimates). Native casinos share revenue locally; the Muckleshoots fund grants to charities, as well as the city of Auburn, its schools, smoking cessation, and problem gambling. In February 2011, the Tulalips (who operate a casino north of Seattle) donated $1.26 million to the Marysville School District.

The 28 Indian casinos in Washington state do not, however, give money directly to state government's general fund. Late in 2011, Gov. Gregoire called upon the tribes to allow "revenue sharing" (i.e., a state tax on their operations). They refused, unless the state gave them exclusive rights to slots. Gregoire refused to allow that. The Washington State Gambling Commission said that of 24 states with tribal gaming, 10 had revenue sharing. Seven years after state voters rejected such an expansion of gaming, the Republicans framed their proposal as a generator of jobs and an attempt to "level the playing field for small, nontribal gambling halls that struggle to compete with glitzy tribal casinos" (Garber and Mapes, 2011). In late 2011, Democrats controlled the Washington State House, Senate and governor's office. "Washington voters have spoken loud and clear that they are comfortable with this kind of gaming being limited in tribal facilities, and I would hope they would look at those past votes," said Brian Cladoosby, chairman of the Swinomish Tribe (Garber and Mapes, 2011). More than 61 percent of voters rejected the 2004 initiative.

GAMING AND ECONOMIC DEVELOPMENT

Republican Dan Evans advocated Native American economic development as a three-term governor of Washington state from 1965 to 1977. He returned to the subject as a U.S. senator. "For a century, frankly, Indian tribes have been screwed by the United States," said Evans. "This gives them a lot more independence, and the potential for economic well-being that is much broader than casino gambling. It will be a huge benefit over time. They are taking the next step. It's precisely what I hoped would happen" (Mapes, 2008).

Indian casinos generated more than $1.3 billion in 2007, two-thirds of all net gambling proceeds in Washington state. State records show tribal casinos had an estimated $1.95 billion in net receipts in fiscal year 2011, up from $1.57 billion in 2009 (Garber and Mapes, 2011). The 2000 census showed that Native

The Casino's marquee.
Photo by John Loftus, Muckleshoot Monthly

Americans were still the least affluent ethnic group, but their income was rising rapidly in Washington state, up 16 percent in ten years. Most of the gain was in the Puget Sound urban area (Mapes, 2008).

The advent of casino gambling fundamentally changed Muckleshoot economic development. During the 1970s, the Muckleshoots had relied on federal grants and contracts. Administrators or consultants wrote proposals to provide reservation services, a procedure that had grown out of the 1960s War on Poverty through programs maintained largely by the Office of Economic Opportunity (OEO) which, for the first time, had provided local communities with resources to develop economic projects. Many Native governments had received OEO funds to combat unemployment, and to utilize reservation resources for various purposes, such as construction of fishing boats. Without self-generated income, resources were difficult to obtain without collateral to back bank loans. Reservation land or resources (defined as federal trust property) was unacceptable because it could not be foreclosed on. Gaming revenue provided independent cash income that met standards as collateral.

Revenue from gaming and other businesses helped meet many needs. More employees were hired to carry on administration of the tribe. A child-care center was constructed entirely from tribal resources. The Philip Starr Building was built to house tribal government. A major portion of funds went into housing to provide living space that had not previously been available to tribal members. Further investment went into construction of the White River Amphitheatre, a major concert venue seating 20,000 people, on the reservation.

The casino's income stream enabled the Muckleshoots to start (or buy) other businesses, including, by 2010, the high-end Salish Lodge in the Cascades (bought for $62.5 million in 2007) and the Emerald Downs racetrack, the largest horse-racing establishment in the Pacific Northwest. The Muckleshoots by 2008 also had become a minority investor in the Four Seasons Hotel and Residences in downtown Seattle. Once the casino began to provide jobs, unemployment compensation fell and taxes paid increased.

Even with gaming's success at Muckleshoot, some of the elders evoke caution. Stanley Moses, who served on the tribal council for many years, said in 2011 that while he likes the fact that gaming income has contributed to Muckleshoot self-reliance, he worries that political winds could shift at the state level. With a scramble in recessionary times for revenue, the state could allow gaming by non-Indians. Moses cautioned that gambling might not be a major revenue base forever, and that the tribe's emphasis on a diversity of income sources must continue.

REFERENCES

Annual Report to the Muckleshoot Community. Auburn, WA: The Muckleshoot Tribe, January 26, 1995.

Annual Report, Muckleshoot Tribal Council, Prepared for the Annual Meeting of the Muckleshoot General Council, January 17, 2005. Auburn, WA: Muckleshoot Indian Tribe, 2005.

Annual Report, 2009: Muckleshoot Indian Tribe. Auburn, WA: Muckleshoot Indian Tribe, January 19, 2009.

Archbold, Mike. [no title] *Valley Daily News*, n.d., A12.

Archbold, Mike. "Muckleshoot Tribe a Top Auburn Employer." *Valley Daily News* (Kent, WA), January 8, 1996, A7.

Archbold, Mike. "Muckleshoots Buying Back Their Reservation Land." *South [King] County Journal*, February 4, 1997, A7.

"Auburn Mayor Not Bullish on Muckleshoot Casino." *Seattle Times*, November 11, 1992. [http://community.seattletimes.nwsource.com/archive/?date=19921111&slug=1524094]

"Casino a Big Winner Coming and Going." *Daily Journal of Commerce* (Seattle), October 31, 1995, n.p.

Connor, Matt. "The Good Neighbor: The Muckleshoot Tribe's Gaming Enterprises Have Helped Foster Good Will with Local Communities." *Muckleshoot Monthly*, September 15, 2002, 3, 12. (Reprinted from Indian Gaming Business, a publication of the National Indian Gaming Association.)

Garber, Andrew, and Linda V. Mapes. "GOP Sees Expanded Gambling as State Budget Solution." *Seattle Times*, December 5, 2011. [http://seattletimes.nwsource.com/html/localnews/2016943073_gambling06m.html]

LaBranche, Janet. [No title.] *New Journal Globe News*, March 14, 1984, D-1.

Mapes, Lynda V. "Tribes Are State's New High Rollers – In Business." *Seattle Times*, February 17, 2008. [http://seattletimes.nwsource.com/html/localnews/2004186688_tribes17m.html]

McMaster, Luci. "Muckleshoot Bingo Celebrates Quarter-Century." *Muckleshoot Monthly*, May 15, 2010, 1, 2.

Moses, Stanley. Interview at Muckleshoot, August 16, 2011.

"Muckleshoot Revenues Soar with Gambling." Portland *Oregonian*, January 21, 1996, n.p. (In LEXIS).

"Muckleshoot Indian Tribe Gives Back to Communities." Muckleshoot Indian Tribe, April 29, 2010. [http://www.muckleshoot.nsn.us]

"Muckleshoot Tribe Gives $5,000 to St. Vincent de Paul to Help Prevent Evictions and Hunger in Seattle and King County." *Auburn Reporter*, February 3, 2011, n.p.

"Muckleshoot Tribe's Revenues Soar with Gambling." *Daily Journal of Commerce* (Seattle), January 11, 1996, n.p.

"Muckleshoots Invest Nearly $3 Million in the State." Auburn *Reporter*, April 17, 2009. [http://www.pnwlocalnews.com/south_king/aub/community/43122972.html]

"Native Legal Advocates Continue Fight with New Beat." Native American Rights Fund. May 8, 2007. [http://narfnews.blogspot.com/2007/05/tribal-organization-using-hip-hop-to.html]

"New Muckleshoot Casino II Open for Business." *Muckleshoot Monthly*, September 25, 2006, 1.

"Opponents, Tribal Members Split over Proposed Amphitheater." *Daily Journal of Commerce* (Seattle), September 24, 1999. [http://www.djc.com/news/business/10058538.html]

Richey, Warren. "Unregulated High-Stakes Gambling Grows on American Indian Reservations." *Christian Science Monitor*, March 25, 1985, 1. (in LEXIS)

Rommel, Bruce. "Tribe's Plan for Bingo Hall Draws Protest." Auburn *Globe*, September 18, 1984, 1.

Sla-hal participant, July 17, 2010 interview, Muckleshoot reservation.

Scanlon, Tom. "Flirt with the Odds or Hit the Dance Floor at Muckleshoot." *Seattle Times*, February 11, 2010. [http://seattletimes.nwsource.com/html/entertainment/2002176626_muck11.html]

Skolnik, Sam. "Tribe Targets Gaming Woes; Muckleshoots Donate to Help Problem Gamblers." *Seattle Post-Intelligencer*, June 11, 2004, B1.

Sneatlum, Lisa. "20th Annual Muckleshoot Easter Weekend Stickgame Event." *Muckleshoot Monthly*, May 15, 2011, 18.

"Tribal Leaders Pave Way for Brighter Future." *Valley Daily News* (Kent, WA), January 10, 1996, n.p.

Valley Daily News (Kent, WA), February 21, 1993.

Wallace, James." Muckleshoots Betting on Casino to Better Their Lot." *Seattle Post-Intelligencer*, September 9, 1995, B-1.

Westneat, Danny and Jim Simon. "Move to Tax Casino Profits Angers Native Americans." *Seattle Times*, November 19, 1995. [http://community.seattletimes.nwsource.com/archive/?date=19951119&slug=2153442]

Chapter 7

Nation-Building at Street Level

Chapter 7

Nation Building at Street Level

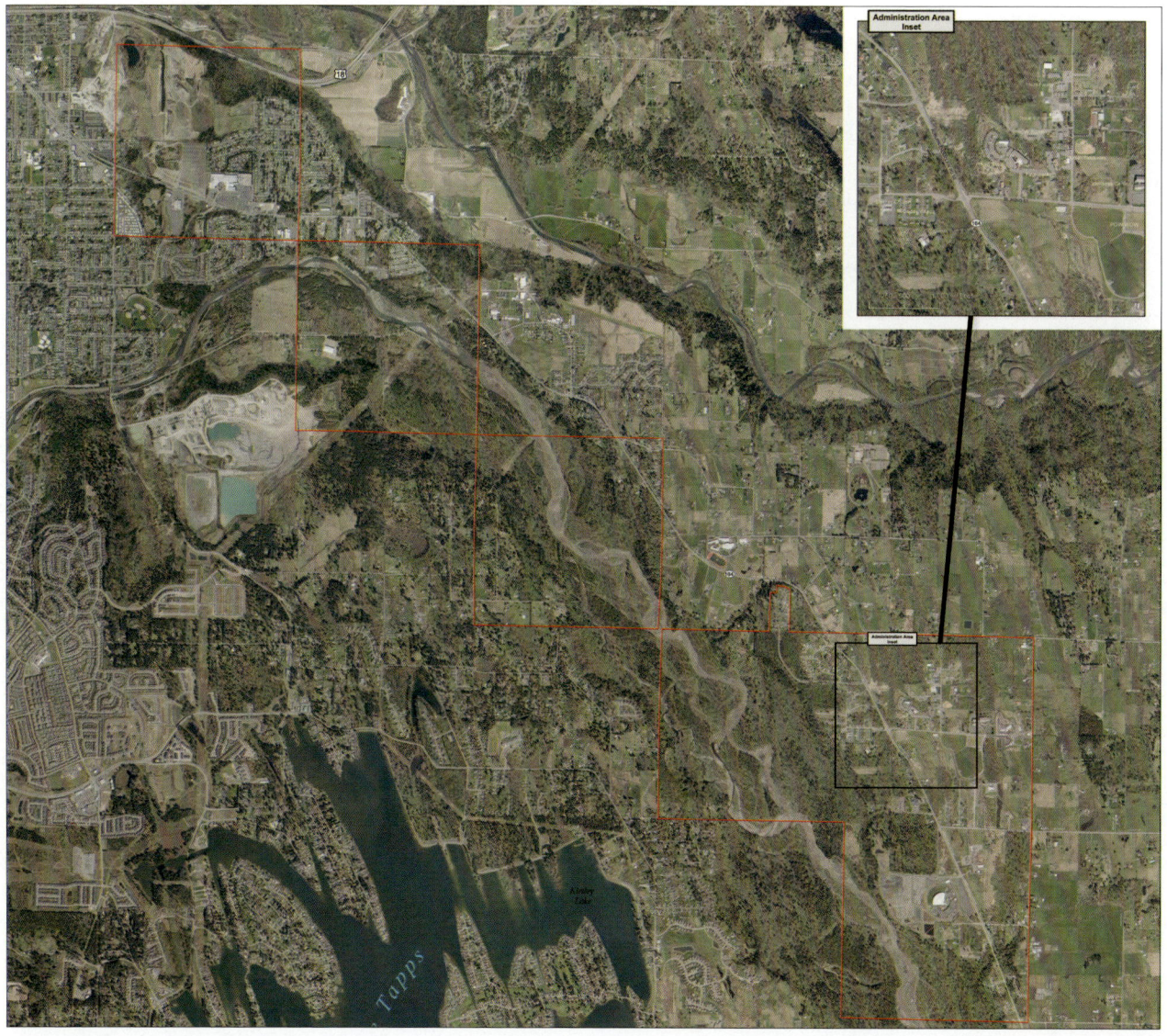

The practical application of economic development for Native people's benefit has made Muckleshoot a national example of nation-building at street level. While other Native people have experienced major problems dealing with a casino revenue windfall (such as the dictatorial policies of Ray Halbritter among the New York Oneidas [Johansen, 2002, 25-46]), the Muckleshoots have applied their new affluence to their people's needs with a minimum of political friction (bearing in mind that resources are never allocated without some debate).

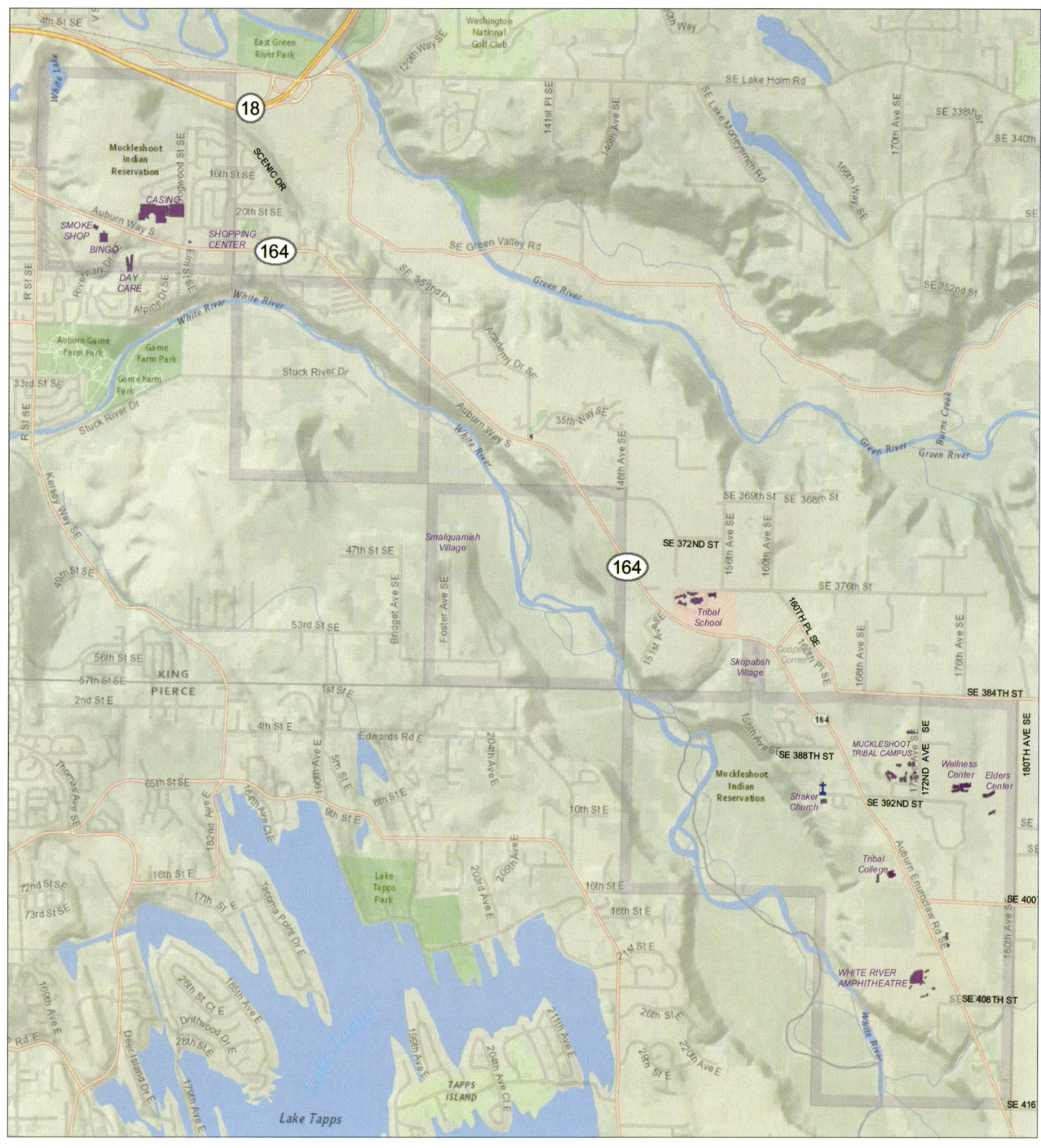

The fact that the Muckleshoot government was providing 90 percent of its budget internally by 2005 is enough by itself to qualify for attention around Indian Country and elsewhere. They have now been involved in street-level nation-building for almost three decades. While about 1970, unemployment

(Opposite page) Muckleshoot reservation map, aerial view, with boundaries, 2013.
(Above) Muckleshoot reservation map, with major construction projects.
Photos courtesy of Muckleshoot Indian Tribe Planning Division

Kelly Lozier holds fireworks at a Muckleshoot stand on July 1, 1981.
Photo courtesy of SeattlePI.com

often reached 80 percent during the winter, by 2010 the Muckleshoots had more jobs than reservation residents or tribal employees. Land holdings are up, as is average income; unemployment is down.

The Muckleshoots' story is remarkable as an ascent from poverty, disease, unemployment, land seizure, land exploitation, racism, and rural isolation. Every step, however, has been met with some resistance from white neighbors who at first have sought to impede the Muckleshoots' economic empowerment, initially seeing a threat. Each economic enterprise was fought by some local non-Indians who beforehand tried to stop or block improvements in Muckleshoots' lives, until they realized that what was good for the Muckleshoots was usually good for them as well. Having prosperous neighbors can be beneficial all around. A sign of the Muckleshoots' growing influence in state politics was provided by the fact that their intergovernmental affairs liaison, Claudia Kauffman, was elected as the state's first Native American female state senator during 2006.

GREAT CHANGE IN A FEW YEARS

Even in the days of poverty the Muckleshoots were enterprising. One of the oldest economic-development activities at Muckleshoot has been the fireworks stands that supply much of the urban area with Fourth of July firepower. Long before the casino, when fishing risked arrest by the state, ranks of wooden stands along Highway 164 came to life for a few weeks before Independence Day when more than 100 entrepreneurs did brisk business.

"Less than a generation ago, the Muckleshoots were one of the poorest tribes in Washington, all but invisible to the outside world," wrote Lynda V. Mapes of the *Seattle Times* in 2002. "Today, the tribe is an economic powerhouse. Its business dealings have earned the tribe a reputation as being tough and professional ... 'It's almost like Muckleshoot, Inc.,' said Ed Fleisher, special assistant for tribal and governmental affairs for the Washington State Gambling Commission. 'They are tough negotiators, but very fair; you can work things through with them. They are very businesslike'" (Mapes, November 27, 2002).

Mapes' account was published two days after the Muckleshoots announced purchase of the 157 acres under Emerald Downs, Washington State's largest thoroughbred racetrack, south of Seattle, which had been part of their traditional territory before European-American

Opening night at Emerald Downs, 2005. Left to right, Muckleshoot Tribal Chairman John Daniels Jr., Emerald Downs President Ron Crockett, King County Councilman Larry Gossett and El Centro de la Raza Executive Director Roberto Maestas.
Photo by John Loftus, Muckleshoot Monthly

immigration beginning in the mid-nineteenth century. The Emerald Downs property is one of the Muckleshoots' most visible acquisitions. "I feel good," John Daniels, Jr., told the *Seattle Times*' Mapes in 2002, speaking as the Muckleshoot Indian Tribe's chairman. "But sometimes it's kind of hard to believe going from a little smoke shop to all of a sudden owning a property like this" (Mapes, November 26, 2002).

As tribal chairman in 2005, Daniels was listed among *Seattle* magazine's 25 most influential people in the Seattle area, along with the state's governor, Seattle's mayor, the managing editor of the *Seattle Times*, and others. The award, based mainly on the Muckleshoots' philanthropy ($6 million in gifts over ten years), was described by Daniels as an honor for "all members of the Muckleshoot tribe," not for himself (Walker, 2006, n.p.). "Our tribe has built upon the strengths of its culture to become more economically independent, and with that influence has come a strong commitment to the broader community," Daniels said (Walker, 2006, n.p.).

Changes for the Muckleshoots have come quickly; Rhonda Harnden Cabanas, director of their jobs-training program, said that she once had to explain where she came from. In Spokane, she said, "Someone said, 'What kind of Indian are you?' Muckleshoot was not even on the map. Well, now who's talking?" (Mapes, November 27, 2002). A full-ride college scholarship program began in 1998; four years later, 130 Muckleshoots were attending college on it. By 2011, a loan program allowed Muckleshoots to borrow as much as $567,000 at 1 percent interest to purchase a house. Every household also is allocated $45,000 toward a down payment and repairs.

Bob Roegner, mayor of Auburn when the Muckleshoot Bingo Hall opened in 1985, seemed to have forgotten his initial doubts about the casino a decade later: "They came to us and said, 'We don't believe we have to follow your land-use laws, or your water and sewer policies or anything else. But how can we set the issue of authority aside and work together and work within your standards?' That made it much easier to work through" (Mapes, November 27, 2002).

Darrell Hillaire, chairman of the Lummi Nation, said in 2002 that the Muckleshoots "are living out their true self-determination. My description of them is they are like an emerging nation. With their economic development they are securing land, and going from economic survival to something more sustainable" (Mapes, November 27, 2002).

Older Muckleshoots who lived through a much different time have been amazed at the pace of change: "No jobs, no economy, no infrastructure; it was lamps, candles and outhouses. Our people worked in the fields, or as loggers," recalled LeeRoy Courville, Sr., who was serving on the Muckleshoot Council in 2002. "It's pretty amazing, like a miracle. … It's nice to finally have what everyone else has." John Halliday, director of economic development for the tribe, said: "My generation grew up in public housing. We joke about having our Indian cars, and living on government programs. But now the tribe is doing for themselves. People are becoming middle class." Gilbert King George, a former Muckleshoot chairman, added: "Look how far we have come, from the old community hall, the amphitheater, right up to the casino. I'll say it out loud: It's something to be proud of. And I pray that our young people will say it proudly: I'm a Muckleshoot" (Mapes, November 27, 2002).

The Muckleshoots realize that their "miracle" has been hardly universal in Indian Country. The combination of location near

Early Muckleshoot license plate.
Photo courtesy of Antton Saez de Gordoa

a major urban area (and gambling market), with sagacious (and relatively harmonious) business management is still an exception on reservations across the United States, where living conditions for many Native people still often resemble the Muckleshoots' conditions 30 to 40 years ago.

The Muckleshoots participated in Harvard University's Project on American Indian Economic Development, which started in 1987 and addressed the popular misconception that all Native peoples have been benefiting from gaming revenues. Successful casinos in urban areas have received extensive publicity, feeding the stereotype. In fact, however, only eight Native nations (of more than 110 with Class III gambling) generated nearly half of total revenues, according to this study. A majority of the 550 Native nations, tribes, and bands recognized by the United States federal government (many others are still unrecognized), especially those in rural areas without a large gaming customer base, remain subject to intense poverty.

WORKING WITH A PLAN

As soon as the Muckleshoots began to develop their economic base with a revived fishing fleet during the 1970s, plans were being made for common development. Administrative capacity was increased as businesses

The Salish Lodge.
Photo by John Loftus, Muckleshoot Monthly

grew. A lending fund was created, offering auto loans of up to $20,000, debt consolidation up to $10,000, and personal unsecured loans up to $2,000. The fishing fleet was further enhanced, and a new cemetery was opened.

An eight-mile sewer system was constructed; additional legal staff were hired; a government-owned public works department was created (instead of sending money outside the community to private construction companies). All of this created long-term, sustainable employment. A child-care center was expanded to an all-day facility to enable mothers to work. A new smoke shop opened in 2005. A hotel at Snoqualmie Falls in the Cascades, the Salish Lodge, which has the highest

Muckleshoot standpipe reservoir, aerial view.
Photo courtesy of Muckleshoot Utility District

room rates of any Puget Sound hotel, was acquired for $62.5 million. The Lodge specializes in no-apologies luxury, offering a distinctly Northwest ambience, with cedar and natural slate floors. At the Lodge's Spa, citing one small example of many, guests' experiences were described by Terry Tazioli, travel editor of the *Seattle Times*:

> The spa design alone is something of an inspiration — slate and madrona floors and soaring cedar ceilings. You will be reminded that the soaking pools, sauna and steam room are silent — meaning keep quiet. If guests must talk, the staff suggests nothing louder than an "intimate whisper." The five-hour Cascade Escape (including foot revitalizer, facial, exfoliation, cocoon and massage) is the top of the line at $508 — the ultimate in spa-ing here and no doubt a major reason some guests might collapse afterward in their rooms. (Tazioli, 2007)

BUILDING A SEWER AND WATER SYSTEM

Many Muckleshoots welcomed the new water and sewer system with joy. Yvonne James said that her drinking water would no longer be contaminated, and the "ferocious odor" from her backyard septic tank would subside. She said that her children could now return to the reservation and build their own homes. The new system thus meant a new life for James, who had housed as many as 18 people at a time in a small house where everyone was forced to boil drinking water (Archbold, 1995, n.p.). The new system, hooked up in 1996, the first infrastructure payoff from casino profits, as well as federal money, involved more than 80 homes and tribal offices in the southeastern corner of the reservation.

Ernestine Starr lived in a trailer with two teenage sons next to her parents' house. She had no water, sewer, or electric power. Outside the trailer, the family used a Spiffy Biffy outhouse that Ernestine emptied every Monday. "I have a lot of friends like that," she said. "My cousin has three children in a camper with no electricity and water." With the new system, she said, "A lot of people are going to be happy" (Archbold, 1995, n.p). The new water system cost $2.5 million and eventually served more than 400 homes. It also provided part of the infrastructure for the amphitheater that opened in 2003.

REGAINING THE LAND

For several years, for-sale signs have been very scarce in the Auburn area around the Muckleshoot reservation, even during a severe national recession and housing bust. The Muckleshoots retain a real-estate agent who finds all listings, and makes offers to buy them — houses, condos, apartments, old farms, and so forth — to recover lands allotted and sold from the original reservation.

The Muckleshoots' biggest single land purchase came in late 2013: 96,307 acres for $313 million, in three counties. Most of the land, 86,501 acres (for $282 million), is in the Cascades (Pierce and King counties) north of Mount Rainier National Park along State Route 410, The remaining 9,806 acres of forest land ($32 million) lies within Lewis County southeast of the park. The property, purchased from investment manager Hancock Natural Resource Group of Boston, has historical and economic value as a "working forest" to the Muckleshoots. In 2013, Hancock was managing $11.5 billion worth of timberland assets.

Muckleshoot Tribal Council Chairwoman Virginia Cross explained the purchase:

> This acquisition is another important step toward the tribe's goals of increasing our land base, reacquiring portions of our homeland, and diversifying our economy ... for the primary purpose of long-term sustainable timber harvest, while preserving natural values, including fish and wildlife habitat, plant resources and areas of cultural importance ... [to] provide jobs and revenue for important tribal government programs now and for future generations ... The White River Forest is an important part of the tribe's homeland ... Bringing this property into tribal ownership is the realization of a long-held goal of our people. (Bhatt, 2013)

Down to less than an acre of common land in 1970, the Muckleshoots had built their holdings base to about 10,000 acres by 2013. In two purchases, that total rose tenfold, to more than 100,000 acres. The new timberlands contain several important sacred, cultural, hunting, and gathering sites. Timber harvest conducted in a manner respectful of the earth will provide income from a renewable resource.

The Muckleshoot usually try to place purchased land into federal trust. Under trust

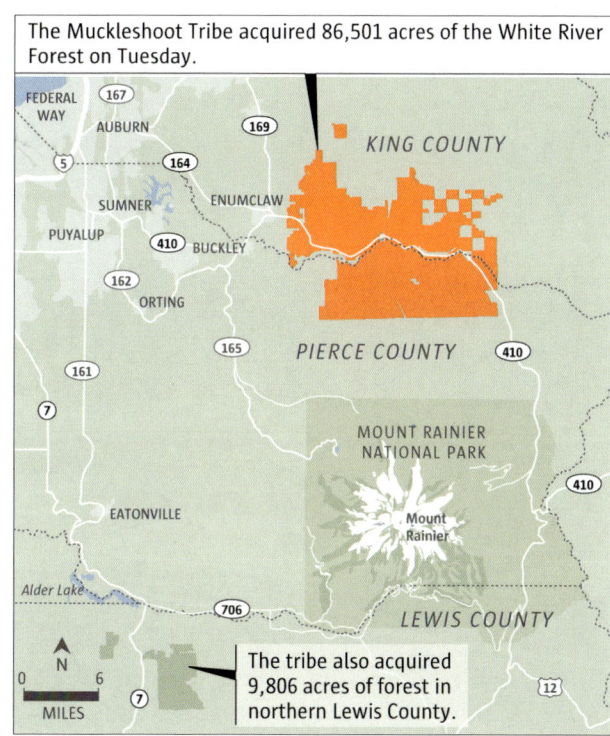

Location of Muckleshoot land purchase in November, 2013.
Photo courtesy of Mark Nowlin / The Seattle Times

status, the it cannot be foreclosed upon, and is exempt from taxes. Placing land in trust is a complicated legal process that requires approval by the U.S. Secretary of the Interior. As the Muckleshoots have bought properties, prices have escalated, a trend that began in a small way during the 1980s, as revenues generated by the bingo hall and smoke shop were used to purchase some of it. As casino revenues have increased, more land has been purchased.

In 1994, a year before the casino opened, the tribe owned 800 acres in common. By 2000, the Muckleshoot government had acquired 1,692 acres of the reservation's original checkerboarded six square miles (with 20 miles of borders), up from the half acre around the community center that had burned 30 years earlier.

During 2002 alone, the Muckleshoots acquired 352 acres, including the land under the Emerald Downs horseracing track, as well as

Emerald Downs from the air.
Photo by John Loftus, Muckleshoot Monthly

a 95-acre gravel pit (known as Miles Sand & Gravel), one acre at the First Avenue Bridge and River Street in Seattle (for expansion of fisheries operations), including a pier and property for a drug and alcohol treatment office on the Auburn-Enumclaw Road (Highway 164). The Emerald Downs purchase not only added revenue generation, but also blunted any future threat of new gaming operations there that could compete with the Muckleshoot Casino. As the race track's landlord, the tribe controlled new activities there (Annual Report, 2003, 4, 10). They held their annual Christmas party for 2002 at Emerald Downs, when 1,400 people inspected the new acquisition.

The gravel pit, located behind the casino's parking lot, was acquired in two purchases (97 and 90 acres, known as the Miles and Meade properties) for future economic development, feeding a rumor that had circulated for several years (without the confirmation of planning studies) that a hotel and resort might someday be built there. Stanley Moses, a member of the Tribal Council in 2002, wrote in a 2003 tribal-government report:

We have been wanting to purchase the Meade property for a long time. That property, when combined with the Miles property, provides the room we need to develop a large-scale destination resort hotel complex. There is nothing to compare with it in the South Sound. ... It will feature a golf course, hiking trails, jogging, boating on White Lake ... This has been a dream. Now it's becoming a reality, and now that we own the land, we can begin to plan. We have to prepare for the day when gaming is no longer profitable by diversifying into other areas, and the recreation and entertainment industry is one of them. (Annual Report, 2003, 10)

As of 2013, however, the hotel and resort had been occasionally talked up, but remained a rumor.

A cultural center and museum have also been discussed for many years, but not yet built. Some Muckleshoots have visited other Native-run museums. "We want our museum to be unique, and an educational place for both kids and adults," wrote Council member Marie Starr in the 2005 *Annual Report*. "We'll have cultural classes there for canning, net-making, and carvings. Some of the kids were really interested in doing silver working and jewelry-making" (Annual Report, 2005, 31).

Property acquisition has been a priority. Combining individual Muckleshoot holdings with land owned by the government, by 2007, Native people possessed more than half of the Muckleshoot reservation for the first time in almost a century. This proportion continued to rise as Muckleshoots identified land with spiritual importance or other deep meaning where their ancestors have lived for thousands of years, a role in family histories, and economic importance.

The Muckleshoots also expressed an interest shortly after 2000 in land at Sand Point, a surplus U.S. Navy station. They considered acquisition of the base for tribal enterprises. Located in Seattle, on Lake Washington, Sand Point had large existing buildings. However, the buildings would have required a great deal of expense to remodel. The Bureau of Indian Affairs also refused to sanction the purchase as trust property. Norm Rice, mayor of Seattle at the time, made a counter offer of $2 million for the Muckleshoot claim, which was accepted.

HOUSING, PAST AND PRESENT

In 1996, a year after the casino opened, a new house was built on the Muckleshoot reservation — not a notable event in many communities, but at Muckleshoot it was the first new residential construction in 17 years. In a Pulitzer-prize-winning series on government mismanagement of Native American reservation housing in the *Seattle Times*, published during 1996, Eric Nalder, Deborah Nelson, and Alex Tizon provided a glimpse into why the Muckleshoots had grown very weary of a system run on cradle-to-grave government control. A century and a half after the treaties were signed, a few months after the casino was embraced as a path out of poverty, the *Times* series, which had a national focus, showed why they needed it. Many Muckleshoots were living in shacks, and counting themselves lucky because they didn't lie down at night in cars or under highway overpasses.

It is not much more than a large plywood box, this house Thelma Moses calls home. To stand outside it is to wonder how such dimensions — 10 feet by 12 feet — can enclose a life. To stand inside is to marvel at how much she has managed to fit in: a bed, a

One of many new Muckleshoot homes.
Photo by John Loftus, Muckleshoot Monthly

recliner, a television, a pile of clothes, a wall of pictures, a fan, a water jug, a hot plate. From the center of the room, she is a step away from almost every object in her house. To use a toilet, she had to step outside to a portable Sani-Can. For water, she must trudge across a littered yard to her son's trailer. For electricity, she must string together extension cords from the trailer to her house.

Moses' house is an example of what Indian-housing bureaucrats call a "substandard" dwelling. Moses herself is more plainspoken. "It's my shack," she said. "Moses, a Muckleshoot Indian, is a crinkly-eyed mother of nine and grandmother of 25 who considers herself lucky to have a house at all. She could be living under a bridge or in a car, like other Native Americans she has known. She has lived on the Muckleshoot Reservation for most of her 56 years. For the past 10, she's been waiting for a government-subsidized house" (Nalder, et al. 1996).

On the Muckleshoot reservation, 100 people were on that HUD [Housing and Urban Development] list, including several of Thelma Moses' relatives. Housing stock at Muckleshoot, according to former housing director Dale Curtis, was "the most dilapidated of any Washington tribe." Nationwide, 40 percent of Native Americans living on reservations in the mid-1990s were housed in overcrowded conditions or in houses with serious physical deficiencies, or both. The national average was 6 percent, according to U.S. Department of Housing and Urban Development and the U.S. Census Bureau. (Nalder, et al. 1996)

In 1996, Thelma Moses stands before her tiny shack on the Muckleshoot Indian Reservation. She had been on a federal government waiting list for low-income housing for 10 years.
Photo courtesy of Greg Gilbert / The Seattle Times

Nalder, Nelson, and Tizon described the scene:

> Scattered along dirt roads are clusters of shacks and broken-down trailers, often connected to the water system via garden hoses. Rusty portable toilets sit between abandoned cars and appliances. Sandra Ross lives in a trailer with her four kids, ages 4 to 8. Part of the trailer is not habitable because of water damage. Some windows are broken and covered by cellophane. The home has no running water or plumbing. Electricity comes in through an extension cord connected to a neighbor's trailer. A portable toilet sits outside the front door. (Nalder et al., 1996)

HOUSING PLEDGED FOR EVERYONE

By 2000, the Muckleshoot government was engaging in several programs to make sure everyone who wanted land suitable for housing could have it. For example, land that was not considered as such could be swapped for areas on which houses could be safely constructed. The Muckleshoot Constitution enables the council to provide land for members. This definition includes families who own land that is not adequate for their needs.

In 2002, a typical year, the Muckleshoots acquired 17 single-family houses: one on five acres, another on three acres, a 19-unit subdivision behind Brown's Corner (Swan Flats), and a seven-unit apartment complex near Brown's Corner (2003 Program Update, 2003, 22–23). The Swan Flats area had lots for 20 houses (two already built, one with a Muckleshoot family in residence), with utilities and streets already installed. An additional 47 houses were planned in 2002 within six years on the former Davis property.

The first 15 homes in the Davis subdivision were completed and occupied during 2006 as rentals, all of them with three, four, or five bedrooms, as well as living, dining, and family rooms. Twenty-five more homes were finished the following year. The same year, a Veterans' Subdivision was constructed just off 164th Street Southeast, near the new Shaker Church. The 12-lot James Daniels West (McCluskey) Project was also being designed, engineered, and mapped in 2006, as water, sewer, telephone, and power lines were installed (Annual Report, 2006, 2).

At this time, the council listed more than 200 families who needed housing, or had

Ollie Wilbur endured many cold winters during the 1990s before she got windows and wall insulation in her house on the Muckleshoot reservation.
Photo courtesy of Greg Gilbert / The Seattle Times

housing and needed extensive repairs for heating systems, roof and window replacements, wheelchair ramps, doors, bathroom, flooring, weatherization, and electrical upgrades ("Our Children," 1997, 58–59). Many Muckleshoots and others were migrating from other areas back to the reservation, returning to take part in the vibrant job market created by the casino and other business development, adding housing demand for families and single workers.

Repairs did not have to be on the reservation. The February 2001 issue of the *Muckleshoot Monthly* carried a letter from Pamela H. Anderson Jackson and Rebecca Anderson Penn, both Muckleshoots living in La Push, on Washington State's coast, sending thanks for home repairs. About 135 units of rental housing maintained by the tribe received insulation and double-paned windows were installed, so that residents "would be warm and comfortable with modest heating bills" (2007 Guide, 40).

Rents have been reduced for elderly, disabled, and low-income people. By 2007, the Muckleshoot government-owned 234 rental properties. Acquisitions were stopped for a time to concentrate on maintenance. "It's a challenge to bring everything up to code and up-to-date with tenants' growing needs," commented council member Virgil Spencer. "So we've invested money in improving the rentals that the tribe currently owns" ("Muckleshoot Tribal," 2008, 29). In 2008, the Muckleshoots constructed 11 elders' and handicapped homes, with seven more built in 2009 (Annual, 2009, 47).

A large proportion of the land purchased by the Muckleshoot government went into housing. People were moved into existing apartments and single-family housing as new units were being constructed. Sometimes new homes and old stood side-by-side, providing a dramatic contrast. Elders (55 years of age or older) were being provided homes free of charge, and younger families were allowed to take out loans at 1 percent with generous allowances toward down payments and repairs. This is a reaction to a time during the bubble years when Native people in the area were sucked into mortgages on double-wide trailers that ballooned to interest rates as high as 29 percent. Emergency home repairs are also provided to members, including the repair of structural damage, roofs and siding, furnaces, windows, and doors, as well as painting, replacing floor coverings, and adding rooms. Remodeled bathrooms and wheelchair ramps accommodate handicapped residents.

Rehabilitation of Muckleshoot housing was still very much a work in progress, however. Old houses were still crowded and prone to fire. In mid-March 2010, for example, a faulty extension cord caused a house fire on the reservation that sent at least 11 people running for their lives at 3:30 A.M., as flames shot 50 feet into the air from the single-floor house, torching nearby trees. All escaped, but the number of people in the house was a surprise to fire officials. "Everyone escaped for the most part unharmed," said Deputy Fire Chief Mike Barlow, with Fire District 44 near Auburn. "Still it's a tragic situation for the family because of all the things that were lost" ("Morning Fire," 2010). Less than two months earlier, another reservation house had been gutted by flames of undetermined origin, killing five-year-old Adrina Lozier and injuring three other children who escaped by jumping out a window (Green, 2010).

CHURCH RECONSTRUCTIONS

Improving infrastructure included a new Shaker Church for congregants who have been active at Muckleshoot for more than a century. After several years of planning, fund-raising, and construction, the new church and its adjoining dining hall opened during 2004. Ken Calvert, a Muckleshoot master carpenter, played a major role in raising the new church. "Wow, what a beautiful building," remarked tribal council member LeeRoy Courville, Sr. "We now have a beautiful facility that can accommodate many more people and will last far into the future" (Annual Report, 2005, 26). On July 11, 12, and 13, 2008, the Pentecostal Church celebrated the grand opening of the new church building.

The reservation's Pentecostal Church has also been reconstructed. A meticulous restoration was completed of the historic Catholic church structure, which was handmade from split cedar boards. The church buildings host a large number of tribal community events (such as dinners and classes) as well as religious services and ceremonies, including weddings and funerals.

(Top) New Muckleshoot Shaker Church under construction. (Bottom) Completed Shaker Church.
Photo by John Loftus, Muckleshoot Monthly

MUCKLESHOOT BUSINESS SAGACITY

As the Muckleshoots began to prosper, they became known for the sagacity of their finances. Such thinking reinforced sovereignty and self-determination. The council did something that was unusual in Indian Country: for several years, it kept individual "per capita" payments small. On other reservations with gambling income many "per caps" were squandered, it was argued. Instead, profits from the tribal bingo hall bought reservation land and supported a youth home and senior center. In April 1995, the day the casino opened, Tribal Chair Virginia Cross said that the ban on "per caps" would continue (small per cap payments began later). "Every dollar this casino makes will go toward building a better future for all Muckleshoots," she said, by which she meant education and business development (Westneat, 1995).

The Muckleshoots' initial policy of depositing revenues of commonly-owned businesses in a tribal treasury, without significant per capita payments, enabled nation-building, as did the Oklahoma Osages' decision long ago to keep their oil revenues in common hands (Trumbly-Lamsam and Johansen, 2004, 271-282). Only in recent years, after income from several businesses in addition to gambling had been secured and much of the reservation's basic infrastructure renovated have "per caps" been offered. In 2011, per caps were paid quarterly and averaged $600 to $700. The money is put in trust for young people until age 18 if they graduate from high school or get a GED, age 21 if they do not.

THE PHILIP STARR BUILDING

The Philip Starr Building, housing administrative offices, opened in 2003. The two-story, 52,000-square-foot building was designed to demonstrate the Muckleshoots' cultural relationship with nature. Housing, Fisheries, Wildlife, and Policy departments, with two water quality and wet/dry research labs, and meeting space for community groups and the Tribal Council. The building was designed to offer a stunning view of Mount Rainier (when the atmosphere cooperates) in the central courtyard and from the lobby, as well as of nearby wetlands.

Day-lighting was used extensively in office spaces around a courtyard that frames interior design of the Starr Building. Its designers also created "a unique 'river' path of slate to guide the visitor to the Fisheries side of the building, while cougar tracks in the slate lead to the Wildlife Department" (Parriott, 2003). The main lobby, circulation, and gathering spaces have floors of Alaskan yellow cedar. According to Breann Parriott, marketing coordinator for Helix Architecture in Tacoma:

> Finally, the connection between culture and structure is realized through the selection of materials used in construction and finishes. The entry/lobby is constructed from heavy timber elements, which stand like tall trees above a large rock fireplace and enclose a spacious gathering place for large groups. Ceremonial meeting rooms maintain traditional patterns, fabrics and colors. Laboratory spaces and associated animal processing are

The Philip Starr Building.
Photo by John Loftus, Muckleshoot Monthly

> located at the rear of the building, the shape of which reflects the curving form of the pond and wetlands beyond … Additional Northwest materials of cedar, Douglas fir and stone are used as finishes throughout the interior and exterior, allowing users to see and touch natural textures and colors. (Parriott, 2003)

Day-to-day infrastructure improvements continued across the reservation, the stuff of everyday life. A water-treatment plant opened in 2009. (Problems with the water were indicated by the fact that the first time the swimming pool was filled at the new Health and Wellness Center the water turned black.) A community garden started in 2009 and a new fire station opened in 2011.

THE MUCKLESHOOT FOOD SOVEREIGNTY PROJECT

The community garden relates to a broader effort to reclaim a traditional diet. The Muckleshoot Food Sovereignty Project, which was funded for two years by the U.S. Department of Agriculture and supported by Northwest Indian College's Traditional Plants and Foods Program, has identified more than 300 types of fish, shellfish, berries, and greens that people ate before the advent of government commodities programs that emphasized processed

Valerie Segrest spokewoman for Food Sovereignty at Muckleshoot.
Photo courtesy of Jonathan Hiskes / Bastyr University

foods, such as the ubiquitous blocks of "commod cheese" that so many Native people came to know so well. A fatty, heavily processed diet has been linked to epidemic levels of diabetes, heart disease, and other problems among Native people, including Muckleshoots (Minard, 2012, 8).

Muckleshoot's coordinator of food sovereignty, Valerie Segrest, has worked as Community Nutritionist and Native Foods Educator for the Northwest Indian College's Cooperative Extension Department in Bellingham, Washington. She also has co-authored a book: Feeding the *People, Feeding the Spirit: Revitalizing Northwest Coastal Indian Food Culture* (2009). On June 1, 2012, she spoke at the White House as part of Michelle Obama's "Let's Move" initiative. With June Kloubec of Northwest Indian College, Segrest documented more than 200 Native foods that contribute to a healthy diet. A basic nutrition curriculum, "Honor the Gift of Food" was developed from the book.

The program includes Northwest Indian College three-credit classes on traditional foodways, such as include hands-on workshops on traditional food principles and a modern approach to a traditional foods diet; opportunities to harvest wild foods; a multi-year Food Action Plan designed to strengthen the Muckleshoot Tribe's food security by using more tribal land; an Annual Harvest Festival at the Muckleshoot Tribal Berry Garden, and support for development of community gardens at the Tribal College, Senior Center and Tribal School ("Food Sovereignty," 2013).

"The foods that were eaten here were a pillar of our culture," said Segrest. Along the way, some traditional foods have taken contemporary twists, such as elk burgers and huckleberry smoothies, kelp pickles, rosehip jam, and nettle pesto. "We're sick of being sick," Segrest said. "We know that diabetes was nonexistent in our communities one hundred years ago, because we ate these [traditional] foods" (Minard, 2012, 8).

SOCIAL AND HEALTH SERVICES

The Muckleshoots' funds have been invested in a wide array of social services that reservation residents did not enjoy when the federal government ran things. An editorial in the Seattle Times enthused that a new Health and Wellness Center, on which planning had begun in 1998 and construction in 2003, was "A Muckleshoot Gem" (2005). The editorial acknowledged that proceeds from the casino largely funded the $19.3 million, 95,000-square-foot facility and its $8 million annual operating costs, including jobs for 30 people (increasing to 110 three years later). The center also began to address a gaping need for medical and dental care, as well as housing physical recreation facilities, including a swimming pool, a racquetball court, a gym, and exercise equipment. Half of the building houses family practice services, dental care, a pharmacy, substance abuse services, massage

Chapter 7

and physical therapy, radiology and optometry services, and mental health counseling.

In 2011, the Health and Wellness Center opened a new 10,000-square-foot Behavioral Health Building with programs that include alcohol and illegal drug prevention, education, and treatment, mentoring, counseling, crisis intervention, psychiatric care, and other services. The Muckleshoots also maintain a live-in Adult Recovery House.

Usage of the Health and Wellness Center increased 43 percent between 2009 and 2010 (2010 Annual Report, 120). Optical services include eye exams, glasses and frames. Dental services provide fillings, crowns, root canals, prevention (exams, X-rays, cleanings, et al.), periodontal care, and orthodontia. Medical services include emergency care, surgery, primary care, pharmacy, referrals to specialists, radiology, vitamins and other supplements, and more.

United States Health and Human Services Secretary Kathleen Sebelius visited the Muckleshoot reservation early in 2011 expressly to see the Health and Wellness Center. The visit, on Tuesday, February 8, was the first by a member of a presidential cabinet to the Muckleshoot reservation. Health and Wellness Center Director Lisa James and Tribal Council Chair Virginia Cross provided a tour. Sebelius also was briefed on the planned Elders' Tribal Complex, to include assisted-living modules and a hospice suite, as well as the new Behavioral Health facility and Early Childhood Education Center.

Health and Wellness Center, front and interior.
Photos courtesy of Muckleshoot Indian Tribe

Muckleshoot Sobriety Pow Wow, July 17-14, 2011.
Photo courtesy of Carol Landau

People welcomed the new services, recalling that for many years, medical care at Muckleshoot had amounted to a combination of home remedies, herbal medicines, midwives, visiting nurses and long drives to federal facilities [elsewhere]. As tribal elder Florence "Dossie" Wynne reminded a crowd of dignitaries and extended tribal families, what passed for medical attention was lots of cod-liver oil and cough syrup. So the tribe relied on its own men and women who knew which plants could "kill the pain, drop the fever and stop the hemorrhaging" ("A Muckleshoot Gem," 2005).

In 1979, when Donna Starr took a job as health administrator for the Muckleshoots, they had access to one doctor and a community-health representative. In 1984, these limited services moved into a building that opened when the tribal smoke and liquor shop moved. Where ranks of liquor bottles once stood, with $53,000 worth of renovations from an annual tribal health budget of $193,000, the building was refurbished with "examining rooms, a small lab, offices, a small X-ray room, a reception area, and a meeting room" (Varney, 1984, n.p.). The clinic, open four days a week, served 2,500 people a year. At the time the facility had no pharmacy, "so the clinic really [wasn't] meeting the needs of the people," said Starr (Varney, 1984, n.p.). It did have one part-time visiting dentist, but he was serving nine other tribes as well.

The new Health and Wellness Center was aimed directly at some of the worst health demographics in North America. Life expectancy for Native Americans, while longer than a few decades earlier, still was shorter than that of any other racial or ethnic group. Diabetes among American Indians and Alaska Natives doubled from 1996 to 2001. Deaths from auto accidents, drowning, and suicide are higher than any other group.

"I have been to so many funerals," said Lisa James, a Muckleshoot who directs the health division of the Health and Wellness Center. "Our tribe doesn't want to take that ... Every family is affected. I don't want it to get to the point where it is just accepted. It is not supposed to be like that" (Mapes, October 17, 2005). James, 47, spent her youth three blocks from the present-day site of the wellness center. Her house had no running water or indoor plumbing; she took a bath once a week in a metal tub. Occasional, rudimentary services usually were provided only by visiting dentists and doctors.

The tribe also provides assistance for expenses related to the death of a close relative, including the services of a funeral home, a handmade wooden casket, a burial plot at White Lake Cemetery, grave digging, motorcade, and food and cooks for a memorial dinner. Some travel expenses are also provided for out-of-town funerals of close family members.

A NEW ELDERS' CENTER

On June 21, 2011, first earth was turned for construction of a new elders' facility east of the Health and Wellness Center, which replaced a seniors' center in one of the oldest buildings on the Muckleshoot government campus. The new center was blessed May 23, 2012; during the second week of June, staff and seniors moved into it. A formal grand opening was held August 22. Elders were welcomed through a covered portal that accommodates buses, into a large entry with a fireplace and seating area.

The new center has the capacity to serve lunch for 300 to 400 people, as well as offices for referrals on special service needs, elder-abuse issues, voucher programs, grocery assistance, and a library. Craft and activity rooms accommodate a wide variety

Grand opening of the Muckleshoot Elders' Center.
Photo by John Loftus, Muckleshoot Monthly

Ollie Wilbur at 100 years of age.
Photo by John Loftus, Muckleshoot Monthly

Elder's Center 2014.
Photo by John Loftus, Muckleshoot Monthly

of cultural practices, including cedar weaving and basketry, canning, sewing, beading, and carving. They also include media space and a small kitchen for cooking and making traditional medicines. Outside, the Elders' Center has medicinal and vegetable gardens, as well as fruit trees providing fresh produce for the lunch program. Salmon and clam pits have been built for cooking these traditional foods.

THE IMPORTANCE OF VETERANS

The Muckleshoot Tribal Government includes a Veterans Affairs Program, with its own building. Veterans have long been an important part of life at Muckleshoot, with an active social life, including regular pow-wows. As with elderly and disabled Muckleshoots, veterans are eligible for new homes. As with all eligible members, they may also take advantage of mortgage assistance, home repair and improvements, down-payment assistance, home loans at 1 percent, or discounted rental housing.

The *Muckleshoot Monthly* described a week of veterans' commemorations: "Honoring veterans is a strongly-held tradition throughout Native America, for who knows better than Native people the importance of defending one's homeland?" ("Veterans," 2011, 1). In 2011, Veterans Day observations took place for a week, beginning on Saturday, November 5, with the 46th annual Auburn Veterans Day Parade.

The *Monthly* reported that:

> It was a perfect day, but as the crowds gathered along downtown curbs a smaller gathering was carrying out a solemn ceremony several blocks away. At 9:45 a.m., the Inter-Tribal Warrior Society presented the colors at the Remembrance Ceremony and Lighting

of the Flame, where a flame is lit and guarded through the night at Veterans Memorial Park. A wreath was placed, followed by a rifle salute, prayers and taps. From there, they proceeded to the parade lineup location to march proudly in the massive mile-long parade. A crowd estimated at 3,000 was on hand to witness the event, which was kicked off by a military C-17 flyover from the U.S. Air Force at Joint Base Lewis-McChord. Muckleshoot Skopabsh Royalty led the Native unit, carrying the banner of the Inter-Tribal Warrior Society. Unit after unit drew applause from the spectators, who also got to wave at lots of dignitaries, including U.S. Senator Maria Cantwell. ("Veterans," 2011, 1)

The Muckleshoots also sponsored a Veterans Day assembly at the Tribal School, a Veterans Day Dinner at the Pentecostal Church, and a Veterans Pow-Wow at the Tribal School. "It always makes me happy to see the veterans [who attend the pow-wow]," said Sonny Bargala, Muckleshoot Veteran Affairs specialist and co-founder of the Inter-Tribal Warrior Society. "We get a nice mix of veterans from all over" (Ramon-Sauberan, 2011). The Muckleshoot Veterans Pow-Wow is the biggest pow-wow on the Muckleshoot Indian Reservation and keeps on getting bigger every year, according to Wendy Lloyd, vice chair of the Pow-Wow Committee. More than 500 contestants participated in the Veterans Pow-Wow in 2011.

After serving in Vietnam, many veterans returned home to take part in fishing-rights activism, just as minority veterans had helped spark the civil-rights movement nationwide after World War II. "It was like living in a deprived, decimated country," said Bargala, 46, a Muckleshoot who was born on the reservation and returned to it in 1970 after fighting in the Vietnam War. "There was not much attempt at government or business. People were hoping for federal money, and that was about it. "We felt we had been systematically wronged so often," said Bargala, who in 1995 was the Muckleshoots' vice chairman and also head of the gaming commission. "It was important to prove that we existed as a government" (Westneat, 1995).

Some Muckleshoots have traveled thousands of miles to commemorate veterans in their families. "Nine hours into our 'red eye' flight from Seattle to Paris, the clouds scattered as morning dawned over the English Channel. Deep emotions stirred as my wife Tallis and I realized that we were descending into France, along much the same route that my father had flown on D-Day, June 6, 1944," wrote Gilbert (Hoagie) King George. His father, Chester Courville, was killed in action June 6, 1944, on the first day of the Normandy invasion.

"On that morning," wrote King George, "Chester Courville, a man I never knew, returned to the country of his Courville ancestors, a Native American man come home, to free a country that had been occupied by the Nazis

The Fallen Four: Melvin Ross, Chet Courville, Turner Martin, and Larry James.
Photo courtesy of Muckleshoot Indian Tribe

for four grim years ... Our trip was our personal memorial to honor my father. More importantly, we traveled to Normandy, guided by our old teachings, to honor those who helped my father on his final journey" (King George, 2011, 1).

Courville was part of the assault by 13,000 paratroopers to capture the French village of Sainte-Mère-Eglise at a supply crossroads where the Germans were expected to send reinforcements after the allied landing at Utah Beach. King George was invited by the Director of Visitor Services, Dwight E. Anderson and his Deputy Director, Shane Williams to help retire the colors as the sound of taps played. "That song has choked me up ever since I was a little boy," he said. "The veterans in our *ad hoc* color guard looked like they were holding back tears as well" (King George, 2011, 5). While in the Normandy area, King George and others also visited the village of Courville, from which members of his family's European side had immigrated to Canada, then to the United States. The mayor gave him a key to the city.

DEALING WITH A "KILLER ROAD"

Improving infrastructure included attempts to address some longtime problems, such as dangerous stretches of State Highway 164, which weaves through nearly the entire reservation, northwest to southeast. Today's State Route 164 follows the route of an Indian trail that became a military road during the Treaty Wars, built to intercept Native movements over a wide area, including Naches Pass. The Fort Muckleshoot blockhouse was built nearby to monitor west-east traffic of "hostiles," including Muckleshoot ancestors.

Traffic deaths at Muckleshoot have been a problem for many decades. In its August 1967 issue (p.3), the *Muckleshoot Messenger* relayed its condolences: "This newspaper shares the grief of the entire reservation at the untimely death of Archie Lobehan, 44, who was killed in a car wreck on August 4, just a little over a week after the birth of his new baby son." "We want the speed limit lowered," Renee Lozier said while watching trucks rumble around a corner. "This is our reservation. This is our community." The Muckleshoot Tribal Council passed a resolution January 17, 1991, that said "poor lighting conditions exist and the absence of 'pedestrian crossing' signs create unsafe living conditions for members of the community." (Foster, 1991, B-1). The Lozier family by 1991 had suffered several deaths and injuries on Highway 164. Sylvia Lozier, Renee's sister, died January 12 of that year, on her 43rd birthday, after she was hit while walking alongside the highway. Five months before her death, Sylvia's son Buddy, 14, was killed while riding a bicycle along the roadway. Sanchez said that her great-uncle and great-grandfather had also been killed on the same road within a year of each other 50 years previously.

Motorists were speeding along Highway 164, a two-lane artery, through what is essentially a residential area and used extensively by Native American children, driving as fast as 75 miles an hour on a stretch that was dangerous even at the posted speed limit of 55 miles an hour. As they had done to recover fishing rights and organize economic muscle, the Muckleshoots in the early 1990s came together to reduce the human carnage in an area they had come to call "Deadman's Corner."

"There's been a lot of non-Indians killed on this highway, too," said Donna Starr, a health administrator with the Muckleshoots. "Fifty-five is freeway speed, and this road is no way close to a freeway. This road is unsafe" (Aweeka, February 14, 1991). From December 1979 to the beginning of 1991, 15 Native Americans were killed in traffic accidents on the Muckleshoot reservation, by Starr's count, some on Highway 164, others elsewhere.

"A lot of people have been hit up there, a lot of people have been killed," said Virginia Cross, serving one of her many terms as Muckleshoot tribal chairperson. `It's just not a safe highway'" (Aweeka, February 14, 1991). The state knew this. Brian Limotti, a spokesman for the Washington State Department of Transportation, told the *Seattle Times* that 15 people had been killed and 561 injured on 10 miles of highway between Auburn and Enumclaw in 10 years (Aweeka, February 14, 1991).

Meanwhile, Cross and other Muckleshoots organized a petition to the state to lower the speed limit from 55 to 45 miles an hour, with better lighting. At the end of February 1991, Renee Lozier organized a march alongside the highway in memory of at least 27 people who had been killed there. "I'm gonna end it with a big dinner at my home to dedicate a memorial that I'm building for my sister," she said. Lozier said that a pedestrian pathway should be built adjacent to the road. "These people are not just another Indian. There's somebody at home that loves that person and is waiting for that person to come home," she said (Aweeka, February 14, 1991).

On February 27, 1991, about 50 people, mostly Muckleshoots, walked ten of the most dangerous miles along Highway 164, carrying signs bearing names of people who had been killed on that road, "keeping to the side of the highway ... past the tribal bingo hall, past boarded-up fireworks stands, and past the freshly installed white crosses that mark the road's victims" (Aweeka, February 28, 1991, B-4). They urged Gov. Booth Gardner to reduce the highway's speed limit to 45 miles an hour. Some carried flowers or pushed baby carriages. Many mourned victims in their own families. "My son got killed. That's why I'm walking," said Rosemary Fryberg. "He was 32 years old in 1986. He was crossing the road and a car hit him [and] killed him instantly" (Aweeka, February 28, 1991, B-4).

The frequency of such deaths was brought home by the routine tone of the lead paragraph in a story describing a death in the South [King] County Journal: "State Route 164 claimed another reservation resident early yesterday when a hit-and-run driver struck and killed an 18-year-old pedestrian" ("Hit-and-Run," 2001, 3). In this case, the victim was Benjamin Ronald Sam, a Tulalip tribal member who grew up at Muckleshoot, whose body was found in the early morning hours of April 5 a short distance from his home on the highway, at about 371st Avenue Southeast, according to the Washington State Patrol. Officers said that the accident had produced no witnesses, and no evidence of who the hit-and-run driver might have been. Family members found Sam dead in the westbound lane.

Born December 20, 1982, Sam was an outstanding basketball player, and very well known around the reservation. His obituary in the *Muckleshoot Monthly* covered an entire page (May 2001, 3). One article, reprinted from the *South* [King] *County Journal*, pointed out that "There are roughly 300 accidents per year on the 15-mile stretch between Auburn and Enumclaw, three times the state average for similar roadways" ("Hit-and-Run," 2001, 3). It continued:

> Family and friends gathered at Sam's home with his mother, Jessica Myer, and stepfather, Joseph Myer. In their living room, three candles burned brightly on a makeshift altar in front of a large white cross. Outside the house, the small, paved basketball court with

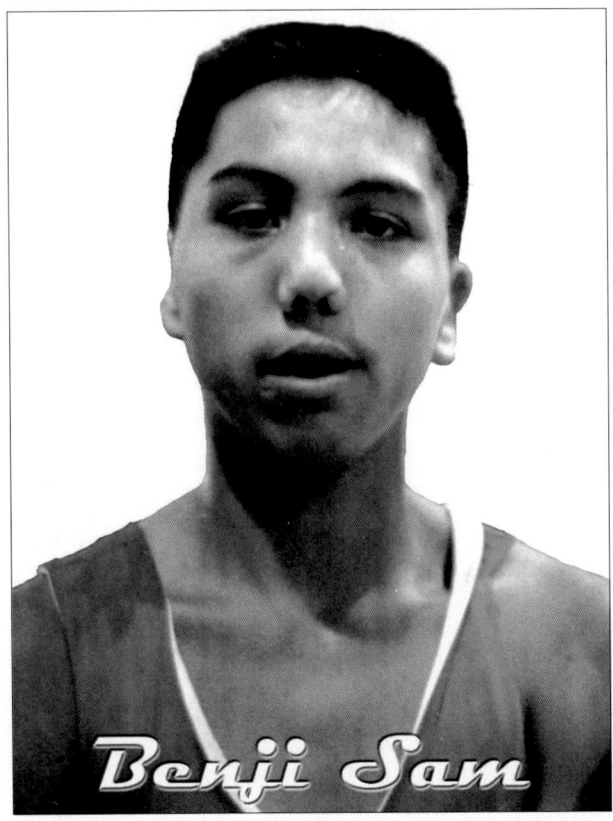

Benjamin Ronald Sam, Victim of hit and run on Highway 164, 2001.
Photo courtesy of Muckleshoot Monthly

a single hoop where Sam — nicknamed Benji — and his buddies played was quiet. ("Hit-and-Run," 2001, 3)

The weekend before he was killed, Sam had been named as a participant in an all-star basketball tournament to be played on the Nisqually and Skokomish tribal reservations, "He made a three-pointer look very easy," his mother said. "His goal was to get to the University of Washington," said Calvin Barr, who helped raise Sam for many years. "He told me that last week" ("Hit-and-Run," 2001, 3). Sam had attended the Muckleshoot Tribal School, and had been a senior at Auburn High School, before he dropped out.

Muckleshoot Tribal Council member Alex Baker said Sam was his young cousin and "a wonderful person" who was just beginning life and now won't be able to enjoy it. He said that no Muckleshoot family has gone untouched by the death on the highway, especially at night. "As a tribal council member, I would like to see the speed limit changed and more lighting," Baker said. "What do we have to do to prevent this from happening to our people, to other people and those who travel through here?"

In the ninth grade, Sam had written a poem

> I AM
> *I am a writer*
> *I wonder if I really can make it to college.*
> *I hear stick game songs.*
> *I see a bunch of Natives fighting each other*
> *(Bloods and Crips)*
> *I want to be a basketball player, a Bingo or*
> *Casino worker.*
> *I am a writer.*
> *I pretend I am brother to my cousins.*
> *I feel happy at Muckleshoot.*
> *I touch a pencil and stay in school.*
> *I worry I am going to drop out.*
> *I cry about family.*
> *I am a writer.*
> *I understand myself.*
> *I say don't do it.*
> *I dream of my future.*
> *I try to stay in school.*
> *I hope to graduate.*
> *I am a writer.*
> — Benjamin Sam, Grade 9
> ("Hit-and-Run," 2001, 3)

During the fall of 2001, a basketball tournament was held at Muckleshoot in Sam's name.

Short of death, the maladies endured on Highway 164 sometimes last a lifetime. Muckleshoot tribal council member Virgil Spencer said in October 2010 that two Muckleshoots, badly injured when they were young, were living out their lives in long-term nursing homes (Spencer, 2010).

Finally, by 2009, after nearly 20 years of effort by the Muckleshoots, Washington State

Senate Bill 5642 designated SR 164 as a Highway of Statewide Significance, which enabled funding to correct problems that had killed or injured so many people.

Stop lights, turn-outs, more street lights, and other improvements were added, and more planned, but Highway 164 remained dangerous, mainly because many drivers exceeded speed limits in residential areas. Even in 2010, Highway 164 was still a very dangerous road, with fresh memorials at roadside. One, erected in mid-October, memorialized a 44-year-old man who had stepped out of his driveway onto the road and was killed by a speeding hit-and-run driver. Terann Hoptowit was killed October 16, just after a dinner with Theresa Hoptowit. Terann had stepped out of their home to buy cigarettes when the driver of a light blue or gray sedan hit him at a high rate of speed, propelling his body into a ditch 15 feet away. The driver never stopped.

Terann A. Hoptowit, victim of a hit-and-run on Highway 164.
Photo courtesy of Muckleshoot Monthly

Theresa heard a loud thud and then, stunned, collided with a closed glass door in her hurry to get to the accident scene. She administered CPR until she realized Terann could not be revived, and then she cried over his motionless body. She then erected a roadside memorial with flowers, candles, and a sign that read: "Terann, I love you." ("Terann," 2010, 22), Services were held October 21 at the Muckleshoot Shaker Church, with burial following at the New White Lake Cemetery. A year and a half later, the Washington State Patrol was offering up to $1,000 in cash for help identifying the driver who had killed Hoptowit.

AN AMPHITHEATER BECOMES A SOVEREIGNTY ISSUE

As an idea, the Muckleshoots' 20,000-seat White River Amphitheatre, the largest outdoor concert venue in Western Washington, originated in 1988, when the tribe was approached by Media One, a regional concert promoter. The size of the planned amphitheater roughly equaled the seating capacity of the Gorge at George, along the Columbia River in a deep ravine east of the Cascades, the state's largest outdoor concert venue. At that time, the Muckleshoot owned no open, available land on which to build such a large structure. The Council negotiated with the Fiori family to acquire the land. Fiori, a local judge who had purchased land from a Native owner years before, sold 324 acres in 1989.

The Amphitheatre opened 14 years later, after strenuous protests that made it a national point issue in the ideological and legal battle over the nature of Native American sovereignty. The battle played an important role in defeating a sitting United States Senator, Slade Gorton, a ceaseless, dogged opponent of American Indian treaty rights.

For two years after the land was purchased, the Muckleshoot Council worked with Don Law, a regional concert promoter in Boston, on an agreement with Bill Graham Presents, a promoter from Northern California. Members of the Tribal Council visited the Great Woods Performing Arts Center in Mansfield, MA, one of Don Law's properties. Bill Graham also visited the Muckleshoot site. In 1991, the tribe entered into a letter of intent to develop an amphitheater on the Fiori property. Law then assigned his letter of intent to Music Corporation of America (MCA) after deciding it could not develop the property from across the United States. After several months of negotiations, the agreement with MCA

White River Amphitheatre under construction.
Photo by John Loftus, Muckleshoot Monthly

collapsed after it decided to purchase the Gorge at George. In 1995, the tribe restarted talks with Bill Graham Presents, signing a management agreement in 1996.

Construction began in 1997, but was halted during June of that year because its opponents, Citizens for Safety and Environment (CSE), asserted that the project might damage a third of an acre of nearby wetlands. In the meantime, opponents of the $20 million amphitheater on November 28, 1997 protested potential traffic congestion with a rolling blockade of 35 to 40 tractors, several pickup trucks, and horse trailers along Highway 164. State troopers and King County police rerouted traffic as some of the Muckleshoots remarked at the irony of creating traffic congestion to protest it. Because it was to be built on a reservation, under principles of tribal sovereignty, the amphitheater required no county permits. Some of King County's legislators then tried to extend its jurisdiction over the reservation, and failed.

Bill Graham Presents was purchased by SFX Entertainment in 1998. The same year a Federal District Court ruled that the Bureau of Indian Affairs must prepare an environmental impact statement on the project as part of its procedure to take the land into trust status. The court did not order a halt to construction, but the tribe and SFX stopped work while the statement was prepared. In 2000, Clear Channel Worldwide, a television, radio, and outdoor advertising company, purchased SFX and created Clear Channel Entertainment (now Live Nation). The Muckleshoots later entered an agreement with Clear Channel for 25 years, providing that the amphitheater be self-financed, with revenues providing funding for its operations.

STAKES OF A LEGAL BATTLE

When Kent Pullen, a member of the King County Council, attempted to impede plans for the amphitheater by advocating extension of county zoning authority over the reservation, the case became a national test of Native American sovereignty. Pullen opposed not only the amphitheater, but also more prosaic infrastructure improvements, such as extension of sewer and water lines on county roads that would allow the Muckleshoots to build new houses and service older ones. He argued that extending sewer and water lines violated county zoning laws that didn't apply on federal trust land. He was able to convince two other members of the County Council to vote with him, but they lost, 9 to 3. The Muckleshoots told Pullen that the county could not legally restrict its work on sewers on sovereign tribal land. The sewers were designed to connect in Auburn with county lines that feed waste into county treatment plants.

Larry Gossett, also a member of the County Council, asserted that an attempt to extend county jurisdiction over the roughly two-thirds of the Muckleshoot reservation within King County would reverse more than 100 years of county policy that respects the semi-sovereign nature of Native nations. If the County Council had approved Pullen's resolution, the Muckleshoot said that they would immediately have filed a federal lawsuit asserting that enforcement of local laws on reservation land infringes its sovereignty as well as its treaty with the United States.

"At stake is the sovereign status of the Muckleshoot Indian Nation," wrote Gossett. "King County has as much right to exert regulatory authority over Muckleshoot Tribal lands as it does for any sovereign nation in the world — absolutely none. The tribe is right in viewing this piercing attack on its sovereignty as an egregious invasion of its standing as an independent government. The Muckleshoot government has the right and power to regulate its own internal affairs — including establishing its own land-use statutes" (Gossett and Devlin, 1997).

Gossett said that the project would be an economic engine, contributing as much as $55 million to the local economy in five years, enlivening local culture, while providing Muckleshoots (and others) with jobs. Two studies already had concluded that environmental impact would be minimal, Gossett said, and that the noise level in surrounding residential communities would be lower than regulations allow. The White River and land in the area would not be disrupted, he said.

Janet Devlin, a resident of Enumclaw and co-chair of Citizens for Safety and Environment, coordinating opposition to the amphitheater, countered that the Farmlands Preservation Ordinance, passed by King County voters in 1979, made the project an illegal disruption, violating the rights of more than 25,000 people who had chosen the "peace, quiet, and safety of rural living that would be in our future. If the Muckleshoot Indian tribe is allowed to continue with construction of [the] ... Amphitheatre ... this region will be adversely impacted and the county changed forever. This facility is being plopped down in one of Western Washington's last agricultural regions," she said (Gossett and Devlin, 1997).

Devlin asserted that existing environmental studies did not adequately address "the safety of the river from runoff, the adequacy of the emergency services and police, the traffic volumes and noise." Local highways "are not equipped to handle the enormous amount of traffic [that the] ... facility would provoke. The Muckleshoots' own Environmental Assessment did not include traffic volumes from similar facilities, and much of the information regarding traffic and the roads was either inaccurate or inadequate" (Gossett and Devlin, 1997).

During March 1998 about 500 people, including many opponents of the project, crammed a hearing held by the U.S. Army Corps of Engineers, urging the agency to withhold approval of the amphitheater because the site, on a former cow pasture between Auburn and Enumclaw, would interfere with a third of an acre of wetlands. The federal Clean Water Act gives the Corps authority to examine impacts on wetlands and surrounding communities.

The Muckleshoots countered that losing a third of an acre of wetlands would not ruin 25,000 people's rural way of life. The opponents' rhetoric sometimes bordered on shrillness, with warnings of "environmental chaos." Very suddenly, ardent advocates of development (when performed by non-Indians) had morphed into tree, marsh, and fish-huggers. People who were otherwise anti-big government, rugged individualists were running to the Environmental Protection Agency and the Army Corps of Engineers to save a third of an acre of wetlands.

One such opponent, U.S. Rep. Jennifer Dunn, a Republican, wrote to President Bill Clinton demanding an environmental review to stall the project, contending that construction was continuing "despite an alarming lack of environmental review" (Muckleshoot Theater, 1997). The Muckleshoots said that they had already worked with federal agencies to build an amphitheater that would have minimal environmental impact. Nonetheless, construction was delayed as the National Marine Fisheries Service and the U.S. Fish and Wildlife Service examined the possible impact on two threatened species in the White River, Chinook salmon and bull trout. The river runs adjacent to the site of the amphitheater. Dunn called the amphitheater an outlaw project, because it lacked county and state building permits. The Muckleshoots replied that Dunn had not expressed similar concerns when a shopping mall owned by non-Indians was built on wetlands nearby. She had not previously been known as an environmental activist.

Regarding the amphitheater controversy, *Seattle Times* columnist Terry McDermott commented:

> King County has never tried to exert authority over tribal zoning. This is not a good time to start. It's true the theater will cause many problems. That's unfortunate. On the other hand, the Muckleshoots no longer own 75,000 acres of the most beautiful real estate in the world. They probably think that's unfortunate, too. (McDermott, 1997)

The 75,000 acres had comprised part of the area that the Muckleshoots used for sustenance, which rapidly shrank to about 3,500 acres in the ensuing century, much of it taken by railroad companies (and, in parcels, then sold to Anglo-American immigrants).

As the debate intensified, Muckleshoot children were taunted and bullied at school bus stops; at times, whites threw rotten produce at them from passing cars. It was much easier to like the Indians, Tim Egan noted in the *New York Times*, "when they were visible only at annual salmon ceremonies" (Egan, March 8, 1998, S-1).

Muckleshoot economic development director John Halliday said that the opponents were being hypocritical because, having damaged the land for economic development for more than a century, they now were complaining about the amphitheater's relatively minor impacts. "The roads? We didn't want the roads in the first place. But you built it [State Highway 164] so Enumclaw could flourish. Now we want the same thing, because we do not want to live in poverty," he said (Murakami, 1998). The King County Council, meanwhile, had declined to act on the proposal to extend its jurisdiction over the Muckleshoots, who said that they were diversifying their economy as gambling came into increasing competition with a state lottery and other casinos.

The Corps of Engineers looked at the situation and declined to stop the project. Opponents then took their case to court, and lost there, too. When they found that Seattle First National Bank was financing the project, they announced a customer boycott. That didn't work, either. The bank politely responded that it valued its relationship with the Muckleshoots. Lena Chavez, a Suquamish Indian who takes care of her grandmother on the Muckleshoot reservation, said: "It's too goddamned bad. We're just using the white man's law to improve our lives and they [whites] don't like it" (Varner, 1997).

ANTE UP AGAINST SENATOR SLADE GORTON

Soon U.S. Senator Slade Gorton, a longtime strident opponent of Native treaty rights on a national level, jumped into the amphitheater debate with his proposal to abrogate sovereign immunity, which Native reservation governments share with many other governmental bodies. Senator Gorton, who began pursuing votes by staking anti-Indian positions as state attorney general during the 1970s with his vociferous opposition to Indian fishing rights, brought the Senate Indian Affairs Committee to the Doubletree Suites in Tukwila, a few miles from the Muckleshoot reservation, where 500 people packed a hearing room so tightly April 7, 1998, that many had to stand outside — all this despite the probability that Gorton's proposal, running counter to more than a century and a half of emphatic legal precedent, had the proverbial snowball's chance in hell of being enacted. This was Gorton's home ground, where Native rights have been a hot issue for decades, with two very well-defined sides. The controversy over the amphitheater lit the fuse on a bomb that soon would blow up in Gorton's face.

The hearing took place in a rancorous atmosphere, "amidst a din of drumbeats on one side and hoots from a flag-waving crowd on the other," filling the hearing room and spilling into a parking lot (Egan, 1998). Hundreds of non-Indians rode in on buses from locations around the Northwest, organized by property-rights groups. "In a bit of political theater," wrote Egan: "they sang *The Star-Spangled Banner*, recited the Pledge of Allegiance, and waved placards like one that read, "White Man's Rights — Pay Taxes, Die" (Egan, 1998). American Indians converged on the hearing from throughout the western United States, drawn by a chance to express their opposition to Gorton. At the hearing, Gorton faced off with former Washington State U.S. Senator Dan Evans, a strong supporter of Native sovereignty and economic development, who testified that Gorton's bill to terminate Native nations' sovereign immunity was a "blunt instrument to ravage tribal independence," and "a solution seeking a problem" (Egan, 1998).

When Gorton entered the amphitheater fight and tried to use it as political kindling in his long-time campaign against Native sovereignty, he seemed not to have realized that Native people in Washington State had acquired quite a bit of political savvy in a few years, as well as the casino-generated cash to make political use of it. The Muckleshoots united with several other Native peoples in the state, then sparked a get-out-the-vote drive that contributed to Maria Cantwell's upset victory over Gorton in the 2000 U.S. Senate race. Cantwell beat Gorton by 2,229 votes, a fraction of one percent.

The First American Education Project coordinated a $100,000 television advertising campaign against Gorton. In 1994, when Gorton had last run for office as U.S. Senator, the Native tribes and nations in his home state had little money or political clout. By 2000, they could afford to place bets on politics; reports were that roughly $2 to $3 million worth of Native American money went into the campaign against Gorton, about half a million dollars of which may have been contributed by the Muckleshoots (Westneat, 1999). In 1998, the Muckleshoots gave $100,000 to 112 candidates in federal and state political races, of whom 104 were elected (Westneat, 1999).

Belatedly realizing that Native people had become formidable adversaries, Senator Gorton quickly used the specter of Native influence to frighten his Republican base. A Gorton fund-raising message in 1999 described "Indian tribes flush with gambling dollars ... Spend[ing] whatever it takes to defeat him." Gorton's advertising mentioned Indian tribes along with other groups: "the trial lawyers, the bosses of big labor, [and] the radical environmental groups" (Westneat, 1999). "That the chronically poor tribes are being mentioned alongside some of the top powers of politics suggests how much has changed since some of the tribes began making money," noted *Seattle Times* writer Danny Westneat (1999).

The mere mention of Gorton's name raised blood pressures across Indian Country because of his long record in opposition to every Native economic initiative in the recent past, beginning with the Boldt fishing-rights decision. As Washington State attorney general, he had been a point man for commercial and sportfishing interests in opposition to Native treaty rights all the way to the U.S. Supreme Court, where he lost. "Slade Gorton's name is known on reservations from Alaska to Florida," said Ron Allen, head of the Jamestown S'Klallam Tribe and president of the National Congress of American Indians in 1999. "If we say we have a chance to beat the dean of the anti-Indian movement, I think tribes everywhere will scramble for money" (Westneat, 1999).

Washington State Native governments spent more than $700,000 in 2002 on lobbying, roughly equal to the $684,000 spent by the Boeing Company, and far more than the $481,538 spent by forest-products multinational Weyerhaeuser. "Campaign contributions is only a part of it," said Allen. "Over time, we have become more astute at playing the political game" (Heffter, 2003).

"... This is a very, very American way to spend your money," said Cate Stetson, who owns Albuquerque-based tribal lobbying firm Legi/X. "It's what Americans have taught tribes to do." Native peoples' loathing for Senator Gorton galvanized the opposition, and Stetson's lobbying firm celebrated Cantwell's win in 2000. Wherever Native Americans gathered in 2000 across the United States, Stetson said, "There were [anti-] Slade Gorton buttons everywhere. The hatred for Slade Gorton was comprehensive, profound and activating, and there was no greater enemy in the eyes of most tribes than Slade Gorton" (Heffter, 2003).

After he left the U.S. Senate, state records indicate that Citizens for Safety and Environment, opponents of the amphitheater, hired Gorton as a lobbyist. "'People are paying me for what I used to do for free' as a $145,000-a-year senator," Gorton quipped (Anderson, 2003, 13). With several clients, Gorton was earning more than $1 million a year pitching the same established interests he had represented in the Senate, doing it with a smile and no apologies. Gorton was not able to reverse the legal tide in favor of the Muckleshoots' amphitheater, however.

AMPHITHEATER CLEARED TO OPEN

In 2002, the BIA decided to take the amphitheater's site into trust, issuing its final impact statement. The Army Corps of Engineers issued a wetlands permit in September 2002, and construction resumed. Opponents took the case to court. After six years of protests, impact studies, and lawsuits that had stalled construction, 15 years after the initial proposal in 1988, and six years after construction had begun, U.S. District Judge John C. Coughenour ruled in March 2003 that previous traffic studies had been adequate, clearing the way for the amphitheater to open on June 14 of the same year. Meanwhile, the cost of the project had risen to $30 million because of the delays. In February 2003, the State Department of Transportation also allowed access to the site from State Highway 16, requiring the Muckleshoots to improve the highway and provide a shuttle service from the Auburn SuperMall. Judge Coughenour also upheld federal agencies' environmental impact statements.

The statement, which ran to almost 1,000 pages and required four years to assemble, detailed 21 pages of stipulations regarding traffic, noise, water quality, the environment, public safety, and the community at large ("Tribe Adds," 2002). To address opponents' concerns regarding traffic congestion around the amphitheater, the Muckleshoot government rented 780 parking spaces at Auburn's SuperMall during concerts. Free shuttles would be provided to the concert grounds along Highway 164. Users of the shuttles would be given seating preference and a head start leaving the site after concerts, reducing traffic congestion by 10 to 15 percent. The White River Amphitheatre Off-Site Community Mitigation Fund added 1.8 percent to the price of tickets to offset the costs to local government agencies' law enforcement, emergency services, traffic issues, and similar needs. The fund added about $200,000 per year to local agencies' budgets ("Tribe Adds," 2002).

David Bricklin, an attorney with Citizens for Safety and Environment, said that Judge Coughenour's ruling was a defeat, but that issues related to noise level had not been addressed. A second lawsuit was filed in King County Superior Court, and an appeal was possible to the Ninth Circuit Court of Appeals. "We lost this round but there are a lot more rounds to go, and we still expect to prevail when it's all over," Bricklin said (Mapes, 2003). Nothing came of any of this.

Opening night at the amphitheater featured the Seattle-area band Heart. "Ozzfest 2003" was booked for July 12, 2003 (MacDonald, 2003). Gene Stout, pop music critic for the *Seattle Post-Intelligencer*, described the amphitheater (2003):

> Built on a sprawling, 98-acre site with stunning views of Mount Rainier, it boasts an acoustically treated metal roof [and] over 8,500 fixed seats, as well as a crescent-shaped lawn area for an additional 11,000 to 12,000 concertgoers. Two 30-by-40-foot video screens flanking the stage will offer close-ups of performers. An elaborate sound system is designed to provide high-quality sound throughout the Amphitheatre.

Farm Aid held its annual benefit concert September 18, 2004, at the White River Amphitheatre, with Willie Nelson, Neil Young,

Chapter 7

Muckleshoot Senior Princess Jolene Lozier shares the stage with the legendary Willie Nelson at Farm Aid concert at the White River Amphitheatre, September 18, 2004.
Photo by John Loftus, Muckleshoot Monthly

John Mellencamp, and Dave Matthews, among others.

In late summer of the amphitheater's first year, September 5 through 7, 2003, the Muckleshoots used it for a huge "family reunion" that brought together all members of the tribe, from the reservation, or afar. The tribal council had sent letters to everyone, inviting them, allowing no impediment: if airfare or gas money was needed, it was provided; if lodging was required, it was found. The result was a familial fair: hundreds of people sharing hugs and memories, some from thousands of miles and decades of time. Photos were shared in a tribally produced memory book, which said: "It was a joyous reunion, and many were reunited with family members they hadn't seen for years. Some tribal members [who] had been adopted out were welcomed back into the fold, meeting relatives for the first time" ("Muckleshoot Family Reunion," 2003, 1). The book is full of Muckleshoot family names: Bill, Calvert, Courville, Daniels, Gonzalez, Halliday, Jansen, Jerry, Lozier, Martinez, Moses, Nelson, Starr, Williams, and more.

The amphitheater encountered some problems along the way. By 2007, due in part to nationwide recession, it was having trouble drawing business, with only eight concerts for the year, plus a few graduations and other small events (Muckleshoot Tribal, 2008). However, the point had been made: the Muckleshoots had planned, fought for, and built another large economic-development project, and made a point about their sovereignty in the process. At the same time, they were helping to reclaim their culture in an intriguing way, in a revival of statewide canoe culture.

PHILIP STARR

Philip Starr was described in 1972 by Barbara Lane as a Muckleshoot leader who was about 68 years of age in 1941, when he and other elders in the region were interviewed by officials of the Bureau of Indian Affairs about traditional Native fishing locations and practices. Starr is recalled as a master multitasker before the idea had that name — a man of many talents and a very hard worker, diligent and physically imposing, a skilled fisherman and farmer who was never without a horse and a canoe, the tools of his many trades. Starr also served on the tribal council through much of the 1940s. His son, Louis (Doc) Starr served on the Council during all of the 1950s. Doc Starr told Lane that his father used a 32-foot canoe to transport WPA workers and their tools to clear driftwood in the White River during the 1930s (Lane, 1980, 57).

Philip Starr on a snub-nosed canoe.
Photo courtesy of National Anthropological Archives, Smithsonian Institute, Arthur Ballard Collection (Public record)

Starr had Cayuse blood and Yakama relations, and was an active Shaker, the reservation's police officer and game warden. The hat he wears for a well-known photo in a shovel-nose canoe is signature headgear for a game warden. Philip Starr had a large garden and an apple orchard, raising sheep and cattle and maintaining a large barn and house. He lost one son in World War II and another in the Korean War. "He was a good guy," recalled grandson Marvin Starr, Sr. "He treated everyone good" (Starr, 2011).

Arthur C. Ballard told the Indian Claims Commission in 1951 that he had met Philip Starr in 1941. Starr pointed out to Ballard several sites that were "usual and accustomed grounds and stations" for fishing (Ballard, 1951, 153-154). These were fishing grounds used by the constituent tribes and bands that came to be called Muckleshoot "from time immemorial" — that is, from their earliest occupancy of the area about 10,000 years ago, or as far into the past as memory extended (Ballard, 1951, 157).

CENSUS STATISTICS – AND QUALIFICATIONS

Measuring economic change among Muckleshoots statistically can be difficult. To begin, the U.S. Census usually tallies for geography, not a single group, in this case, the "Muckleshoot Reservation and Off-Reservation Trust Land." In addition, the most detailed census statistics are often not direct counts, but estimates extrapolated from surveys. Small sample sizes increase the margin of error.

Of the 4,100 people who lived on Muckleshoot Reservation and Off-Reservation Trust Land in 2009, about half were Caucasian. About one-fourth were American Indian and Alaska Native, not all of them Muckleshoot. The tribal government estimates that about 800 of 2,200 enrolled Muckleshoots lived on the reservation and trust lands in 2012.

Many Muckleshoots do not live "on the rez," but in nearby communities. About one-fourth of the reservation and trust land population is non-Caucasian and non-Indian, mainly Latin American (the largest nationality being of Mexican heritage) and Asian (most having Chinese or Japanese roots). Some people are mixed. Those born outside the United States were about 40 percent Latino and 40 percent Asian (*Muckleshoot Reservation*, 2005-2009).

Given these qualifications, trends emerge over time. The number of people has risen, a fact reflected by growing numbers of houses and trailer homes. The median family annual income was about $60,000 in 2005-2009; mean family income was about $78,600. Median household income was $48,000; mean household income was $67,200. Per capita income was $22,056. Median income for people with employment was $30,200 (*Muckleshoot Reservation*, 2005-2009).

The income numbers have risen sharply with the Muckleshoots' economic recovery. These numbers are not adjusted for inflation, but they easily eclipse it. During the mid-1980s, among the population of King County in which the Muckleshoot reservation is located, its residents had the lowest income of any group. In 1986, the average Muckleshoot household income was $6,552 compared to $33,210 in Seattle. The Muckleshoots reported that in 1990 household income for a family was $7,400 compared to $34,178 for a household in Auburn, according to the 1990 U.S. Census. Per capita income at Muckleshoot was reported at $3,669 in the 1990 Census, less than one-fourth of the statewide $14,923 average. In 1990, 43 percent of Muckleshoot households had incomes below the federal poverty level. Per capita income was $3,711 on the reservation compared to $18,308 for the city of Seattle, according to the *County and City Data Book* (1994) and *State and Metropolitan Area Data Book* (1991). According to the 1990 U.S. Census, unemployment on the Muckleshoot reservation was 58 percent.

The Caucasian proportion of population on the reservation and trust lands declined slightly during the first few years of the 21st century. As recorded by the 2000 Census, 2,073 of the 3,605 people were "white alone," (including 503 of German ancestry, 322 "English," 319 "Irish," 124 "Norwegian," 76 "Swedish," and 115 "United States") while 1,029 were American Indian or Alaska Native, 117 African American or black, 96 Asian, 15 Native Hawaiian or other Pacific Islander, and 70 listed themselves as "other race" (U.S. Census 2000, 1).

The differing economic status of ethnic groups on the reservation was reflected in the proportion of people whose incomes fell below the poverty level in 2000 — 7.4 percent for whites (and 4.2 percent for Asians), 21.4 percent for Latinos, 29.3 percent for American Indians and Alaska Natives, and 56 percent for blacks. The reservation-wide proportion of people living below the poverty level was 16 percent (U.S. Census 2000, 52). Of 550 white families on the reservation, 17 lived in poverty, while 69 of 241 American Indian families were defined as poor, and two-thirds of the 31 black families (U.S. Census, 2000,11). Unemployment rates struck a similar profile: 6.4 percent for whites, 13.6 percent for American Indians and Alaska Natives, 16.7 percent for Latinos, and 21.4 percent for blacks (U.S. Census, 2000, 40). Per capita annual incomes showed the same disparity: $21,696 for whites, $18,555 for Asians, $12,073 for Latinos, $10,810 for blacks, and $9,194 for American Indians. The reservation-wide average was $16,890 (U.S. Census, 2000, 9).

REFERENCES

2003 Program Update; Muckleshoot Tribal Administration. Auburn, WA: Muckleshoot Indian Tribe, 2003.

2007 Guide to Tribal Programs and Annual Progress Report. Auburn, WA: Muckleshoot Indian Tribe, 2007.

2010 Annual Report: Muckleshoot Indian Tribe. Auburn, WA: Muckleshoot Indian Tribe, 2011.

Anderson, Rick. "Slade's Slate." *Seattle Weekly*, January 1, 2003, 13 (in LEXIS).

Annual Report: Muckleshoot Tribal Council, January 20, 2003. Auburn, WA: Muckleshoot Indian Tribe, 2003.

Annual Report, Muckleshoot Tribal Council, Prepared for the Annual Meeting of the Muckleshoot General Council, January 17, 2005. Auburn, WA: Muckleshoot Indian Tribe, 2005.

Annual Report for 2006: Muckleshoot Tribal Council. Auburn, WA: Muckleshoot Indian Tribe, 2006.

Annual Report, 2009: Muckleshoot Indian Tribe. Auburn, WA: Muckleshoot Indian Tribe, January 19, 2009.

Archbold, Mike. "'People Are Going to Be Happy' Muckleshoots Eagerly Look Forward to Water, Sewer Systems," *Auburn Valley Daily News*, October 9, 1995, n.p.

Aweeka, Charles. "Traffic Deaths Spur Muckleshoot Drive for Safety Measures on Highway 164." *Seattle Times*, February 14, 1991.
[http://community.seattletimes.nwsource.com/archive/?date=19910214&slug=1266240]

Aweeka, Charles. "50 March for Safer Highway: Muckleshoots Want Speed Limit Reduced." *Seattle Times*, February 28, 1991, B-4.
[http://community.seattletimes.nwsource.com/archive/?date=19910228&slug=1268879]

Ballard, Arthur C. Testimony, Indian Claims Commission of the United States. *The Muckleshoot Tribe of Indians on Relation of Napolean Ross, Chairman of the General Council, Claimant, vs. The United States of America, Defendant*, Seattle, WA, November 26-28, 1951. 2 vols. (1 to p. 256; 2: 257-466).

Bhatt, Sanjay. "Muckleshoots Buy Huge Forestland in 3 Counties." *Seattle Times*, November 6, 2013.
[http://seattletimes.com/html/businesstechnology/2022202267_muckleshoottribepurchasexml.html]

Egan, Timothy. "New Prosperity Brings New Conflict to Indian Country." *New York Times*, March 8, 1998, A-1.

Egan, Timothy. "Debate About Tribal Rights Turns Rancorous." *New York Times*, April 8, 1998.
[http://www.nytimes.com/1998/04/08/us/debate-about-tribal-rights-turns-rancorous.html]

"Farm Aid 2004 Heads to Seattle: Willie Nelson, Neil Young, John Mellencamp and Dave Matthews to Headline West Coast's First-Ever Farm Aid Benefit Concert." *Muckleshoot Monthly*, August 15, 2004.

Food Sovereignty Project. Muckleshoot Indian Tribe. Accessed April 20, 2013.
[http://nwicplantsandfoods.com/muckleshoot]

Foster, George. "Death's Highway: Tribe Wants Lower Speed Limit." *Seattle Post-Intelligencer*, February 14, 1991, B-1.

"General Population and Housing Characteristics." U.S. Census, 1990. Muckleshoot Reservation. Washington State Office of Financial Management. 1991.
[http://www.ofm.wa.gov/pop/census1990/reservation/default.asp]

Gossett, Larry, and Janet Devlin. "Pro/Con — The Muckleshoot Amphitheatre Project." *Seattle Times*, November 13, 1997.
[http://community.seattletimes.nwsource.com/archive/?date=19971113&slug=2571967]

Green, Sara Jean. "Body Found After Muckleshoot House Fire; 3 Children Injured." *Seattle Times*, January 22, 2010.
[http://seattletimes.nwsource.com/html/localnews/2008658954_webauburnfire22m.html]

Heffter, Emily. "Tribes Becoming Political Players with Casino Cash." *Seattle Times*, November 17, 2003.
[http://community.seattletimes.nwsource.com/archive/?date=20031117&slug=tribes17m]

"Hit-and-Run Driver Kills Teen; Basketball All-Star Hoped to Attend UW." *Muckleshoot Monthly*, May 2001, 3.

Johansen, Bruce E. "The New York Oneidas: A Case Study in the Mismatch of Cultural Tradition and Economic Development." *American Indian Culture & Research Journal* 26:3 (2002), 25-46.

King George, Gilbert. "Journey to France: Searching for the Father I Never Knew." *Muckleshoot Monthly*, November 2011, 1.

Lane, Barbara. "The Muckleshoot Indians and the White River: A Report Prepared for the Muckleshoot Indian Tribe." September 1980. In Muckleshoot Preservation Program Archives.

Lewis, Peter B. "The High Costs of a Killer Road." *Seattle Times*, October 1, 2003.
[http://community.seattletimes.nwsource.com/archive/?date=20031001&slug=highway01]

Loftus, John. "A Brief History of *The Muckleshoot Monthly*, and Other Things ..." *Muckleshoot Monthly*, May 15, 2008, 16.

MacDonald, Patrick. "Ozzfest 2003 to Rock Muckleshoot Arena." *Seattle Times*, February 25, 2003.
[http://community.seattletimes.nwsource.com/archive/?date=20030225&slug=ozzfest27]

Mapes, Lynda V. "Tribe Buys Racetrack Property in Auburn." *Seattle Times*, November 26, 2002.
[http://community.seattletimes.nwsource.com/archive/?date=20021126&slug=emerald26m]

Mapes, Lynda V. "Once Invisible, Muckleshoots Are Now an Economic Force." *Seattle Times*, November 27, 2002.
[http://community.seattletimes.nwsource.com/archive/?date=20021127&slug=tribe27m]

Mapes, Lynda V. "Green Light for Muckleshoot Amphiteater." *Seattle Times*, March 25, 2003.
[http://community.seattletimes.nwsource.com/archive/?date=20030325&slug=mucks25m]

Mapes, Lynda. "Tribe Counting on New Facility to Lift Members' Overall Health." *Seattle Times*, October 17, 2005.
[http://community.seattletimes.nwsource.com/archive/?date=20051017&slug=health17m]

McDermott, Terry. "The Land Is the Muckleshoots', So Get Used to It." *Seattle Times*, December 16, 1997. [http://community.seattletimes.nwsource.com/archive/?date=19971216&slug=2578369]

Minard, Anne. "Food Empowerment: The Muckleshoot Tribe Reintroduces Traditional Fare." *Indian Country Today in Muckleshoot Monthly*, March 15, 2012, 8.

"Morning Fire Destroys House, Displaces 11 on Muckleshoot Reservation." *Seattle Times*, March 16, 2010. [http://seattletimes.nwsource.com/html/localnews/2011358101_auburnfire16m.html]

Muckleshoot Family Reunion, 2003. Auburn, WA: Muckleshoot Tribe, 2003.

"A Muckleshoot Gem." [Editorial] *Seattle Times*, June 14, 2005. [http://seattletimes.com/html/editorialsopinion/2002334856_mucked14.html]

Muckleshoot Reservation and Off-Reservation Trust Land: Selected Social Characteristics. American Fact Finder. U.S. Census Bureau. 2005-2009.

"Muckleshoot Theater Decried." *Seattle Times*, November 29, 1997. [http://community.seattletimes.nwsource.com/archive/?date=19971129&slug=2575144]

Muckleshoot Tribal Council: Annual Report for 2007. Auburn, WA: Muckleshoot Indian Tribe, January 21, 2008.

Murakami, Kerry. "Opponents of Theater Counting on Corps — Hundreds Attend Hearing on Muckleshoot Project." *Seattle Times*, March 28, 1998. [http://community.seattletimes.nwsource.com/archive/?date=19980326&slug=2741699]

Nalder, Eric, Deborah Nelson, and Alex Tizon "The Muckleshoots — HUD Program Undermined, While Many Remain in Shacks." *Seattle Times*, December 1, 1996. [http://community.seattletimes.nwsource.com/archive/?date=19961201&slug=2362670]

"Overview: The Muckleshoot Indian Tribe." Accessed January 3, 2010. [http://www.muckleshoot.nsn.us/about-us/overview.aspx]

Parriott, Breann. "Muckleshoot Project Blends Culture with Design: Philip Starr Building Reflects Tribe's Relation to Nature" *Daily Journal of Commerce* (Seattle), November 20, 2003. [http://www.djc.com/news/ae/11151123.html]

"President Obama's Secretary of Health & Human Services visits Muckleshoot Tribe." *Muckleshoot Monthly*, March 2011, 1-2.

Ramon-Sauberan, Jacelle. "Inside the Muckleshoot Veterans Pow Wow." *Indian Country Today*, July 3, 2011. [http://indiancountrytodaymedianetwork.com/2011/07/inside-the-muckleshoot-veterans-pow-wow]

"Reservation Left out of First Phase of SR-164 Study; High-Accident Road Way Splits Muckleshoot Land for 4 Miles from Auburn to Enumclaw." *Muckleshoot Monthly*, July 2000, 2. Reprinted from the *South County Journal*, n.p., n.d.

Segrest, Valerie. and June Kloubec. *Feeding the People, Feeding the Spirit: Revitalizing Northwest Coastal Indian Food Culture*. Bellingham, WA: Northwest Indian College, 2009.

Spencer, Virgil. Interview at Muckleshoot, October 22, 2010.

Starr, Marvin, Sr. Interview at Keta Creek Hatchery, August 16, 2011.

Stout, Gene. "Heart Is Ready to Rock and Roll Up the Curtain at White River." *Seattle Post-Intelligencer*, June 13, 2003, What's Happening, 7.

Tazioli, Terry. "A look at Salish Lodge, Snoqualmie Falls' high-end hideaway." *Seattle Times*, May 10, 2007. [http://seattletimes.com/html/outdoors/2003698889_nwwsalish100.html]

"Terann Hoptowit Killed by Hit-and-Run Driver." *Muckleshoot Monthly*, October 2010, 22.

"Tribe Gets Approval for Sewer, Water System." *Seattle Times*, May 16, 2000. [http://community.seattletimes.nwsource.com/archive/?date=20000516&slug=4021210]

"Tribe Adds New Features to Amphitheatre Plan." *Muckleshoot Monthly*, February 2002, 2.

"Tribe's Request Advances." *Seattle Times*, March 24, 2000. [http://community.seattletimes.nwsource.com/archive/?date=20000324&slug=4011774]

Trumbly-Lamsam, Teresa and Bruce E. Johansen. "How the Osages Kept Their Oil," in Bruce E. Johansen, ed. *Enduring Legacies: Native American Treaties and Today's Issues*. Westport, CT: Praeger, 2004, 271-282.

"U.S. Census: Muckleshoot Reservation and Off-Reservation Trust Land." Accessed September 1, 2010.

U.S. Census 2000, Summary File 3. Muckleshoot Reservation. Washington State Office of Financial Management. September 17, 2002. [http://www.ofm.wa.gov/pop/census1990/reservation/default.asp]

Varner, Lynne K. "Culture Clash Along the White River — Rural Residents Say Lifestyle Threatened by Muckleshoots' Plans for Amphitheater." *Seattle Times*, November 9, 1997. [http://community.seattletimes.nwsource.com/archive/?date=19971109&slug=2571252]

Varner, Lynne K. "Tribal-Immunity Issues Debated — A Hearing on Sen. Slade Gorton's Proposal to End Protection from Lawsuits Draws a Spirited Response." *Seattle Times*, April 8, 1998. [http://community.seattletimes.nwsource.com/archive/?date=19980408&slug=2744020]

Varney, Val. "Muckleshoots Get a New Health Clinic." *Seattle Times*, November 28, 1984, n.p.

"Veterans Are Honored." *Muckleshoot Monthly*, November 2011, 1.

Walker, Richard. "John Daniels, Jr. Named to *Seattle* Magazine's 'Most Influential' List." *Indian Country Today*, January 30, 2006, n.p.

Westneat, Danny. "Muckleshoot Tribe Rises from Ashes of 1970 Fire." *Seattle Times*, July 26, 1995. [http://community.seattletimes.nwsource.com/archive/?date=19950726&slug=2133476]

Westneat, Danny. "Tribes Target Gorton with Casino Money." *Seattle Times*, April 4, 1999. [http://community.seattletimes.nwsource.com/archive/?date=19990404&slug=2953279]

Chapter 8

Canoe Journeys and Cultural Revival

Chapter 8

Canoe Journeys and Cultural Revival

Jack Adams' racing canoe, Portage Bay, Seattle, 1909.
Photo courtesy of Museum of History and Industry, Seattle / SHS11726

During the Washington State Centennial celebration in July 1989, Native American peoples decided to revive a distinctive mode of transport — long-distance journeys by canoe — along with an entire associated culture. Born as the "Paddle to Seattle," Tribal Canoe Journeys in two decades became a summer-time staple for Native peoples as well as thousands of non-Indian tourists in Washington, Oregon, and British Columbia, with some participants arriving (not by canoe) from as far away as Florida (Seminoles) and New Zealand (Maoris).

In 1989, Hoh and Quileute canoes carved by traditionalist David Forlines, skippered by him, Tom Jackson, Fred Eastman, and others, also plied the open ocean for the first time in several decades. These are not little, local-lake canoes, but craft capable of traveling hundreds of miles over saltwater straits and oceans, which demands respect; "pullers," as members of canoe crews are called, have died at sea.

The Muckleshoot hosted the journey in 2006, titling it "Past and Present — Pulling Together for Our Future." Over the years, the

2011 Canoe Family, Journey to Swinomish.
Photo by John Loftus, Muckleshoot Monthly

Muckleshoots acquired three canoes: Eagle Spirit, Grandmother (for the late Yvonne James), and Shaman (for the late John Daniels, Sr.).

Today's pullers are not purists. They may call for help to chase boats with GPS, trucks follow them on shore with sleeping bags and other supplies, and the United States and Canadian coast guards can offer help if needed. This is not your great-great-grandfather's canoe journey, but it is a revival of culture and, to some extent, indigenous languages.

The craft and the rituals attending them are maintained in each Native tribe or nation by "canoe families" that put boats into the water for an annual journey, which ends at the homeland of a different host nation each summer, usually in late July and early August. The canoe families meet regularly, year round, to organize the making of regalia and drums used in canoe-culture songs and dances. Children may take part in singing and dancing, and in practice "pulling," but no one less than 14 years of age goes to sea in an open boat. As they learned the ways of canoe culture, the Muckleshoot Canoe Family was mentored by others, most notably the Tulalips, one of the largest, with between 100 and 200 members.

The Muckleshoot Canoe Family also engages in other events that bring honor to the community and to revive traditional culture. They opened a local Farm Aid Concert, participated in a 2005 film festival, and in many other cultural activities. Members of the Canoe Family also conduct paddle-carving workshops at the Tribal College. Canoe Family membership is a way of life, a code of behavior. Paddlers vow to be clean and sober to combat alcoholism and abuse of other drugs. Elders and other people reinforce clean living during the journey. The Muckleshoot government, realizing the value of the Canoe Family, provides financial support on a regular basis.

REVIVAL IN BRITISH COLUMBIA

A few years before the canoe-culture revival began in Washington State, Native nations along the western coast of British Columbia started to carve new canoes. They recalled legends describing a great flood that people survived by linking their canoes to a mountaintop. The canoes thus became a cultural

Chapter 8

2012 Muckleshoot Canoe Family, Journey to Squaxin.
Photo by John Loftus, Muckleshoot Monthly

and spiritual metaphor for emerging from the oppression that followed the immigration of European-Americans. "The canoe is a metaphor for community," wrote David Neel, a Fort Rupert Kwakiutl photographer and writer who carved his own canoe, in *The Great Canoes: Reviving a Northwest Coast Tradition*, in 1995. "In the canoe, as in any community, everyone must work together ... The canoe is helping us to be more human again. We work for something besides income; for a few precious days or weeks we forget about the clock, [and] live by the tides" (Neel, 1995, 2). On one occasion, 50 people of the 140-member Comox band traveled southeastward along the east coast of Vancouver Island to Vancouver, B.C. (Neel, 1995, 99).

The renowned Haida artist Bill Reid, working with Guujaaw (Gary Edenshaw), and Simon Dick (as well as several other people) began, during 1985 and 1986, to create the 50-foot LooTaas ("Wave Eater"). They first studied old canoes in museums. Along the way, they found a Haida canoe in New York City's American Museum of Natural History that had been built backwards, with its bow cut from the butt of a log (Neel, 1995, 23). They then built a model before attempting a full-scale craft. The builders learned that the creation of a canoe took over their lives. "A canoe demands your undivided attention," said Guujaaw. "A canoe gets jealous" (Neel, 1995, 36). "This ocean is our highway, our lifeline, our bloodline," wrote Neel (1995, 39).

The Heiltsuk people traveled in a canoe from Bella Bella, about 100 miles north of Vancouver Island's northern tip, to the Vancouver World's Fair in 1986, a distance of about 400 miles. Canoe families from Washington State established connections with people in Bella Bella, about 500 miles away, during 1993. The trip took two and a half months. Pullers slept on beaches or were invited into the bighouses of native bands along the way (Neel, 1995, 4-6, 126, 131). Most of the canoes took the inland passage north and westward along the east coast of Vancouver Island, but the Makahs, following their ancestral route, made the much more dangerous and demanding journey in the open ocean along the island's west coast, disregarding Coast Guard warnings. When they reached Bella Bella, emerging

Swinomish men behind racing canoe, La Conner, Washington, ca. 1895.
Photo courtesy of University of Washington Libraries, Special Collection / NA684

from savage seas and 30-mile-an-hour winds, "They were lifted, still in their canoe, and carried by the people of Nuu-chah-nulth into the bighouse" (Neel, 1995, 131).

THE OLD CANOES RETURN

In pre-contact times, the Muckleshoot navigated rivers and fished on Puget Sound, using cedar, their best wood, for canoes. Canoemaking was an intricate and complicated craft, practiced by people who learned it from older experts. Cedar trees large enough to serve as canoes are very rare in our time. Smaller ones may leak or fall apart. Many of today's canoes appear to be made of wood but are actually fiberglass.

During the first few decades after initial European-American immigration to the Pacific Northwest canoe culture not only survived, but thrived, with whites' encouragement. "Native Americans developed a new and exciting 'racing' type of canoe that was sleeker and faster than any of their traditional designs," wrote Will Sarvis (2003, 77). Competition in canoe racing flourished for a time. Native builders retained their skills until the late 1880s. By the 1920s, canoe culture was dying rapidly as massive logging of old-growth red cedar destroyed the centuries-old spiritual relationship between canoe craftsmen and the trees. This decline went hand-in-hand with increasing pressure to assimilate Native peoples by others means, such as forced attendance at U.S. government boarding schools.

Gradually Native peoples adapted to new technology during the twentieth century, using boats made of planks and powered by outboard motors. The old canoes were nearly gone, except in museum exhibits and photographs, when Emmett Oliver of the Quinault Nation came up with the idea of the Paddle to Seattle in 1989, after he had retired as supervisor of Indian education with the Washington State Superintendent of Public Instruction, during the early 1980s. Oliver was raised during a time when money was very scarce, according to Willard Bill, Sr.'s unpublished manuscript. He had a tough childhood, but he was an outstanding athlete at Bacone College in Oklahoma, where he played a variety of sports. After many years as a schoolteacher in Shelton, Washington, Oliver became a teacher and counselor in California, as well as Director of Indian Education at U.C.L.A. During the 1970s, he returned to Western Washington as Supervisor of the Indian Division in the Office of Minority Affairs at the University of Washington.

Oliver began "pulling" during the summer of 1934, when he took a seat in the eleven-man Lummi racing canoe Lone Eagle, "honored to replace a man who been killed in a logging accident." He sat second from the stern, directly in front of the skipper. "Little did I know that that position would make me the object of particularly clear and dedicated attention," Oliver said more than 50 years later. "I can still hear the skipper, Bunny Washington, yelling, 'Come on, Emmett — PULL!'" (Oliver, 1991, 248-249).

Oliver consulted the U.S. Forest Service, which located, harvested, and donated an old-growth cedar log that was trucked to the Quinault Reservation for carving. He then found a carver who created the first craft for the modern Canoe Journey, which brought together a few Native peoples from the Washington coast, the Strait of Juan de Fuca, and Puget Sound. Oliver traveled around the northern and western coasts of the Olympic Peninsula talking up the idea of reviving canoe journeys, enlisting 30 Native nations and tribes. Coastal peoples paddled from the ocean shore through the strait to Seattle. The first "Paddle" concluded at Seattle's Shilshole Bay and Golden Gardens, (about six miles northwest of downtown Seattle on the western shore of Puget Sound), with singing, dancing, and a salmon feast.

In subsequent years the event grew, and with it a cultural revival in canoe construction, canoe society structure, traditional clothing, drums, songs, and even languages. Pullers were welcomed ashore as honored visitors according to traditional protocols.

The new wave of canoe carving also was stimulated by museums and other contractors that bought canoes for display. Some art centers have donated use of their land for carving. The United Indians of All Tribes in Seattle provided covered carving space near its ceremonial grounds; increasing numbers of people, both Native and non-Native, watched the craftsmen at work. Some Native peoples, such as the Makah, from the westernmost tip of Washington State, contributed canoe-carving knowledge that they had retained from a whale-hunting tradition.

The revival of canoe journeys also provided new attention to traditional crafts, such as the making of that ancient wet-weather accessory, the cedar hat, as useful for shedding water today as centuries ago. Instructor Yvonne Peterson taught cedar hat–making classes at the Muckleshoot Senior Center. Muckleshoot elders picked up this ancient art quickly, as if their fingers remembered it. In times past, the Coast Salish peoples used cedar for many things in their everyday lives, from houses and canoes to clothing. Unlike leather, which tends to get soaked in the rain, cedar garments shed water and keep the person inside dry.

Louis "Doc" Starr passes on techniques for creation of dugout canoe.
Photo courtesy of Mike Levy / The Seattle Times

"DOC" STARR AND THE PADDLE TO SEATTLE

The old technologies were carried on by elders such as Alex Starr, who, at age 65 in 1968, was described as one of the few Muckleshoots who could carve a traditional canoe. He also regularly built and used traditional fishing spears. "Uncle Alex" said he used deer and antelope antlers donated by hunters, trimmed tree branches, metal points, and an 18-inch whipcord to make a tool that could spear a large salmon in its side and put food on the table (Jeffords, 1968, n.p.). Starr was a logger by trade, took part in construction of the Auburn-Enumclaw Highway, and was a cook of unusual skill. He was always making something, his family said — always passing along history, and the cardinal values of respect, and what was right and wrong.

In 1989, with an $18,000 grant from the State Centennial Commission, Louis "Doc" Starr (called "Poshnikai" within the tribe), then 90 years of age, and his son Marvin (Cubby) Starr, Sr. hand-carved a 26-foot red cedar canoe "identical to the canoes that the Muckleshoots used for fishing and trapping along the Green, White, and Cedar rivers before white settlement" (Danelski, 1989, A-1). Doc Starr was carving his first canoe in more than 50 years, as he mused that the state was now paying him to create the type of craft that state game agents had seized and chopped up in the 1920s and 1930s. The log for the canoe was provided by the U.S. Forest Service from public lands north of Shelton. A team of six Muckleshoot pullers (Todd LaClair, Donnie Jerry, Roy Starr, Petro ("Zeffa") Pedro, John Starr, and Marvin Starr, Jr.) took the craft from its first launch in the Green River to Seattle's Shilshole Bay, where, on July 21, 1989, they joined 24 other tribes in the "Paddle to Seattle."

Doc and Cubby worked an entire summer, usually ten hours a day, to get the canoe ready, and even then it was not completely finished. Work was delayed when Doc and Cubby found that their cedar log, hewn at Skykomish, had a hole, which they plugged. Cubby worked with a chain saw, hand tools and a great deal of pride. After the Paddle to Seattle, however, the canoe was neglected. Cubby discovered that it had been left in the sun, causing a damaging crack (Starr, 2011).

Less than two years later, "Doc" Starr passed away of pneumonia at age 92. Danny Westneat of the *Valley Daily News* wrote: "Carrying a simple pine coffin, a procession of Native Americans from all over the state ringed the inside of the Muckleshoot Shaker Church Wednesday, singing and crying … bringing the coffin around the circle three times … [and said] a final farewell" (Westneat, 1991, A-1). Several hundred people attended the funeral.

THE SPIRITUAL DIMENSION

The canoe-culture revival also began a restoration of the entire spiritual dimension of paddling, "including prayers in log felling, blessing of the fallen log, recognition and appreciation for the unique spirit of each canoe, spiritual communication between wood and human, the sacredness of canoe travel as moving over water and through time, and a stress on the importance of personal purity," wrote Will Sarvis (2003, 78).

The log that becomes a canoe is treated as a living being with a spirit. David Neel wrote that "a canoe, coming from a soul sometimes more than a thousand years old, is a spiritual being" (1995, 6). A canoe carver begins long before locating a suitable log with fasting and prayer, inside and outside of a sweat lodge. During this time, the traditional carver avoids sexual activity and does not comb his hair, believing that doing so could cause cracks in the canoe that would ruin months of work.

Having located a suitable tree, a carver tests it for inside rot using an elbow adze and chisel before the difficult job of felling the tree. Centuries ago, the entire felling was done with hand tools. Today, power saws may be used, but very carefully. The wrong angle of cut with a chain saw may split a centuries-old log. The tree is thanked for its sacrifice. Construction of a canoe traditionally requires parts of two years. At first, bark and sapwood is stripped with an elbow adze and axe, then, with a rough carving, the log begins to take the shape of a canoe. It is then left to season over a winter so that cracks will not ruin it during the detailed carving to come. Centuries ago, the log would remain in the forest near the site of its felling for the first year, after which a team of men would push it into a stream and float it to their village for the detailed finishing work (Neel, 1995, 5). Today, logging trucks carry them to carving sites. The bow of an old canoe may be used on a new one to maintain continuity. Once finished, canoes are launched with considerable ceremony (Neel, 1995, 6).

CAPTURING THE MOOD

The canoe journeys raised Native spirits, and connected pullers, their supporters, and observers with a sense of cultural continuity. A poem by Suquamish Peg Deem (relayed by Willard Bill, Sr.) captured the mood:

> *I want to see the canoes again*
> *I need to feel the rain on my face*
> *And wipe the drops from my eyes*
> *Hug my drum under my jacket*
> *Sing with Lela May*
> *Wake up in the tent*

Break camp
Find the next beach
I would like to stand on the sand
With all the other Tribes
And watch, proud
And full of understanding
As the canoes
Once again bring to us
Our culture
Our future
Our dignity
Look, get your songs ready
See the canoes come
Around the point!
Again.
This is our ancestors
And our future.
Sing out with pride
Again
(Bill, 2005, n.p.)

Virginia Cross, who has been active in Muckleshoot revival for more than a half century, joined land-based support efforts for the Muckleshoots' first canoe journey after the Paddle to Seattle, in 2002. The Muckleshoots' 2002 entry in the Tribal Canoe Journey was a hand-carved craft purchased at Clayoquot Sound on the west side of Vancouver Island. At first the canoe didn't have a name, but after a seal followed them for several days on the journey, the crew decided to call it The Great Seal Spirit. In January 2012, Seal Spirit was one of three canoes (the others were Cowlitz and Puyallup) installed in the lobby of the Tacoma Art Museum. "The canoe has been a part of bringing back our language, our songs, our regalia, our dancing," said Connie McCloud, who is Puyallup. "The Tacoma Art Museum festival is a way to show what we've done" (Ponnekanti, 2012).

"I spent two weeks with the Canoe Journey, from Port Angeles to Quinault," Cross wrote in an annual report for the year 2002

Filmmakers of "Pulling Together" interview David Hudson.
Photo by John Loftus, Muckleshoot Monthly

compiled by Tribal Council members. "It was quite an adventure. I haven't slept in a tent for 30 years, or stayed up until four o'clock in the morning. I thought it was really good for the kids and the adults who took part. It brought them together in a way I haven't seen before" (Annual Report, 2003, 25).

James M. Fortier directed *Pulling Together*, a Muckleshoot-sponsored documentary film about the 2003 canoe journey, which illustrates the scope of the undertaking as much more than assembling some "pullers" and putting a canoe in the water. The journey requires appropriate clothing. Air above the waters is cool to cold, even in summer; the water (into which pullers are sometimes dunked) is even colder. Life jackets are required, as are tents and sleeping bags. A support boat (actually a moderate-sized yacht) is required, an investment of tens of thousands of dollars. Pullers are also sustained onshore, when they stop for the night between major festivals, by a support truck that hauls food, camping gear, and other provisions. At a major stop, at which everyone convenes, hosting even one meal is a formidable task, as hundreds of pounds of salmon must be grilled.

Chapter 8

Soundman Eric Soma, on left, with filmmaker James Fortier on the 2003 Canoe Journey. *Photo by John Loftus, Muckleshoot Monthly*

Fortier was one of Indian Country's best-known filmmakers by the time the Muckleshoots asked him to film the canoe journeys. He was renowned for *Alcatraz Is Not an Island*, depicting the American Indian occupation of San Francisco Bay's Alcatraz Island and its abandoned federal prison between 1969 and 1971. The film was televised nationally on PBS and screened at the Sundance Film Festival. Having created *Pulling Together*, Fortier and his crew followed up with *Gathering Together*, a sequel about the 2006 Canoe Journey, which the Muckleshoots hosted.

The canoe journey is not a race, nor a contest. It *is* something of a feat of physical endurance. *Seattle Times* columnist Danny Westneat, who was invited to paddle in the 2006 Canoe Journey, recalled:

> It's not easy doing things the Indian way. This dawned on me about 20 minutes into paddling a 26-foot homemade cedar canoe across Puget Sound. It was 7 A.M., and already I'd done the hardest, fastest paddling of my life. Then the skipper, a Quileute Indian named Liz Ward, inquired sweetly if the crew might be warmed up yet and ready to actually start pulling hard. (Westneat, 2006)

To make *Pulling Together*, Fortier and soundman Eric Soma were "embedded," as they worked aboard canoes, recording more than 65 hours of film. Members of the crew were a bit self-conscious at having a film crew in their midst at first, but soon forgot the cameras' presence, "enabling them to capture a true insider's look at both the success and the struggles of the Canoe Family as its story unfolded" (Fortier, 2004, 1). There was no script; the story told itself.

Having originally planned a 20- to 30-minute film, Fortier found the story so compelling that even a three-hour "rough cut" was worth an audience. Finally, the documentary was cut to a 94-minute feature-length documentary film. Fortier and Soma followed the Canoe Family's preparations, then their journey from Neah Bay at the confluence of the Pacific Ocean and the Strait of Juan de Fuca, eastward in the strait past Port Angeles and Port Townsend, and across Puget Sound to Tulalip Bay where, on July 28, 2003, more than 65 canoes met a cheering crowd of about 10,000 people ("Premiere Showing," 2004, 1, 2). *Pulling Together* and *Gathering Together* have been continually shown around the world in the decade since they premiered at the Palm Springs American Indian Film Festival. They have screened in Italy, Spain, Germany, and Jordan, and have been used in university courses across the United States and Canada.

Problems sometimes arose. During the 2003 Journey, drunk vandals poured beer and urinated in some of the canoes at Hollywood Beach, near Port Angeles. A healing ceremony was performed to restore the spirit of the canoes, which are regarded as sacred, living beings. (Canoes, as living things, are said to "wake up" in March and "go to sleep" in late fall.) The Muckleshoots had two canoes in the 2003 Journey, "Grandmother," named for a member of the tribe, and "Eagle Spirit," so named because an eagle was sighted soaring while the Canoe Family was searching for a name.

Muckleshoot canoe Eagle Spirit on Elliot Bay near Seattle, summer 2014.
Photo by John Loftus, Muckleshoot Monthly

"Pulling" a canoe several hundred miles over the course of a week or more between southern Puget Sound, through the Strait of Juan de Fuca, to the coast and back is an arduous task that involves stamina and teamwork as long as ten hours a day. Conditions can range from nearly flat water and warm, clear weather to chilly days with fog and roiling seas that can dunk pullers in the cold saltwater and leave them wondering where they are going, even with modern conveniences such as support boats with GPS service. Today, as in the past, balance is very important, down to placing pullers of similar weight opposite each other. Imbalance may cause a canoe to roll over in rough seas.

The pullers are led by a "skipper," who stands at the back of the canoe, using a paddle as a keel or rudder, maintaining direction. Rookie pullers are called "babies." Pulling in a unified way requires coordination. Pullers who do not coordinate go nearly nowhere. Many young people take part in the Journey, as pullers, support workers, or observers, an exercise which reinforces traditional culture. It is said that one stroke can cleanse a person. Drugs, smoking, and even swearing are forbidden. Ashore, ceremonies are more than feasts. They also require songs that sustain culture. One Muckleshoot said in the Fortier film: "We are poor in songs. We have lots of money, but you can't just buy songs" (Fortier, 2004).

The Tribal Canoe Journey also involves recovery of culture, including protocols for entering another tribe's territory, and leaving it. Generally, a crew requests permission to come ashore, having had a long, difficult, tiring day without food. Protocol calls for the pullers to approach the shore, explain who they are (usually with details about how they have become cold, wet, and hungry after several hours of hard work over their paddles), then ask permission to make landfall. Permission is granted by the hosts. The host village then welcomes them. The pullers haul their canoes onto the beach where they remain until the crew is ready to pull out again. On leaving, the process is reversed. In recent years, the landing ritual has been refined to fit cultural antecedents — speaking Native languages, and acting in a mature and respectful manner. During the 2003 Journey, this ritual was performed in the Muckleshoot language as well as in English.

NEW CEDAR CANOES

Many people had assumed until 2005 that cedar trees of a size needed to carve canoes the old way were a thing of the past. Muckleshoot Language Instructor Donna Starr put some money in her budget, however, and then prayed and looked — and found a number of cedar logs on the Quinault reservation (on the Pacific Coast of Washington State) that had grown from seed before Columbus reached the Americas, more than 500 years ago ("Logs," 2006, 1).

"We have fiberglass canoes and strip canoes," she said, "And we wanted Muckleshoot to have all cedar-made canoes. I didn't know where we were going to get the logs," Starr continued. "I didn't even think there was any old-growth left in the State of Washington ... And then I ran into Mike Curley, and I said, 'Hey, do they have any old-growth over in Quinault?'" to which Mike responded: "Yeah, they do. As a matter of fact, they're logging off my property now, and they have some old-growth coming out of there." Donna asked, "How old are these trees?" And the woodcutter replied: "They were standing before Columbus landed" ("Logs," 2006, 1). A logging truck groaning under the weight of three huge cedar logs delivered one to master canoe carver Theron Parker at Neah Bay, on the northwest tip of the state, and took the other two to the Muckleshoot reservation.

THE SEA IS A TOUGH MASTER

The ocean is a tough master, and the Muckleshoot paddlers, many of whom had grown up in or near cities, quickly came to respect it. Paddlers who navigate canoes from the relatively calm Puget Sound must learn how to navigate outside of local bays and rivers in open water. The Strait of Juan de Fuca's winds, rip currents, and waves can easily swamp a canoe. In 2004 and 2005, the Muckleshoots' novice pullers practiced by paddling across the Strait of Juan de Fuca from the Washington shore to British Columbia, which can require navigating extremely rough water for hours at a time. Seas can change from smooth to rough in a matter of minutes, and disorienting fogs can roll in across the water, chilling even warm, calm summer days, and causing pullers to lose their sense of direction — and to wonder how their ancestors survived such ordeals in the days before modern technology.

These days canoes caught in rough seas can be hauled out of the water and loaded onto motorized trailers. Chase boats accompany the canoes during the entire journey, offering a break to pullers worn out after hours of hard work. Even one afternoon on the water can leave a young Native person (or anyone else) in awe of his or her Coast Salish ancestors who traveled, traded, and socialized by canoe.

CANOEING AND PERSONAL PURITY

Personal purity has long been important throughout the carving and use of canoes. Participation in a canoe family has become a profound type of therapy for young people involved with illegal drugs and gangs, and those whose lives have been ruined by alcohol. Several people said that the act of carving a canoe was profoundly curative. In *The Great Canoes: Reviving a Northwest Coast Tradition*, Lummi elder Joe Washington described the way in which the Tribal Journey had rehabilitated drinkers: "Drinking means nothing to my son now. All he wants to do is get in that canoe. He's out in the water, paddling. He wants to carve. He wants to know the cedar" (Neel, 1995, 125).

Tensions have developed for some young men between youth gangs and the tradition-reviving efforts of canoe culture, with its rejection of drugs and embrace of respect for ancestors and elders. "Every step of the way your ancestors will be with you," they were told. "Respect the Earth and the power of the water. Learn the songs, learn the dances, learn who you are as Muckleshoot ... These canoes have the power to heal" (Fortier, 2007). Canoe family members learn how to get along with others and how to stay clean and sober during journeys where they represent their nation. Many elders cried with joy when they saw the children rediscovering traditions that they had thought might be dying.

The young people also learn how to deal with conflicts that arise from living in close quarters and pulling canoes for hours at a time, day after day. Elders are available to meet with them at sharing times and encourage them to get along and participate in a responsible manner. The whole exercise empowers the young and old alike, reinforcing pride and respect between age groups. Many of the elders have a long history of involvement with Muckleshoot, having grown up on the reservation, or having returned after careers elsewhere. Elders practice protocol, and pass along traditional songs, dances, and other traditions.

THE 2005 PADDLE: SEATTLE TO PORT ANGELES

In 2005 the Lower Elwha Tribe, whose reservation straddles the river of the same name between Port Angeles and Neah Bay (on the Strait of Juan de Fuca) was the Canoe Journey host. On August 2, 2005, the Muckleshoot Canoe Family, nearing Lower Elwha, joined 60 watercrafts in a landing at Port Angeles, Washington. Newspapers reported that several thousand people welcomed them to the beach. Some of the Native peoples put canoes in the water for the first time in 60 years or more. A 900-hundred year old tree was donated to the Suquamish Tribe for a new canoe. The sight of the vessels landing in the sunlight on shore in the traditional homeland of Puget Sound Indians was a dramatic illustration of a Native cultural renaissance. The canoes had pushed off at Seattle's Golden Gardens Park, then moved across Puget Sound, westward, to Suquamish, thence to Port Gamble, Port Townsend, Jamestown, Port Angeles and then Lower Elwha.

At Port Angeles, the canoes landed on Hollywood Beach, one after another, taking several hours to observe protocol as paddlers were welcomed ashore. They then pulled their vessels onto the sandy beach and appointed security guards to watch them during evening hours. Paddlers rose early the next day and participated in a wake-up call by jumping into the strait (cold enough to test one's endurance even in midsummer) for swimming.

The 2005 Canoe Journey became national news because the Lower Elwha tribe had recently stopped construction of a major development project across their traditional burial grounds containing many family artifacts (dating back at least 300 years) near Port Angeles. An archeologist was brought in to identify graves, as ceremonies were held to honor the Lower Elwha ancestors who had been buried there.

MUCKLESHOOTS HOST 2006 CANOE JOURNEY

What had begun as a rather small-scale revival of canoe journeys by a few teams of pullers in 1989 by 2006 had become a very large-scale affair. In 2006, the Muckleshoots hosted 70 canoes and tens of thousands of guests. The Muckleshoots also often provided money for hostings by other tribes. For example, in 2005, they provided $30,000 toward the journey-concluding feast, singing, and dancing. In 2006, they hosted participants from the Oregon Coast, Washington, British Columbia, and the Alaska Panhandle.

The Muckleshoots hosted the tribal Canoe Journey in 2006.
Photo by John Loftus, Muckleshoot Monthly

Muckleshoot Walter Pacheco, who had worked on the reservation since the 1980s, was captain of the Canoe Family for the 2006 Journey, a role that Willard Bill, Jr. had filled in 2005. The hosting was a cultural rediscovery for the Muckleshoots, teaching them how to dress, how to recover the songs and dances that once had been banned by Canadian and United States governments. How would they welcome ashore the various peoples, and do it in their own languages? The elders were called upon to share their cultural knowledge with the young people through the Muckleshoot school system. "We had to teach ourselves what we used to wear," said one participant (Fortier, 2007).

Muckleshoot plans for the 2006 Canoe Journey began a year in advance, just after the 2005 journey ended, locating camping grounds for several thousand people, ordering food for several thousand meals, making plans for security of the canoes, and setting up transport from locations on Puget Sound, where the canoes came ashore, to meeting grounds at Muckleshoot, which is inland. The theme for the 2006 Canoe Journey, chosen from 92 ideas, was "Past and Present — Pulling Together for Our Future," submitted by Autumn Judge Fish.

When the Muckleshoots hosted the event, canoes passed through Seattle's Ballard Locks into Lake Washington, landing at Sand Point, greeted by several thousand people many of who also traveled to Muckleshoot for a week of songs, dancing, and celebration. This was a major logistical undertaking. The Muckleshoots prepared an average of 4,200 breakfasts each morning, 3,400 lunches, and 6,100 evening meals. On the peak day, Saturday, 8,100 meals were prepared. The Muckleshoots also created, by hand, 5,000 necklaces, 110 drums, about 125 sets of regalia, more than 50 cedar hats, 30 dance paddles, six woven Salish robes, and 800 carved regalia paddles (2007 Guide, 2007, 14). Hosting the Journey also entailed erection of a 30- by 90-foot tent to house singing, dancing and feasting, as well as the logistics of sanitation for a huge campground.

CANOE JOURNEY 2006 MARRED BY DEATH OF JOSEPH ANDREW "JERRY" JACK

Joseph Andrew "Jerry" Jack, 68, a hereditary chief of the Mowachaht/Muchalaht First Nation tribe in Gold River, British Columbia, died July 22, 2006, after the Makah canoe in which he was paddling capsized in rough water west of Dungeness Spit. Jack, who drowned, was the only water fatality in nearly two decades of tribal canoe journeys. "We don't say died — we say went home. He went home doing exactly what he wanted," said Colleen Pendleton, Jack's eldest daughter, who lives in Neah Bay, on the Makah reservation. "He lived and breathed tribal journeys," Jack Jr. told the *Times Colonist* of Victoria (Casavant, July 28, 2006).

Jack was paddling with a six-person crew in the Makah canoe Hummingbird. The other five pullers were rescued; three of them were hospitalized with hypothermia, but recovered. Jack's paddle was carried to Seattle on a Makah canoe at his family's request. He was a second chief, a position he inherited from his grandfather, Captain Jack Pendleton said. The second chief is the "keeper of the beach," who greets and feeds visitors.

Following Jack's death, U.S. and Canadian coast guards increased their vigilance during the canoe journeys. "The U.S. Coast Guard is ready to assist tribal leaders and event organizers to ensure this important maritime journey is always carried out in ways that are meaningful, enjoyable and as safe as possible," wrote 13th District Coast Guard commandant Rear Admiral Richard Houck (Casavant, July

Button, 2006 Canoe Journey hosted by Muckleshoot.
Photo courtesy of Tribal Journeys Wordpress

27, 2010). A year later, in 2007, the Lummis, who live near the Canadian border north of Bellingham, hosted the event, and celebrated their first potlatch since 1937.

On July 28, 2008, 109 canoes arrived at Cowichan Tribes Territory, British Columbia, Canada, near Duncan, on Vancouver Island, with Canoe Protocol continuing to August 1. In 2009, the Canoe Journey celebrated the 20th anniversary of the Paddle to Seattle, with commitments from all the original crewmembers to take part in the new journey. Quileute elder Frederick "Sonny" Woodruff, of La Push, Washington, former chairman of the Quileute Tribal Council, who played a key role in reviving canoe journeys, died 20 years after the revival began, September 29, 2009, of a heart attack at age 58 in a Seattle hospital. A fisherman, he had used dugout cedar canoes much of his life.

"Sonny's contributions to the revival of the Tribal Canoe Journeys 20 years ago were instrumental to its current-day success," said Jackie Jacobs, tribal publicist ("Frederick

Landing of canoes at Neah Bay, 2010.
Photo by John Loftus, Muckleshoot Monthly

'Sonny' Woodruff," 2009). In July, during this year's Tribal Canoe Journey, Mr. Woodruff called the event a "rebirth of our culture." Quileute Chairwoman Carol Hatch, Mr. Woodruff's niece, said: "Sonny was a strong leader and mentor for our youth, encouraging them to walk a clean, alcohol-drug-free path," Hatch said. "He understood the significance and importance of sharing our cultural and spiritual values with the younger generations, so they would always have a solid foundation from which to stand" ("Frederick 'Sonny' Woodruff," 2009).

THE MAKAH HOST 2010 JOURNEY

The 2010 journey, hosted by the Makahs, included 86 canoes. It began July 9 with canoes setting out from their home ports for Neah Bay, at the very northwestern tip of Washington State, with arrivals July 19. The Muckleshoot delegation had expanded to three canoes with 25 to 30 pullers who embarked on the South Puget Sound route with the Squaxin, Nisqually, and Puyallup. They converged at Seattle's Golden Gardens Park July 10, with food, song, and dancing ("Tribal Canoe," 2010, 4). By 2010, about 10,000 people were pulling, providing support, or watching the journey. The "Paddle to the Beginning of the World" ended as Neah Bay swelled to several times its usual population for nearly a week of feasting, dancing, and singing by more than 50 Native nations, tribes, and bands July 19 through 25 (Leach, 2010).

The Makah reservation added infrastructure (including a new gym, new access ramps to the beach, and an expanded senior citizens' deck) to host the event, with an eye toward improvements that would be useful for many years. "During the canoe journeys, we're able to build things that are long-lasting within our community. It's like the World's Fair or the Olympics — we took that same kind of idea and did that here, making some infrastructure improvements," said Crystal Denney, the tribal journey coordinator. The revival of culture infuses every Native community that hosts a canoe journey as well, "It's helping to revitalize and reinforce a culture that's already pretty strong," she said. "Hospitality is a big portion of our culture." (Leach, 2010). Awaiting the first canoe landings, roughly 100 Makah women danced in a line on the beach, inviting onlookers seated on bleachers, logs, or in the sand to join in songs of welcome.

After formal greetings on the beach, each canoe family told stories, accompanied by songs and dances in a very large tent on the Neah Bay High School football field from 10 A.M. to midnight each day. A street fair with 82 vendors surrounded the football field. The *Peninsula Daily News* characterized the event as occurring in "a carnival-like atmosphere" ("Neah Bay Packed," 2010). Under the direction of Makah Joe Jimmicum, volunteer cooks and young helpers attached filets of 300 large coho and king salmon onto large skewers and cooked them over an open flame near the landing site. Drums accompanied Native songs and the occasional beat of hip-hop music.

Rob Ollikainen of the *Peninsula Daily News* reported: "The summer breeze blowing off Neah Bay on Monday was the last obstacle for 86 canoe teams at the end of the 2010 Tribal Canoe Journey. Each canoe looped in front of a sun-splashed beach, which was packed with several thousand onlookers, in a four-hour landing ceremony. The canoes then anchored to a rope about 50 yards offshore to prepare for the traditional protocol. A member of each canoe team asked the Makah for permission to come ashore, as is traditional." "We're glad you're here. Thank you for your journeys here today," said Joe McGimpsy, who welcomed each canoe over a public address system (Ollikainen, 2010).

Makah teacher Maria Parker Pasqua greeted the pullers in each canoe in the Makah language, followed by translation into English by Tribal Chairman Michael Lawrence. "On behalf of the people of the cape, I am honored for your presence," Lawrence said from atop a longhouse replica. Ollikainen reported:

> Tribes from the Pacific Coast of Washington, including the Quinault, Quileute and Hoh, followed the Makah tribe's Parker family escort canoe to the staging area at 3:30 P.M. Next came canoes from inland, including the Lummi, Suquamish, Nisqually, Nooksack, Muckleshoot, and Tulalip. A Jamestown S'Klallam canoe made its initial pass about 3:45 P.M. Three Lower Elwha Klallam canoes — including the "Pink Paddle" healing canoe intended to raise breast cancer awareness — arrived shortly after 4 P.M. The Salish canoes came ashore at 6:45 P.M. "It has been an honor to travel in your sacred waters," said Phil Charles, skipper of the Lower Elwha Klallam Lightning canoe. Rose Wilson, a 14-year breast cancer survivor, asked the Makah for permission to land before a puller in the Pink Paddle released four pink balloons in honor of breast cancer victims. (Ollikainen, 2010)

By 2013, the Canoe Journey was up to 18 days (July 14–August 1), and was drawing about 100 watercraft with several hundred "pullers" (plus several hundred support workers and thousands of spectators) from the length of Puget Sound, coastal British Columbia, and the Alaska Panhandle, through the Strait of Juan de Fuca and along the inland passageways east of Vancouver Island, then southeastward along the Pacific Coast to Quinault. Twenty-four years after Quinault elder Emmett Oliver organized the "Paddle to Seattle" in 1989, the event had come home.

REFERENCES

2007 Guide to Tribal Programs and Annual Progress Report. Auburn, WA: Muckleshoot Indian Tribe, 2007.

Annual Report: Muckleshoot Tribal Council, January 20, 2003. Auburn, WA: Muckleshoot Indian Tribe, 2003.

Bill, Willard, Sr. Unpublished Muckleshoot history files. 2005, unpaginated.

Casavant, Vanessa Renee. "U.S., Canadian Coast Guards Offer Help with Future Canoe Journeys." *Peninsula Daily News,* July 27, 2006. [http://www.peninsuladailynews.com/apps/pbcs.dll/article?AID=2006607270305]

Casavant, Vanessa Renee. "Canoe Victim's Personal Paddle to Be Carried in His Honor to End of Journey." *Peninsula Daily News,* July 28, 2006.

Danelski, David. "Classic Canoe: Aging Muckleshoot Passes on Design, Technique of Dugout." *Valley Daily News,* July 13, 1989, A-1, A-4.

Fortier, James M., director. *Pulling Together.* Muckleshoot Indian Tribe. 2004. Turtle Island Productions (Film).

Fortier, James M., director. *Gathering Together.* Muckleshoot Indian Tribe, 2007. Turtle Island Productions (Film).

"Frederick 'Sonny' Woodruff: Quileute Elder Who Helped to Start Canoe Journey Dies." *Peninsula Daily News,* September 30, 2009. [http://www.peninsuladailynews.com/apps/pbcs.dll/article?AID=2009309309983]

"James Fortier: The Award-Winning Filmmaker Behind 'Pulling Together.'" *Muckleshoot Monthly,* March 15, 2004, 1, 2.

Jeffords, Edd. "'Uncle Alex' — His Primitive Tackle Gets the Big Ones." Tacoma *News-Tribune,* May 6, 1968, n.p.

Leach, Leah. "Makah to Welcome 100 Canoes Today." *Peninsula Daily News,* July 19, 2010. [http://www.peninsuladailynews.com/apps/pbcs.dll/article?AID=2010307199990]

"Logs for Carving Canoes." *Muckleshoot Monthly,* March 15, 2006, 1.

"Making Cedar Hats." *Muckleshoot Monthly,* February 2001, 17.

"Neah Bay Packed and Prepared for Arrival of Tribal Canoe Journey." *Peninsula Daily News,* July 20, 2010. [http://www.peninsuladailynews.com/apps/pbcs.dll/article?AID=2010307209994]

Neel, David. *The Great Canoes: Reviving a Northwest Coast Tradition.* Seattle: University of Washington Press, 1995.

Oliver, Emmett. "Reminiscences of a Canoe Puller," in Robin K. Wright, ed. *A Time of Gathering: Native Heritage in Washington State.* Seattle: Burke Museum/University of Washington Press, 1991, 248-253.

Ollikainen, Rob. "Makah Welcome Tribal Canoe Journey to Neah Bay." *Peninsula Daily News,* July 20, 2010. [http://www.peninsuladailynews.com/apps/pbcs.dll/article?AID=2010307209995]

Ponnekanti, Rosemary. "Celebration Connects Tribes, Boats and More at Tacoma Art Museum." Tacoma *News-Tribune,* January 27, 2012. [http://www.thenewstribune.com/2012/01/27/2001039/dock-at-tam.html#storylink=misearch]

"Premiere Showing of New MIT Film Set for April 20: Feature-Length Documentary Tells Story of 2003 Canoe Journey." *Muckleshoot Monthly,* March 15, 2004, 1, 3.

Ratliff, Pat. "50-Canoe Flotilla Mukilteo-Bound; 'I Hope This Will Give the City Some Perspective.'" *Mukilteo* [Washington] *Beacon,* July 18, 2007. (in LEXIS).

Sarvis, Will. "Deeply Embedded: Canoes As an Enduring Manifestation of Spiritualism and Communalism Among the Coast Salish." *Journal of the West* 42:4 (2003), 74-80.

Starr, Marvin, Sr. Interview at Keta Creek Hatchery, August 17, 2011.

"Tribal Canoe Journey to Neah Bay Prepares to Get Underway." *Muckleshoot Monthly,* June 15, 2010, 4.

Westneat, Danny. "Farewell to the Old Chief: Tribes Pay Respects to Muckleshoot Leader." *Valley Daily News,* July 4, 1991, A-1, A-5.

Westneat, Danny. "'Indian Pilgrimage' Reaches Beach in Triumph and Tiredness." *Seattle Times,* August 1, 2006. [http://community.seattletimes.nwsource.com/archive/?date=20060801&slug=danny01m]

Chapter 9

Education and Self-Determination

Chapter 9

Education and Self-Determination

School complex from the air under construction.
Photo courtesy of Muckleshoot Indian Tribe

In planning the distribution of casino profits, the Muckleshoots' first priority has been education, on which nearly a quarter of its profits have been spent. The development of a formalized, tribally controlled, educational system is a dream realized that has been built step-by-step for a half century, from Head Start (Muckleshoot Early Learning Academy) through community college. At first schools were started in temporary quarters, but by 2010, students were housed in a new complex of Muckleshoot-run schools that equaled or surpassed anything that public schools offered, with one important difference: curricula were designed to reinforce Native identity and keep students in school. A few years before the casino opened in 1995 the Muckleshoots also started a scholarship and financial aid program to provide funds to Muckleshoot students at any four-year college or university in the United States.

SEAMLESS PATHWAYS

The Muckleshoot Tribal School, kindergarten through 12th grade, has expanded steadily. From the opening of the first classrooms, kindergarten through fourth grade in 1984-1985 in the old Muckleshoot Community Center, the school continued to grow. Fifth grade was added in 1985-1986, and one additional grade each year until 1992-1993, with 12th grade. The first high school students, Ginger Allen and Matt Allen, graduated in June 2001.

A new 37-acre, 113,000-square-foot, consolidated K-12 school was opened in 2009. The Muckleshoot Early Childhood Education Center — housing the Birth to Three Program, Head Start (ages three through five), and Muckleshoot Childcare Development Fund — opened its own 20,000 square foot building in October 2010. According to Joseph Martin, this completes the seamless pathway that is birth through grade twelve on one world-class, culturally relevant campus. Martin has been Assistant Tribal Operations Manager (ATOM) for Education for ten years (2004-2014). The ATOM-Education position serves as the chief administrator in charge of all education programs for the Muckleshoot Indian Tribe, including the Early Childhood Education Division, K-12 Tribal School Division, the Higher Education Division, and the Financial Aid Division. The Muckleshoot Tribal College (Higher Education Division) moved into a new and larger temporary building in 2004.

"When we had bingo, we could help out a little. But now ... it's covered. And if we had a cutback, that [education] would be the last

Artist's rendering of the new K-12 Muckleshoot Tribal School, with Mt. Tahoma (Rainier) in the background.
Photo courtesy of Muckleshoot Indian Tribe

one," said John Daniels, Jr., tribal council chairman in 2002. Casino money also buys supplies and new clothes for children "so they can go to school with their heads up," Daniels said (Mapes, November 3, 2002). By 2012, the Muckleshoot Department of Education employed 374 people. When budget cuts hit the Auburn public schools, the Muckleshoots stepped in with aid. In addition, the Muckleshoot Indian Tribe cooperates with the Auburn School District to support Native students in public schools with several hundred thousand dollars per year for added staff and Indian education programs.

The tribe has an inter-local agreement with the Enumclaw School District, first established in 2005, providing enhanced services to 96 Native American students, 13 of them Muckleshoot. The agreement has been renewed through 2014, and by 2012 served about 125 Native American, about 25 of them Muckleshoot-descended. The grant money, amounting to several hundred thousand dollars over several years, has been allocated to aid specific programs (such as annual salaries of Native American educators, field trips

Chapter 9

The Muckleshoot Tribal School's 2007 High School graduating class.
Photo by John Loftus, Muckleshoot Monthly

Denise Bill.
Photo by John Loftus

and expenses for the school's Native American song and dance group) that benefit all students who take part in them. For this agreement (among other work) the Muckleshoots earned in 2010 a community recognition award from the Washington Association of School Administrators, which cited their role in teaching "our children about the cultural values of generosity, honoring elders, and education" ("Enumclaw Schools," 2007, 1; "Enumclaw," 2010).

The value placed on education was reflected by the lead story in the *Muckleshoot Monthly*, June 15, 2002, an edition filled with photographs of graduates from Head Start to college: "The first two weeks of June featured a nearly non-stop parade of events honoring graduates from the Muckleshoot Tribal Community, as well as other area Native American students" ("Muckleshoot Celebrates," 2002, 1).

Muckleshoot Assistant Tribal Operations Manager for Education Joseph Martin speaks to graduates of the Muckleshoot Tribal School's kindergarten.
Photo by John Loftus, Muckleshoot Monthly

Graduation from Head Start, as from college, is celebrated with a cap, gown, and diploma. The special section has become a regular annual feature of the newspaper, celebrating a week when graduation from all manner of schools is the main business of the reservation.

By 2010, what had come to be known as "Graduation Season" produced the Muckleshoot school system's largest high-school commencement ceremony, with 19 graduating seniors, compared with a total of 32 in the preceding nine. In 2011 the Muckleshoot schools graduated 19 high-school seniors for the second year in a row. That same year, eight Muckleshoots earned master's degrees in cooperation with Antioch University — Charles Gordon (environment and community), Mitzi Judge (management), Leo V. LaClair and Todd LaClair (strategic communication), Ada McDaniel (environment and community), Noreen Milne, Dena Starr, and Linda Starr (all in management).

A total of 224 Muckleshoots graduated at various stages of their educational careers in 2011 — Head Start 40, Kindergarten 34, 5th grade 18, 8th grade 18, high school 19, other local high schools, 13, college degrees 21, post-secondary certificates 37, GEDs, 24 — a 20 percent increase in a year (Martin, 2011, P-1). "'All our students are provided the tools and skills they need for academic success in a culturally relevant setting. ... education is a life-long journey,' said Martin" (2011, P-1).

In 2012, 252 tribal members celebrated graduation, a 12.5 percent increase compared to the previous year. That number included 16 high school seniors at the Muckleshoot Tribal School, bringing the total to 54 since the opening of the new school complex. That year, the Muckleshoots also celebrated Denise Bill's doctorate in education from the University of Washington (following in the footsteps of her father Willard Bill, Sr.), as well as Bobbi Keeline-Young's master's degree in leadership and organizational development from Saybrook University. In addition, 33 Muckleshoots earned college degrees, a record. In 2013, the Muckleshoot school system produced another 15 high school seniors, and recognized 241 diploma-earning students at all levels. Twenty-seven Muckleshoots graduated with college degrees with several at post-graduate-level: Anita Mitchell (Juris doctor, Syracuse University); Valerie Segrest (MA, Antioch); Romajean Thomas (MA, Antioch), and Samantha McGee (MA, Jones University).

By 2013, the Muckleshoot school system had graduated 69 high school seniors in four years. 241 students graduated at all levels that year.

FULL ACCREDITATION

During late spring 2011, the Muckleshoot schools reached a milestone: full recognition by the Northwest Accreditation Commission (NAC). The school system had operated under provisional accreditation for several years as it built a new facility and increased

Joseph Martin (at right) sings an honoring song at the commencement ceremonies for The Muckleshoot Tribal School's Class of 2013, June 7.
Photo by John Loftus, Muckleshoot Monthly

enrollment. "Receiving formal accreditation is an incredibly significant accomplishment. It means that MTS [Muckleshoot Tribal Schools] has achieved the rigorous teaching and learning standards, support standards, and continual improvement standards established by the NAC. Accreditation certifies that the school has undergone a process of intense self-examination that has been validated by an outside team of educational experts. In addition, NAC accreditation will ensure that academic credits earned at MTS will be fully transferable to all other accredited high schools and will be accepted by colleges and universities," said Martin ("Tribal School," 2011, 1).

PRE-CONTACT EDUCATION: LESSONS OF THE CRADLEBOARD

Like many other Native American peoples, the Muckleshoot passed their culture to succeeding generations with stories and practices that emphasized order and compliance, the value of tradition, and the common identity of the people who comprised the nation.

A Native child was born into a family with long experience raising children in a group. Babies were placed on cradleboards early in life, often strapped to a mother's back, keeping the baby close to its mother for extended periods of time. The cradleboard had a solid back, and contained crisscrossing leather ties that held the baby secure. A type of roll bar at the level of the baby's head provided support if it slipped. Parents used blankets during the winter months to provide warmth; it could also be ventilated as the weather warmed. Cradles were decorated with colorful ribbons, beads and other objects. Cradleboards freed a mother's hands for other work. It could be set on the ground while parents worked in vegetable or berry fields.

Education of Muckleshoot children began with cradleboards, which taught some important lessons. First, a child learned limits on behavior because he or she was confined. At the same time, the board provided a secure feeling because the infant was held in a firm position. This education was designed to identify gifts, which came naturally to them, focusing on enhancing each person's talents. Childhood education focused on survival as a responsible, productive member of the group. Each step of child-rearing reinforced mores and morals of the community. Growing up, children were taught to subsume individual needs to the group. The cradleboard was an initial wake-up call for children to join their group and conduct themselves to benefit others.

Muckleshoot education involved tutoring by the extended family. Early in life, children were given roles during important activities, such as river fishing. Fishermen set their nets across rivers. Children were sent upriver to throw rocks that would scare fish into swimming downstream and into the nets, knowing that they were taking part in an important family activity. In a similar manner, after farms spread over the Muckleshoot homeland, children took part with their families in berry picking. They also learned how to peel cedar bark for weaving baskets and clothes and to cut cedar planks for houses. As adults, they employed survival skills learned in childhood to build their own homes and make family clothing.

Muckleshoot children also learned at play, as they were taught to make toys and other playthings from natural materials. They made whistles from small pieces of wood and used reeds that, folded in a certain way, produced whistling sounds. Children also made slingshots as they learned the first fundamentals about hunting.

Slingshots could be fashioned from any piece of wood that formed a "Y." Materials were found to make the bands, such as thin pieces of old, pliable leather or, after contact with whites, parts of used bicycle tubes. Children trapped small animals such as beavers and mink in cages built from sticks, twine, and other things. Beavers were trapped and cooked for dog food. Mink were sold to companies that used them for making clothing items.

Individual initiatives and talents were celebrated in stories, especially those that aided the group. People with certain kinds of expertise or talents made their mark as artisans, warriors, healers, orators, or in other ways. The naming of children (finding available and appropriate ancestral names) was given considerable attention.

Until the nineteenth century, much of Muckleshoot culture was relayed orally, from the elders to the young. Bertha McJoe and Bernice White remember evening stories related by their fathers and grandfathers. These were so engrossing that children begged to stay up late to hear one more; they were sent to bed with the promise of another story the next evening. Most of them had a moral, and were told to shape correct behavior. They were, in today's sociological jargon, vehicles of socialization (Noel and Cross, 1980, 7).

While training children to put group needs before their own, traditional child-raising practices also identified leadership abilities. Elders and other members of their extended families (aunts, uncles, and grandparents were active in child rearing) observed children's behavior very carefully and noted how they interacted with others. Adults augmented these skills and talents as children grew into their adulthood, and positions of leadership. The idea was to enhance the contributions of individuals to the group.

BOARDING SCHOOLS AND FORCED ASSIMILATION

Like many Native peoples, the Muckleshoots were unprepared for contact with English-speaking European-Americans, who relied on a written language with emphasis on acquiring individual land ownership. They also did not ask to be subjected to the immigrants' educational institutions, which were set up to eradicate culture and Native values within a generation or two. By 1880, this new regime had arrived in the Pacific Northwest, under the aegis of the U.S. government and churches. Federal government reports listed a dozen boarding and day schools in Western Washington, enrolling about 300 Indian children of 1,700 deemed to be of school age (Marino, 1990, 173).

During their early years, children were dressed in uniforms, forced to speak English, and required to attend chapel services several times a week. Students were provided a diet of mass-produced food that was completely different from their traditional diet of fish, deer and elk, fruit, and berries. Joe Washington, a Lummi, said during a workshop with Auburn School District teachers, that speaking his native language in boarding school was punished by having his tongue burned with matches and his ears cut with scissors. He was left outside for two weeks with only bread and water, during which nuns at the school pressed his tongue against frozen pipes (Noel and Cross, 1980, 43).

Young men's hair was cut to fit a military style. Many of these men were members of cultures in which hair was not cut unless they were grieving the loss of a family or community member. Many boarding-school students were removed from their homes and villages for at least nine months of the year and allowed to go home only during the

Chapter 9

Children in front of girls' dormitory building, Tulalip Indian School, ca. 1912.
Photo courtesy of Museum of History & Industry, Seattle / Ferdinand Brady Collection 1988.11.13

summer. Other children who lived closer to their schools were allowed to go home on weekends. As late as the 1960s, some Muckleshoot children were sent to boarding schools as far away as Oklahoma. Students were instructed to ignore Native culture and conform to the assumptions and standards of European-American education. For many students, the cultural shock of induction into such a foreign way of life provoked depression and (for some children) suicide.

The boarding schools operated on a model that was considered appropriate for training a factory workforce during the late nineteenth century. Thus, the communal lifeways of many American Indians were replaced by an emphasis on individual labor regarded as a commodity in the capitalistic marketplace. Col. William Pratt, the U.S. Army officer who invented the boarding schools on a military model, continuously stressed the value of boarding-school education as a route to the white man's world of work, to eradicate what he regarded as obsolete cultural traits. "Kill the Indian," he said; "Save the Man."

Many Muckleshoots attended boarding schools in different parts of Washington and Oregon, from the nearby St. George's Indian School in Milton, near Tacoma (operated by the Catholic Church), to the Tulalip Agency school north of Seattle, and the Chemawa Indian School in Salem, Oregon. During the early and middle 1930s, the state of Washington closed boarding schools and directed Native Americans toward public schools. Tulalip, a major physical complex housing doctors, teachers, cooks and other personnel was closed during that time.

Kitchen girls, Tulalip Indian School, c. 1912.
Photo courtesy of Museum of History & Industry, Seattle / Ferdinand Brady Collection 1988.11.16

THE CHEMAWA INDIAN SCHOOL

The Chemawa Indian Training School opened on February 25, 1880, the second "Indian industrial school" in the United States in what became a nationwide system (the first, in Carlisle, Pennsylvania, Col. Pratt's flagship, had opened a year earlier). Chemawa was built at nearly the same time as Carlisle, under the supervision of Col. Wilkinson (first names were not used for senior officers at the school).

During its history, Chemawa has been known by several names: Harrison Institute, Salem Indian Industrial and Training School, and United States Indian Training and Normal School. The school was first located on four acres in Forest Grove, built by a team of Puyallup boys under the direction of General O. O. Howard, with a $5,000 federal grant in 1880. The first class, 18 students (14 boys and four girls) all came from Washington State, 17 Puyallups and one Nisqually. By the early 1880s, with increasing appropriations from Congress, the school was looking for a larger site that could accommodate farming. A 171-acre site was chosen in 1885 five miles north of Salem. The first wooden buildings were demolished after a few years as brick structures replaced them. Farming, including animal husbandry, poultry raising and dairy, became the mainstay of the school.

Male and female students were taught geography, history, English, and arithmetic. The boys were also taught agriculture, blacksmithing, wagon-making, electrical engineering, plumbing, shoe and boot manufacturing, tinsmithing, gardening, tailoring, and carpentry. Girls were taught cooking, sewing, painting, nursing, vocal and instrumental music, and

Chapter 9

laundering. The boys grew most of the food that the students consumed, and the girls cooked it (Marino, 1990, 174).

Chemawa maintained 345 acres of farmland by 1905, half of which had been donated by the City of Salem. Pupils and alumni pooled their savings from picking hops to buy 84 acres. The farm also maintained orchards that produced plums, apples, strawberries, blackberries, raspberries, pears, and cherries "in profusion" (Chemawa, 1905, 9). Four literary societies met in the evenings, with public debates governed by parliamentary procedure. On Sundays, attendance at church and Sunday school was mandatory. The football and baseball teams were competitive with many non-Indian schools in southern Oregon. In 1905, Chemawa assembled a large display to celebrate the 100th anniversary of the Lewis and Clark expedition.

In 1905, the school also celebrated its silver (25th) anniversary with a special edition of its weekly newsletter, *The Chemawa American* (7:56, March 3, 1905). This issue included several advertisements from local businesses — grocers, furniture stores, men's clothiers, booksellers, jewelers, bakers, beekeepers, photo studios, and the Northern Pacific Railroad, which maintained a station near the school on its Portland-to-San Francisco line. "Chemawa's beautiful grounds and rose-covered gardens have given the school the name of being the most beautiful in the Indian Service," the newsletter said. "Flowers bloom nearly the whole year round, and the grass is always green, studded with tall firs ... due to the warm, mild climate of Oregon" (Chemawa, 1905, 5). Durning that same year, a hospital was under construction at Chemawa.

Chemawa reported 690 students in 1913 from a wide geographical area, including 175 Alaska native children. By 1922, 70 buildings had spread over 40 acres as the school's land base grew to more than 400 acres. In 1926, the school enrolled more than 1,000 students. In 1927, it became a fully accredited high school, and dropped its elementary grades. During the early 1930s, however, Chemawa nearly closed due to federal funding cuts, but pressure from local political figures and newspapers kept it open, with about 300 students. It remained open after boarding schools in Washington State closed. After the Carlisle school closed, Chemawa became the oldest Indian boarding school in the United States with a record of continuous operation.

Muckleshoot children sometimes ran away from the Chemawa School, walking and hitchhiking home. Sometimes parents hid their six-year-old children to avoid having them taken away. Lawney Reyes (brother of Seattle activist Bernie Whitebear), who attended Chemawa, wrote that by 1950s the school had relaxed prohibitions on the practice of Native cultures:

> I did not experience any harsh restraint against Indian culture or tradition at Chemawa. Generations of Indians before me had already felt the full force of that practice. I learned that in earlier years, speaking the Indian language had been forbidden. White authority had dealt harshly with Indian dancing, singing, and drumming. Students were not allowed to braid their hair or wear any ornaments with Indian design motifs. During my time, efforts to teach the white way were still in force, but attempts to abolish or restrain Indian culture were past. The practice of Indian culture, however, was not encouraged or discussed. (Reyes, 2002, 117)

During the late 1970s, Chemawa built a new campus; most of the original brick buildings were removed. Four buildings that were not destroyed were listed in the National Register of Historic Places in 1992. Today, Chemawa numbers its alumni in the thousands.

THE ST. GEORGE'S INDIAN SCHOOL

The St. George's Indian School was the first educational institution in or near the small town of Milton, near Tacoma, which was first called Mill Town, after its main industry. As the town's residents sought to incorporate, they discovered that the U.S. Post Office would not award a fourth-class office to a town with more than one word in its name. The name thus became "Milton." The St. George's Indian School was endowed in 1878 by Katharine Drexel, an heiress from Philadelphia, who also founded the Catholic religious order that constructed it (Olive, 1982, 2). The school was built mainly to educate Indian children in reading, writing, and agriculture. St. George's was designed to be as self-sufficient as possible. The boys farmed, and the girls, even the youngest, processed food and cooked it. The school enrolled European-American immigrants' children as well as Indians until shortly after 1900, as Milton, in its earliest years, had no schools of its own. They studied side by side through the first eight grades. The whites then went to Stadium High School in Tacoma, and the Native students to Cushman School, until it was closed in 1920. (A hospital by the same name operated on the Puyallup reservation from 1929 to the late 1950s).

The most prominent headmaster of the school in its early days was Father Hylebos,

St. George Indian School c. 1880.
Photo courtesy of Muckleshoot Preservation Program Archives

an immigrant from Belgium, born in 1848, one of the first Catholic missionaries at St. George's. Hylebos was ordained as a priest in 1870, and began his trek to Puget Sound as a divine calling. In addition to the St. George's School, he started hospitals and homes for orphans and destitute women. When people in Tacoma tried to expel Chinese immigrants, Hylebos defended them with a plea for interethnic peace. A local creek named after Hylebos was known as such a rich source of salmon that local people said they could hear them roiling the water during spawning season.

An electric commuter railway, the Interurban, connected Milton with Tacoma and Seattle. It supplied a cheap ride (15 cents, transfers free). Young people were not always told to avoid the train's dangerous charged third rail. A young Native boy, a student at St. George's, was long remembered after he dragged a wet salmon over the third rail on a line, not realizing the current would kill him (Adams, 1948, 12; Olive, 1982, 6).

Many Native elders became dubious about education because of their experiences in boarding schools. They recalled being told that their cultures, languages, and families were not valued, as they lived for years in an atmosphere that repressed the very cultural attributes that had helped their ancestors survive for thousands of years.

The parents of the generation who built Muckleshoot schools had been forced to wear military uniforms, march in ranks, and suffer punishment for speaking their Native languages. At the same time, many children were taken from parents and placed in non-Indian foster homes during the 1950s and 1960s, away from their reservations' extended families, and culture. The Indian Child Welfare Act (ICWA, 25 USC 1901) was adopted in 1978 to deal with these issues. The Muckleshoot Indian Tribe took advantage of the law in 1979, writing its own Youth Code and taking jurisdiction over dependencies involving tribal children.

The Muckleshoot schools were designed as an alternative to public schools, and government boarding schools, part of a widespread movement since the early 1970s among Native peoples across North America that included teaching of American Indian culture to improve overall academic achievement. This was a reaction to a facet of colonialism that dictates what children would learn, and in what cultural framework, as in the boarding school system. When traditional forms of education were destroyed, so were Native societies' methods of raising up leaders. The new systems restore these traditions in a modern context.

PRIDE IN HEAD START

The path to self-determination in education began with the youngest of pupils. The Head Start program, directed by Muckleshoot Virginia Cross, a 1957 Auburn High School graduate, became a point of pride and self-determination on a reservation of about 300 people where by the late 1960s community organization was becoming widespread.

Interest in a Muckleshoot preschool had begun five years before the Head Start program was funded with help from the Saltwater Unitarian Universalist Church in Des Moines, Washington, a suburb south of Seattle. A number of women from several churches were taking part with Muckleshoot women in a quilting circle at which they discussed the fact that Muckleshoot children were lacking preschool skills. These discussions preceded the establishment of a preschool on the reservation with cooperation of the tribal government, the Saltwater Unitarian Church, the Family Life Group of the Seattle Public Schools, the American Friends Service Committee (Quakers), and Erna Gunther, a well-known anthropology professor at the University of Washington. The Muckleshoot Preschool, which enrolled about 30 children a year, meeting in an old Government Services Administration building owned by the Auburn School District, started in 1958 with donations from local churches and volunteer teachers.

Virginia Cross and daughter Ronette, 1959.
Photo courtesy of Muckleshoot Preservation Program Archives

Several churchwomen (Marian Fairbanks, Doreen Johnson, Carolyn McMichael, and Lee Landrud) served as teachers at the school, and enrolled their own children in it. After three years of volunteer efforts, the school received financial support from the Auburn School District. Many Muckleshoot educational leaders assumed their roles as educational activists in that Head Start program. Certification and training through that program became a basis for development of the entire Native-run system of today.

In 1965, Muckleshoot, with about 300 enrolled members, received one of the first two federal Head Start grants for Native Americans (the Navajo, the largest Native nation in the United States, was the other funded program). This has been a point of pride at Muckleshoot for decades, the beginning of education defined and controlled by the tribe. The $24,000

Marie Starr teaching Head Start during the early years. In 2013, she recalled: "We are having lunch and it is Head Start and the other person is Yvonne James. It looks like I have pitchers of milk. At lunch time we taught children how to serve themselves and also to talk about the day's events."
Photo courtesy of Muckleshoot Preservation Program Archives

annual Head Start grant was often placed in jeopardy because of politics in Washington, D.C. For several weeks in 1967, the funds were delayed, as mothers and teachers, according to a report in the Tacoma *News-Tribune*, "ran the program on their own time" (Jeffords, 1968, n.p.).

Parents helped to make the 25 percent non-federal match by volunteering, fundraising and obtaining donations. They held raffles, bake sales, cakewalks, rummage sales and Indian taco sales. Some even raffled off blankets, rugs, beadwork, vests, lamps, horses, cars, bikes, radios and television sets. From the start, Head Start enrolled Muckleshoot children, as well as some from other Native tribes, along with Blacks, Latinos, European-Americans, and Asians. The staff also has long been ethnically mixed.

The Head Start program had a unique requirement: mothers were required to accompany their children to school at least once a week. The mothers worked as teachers' aides, kept the students "at ease," and "picked up an interest in what the children are accomplishing," according to the newspaper report (Jeffords, 1968, n.p.). Robert J. Terrell, principal of Chinook Elementary School, where most of the children went to school after Head Start, told the Tacoma *News-Tribune* that "Prior to the Head Start program, the Muckleshoot children usually were a little behind in their learning, but never in intelligence. Now the situation really is improving and the Indian children are catching up much quicker" (Jeffords, 1968, n.p.).

On April 13, 1967, John Baird of the Auburn Public Schools invited staff and parents to a meeting, and proposed a merger of Head Start programs in Auburn and at Muckleshoot, fearing that without a merger Auburn Head Start would lose its federal funds. "After a heated discussion," according to an account in the first issue of *Muckleshoot News*, "It was decided that only the mothers of both groups would meet again to see what solution could be made" (Brown, 1967, 5). On April 17, the Muckleshoot mothers turned down Baird's proposal. At about the same time, teachers and mothers attended Head Start workshops at Seattle University, March 13, 14, and 15. The preschool students, teachers, and mothers also took a day trip to Seattle where they rode the Monorail to the Seattle Center and ascended the Space Needle, then visited the Woodland Park Zoo.

The Muckleshoots' Head Start program has long been notable for its excellence. In 2000, a federal audit praised it. "I see this as a model program," reported one auditor. "The curriculum is excellent ... the literacy component is powerful ... the staff should be commended for all the work and effort involved in successfully implementing the curriculums." This auditor said that the program's focus on literacy and reading would have long-term effects. "As a result of what you're doing, these kids are going to grow up and make it," he said (Coolidge, 2000, 7). The director and staff were also commended for their efforts towards learning the Muckleshoot language, and for their commitment in providing Muckleshoot culture and language to children. In 2010, new facilities opened with 80 to 90 children between the ages of three and five, continuing one of the oldest early childhood education programs in the state of Washington.

From the beginning, the Muckleshoots utilized a combination of new technology and elders' knowledge to make the schools a cultural conduit, passing traditional dances, arts, and customs to a new generation. Children were taught the "Paddle Dance" (using drainage pipes if no canoe paddles were available). Software was developed to teach the language by computer, creating a dictionary of the Muckleshoot language, "a keyboard with the 45 characters and an audio program that would pronounce words correctly for the user at a touch of a key" (Jung, 1993). Meanwhile, the students learned to sing ancient songs that accompany the picking of berries, fishing, and cooking. Students, having heard old stories, create clay murals that depict them visually. They design dance blankets of canvas (to repel the Northwest's rainfall) and decorate them with painted images.

Nearly forgotten songs have been revived, said Virginia Cross, Muckleshoot Indian Tribal Council chairwoman. "I think if we don't retain it, it will be gone forever" (Pemberton-Butler, 2001). With the songs come memories and reconstruction of history. One teacher who has helped recapture culture has been David Horsley, formerly a Federal Way educator, a non-Indian who gained his knowledge through research. Early curricula that include emphasis on culture, such as traditional arts and the Muckleshoot language, reduce drop-out rates. Roberto Enríquez, a teacher in the Muckleshoot schools, said: "We're about our culture, our language, we're about promoting pride in one's cultural identity," he said. "When people have a healthy identity of themselves and where they came from, I think they're going to be more positive" (Pemberton-Butler, 2001).

A NEW SCHOOL OPENS: A DREAM REALIZED

Ground was broken on a sunny, crisp Friday morning, November 9, 2007, for the Muckleshoots' $40 million K-12 school complex. Children were let out of school as tribal members and dignitaries with ceremonial first shovels assembled on a large vacant pasture near Cooper's Corner. A little less than two years later, early on September 9, 2009, the Muckleshoots moved their school from the community center, where students had gathered for 25 years, to the new 113,000-square-foot building. Teachers, students, and leaders joined local and state dignitaries to celebrate. "This ... has been a dream for decades," said Joseph Martin (Whale, 2009a).

Kindergarten students made a quilt for the elders at a Muckleshoot Tribal School Potlatch in 2005.
Photo by John Loftus, Muckleshoot Monthly

Martin, the Muckleshoot's education director who is Comanche, was born and raised in Western Washington. He graduated with a BA with honors from the University of Washington in international studies, with an emphasis in international trade and investment. He is also an accomplished traditional singer, gourd dancer, and coach of basketball and soccer.

Martin and his wife Toni, daughter Mikayla, and two sons, Marcus and Jordan, lived in Tucson, Arizona, for five years before moving to Muckleshoot in 2002. There, as a Gates Millennium Scholar with the Bill and Melinda Gates Foundation, Martin completed his Master of Arts degree in American Indian Studies with an emphasis in American Indian Education with honors at the University of Arizona in 1999. He then completed all but the dissertation of a PhD in American Indian studies with an emphasis in American Indian education, also at the University of Arizona. During graduate studies, he received the university Outstanding Native American Graduate Academic Award for 2000-2001 and its Dr. Martin Luther King, Jr. Distinguished Leadership Award in 1999 (Martin, 002, 7).

Martin started his career at Muckleshoot as Tribal College's program development coordinator in February 2002. In January 2004 he was promoted to Assistant Tribal Operations Manager for Education. Martin began with 130 employees; by 2012 the department employed 374 people.

Five very busy years after becoming the ATOM-Education, Martin and the Muckleshoot community celebrated the opening of the new Muckleshoot Tribal School. The new complex includes several buildings housing administration and elementary classrooms, a middle school, a high school, and a gymnasium-cafeteria building, as well as a library, computer labs, two gymnasiums, a media production center, occupational education shops, a field for track, football, softball, soccer, and baseball, a children's covered play area, and nature trails.

The school offers an extensive native cultural program, including instruction in the Muckleshoot language, as well as general academics for 400 students from kindergarten through 12th grade. It is funded by the Muckleshoots and the Bureau of Indian Affairs.

Washington State Governor Christine Gregoire, an Auburn High School alumna with

The Muckleshoot Tribal School opened Fall 2009.
Photo courtesy of Muckleshoot Indian Tribe

current Muckleshoot Chairwoman Charlotte Williams (both class of 1965), were present at the school's opening in 2009. "Having a tribal school where classroom instruction can be infused with native culture, the Muckleshoot language and history has been a dream of the tribe for many years, and today that dream becomes a reality. These beautiful buildings, this wonderful campus represent so much more than simply a new structure, much more than just another tribal project," Williams added. "These buildings represent the culmination of years of planning and hard work and steadfast dedication of the past and current tribal council, the past and current school board, the past and current students and their families" (Whale, 2009b).

It is difficult to overstate the eagerness with which the Muckleshoots greeted the opening of the new school. After the new complex was dedicated before an overflow crowd of 600 people, the front page of the *Muckleshoot Monthly*'s September 2009 issue, headlined: "THE DAWN OF A NEW ERA." An editorial on page 2 was headed "A VERY GRAND OPENING." Martin thanked the students, parents, leaders, elders, and other community members for their roles in "our long-held dream that has come to fruition — to have a tribal school where all of our students are provided the tools and skills they need for academic success in a culturally-relevant setting" (Martin, 2010, 1). He continued:

> The grand opening of our new Muckleshoot Tribal School represents the result of decades of carefully measured and calculated community advocacy and planning. This ... has been a dream of the Muckleshoot Community for decades ... and now the dream has officially come to realization. As an educator, I am humbled by the fact that the Muckleshoot Indian Tribe has made education its number-one priority. Muckleshoot has fully embraced its responsibility for successfully educating tribal members and is truly a place where the talk about putting more money into education is being walked. Hard work, perseverance and a "never give up" attitude are all hallmarks of the Muckleshoot Community ... that has increased enrollment capacity from 140 to 500 students — meaning

that right now — the Muckleshoot Indian Tribe has a K-12 school facility that is large enough to hold the vast majority of our school-age tribal members. (Martin, 2009, 17)

Gov. Gregoire hugged Charlotte Williams and extended best wishes: "Back in high school, how many of you actually thought I'd be governor and she'd be chair? Our teachers didn't think that," said Gregoire, evoking laughter. "This is a great day for our children, this is a great day for the Muckleshoot Tribe. The central part of most of our communities is the school. It is the heart and soul of a community, and that's exactly what this school is going to be here — the heart and soul of this community," Gregoire said (Whale, 200b). Auburn *Reporter* staff writer Robert Whale wrote that, "As the governor spoke, the happy squeals of children on the playground could already be heard" (Whale, 2009b).

Higher Education Banquet, Muckleshoot School, 2009.
Photo courtesy of Joseph Martin

Butch Reifert of Mahlum Architects, which played a major role in designing the new educational complex, called upon Muckleshoot elders for advice, and developed a design for the education center that is

... [R]ich in symbolism, referencing the geography of the tribe's land between two rivers as well as the path that children take toward adulthood. The school will also pay tribute to the four seasons. The design of each building in the four-building complex will support tribal identity and traditions. And each building will represent a step in the development of a child, a deliberate hierarchy that brings children into contact with older children and ultimately adults. An exterior fire pit and story circle as well as a freestanding fireplace in the library will support the tribe's oral tradition.

The elementary school building will evoke images of spring — Chinook [salmon], new fawns, first winds, new foliage of greens and yellows — while the middle school building will reference summer — sockeye, fishing, berry picking, dark greens and berry reds. The high school building will reflect autumn — coho, fishing, hunting, and the fall colors of red, yellow and orange. The fourth building will include a commons, library and gymnasium that can accommodate large potlatches or community celebrations. These public spaces will convey images of steelhead, storytelling, dancing and the winter colors of smoked salmon, dark greens and browns. All public spaces will open onto a central courtyard that looks toward Mount Rainier and the Cascade foothills. The buildings will be timber-framed and clad with cedar, reflecting the tribe's tradition of building with wood (Reifert, 2008).

On June 15, 2010, more than 60 students and community members gathered to celebrate the launch of Muckleshoot Tribal College's magazine *The Muckleshoot Review* a collection of prose and poetry edited by Alicia Woods and Northwest Indian College students, including Elise Bill-Gerrish, Lannessa Brown, Richelle

Brown, Danny Leonard, Chadrick MaGee, Ester McCluskey, Lisa Miller, Anthony Nichols, Deborah Saluskin, Leo Sanchez, Kristopher Spiker, Mary Starr, and Sidney Williams, Jr. The launch of the magazine was partly the result of a grant for Woods' writing-instructor position by the Gates Foundation and Lumina, from which she provided workshops and individual instruction for students at all levels. Replacement funding was being sought.

The Muckleshoot Tribal College also maintains curricular relationships with the Northwest Indian College (on the Lummi reservation near Bellingham), Evergreen State University, near Olympia, and Antioch College's branch in Seattle, each of which offers course work related to Native American language, literature, and history. The Evergreen State University program offers a liberal arts BA degree. Antioch's program also serves teachers studying Native American communities, values, and traditions.

In 2010, the school complex added an Early Childhood Education Center, housing the Muckleshoot Birth to Three, Head Start, and Child Care Development Fund (CCDF) Programs with eight toddler/pre-K classrooms, one infant room and support-service areas. Opening the new 20,000-square-foot Early Childhood Education Center October 1, 2010, Virginia Cross was assisted by eight Head Start pupils as she read the names of people who had played a key role in Muckleshoot education of young children, reaching all the way back to the first Head Start class in 1966. At the opening, several adults, including three of the Tribal Council's nine members, recalled what they had learned in Head Start. Marie Starr recalled that the program had started in an old garage. Lessons were basic: each Christmas the children used old work socks to make monkey dolls ("Early," 2010, 1).

Muckleshoot Early Childhood Education Center from the air.
Photo by John Loftus, Muckleshoot Monthly

The Muckleshoot Birth to Three Program provides a safe, nurturing environment that promotes the language, motor, social, emotional, adaptive, and cognitive development of young children. The children have the opportunity to explore their Native American heritage through drumming, exposure to the Muckleshoot language and participation in cultural activities, as well as sports.

CULTURAL EXCHANGES WORLDWIDE

The Muckleshoot tribal schools exchange cultural visits with indigenous peoples worldwide. Cultural exchange with the Maoris of New Zealand went both ways. They first came to Muckleshoot, where students learned some of their songs and dances, before the Maoris embarked on a tour of the American West, performing on reservations as far away as South Dakota. The New Zealanders came again years later. In the meantime, three Muckleshoot young people had an unforgettable experience in 2007. Neil Foulkes, his sister Hannah, and Eric Pacheco traveled to New Zealand under a special cultural exchange program funded by the Tribal Council to learn the culture of the Maori.

Another visitor was one of Chile's best-known poets, Elicura Chihuailaf, a Mapuche, who has used his many volumes of prize-winning verse to highlight the beauty of his Native cultures and thus help to preserve them. Chihuailaf was escorted by diplomats from the Chilean Consulate in Seattle. Roberto Maestas, longtime executive director of Seattle's El Centro de la Raza, served as his interpreter.

SCHOLARSHIPS CHANGE LIVES

By 2002, the Muckleshoots were converting $1 million a year worth of casino profits and other business income into college scholarships for 132 students. Behind every one was a personal story. Lynda Mapes of the Seattle Times described Denise Dillon, the first member of her family to enter college, who became the first Muckleshoot to earn advanced degrees from large institutions of higher learning on the East Coast of the United States. Behind her was a determined mother, Cathleen Schultz, whose education had ended in the eighth grade, who decided that college was not a question of "if," for her daughter, but "when."

The odds were long. In Washington State, during the late 1990s, when Dillon began her college career, about 4 percent of Native Americans earned graduate or professional degrees (Mapes, November 3, 2002). Attending Western Washington University in Bellingham, on a full-ride Muckleshoot scholarship, she earned a bachelor's degree. Then she completed a master's in health sciences at Duke University and, in 2002, a physician assistant's surgical residency program through the Yale School of Medicine.

Dillon's mother, as a child, had used empty milk jugs to collect drinking water on the site that now houses the Muckleshoot Casino. Mapes wrote:

> Once a week, the water went on the woodstove for bathing by the light of a kerosene lamp. "When we grew up there was no running water, no lights," Schultz said. "We didn't think of ourselves as poor. We had the woods, the family, the church — it was fun. We didn't know we were poor, until we left the reservation." Schultz, 54, never made it to high school. She cleaned houses, managed restaurants, and later dealt blackjack at the tribal casino. (Mapes, November 3, 2002)

All her life, Schultz was an avid reader who shared her passion with her daughter. Denise was seriously injured by a drunk driver when she was 17 years old, concluding her senior year wheelchair-bound. "After bone grafts, surgery and an assortment of rods and pins in both legs, Dillon accepted her diploma from Yelm High on her feet," Mapes wrote (November 3, 2002).

Raised in a tradition of modesty and cooperation, Dillon found Yale's competitive atmosphere daunting. "You have to be much more aggressive, and that is not something we are taught. We are taught to cooperate and work as a team," she said. "Surgery was very different, very competitive, very cutthroat. That's not the type of person I am, but I had to hold my own" (Mapes, November 3, 2002).

Mapes wrote:

> It's a big step up, [Muckleshoot chairman John] Daniels said, from when there was only one car per neighborhood on the reservation and tribal members took turns pushing it through rutted mud driveways to get to the grocery store. He remembers having outhouses, and how the septic tanks were dropped off in tribal members' yards by the federal government but never installed. "We used to play on them," Daniels said. He looks at Dillon with pride and affection, saying simply, "She has done great." A tan baseball cap Dillon brought him, emblazoned YALE, sits on the shelf above his [Daniels']

desk. It's displayed along with his other prized possessions, a totem of mainstream success not only for Dillon, but for the entire tribe. (Mapes, November 3, 2002)

By 2007, more than 700 students held Muckleshoot scholarships (Annual Report 2007, 73). In 2008, 564 students were on scholarships. The program was producing long-term results as well. The annual graduation dinner in 2008 recognized five students who had earned master's degrees in the previous years, as well as several others who had completed college programs (Annual Report, 2009).

During 2012, the Muckleshoots extended scholarship aid to Native American college students in Washington State generally, under a higher education scholarship program at 12 state universities, community colleges and technical colleges. "This new program reflects the Muckleshoot Tribe's strong commitment to education," said Muckleshoot Tribal Council Chairwoman Virginia Cross. "This is especially important at a time we see the cost of higher education increasing at the same time state support is declining. The Muckleshoot Tribe views education as a life-long pursuit," said Cross ("Muckleshoot Tribe Establishes," 2012). The program provided approximately $3 million during the 2012 school year for 80 scholarships.

NEW CURRICULA REACH OFF-RESERVATION PUBLIC SCHOOLS

By 2002, curricula based on Native American cultures were being used in many Washington State public schools with sizable numbers of Indian students, where textbooks with stereotypical images of Indians had once

Sherri Foreman's 6th Grade class, Muckleshoot School, at White River, June 10, 2005.
Photo courtesy of Joseph Martin

been used. At Chinook Elementary, in the Auburn School District (built on land ceded by the Muckleshoots), children from 31 Native tribes and nations have responded so favorably to culture-based education that reading scores jumped from much below to at or above state averages within two years after a reading curriculum designed with the help of elders and spiritual leaders living on the Muckleshoot reservation was adopted. Having been classified before the 2002–2003 school year as a failing school because of its students' low standardized test scores, Chinook Elementary's teachers and administrators watched test scores race upward. At Chinook, more than 100 Native students were staying after school four days a week for intensive reading, not because they have been told to, but because they asked for it.

The supplemental curriculum develops writing and reading skills with three sets of activities: the drum, the canoe, and the hunt. Native elders, parents and other community people also have been invited into classrooms as teachers lead lessons with 22 storybooks illustrated and written by Native people in the Northwest that are shared through a state-sponsored program with other schools that have large numbers of Native students.

The new focus on Native culture is a far cry from the curricula of boarding schools, with their emphasis on assimilation into a European-dominated melting pot. A generation or two ago, public schools used the same model, and Native young people often were bullied in stereotypical terms — so much, at times, that many preferred boarding schools.

There they lived and learned with other Native American students, as degrading as the experience was, as their hair was cut, their names were changed, and the languages of their parents were forbidden. In public schools, "The people called us terrible names," said Sharon LaClair, 53, a Muckleshoot who grew up in Auburn amidst billboards covered with graffiti reading "Dirty Mucks," and other slurs. "At the boarding school I met my own people. People with the same skin, the same hair color, I came out of my shell" (Mapes, November 5, 2004).

Parents silently shouldered the racism, stereotypical textbooks, and ignorance of their cultures in all of the schools. Thus the enthusiasm at Muckleshoot for education *their* way. Lynda Mapes described the new atmosphere at Chinook Elementary in the *Seattle Times Pacific Northwest Magazine*.

> "... When the kids from Chinook take the stage to perform, their parents, relatives, snowy-haired elders and tribal-council members are there to applaud along with the superintendent for the school district, many of the kids' teachers and their principal ... as kids from the fourth-grade culture class perform a traditional song, with its dignified dance, and drumming soft as the beating of their mother's heart. The audience stills, as if to soak up the kids' moment on stage." (Mapes, November 5, 2004)

"So much of it is the self-esteem thing, feeling good about themselves," said Dennis Grad, who was principal at Chinook before moving to a similar job at a middle school in 2003. Grad recognized each student at Chinook by name, and stood at the main door to greet them each day. The best students were rewarded with lunch in his office — a new curriculum and a new attitude.

Chapter 9

Virginia Cross, with beaded purse.
Photo by John Loftus, Muckleshoot Monthly

VIRGINIA CROSS'S ROLE IN EDUCATIONAL REVIVAL

Like many of today's Native elders, Virginia Cross came from humble beginnings, and used hard work, determination, vision, and compassion, to help raise her people from poverty.

"We didn't have much," she recalled of her childhood. "We didn't have electricity or running water; but we didn't feel that we were poor. Everybody else lived the same way we did" ("Virginia Cross," 2012, 1). One of her jobs was to fetch water from the small stream that flowed past their home. She and her four sisters all slept in the same bed.

Cross, a longtime member (and often chair) of the Muckleshoot Tribal Council, has been challenging the status quo for more than 40 years. She was part of a pioneering group of Native Americans (mainly women) who helped transform Indian education in a context of self-determination, on a nation-wide scale, and as one of many facets of the Muckleshoots' dramatic revival. Starting in the 1960s, Cross and her colleagues throughout the United States fought for recognition of Indian education and forged a network of programs that are now used in many public school districts that have significant Native American population, as well as in the growing numbers of reservation schools built by Native peoples.

Cross graduated from Auburn High School in 1957. She was later one of the women who began the much-heralded Head Start on the reservation during the 1960s, and its first director. She also served as Director of Indian Education for the Auburn School District for 22 years. In addition, she coordinated the Auburn School District's Muckleshoot Re-Entry Program, to bring young people who had dropped out back to school. The National Congress of American Indians selected Cross as 1998 National Elder of the Year, to which she replied: "I'm really not that important" (Bartley, 1999). On her 60th birthday, Cross was feted with drumming and singing in the Muckleshoot language, a fitting celebration for a woman who fought so hard to revive it. Today the language is taught not only in tribal curricula, but also in the Auburn public schools.

Cross is known for giving students what they need on a very personal level: "Whatever it takes to motivate students — transportation, medical help, clothing or help with homework — she finds a way," said Auburn Superintendent of Schools Linda Cowan. If a student misses school, Cross goes to his or her house and finds out why. And thanks to Cross's involvement, the number of Muckleshoot students graduating from high school "'has increased tenfold,"' Cowan said (Bartley, 1999). Noreen Milne remembered her aunt Virginia advocating education on all fronts even as a young woman: "Growing up, I remember her going to college all the time and working during the day. She was the one who started the JOM [Johnson-O'Malley] program with the native students." Johnson-O'Malley is a federal government program that provides basic school supplies and clothing for Native students. "When I was in grade school she would arrange for all Muckleshoot students to purchase shoes. She would also hand out new school coats once a year," Milne recalled (Milne, 2002, 4).

In 2012, Virginia Cross was inducted into the Auburn High School Hall of Fame — only the sixth inductee in the school's 106-year history. The other five AHS Hall of Fame inductees are Gordon Hirabayashi, a winner of the Presidential Medal of Freedom, Dick Scobee, a NASA astronaut, Christine Gregoire, Washington State governor, and Judy Roland and Frank Warnke, Washington State legislators. She was inducted during the school's graduation ceremony June 15 at Auburn Memorial Stadium.

Virginia Cross greets President Barack Obama.
Photo courtesy of Muckleshoot Monthly

REFERENCES

2003 Program Update; Muckleshoot Tribal Administration. Auburn, WA: Muckleshoot Indian Tribe, 2003.

Adams, Vera S. "Early History of Milton, Washington." Milton, WA: unpublished, 1948. Manuscript in City of Milton archives.
[www.cityofmilton.net/file_viewer.php?id=2095]

Annual Report: Muckleshoot Tribal Council, January 20, 2003. Auburn, WA: Muckleshoot Indian Tribe, 2003.

Annual Report for 2007: Muckleshoot Indian Tribe. Auburn, WA: Muckleshoot Indian Tribe, 2007.

Annual Report, 2009: Muckleshoot Indian Tribe. Auburn, WA: Muckleshoot Indian Tribe, January 19, 2009.

Bartley, Nancy. "Educator Honored for Tribal Activism." *Seattle Times*, June 17, 1999.
[http://community.seattletimes.nwsource.com/archive/?date=19990617&slug=2966998]

Brown, Virginia. "Pre-School Controversy." *Muckleshoot News* 1:1, May 1967, 5.

Chemawa American, Anniversary Number, 7:56 (March 3, 1905). Copy in Muckleshoot Preservation Program Archives.

Coolidge, Jane. "Head Start Impresses Federal Audit Team." *Muckleshoot Monthly*, July 2000, 7.

"Early Childhood Education Center Celebrates Grand Opening." *Muckleshoot Monthly*, October 2010, 1.

"Enumclaw School District Extends Agreement with Muckleshoot Tribal School." *Enumclaw Courier-Herald*, May 19, 2010.
[http://www.courierherald.com/news/94273529.html]

"Enumclaw Schools Native American Program Receives Funding from Tribe." *Muckleshoot Monthly*, July 1, 2007, 1, 3.

Jeffords, Edd. "Muckleshoot Preschool Prepares Tots for Burgeoning Education." Tacoma *News-Tribune*, May 12, 1968, n.p.

Jung, Helen E. "Computers, 'Canoes' Pass On Traditions — Muckleshoot School Brings History to Life." *Seattle Times*, May 10, 1993.
[http://community.seattletimes.nwsource.com/archive/?date=19930510&slug=1700545]

Lazzar, Delilah. "'Broken Chains' Shares Maori Culture." *Muckleshoot Monthly*, February 2001, 6.

Mapes, Lynda V. "Washington Tribes Invest Casino Proceeds by Sending Members to College." *Seattle Times*, November 3, 2002.
[http://community.seattletimes.nwsource.com/archive/?date=20021103&slug=yale03m]

Mapes, Lynda V. "Teaching the Teachers: In a New Kind of Indian Education, Lessons for Us All." *Seattle Times, Pacific Northwest Magazine*, November 5, 2004.
[http://community.seattletimes.nwsource.com/archive/?date=20041105&slug=pacific-pindianed07]

Marino, Cesare. "History of Western Washington Since 1846," in Wayne Suttles, Ed. *Handbook of North American Indians: Northwest Coast.* Vol. 7. In William C. Sturtevant, General Ed. *Handbook of North American Indians.* Washington, D.C.: Smithsonian Institution, 1990, 169-179.

Martin, Joseph J. "Dear Members of the Muckleshoot Community." *Muckleshoot Monthly*, September 2009, 17.

Martin, Joseph J. "Graduations 2010: MIT Takes a Giant Step Forward." *Muckleshoot Monthly*, July 2010, 1.

Martin, Joseph J. "Graduations 2011: MIT Enjoys Another Excellent Graduation Season." *Muckleshoot Monthly*, August 2011, P-1.

Martin, Joseph J. "Joseph Martin Hired [as] Program Development Coordinator for Tribal College." *Muckleshoot Monthly*, April 15, 2002, 7.

Milne, Noreen. "My Aunty, Virginia Cross." *Muckleshoot Monthly*, April 15, 2002, 4.

"Muckleshoot Celebrates Educational Achievement." *Muckleshoot Monthly*, June 15, 2002, 1.

"Muckleshoot Tribe Establishes Higher Education Scholarship Program: $175,000 Pledged to Washington Universities, Community and Technical Colleges." Muckleshoot Tribal e-Newsletter, June 2012, 1.

"Native Poet from Chile Visits Tribal School; A Visit from Elicura Chihuailaf, Mapuche Poet, of Temuco, Chile." *Muckleshoot Monthly*, November 15, 2002.

Noel, Patricia Slettvet and Virginia Cross. *Muckleshoot Indian History*. Auburn, WA: Auburn Public School District No. 408, 1980.

Olive, Shirley. "Milton, Washington: The Early Days." Historic Tacoma, Instructor: Chris Cherbas, July 1982. Manuscript in City of Milton archives.
[www.cityofmilton.net/file_viewer.php?id=1668]

Pemberton-Butler, Lisa. "Huge Day for Muckleshoot School: Its First Two Grads." *Seattle Times*, June 19, 2001.
[http://community.seattletimes.nwsource.com/archive/?date=20010619&slug=muckleshoot19m]

Reifert, Butch. "Tribal Schools Expand Role Preserving Native Cultures: New Designs Focus on Symbolism, Tribal Rituals and Eco-Friendly Features." *Daily Journal of Commerce* [Seattle], August 28, 2008.
[http://www.djc.com/news/co/11203987.html]

Reyes, Lawney. *White Grizzly Bear's Legacy: Learning to be Indian.* Seattle: University of Washington Press, 2002.

"Tribal School Receives Accreditation." *Muckleshoot Monthly*, June 2011, 1.

"Virginia Cross Inducted into Auburn H.S. Hall of Fame." *Muckleshoot Monthly*, June 2012, 1.

Whale, Robert. "Tribe Opens Doors to New, Expansive School." *Auburn Reporter*, September 9, 2009. (2009a) [http://www.pnwlocalnews.com/south_king/aub/news/58196072.html]

Whale, Robert. "Dream Comes to Life for Tribe: New School Officially Opens." *Auburn Reporter*, September 10, 2009. (2009b) [http://www.pnwlocalnews.com/south_king/aub/news/58207197.html]

Chapter 10

Muckleshoot Language Revival: Learning bəqəlšuɬucid

Muckleshoot Language Revival: Learning bəqəlšuɫucid

One of the boarding schools' primary missions was to obliterate Native American culture, and banning language was key. Students were forced to speak English exclusively. This was militantly enforced monolingualism — an effort, as boarding school founder William Henry Pratt put it in a paper he presented at the 19th Annual Conference of Charities and Correction, Denver, in 1892, to "kill the Indian in him, [and] save the man." That is, kill the culture, assimilate the people. Native people living on their own terms was not permissible at that time. The curriculum was designed to sever cultural transmission from one generation to another, and thereby kill it.

Many Muckleshoot youth spoke their native language when they entered boarding or public schools. Elders such as John Daniels, Sr. and Iola Bill did not speak any English when they attended these schools early in the twentieth century. The speaking of Indian languages was punished. During that time, many parents did not want their own children to go through what they had experienced, so they chose not to teach their children a language that had been targeted for elimination by the federal government.

Present-day Native education is reversing that process. Reclaiming language is important to reconstruction of culture and educational systems. Willard Bill, Sr. the Muckleshoots' historian until his death late in 2007, was saddened by the fact that he could not speak the language, but was encouraged by its revival. "My mother really understood the language, but then she went

Donna Starr singing.
Photo by John Loftus, Muckleshoot Monthly

to boarding school, and, of course, the Indian language was not allowed. That's when the cycle was broken," he said (Lacitis, 2005). Erik Lacitis of the *Seattle Times* wrote that "Bill takes solace in hearing small success stories about preserving the language. He had heard that some kids were using it to talk on the playground, he said. 'Day-to-day conversation. That's really a breakthrough.'" (Lacitis, 2005).

The Sapir-Whorf hypothesis states that language is the vessel of culture. If the language dies, culture dies. Some ideas exist only in language. Donna Starr, who has taught the language to many Muckleshoot young people, said: "I tell my classes [that] the language is in your blood. It's already in your tongue, but your ears haven't [yet] heard it. It's sleeping, but it is waking up. By hearing it, the language comes back ... and makes you a stronger person" (Waterman, 2002).

LANGUAGE BASICS

The Muckleshoot language is a dialect of Puget Sound Salish (Lushootseed), one of the twenty-three languages in the Salishan family. Varieties of Lushootseed are spoken throughout the Puget Sound country from the Skagit River Valley to Olympia. The word "Lushootseed" itself is anglicized from root words indicating the region surrounding the body of water that Anglo-Americans named Puget Sound and "language of." No collective name exists in their own language for Lushootseed-speaking people (Suttles and Lane, 1990, 501). "Coast Salish" is an anthropological invention. Marian Smith wrote that the languages of Puget South Salish from the Snohomish southward were mutually intelligible (1940, 20). The entire range of the fourteen Coast Salish languages (northward across Vancouver Island), however, were about as different as English is from German (Suttles, 2008, 60).

Although each Puget Sound tribe or nation has its own dialect, most of them can be understood by speakers of the others with minimal study. A northern dialect is spoken by the Snohomish, Skagit, Sauk-Suiattle, Kikiallus and Swinomish; speakers of a southern dialect include the Sahewamish, Nisqually, Steilacoom, Puyallup, Suquamish, Duwamish, Snoqualmie, Skykomish, and Muckleshoot. Franz Boas, the noted anthropologist, described the Salish language family, as did Erna Gunther and Viola Garfield, who studied and recorded the Muckleshoot language.

Tens of thousands of people spoke Lushootseed's many dialects during the 1770s. The language that remains today is much less complex than its historical form. As populations declined due to disease, immigrant pressure, elimination of speakers through educational assimilation, alcoholism, and other reasons, Native societies' linguistic memory was reduced, restricting the languages' vocabulary and grammatical complexity. Entire dialects vanished. The roughly 20 dialects of Lushootseed in historic time have been reduced to about 12 today, and some of them have become endangered as old speakers pass away. (The languages have also added words from English, of course.)

In 1996, instruction in the language became mandatory in Muckleshoot schools. "The elders are passing away, and we must try to retain our original language," said Virginia Cross, chairwoman of the Muckleshoot Tribal Council (Gong, 1996). At that time, some elders, including Blodgett (Harold Moses) still spoke (and told jokes) in the language. Arthur Ballard had created his own linguistic orthography for the language as he studied it at Muckleshoot. Because it was not standard, his system was not widely used by other linguists.

Audrey Leach, left, studies the Muckleshoot language at the Muckleshoot Tribal College.
Photo courtesy of Greg Gilbert / The Seattle Times

Studies of Puget Sound Salish have been published, the oldest dating to the nineteenth century. George Gibbs published *The Dictionary of the Niskwali Indian Language* by 1877. The language had no widely available written form until 1976, however, when Thomas Hess, linguistics professor at the University of Victoria, British Columbia published *The Dictionary of Puget [Sound] Salish*. *The Lushootseed Dictionary*, compiled by Dawn Bates, Hess, and Vi Hilbert, was updated in 1994 from the earlier edition by Hess. The language was recorded during the 1960s and 1970s with internationally known phonetic symbols, led initially by Hess, who was aided by a small group of Native elders as he compiled the first Lushootseed dictionary.

Any language illustrates what is important in its culture. For example, regional Native peoples' languages have several words, a dozen or more, for salmon and trout. "Salmon were so very important to their way of life," said Hess. "They would refer to the different species, sex, degree of maturity, times of the year they returned, whether they came back on schedule or out of schedule" (Lacitis, 2005). The language lives on in many place names. Many locations in the Puget Sound area have the suffix "mish" — e.g., Snohomish, Suquamish, Duwamish and Sammamish — which means "people of [a place]" in Lushootseed, signifying the homeland of a certain group, usually along a river. "Puyallup" means curving or winding river; the Puyallup River winds and curves into Commencement Bay in the City of Tacoma. "Puy" refers to a bend or curve. "Up" is what remains of the ancient suffice "aps" which means river. The syllable in the middle (al) joins the beginning and ending segments of the word. The Puyallup people are, therefore, "the people of the winding river."

Aside from place names, European-American immigration and assimilating effects of a foreign educational system nearly eliminated the Muckleshoot language. In some cases, only words and phrases remained, but full-scale fluency became very rare. The most fluent speakers are the eldest Muckleshoots who learned to speak at home with parents and extended family. Just as language revival became important, many of these elders are passing away. A documentary, *Muckleshoot: A People and Their Language*, was produced in 2000, which contains interviews of several Muckleshoot people, describing loss of language during the twentieth century and the later revival. In 2001 the film was exhibited at the National Indian Film Festival in San Francisco.

TEACHING THE LANGUAGE

The Muckleshoot designed their schools to include instruction focused on traditional culture, language included. Eva (King George) Jerry, who taught language for 20 years prior to her passing in 1992, at age 77, led instruction. She was one of the elders who raised the language literacy level in the schools. She also passed on lifelong devotion to language revival to her daughter Donna (Jerry) Starr and granddaughter Roberta "Birdie" Lynn (Starr) Pierce.

One of the best known language teachers, Birdie passed away of pulmonary embolism on September 28, 2009, at Valley Medical Center in Renton, Washington, at age 35, 10 days after she lost twins, Kylee and Reggie, in childbirth. Birdie's greatest passion in life, aside from her family, was the culture and language of her Muckleshoot people. Following the example of her mother and grandmother, both known by the title *Kiyah* (esteemed grandmother) Birdie was a keeper of the Muckleshoot language much of her life. She also taught children and

Eva Jerry.
Photo courtesy of Virginia Cross

Birdie Starr-Pierce (right) and son Harvey Starr.
Photo by John Loftus, Muckleshoot Monthly

community members other traditions, such as drum making and cedar weaving. Each year, Birdie conducted a language camp. She also raised her children to speak in the language from birth.

Muckleshoot teachers started with students who had some knowledge of the language, emphasizing its use in everyday life, making it a useful, living realm of expression. For example, when a person bought a loaf of bread he or she was taught to practice the Native language, even if doing so required extra time and effort.

"Everybody loved her," said Pat Noel Fleming, a teacher who worked with Mrs. Jerry at Chinook Elementary School in Auburn, very close to the reservation, with many Muckleshoot pupils. "She was *Kiyah* to the whole school. Kids loved to go to her. It wasn't just a class, they were talking to their grandmother."

She started because she knew her language was dying, and she didn't want it lost" (Lane, 1992).

Mrs. Jerry was born on the Muckleshoot reservation and heard only the Muckleshoot language at home until age six, when she was sent to a Bureau of Indian Affairs boarding school on the Tulalip reservation, north of Seattle. "We had to learn English fast or we would get in trouble," she told Ann Strosnider of the *Auburn Daily Globe-News* (1985, 1). Jerry and her sisters spoke the native language on the sly, however. Once caught, the sisters were spanked. Even though Jerry was punished for using the Muckleshoot language and forced to speak English, "she remembered the language," said Virginia Cross, her niece (Lane, 1992).

Jerry first taught the language to her grandchildren. Then she was asked to teach summer classes in the Auburn schools. Finally, she began teaching half-time during the school year at Chinook Elementary School, in Auburn, and at the Muckleshoot Tribal School. Jerry started teaching at a time when the number of speakers could be counted on one hand, and all of them were elderly. She also worked with University of British Columbia scholars to develop the first written version of the Muckleshoot language.

As she taught, Jerry's vocabulary grew as words came back to her. In 1985, only two or three Muckleshoot elders retained enough of the language to converse in it (Strosnider, 1985, 1). That same year, at age 71, Jerry received the Elder of the Year award from the National Indian Education Association, for teaching Muckleshoot language and culture at Chinook Elementary.

More than 400 family members, friends, and others attended a funeral service for Jerry in the Muckleshoot Tribal School Gymnasium after she passed away April 16, 1992. She was buried at the White Lake Cemetery on April 22. An account in the *Valley Daily News* said that Jerry "made her final trek to the land of her forefathers as storm clouds blew over the reservation." She was buried in a simple wooden casket inscribed "Kiyah." "She was a grandmother to all the Muckleshoots," said Virginia Cross. "Everybody called her that" (Bond, 1992, A-6). Her casket was carried into the Muckleshoot Shaker Church in a dense drizzle.

Gilbert King George, Jerry's eldest son, gave away her personal items to family and friends. Items not given away were burned. All photos of Jerry were removed for a year, in Shaker tradition. She was the widow of Donald Jerry. Survivors included seven children, Henry King George, Gilbert King George, Pete Jerry, Donna Starr (who carried on her work in language restoration), Mary Ross, Theresa Moses, and Frank Jerry, all of whom lived in the Auburn area.

EXPANDING LANGUAGE LESSONS

Eva Jerry's work continued as language instruction expanded at Muckleshoot. In 1994, the Muckleshoots were among the first eight Native nations and tribes to receive funds from the Administration for Native Americans' new Native Language Preservation Program. The grant of $373,253 over three years from the Department of Health and Human Services Administration for Native Americans (ANA) funded the Whulshootseed Language Preservation Program, including the archiving of the language with computer programs. The 1995 Muckleshoot Tribal Council annual report included a children's section with excerpts of basic phrases. The language was being taught to adults of all ages as well, as part of school curricula.

Valerie Bellack.
Photo by John Loftus, Muckleshoot Monthly

By 1996, a first book of five planned volumes for the preservation project had been assembled. Audiotapes were completed as well. The language was being archived digitally, and tapes were being acquired from local sources, such as the King County Library and the University of Washington's Burke Museum. Songs were transcribed as well. Courses were being held for 15 to 20 students each. Muckleshoot language place names compiled by T. T. Waterman were being put into a database with English translations ("Our Children," 1997, 28-29).

The revival of canoe journeys beginning in 1989 also provided aid to recovery of the language. Valerie Bellack, coordinator of the Muckleshoot Language Program, recalled the

Muckleshoots' hosting of the 2006 journey with fondness as a cultural event, having watched "the protocol speeches and dance performances in the language at the canoe hosting at Sand Point ... None of this could have been possible without the assistance of all of the language teachers ... and community effort" (2007 Guide, 2007, 82). Eileen Richardson, working in early childhood education, gained considerable proficiency in the language and, after a lengthy process, was selected to serve as the overall head of the Muckleshoot Language Program. In March 2014, the Language Program staff was composed of Richardson, Morgan Sohappy, and Mary Ross, Jr.

Since 1997, several people have been involved in teaching the Muckleshoot language. The Muckleshoot Tribal School hired Bernedette Starr and Marie Johnson, both of whom worked with students' fluency. Starr had learned the language from her mother.

From time to time, the Muckleshoot language "doctor," Doris Allen, even made house calls. In June 2001, the *Muckleshoot Monthly* published a notice:

> The Language Program is starting a new project to teach the language to community members in their homes. We are experimenting with this idea to see if our Indian people will be more willing to learn their language if it is taught in the familiar setting of their homes. We want to teach the basic communication commands that you would normally use with family members in the home, and give you the opportunity to use what you learn. Please call Valerie Bellack at the Muckleshoot Tribal College. ("Doris Allen," 2001, 4)

The Muckleshoot language also has been set in type, employing a special font called

Donna Starr.
Photo by John Loftus, Muckleshoot Monthly

Fontootseed. Starr and Johnson, lifelong residents of the Muckleshoot reservation, were instrumental in its development, which is based on international phonetics, and is appropriate for all Puget Sound Native languages. Following adoption of the font, more people began teaching the language at Muckleshoot, including Marie Johnson, Doris Allen, Theresa Jerry, Roberta "Birdie" Starr, Tami Cooper, Nancy Jo Bob, Eileen Richardson, Morgan Sohappy, Autumn Judge, and Teresa Allen.

Donna Starr told a story to Willard Bill, Sr. May 24, 2005, describing how when her mother passed away there was a giveaway during which family members distributed possessions. She chose five books written in the Muckleshoot language because they meant so much to her. She made hundreds of copies that she used for instruction. The Muckleshoot government also made available $81,000 to develop a language curriculum. Starr recruited students and had as many as 100 people in her classes. She also taught at Olympic Middle School. She has been very successful promoting language, and continues her instruction at

Muckleshoot Tribal College, using a language lab built for that purpose.

The Washington State Board of Education during January 2003 approved a three-year pilot program for indigenous language teachers, which extended full privileges to Native educators in public schools, including teaching certification (2004 Program Update, 2004, 22). In February 2003, Harold Moses, one of the last fluent speakers of the language, passed away. "His gentle spirit, his warm smile and words of encouragement to me will be greatly missed," wrote Valerie Bellack, who was working with the language preservation program (2004 Program Update, 2004, 22).

Also, during February 2003, Donna Starr and Marie Johnson initiated a language class in the Muckleshoot Seniors Building. They put the word out, expecting a few students, but got 37, "standing room only … grandparents with grandchildren, parents with children, and aunts and uncles!" ("2004 Program Update," 21). The age range was two to 67 years of age. Soon the Tribal Council found some money to pay them for two evening classes per week, and they began with the basics: introductions, counting, animals' names, food, clothing, and other "words of the house" ("2004 Program Update," 2004, 21). A compact disc was prepared and more instructors were recruited. Jackets were presented to "Keepers of the Whulshootseed Language," and high-school credit was awarded for learning it. By August 2004, when the third and final year of its grant ended, the Language Program had compiled an updated dictionary.

Faith Minthorn, 19, one of the students in the language class, is an enrolled Yakama, but with family background among the Muckleshoots. She used words and fragments of Muckleshoot language words with a nephew, who was two years of age, "Little words, like 'animals' and 'sit down,' 'stand up.'" That's

Ellen "Bena" Williams, 81, was honored by the Muckleshoot Tribal College for being the last one on the Muckleshoot Reservation who can fully understand and speak the Muckleshoot language.
Photo courtesy of Muckleshoot Monthly

how she practices her language skills, she said. "I enjoy being part of bringing our culture back to life" (Lacitis, 2005). Even today, the language evolves to encompass new technology and experiences. "Refrigerator" is translated as "by means of making things cold." "Stove" is translated as "making things with fire" (Lacitis, 2005).

At age 90 in 2014, Ellen Williams (who is known as "Bena") is the eldest member of the tribe as well as the oldest living speaker of the Muckleshoot language, "with its clicking and consonants with popping sounds, is so vastly different from English" (Lacitis, 2005). Bena — no one knows her as "Ellen" — is a

Snoqualmie who has been living with the Muckleshoots since 1945 when her parents moved to Auburn. Bena is a cultural treasure who has long mentored teachers in the reservation school, and is a major contributor in language revival at Muckleshoot.

The children in Head Start and the Virginia Cross Educational Center have found many ways to increase their vocabularies in the Muckleshoot language. They practiced at school, of course, with songs, counting, learning names of animals and body parts, family members, greetings, partings, and colors. They also take field trips to the Muckleshoots' shellfishery on Vashon Island and used "words of the beach." They gather at Donna Starr's house for breakfast, and afterwards tour the local flora, looking for "Indian medicines."

"Without the language," wrote Donna Starr in the *Muckleshoot Monthly*, "We are just

Muckleshoot Tribe teens meet four days a week at the Muckleshoot Tribal College to learn the language. Teacher Donna Starr (left) learned the language from her mother. She finishes the class with a drumming ceremony.
Photo courtesy of Greg Gilbert / The Seattle Times

postids with brown skin" (Starr, 2008, 8). "Postid" is the Muckleshoot language rendering of "Bostons," the word used for the earliest non-Indian colonizers of the Pacific Northwest, who had sailed to present-day Seattle from that city.

Eileen Richardson.
Photo by John Loftus, Muckleshoot Monthly

MUCKLESHOOT LANGUAGE REVIVAL: A PROGRAM ESTABLISHED AND A DIRECTOR HIRED

In the continuing revitalization of the Muckleshoot language, the tribe announced on April 8, 2013, that Eileen Richardson had been hired as the first Muckleshoot Language Program Director. This move shows the tribe's determination and dedication to reuniting the people with their language. Eileen had previously served in the Muckleshoot Department of Education for thirteen years. From 2007 to the present, she worked as the Muckleshoot Language Specialist teaching language in all the MIT Early Childhood Education programs. From 2005-2007, she taught at the Muckleshoot Tribal School; from 2003-2005, she worked as a bus driver and classroom assistant for the MIT Birth to Three Program, and from 2000-2003, as an instructional assistant for the Muckleshoot Head Start Program. Eileen's entire professional career has been committed to achieving educational excellence for the Muckleshoot Indian Tribe.

REFERENCES

2004 Program Update: Muckleshoot Tribal Administration. Auburn, WA: Muckleshoot Indian Tribe, 2004.

2007 Guide to Tribal Programs and Annual Progress Report. Auburn, WA: Muckleshoot Indian Tribe, 2007.

Bond, Jeff. "Overnight Vigil Honors Muckleshoots' 'Kiyah.'" *Valley Daily News*, April 22, 1992, A-6.

"Doris Allen to Teach New In-Home Language Program." *Muckleshoot Monthly*, June 2001, 4.

Gong, E.J., Jr. "Reviving a Dying Tongue — Muckleshoots Hope Language Lessons Will Preserve Fading Culture." *Seattle Times*, August 7, 1996. [http://community.seattletimes.nwsource.com/archive/?date=19960807&slug=2343017]

Lacitis, Erik. "Last Few Whulshootseed Speakers Spread the Word." *Seattle Times*, February 8, 2005. [http://seattletimes.nwsource.com/html/localnews/2002173798_muckleshoot08m.html]

Lane, Bob. "Eva Mae Jerry; Focused on Saving Muckleshoot Language, Culture." *Seattle Times*, April 30, 1992. [http://community.seattletimes.nwsource.com/archive/?date=19920430&slug=1489202]

Our Children Are Our Future: Muckleshoot Indian Tribe. Annual Report to the Muckleshoot General Council. January 20, 1997.

Smith, Marian W. *The Puyallup-Nisqually.* (Columbia University Contributions in Anthropology, 32.) New York: Columbia University Press, 1940.

Starr, Donna. "Whulshootseed Language Being Taught at Head Start and VCEC [Virginia Cross Education Center]." *Muckleshoot Monthly*, May 15, 2008, 8.

Strosnider, Ann. "Working to Preserve a Culture: Muckleshoot Woman Receives Award from National Indian Education Group." Auburn *Daily Globe-News*, October 29, 1985, 1.

Suttles, Wayne. "The Recognition of Coast Salish Art," in Barbara Brotherton, ed. *S'abadeb, the Gifts: Pacific Coast Salish Art and Artists.* Seattle: University of Washington Press, 2008, 50-67.

Suttles, Wayne and Barbara Lane. "Southern Coast Salish," in Wayne Suttles, Ed. *Handbook of North American Indians: Northwest Coast.* Vol. 7. In William C. Sturtevant, General Ed. *Handbook of North American Indians.* Washington, D.C.: Smithsonian Institution, 1990, 485-502.

Waterman, T. T. *Puget Sound Geography.* Original manuscript from T. T. Waterman. Ed. with additional material from Vi Hilbert, Jay Miller, and Zalmai Zahir. Zahir Consulting Services, 2004. Copy in files of Muckleshoot Preservation Program Archives.

Selected Bibliography

2003 Program Update; Muckleshoot Tribal Administration. Auburn, WA: Muckleshoot Indian Tribe, 2003.

2004 Program Update: Muckleshoot Tribal Administration. Auburn, WA: Muckleshoot Indian Tribe, 2004.

2007 Guide to Tribal Programs and Annual Progress Report. Auburn, WA: Muckleshoot Indian Tribe, 2007.

2010 Annual Report: Muckleshoot Indian Tribe. Auburn, WA: Muckleshoot Indian Tribe, 2011.

"A.C. Ballard, Authority on Indians, Dies." *Seattle Times*, May 13, 1962, n.p.

Alexie, Arnold. "Florence 'Dossie' Wynne: Once Bitten, Twice Shy." *Muckleshoot Monthly*, February 2012, 3.

American Friends Service Committee. *Uncommon Controversy: Fishing Rights of the Muckleshoot, Puyallup, and Nisqually Indians.* Seattle: University of Washington Press, 1970.

Amoss, Pamela T. "The Indian Shaker Church," in Wayne Suttles Ed. *Handbook of North American Indians: Northwest Coast.* Vol. 7. In William C. Sturtevant, General Ed. *Handbook of North American Indians.* Washington, D.C.: Smithsonian Institution, 1990, 633-639.

Anderson, Rick. "Slade's Slate." *Seattle Weekly*, January 1, 2003, 13. (in LEXIS)

Annual Report 2000. Auburn, WA: Muckleshoot Indian Tribe, 2000.

Annual Report: Muckleshoot Tribal Council, January 20, 2003. Auburn, WA: Muckleshoot Indian Tribe, 2003.

Annual Report, Muckleshoot Tribal Council, Prepared for the Annual Meeting of the Muckleshoot General Council, January 17, 2005. Auburn, WA: Muckleshoot Indian Tribe, 2005.

Annual Report for 2006: Muckleshoot Tribal Council. Auburn, WA: Muckleshoot Indian Tribe, 2006.

Annual Report for 2007: Muckleshoot Indian Tribe. Auburn, WA: Muckleshoot Indian Tribe, 2007.

Annual Report, 2009: Muckleshoot Indian Tribe. Auburn, WA: Muckleshoot Indian Tribe, January 19, 2009.

Annual Report, Muckleshoot Tribal Council, Prepared for the Annual Meeting of the Muckleshoot General Council, January 17, 2005. Auburn, WA: Muckleshoot Indian Tribe, 2005.

Annual Report to the Muckleshoot Community. Auburn, WA: The Muckleshoot Tribe, January 26, 1995.

Archbold, Mike. "'People Are Going to Be Happy': Muckleshoots Eagerly Look Forward to Water, Sewer Systems," *Auburn Valley Daily News*, October 9, 1995, n.p.

Archbold, Mike. "Muckleshoot Tribe a Top Auburn Employer." *Valley Daily News* (Kent, WA), January 8, 1996, A-7.

Archbold, Mike. "Muckleshoots Buying Back Their Reservation Land." *South [King] County Journal*, February 4, 1997, A-7.

Archbold, Mike. "Auburn's History Shaped by Violence and Courage." *King County Journal*, October 28, 2005, A-1, A-15.

Asher, Brad. *Beyond the Reservation: Indians, Settlers, and the Law in Washington Territory, 1853-1889.* Norman: University of Oklahoma Press, 1999.

"Auburn Mayor Not Bullish on Muckleshoot Casino." *Seattle Times*, November 11, 1992. [http://community.seattletimes.nwsource.com/archive/?date=19921111&slug=1524094]

Aweeka, Charles. "Traffic Deaths Spur Muckleshoot Drive for Safety Measures on Highway 164." *Seattle Times*, February 14, 1991. http://community.seattletimes.nwsource.com/archive/?date=19910214&slug=1266240]

Aweeka, Charles. "50 March for Safer Highway: Muckleshoots Want Speed Limit Reduced." *Seattle Times*, February 28, 1991, B-4.

Ballard, Arthur C. "Some Tales of the Southern Puget Sound Salish." *University of Washington Publications in Anthropology* 2:3 (December 1927), 35-41; 57-81. Seattle: University of Washington Press, 1927.

Ballard, Arthur C. "Mythology of Southern Puget Sound." *University of Washington Publications in Anthropology* 3:2 (December 1929), 31-150. Seattle: University of Washington Press, 1929.

Ballard, Arthur C. "Southern Puget Sound Salish Kinship Terms." *American Anthropologist* 37:1 (January-March 1935), 111-116.

Ballard, Arthur C. "Calendric Terms of the Southern Puget Sound Salish." *Southwestern Journal of Anthropology* 6 (1950), 79-99.

Ballard, Arthur C. "Notes on Data Concerning Informants in Mythology of Southern Puget Sound, Vol. 3, No. 2, *University of Washington Publications in Anthropology*." May, 1949. Manuscript copy in Muckleshoot Preservation Program Archives.

Ballard, Arthur C. Testimony, Indian Claims Commission of the United States. *The Muckleshoot Tribe of Indians on Relation of Napolean Ross, Chairman of the General Council, Claimant, vs. The United States of America, Defendant*, Seattle, WA, November 26-28, 1951. 2 vols. (1 to p. 256; 2: 257-466).

Selected Bibliography

Ballard, Arthur C. "The Salmon Weir on Green River in Western Washington." *Davidson Journal of Anthropology* 3:1 (Summer 1957), 37-53. Copy in files of Muckleshoot Preservation Program Archives.

Bargala, Sonny. "The Passing of a Great Leader." *Muckleshoot Monthly*, February 2012, 3.

Bartley, Nancy. "Educator Honored for Tribal Activism." *Seattle Times*, June 17, 1999.
[http://community.seattletimes.nwsource.com/archive/?date=19990617&slug=2966998]

Bells, Myron. "Decrease of Population Among the Indians of Puget Sound." *American Antiquarian* 9:4 (September 1887), n.p.

Bells, Myron."The Religion of the Indians of Puget Sound." *American Antiquarian* 12:2 (March 1890), n.p.

"Bernice White." *Muckleshoot Monthly*, June 2009, 3

"Bernice White Park on Duwamish Is Dedicated." *Muckleshoot Monthly*, December 20, 2013, 1-2.

Bhatt, Sanjay. "Muckleshoots Buy Huge Forestland in 3 Counties." *Seattle Times*, November 6, 2013.
http://seattletimes.com/html/businesstechnology/2022202267_muckleshoottribepurchasexml.html

Bill, Willard, Sr. Unpublished Muckleshoot history files. 2005, unpaginated.

"Biologists Probe Fate of Last Year's Sockeye Run; Half of Run Failed to Reach Spawning Grounds Due to Freshwater Mortality; Fishing Prospects Grow Dimmer." *Seattle Times* in *Muckleshoot Monthly*, July 15, 2005, 4.

Bond, Jeff. "Overnight Vigil Honors Muckleshoots' 'Ki-yah.'" *Valley Daily News*, April 22, 1992, A-6.

Boyd, Robert. *The Coming of the Spirit of Pestilence: Introduced Infectious Diseases and Population Decline Among Northwest Coast Indians, 1774-1874*. Seattle: University of Washington Press/Vancouver: University of British Columbia Press, 2000.

Brodeur, Nicole. "Limelight? This Leader Won't Bask." *Seattle Times*, June 17, 2003.
[http://community.seattletimes.nwsource.com/archive/?date=20030617&slug=brodeur17m]

Brotherton, Barbara, ed. *S'abadeb, the Gifts: Pacific Coast Salish Art and Artists*. Seattle: University of Washington Press, 2008.

Brown, Bruce. *Mountain in the Clouds: A Search for the Wild Salmon*. New York: Simon & Schuster, 1982.
[http://www.astonisher.com/archives/mitc/mitc_ch1.html]

Brown, Larry. "4 Indians Convicted on Fishing Charge." *Seattle Times*, January 11, 1968, n.p.

Brown, Virginia. "Pre-School Controversy." *Muckleshoot News* 1:1 (May 1967), 5.

Burtchard, Greg C. "Holocene Subsistence and Settlement Patterns: Mount Rainier and the Montane Pacific Northwest." *Archaeology in Washington* 13 (2007), 3-44.
[http://www.nps.gov/mora/historyculture/upload/AIW-Burtchard2007.pdf]

Burtchard, Greg C. Mount Rainier National Park. Archaeology. U.S. National Park Service. May 27, 2011. Accessed September 10, 2011.
[http://www.nps.gov/mora/historyculture/archaeology.htm

"CAP Survey." *Muckleshoot Messenger*, 1:3 (July 1967), 6.

Carson, Jerry. "Indians Face Court Battle over Puyallup Fishing," *Seattle Times*, September 10, 1970, B-10.

Casavant, Vanessa Renee. "U.S., Canadian Coast Guards Offer Help with Future Canoe Journeys." *Peninsula Daily News*, July 27, 2006.
http://www.peninsuladailynews.com/apps/pbcs.dll/article?AID=2006607270305

Casavant, Vanessa Renee. "Canoe Victim's Personal Paddle to be Carried in his Honor to End of Journey." *Peninsula Daily News*, July 28, 2006, n.p.

"Casino a Big Winner Coming and Going." *Daily Journal of Commerce* (Seattle), October 31, 1995, n.p.

Caster, Dick. *Native American Presence in the Federal Way [Washington] Area*. Federal Way, WA: Historical Society of Federal Way, 2005. Copy in files of Muckleshoot Preservation Program Archives.

Castille, George Pierre. *The Indians of Puget Sound*. Seattle: University of Washington Press, 1985.

Chemawa American, Anniversary Number, 7:56 (March 3, 1905). Copy in files of Muckleshoot Preservation Program Archives.

"City of Auburn, Washington. 2009-2010 Biennial Budget." Prepared by Department of Finance. February 23, 2009. Accessed December 10, 2010.
[www.auburnwa.gov/Assets/Finance/AuburnWA/.../2009-10_Budget.pdf]

Clements, Barbara. "Muckleshoot Leader Dies in Boat Accident." *Valley Daily News*, October 22, 1986, A-2.

Cohen, Fay G. *Treaties on Trial: The Continuing Controversy over Northwest Indian Fishing Rights: A Report Prepared for the American Friends Service Committee*. Seattle: University of Washington Press, 1986.

"A Computer in Every Home." *Muckleshoot Monthly*, October 2003, 1.

Connor, Matt. "The Good Neighbor: The Muckleshoot Tribe's Gaming Enterprises Have Helped Foster Good Will with Local Communities." *Muckleshoot Monthly*, September 15, 2002, 3, 12. (Reprinted from *Indian Gaming Business*, a publication of the National Indian Gaming Association.)

Coolidge, Jane. "Head Start Impresses Federal Audit Team." *Muckleshoot Monthly*, July 2000, 7.

Cook, Sherburn F., Jr. "The Little Napoleon: The Short and Turbulent Career of Isaac Stevens." *Columbia* 14:4 (Winter 2000), 17-20.

"Court Move Could End Fishing Dispute." Tacoma *News-Tribune*, March 18, 1968, n.p.

Cross, Lorraine. *History of Puget Sound with a Viewpoint Towards Understanding What Has Happened to the Indians of the Muckleshoot Indian Reservation*. Paper presented for the B.A. degree, University of Washington, 1975.

Cross, Virginia and Patricia Slettvet Noel. *Muckleshoot Today*. Auburn, WA: Auburn School District no. 408, 1981.

"Cultural Program Steaming Ahead." *Muckleshoot Monthly*, May 2000, 6.

"Cultural Treasures Come Home to Muckleshoot." *Muckleshoot Monthly*, November 15, 2005.

D'Ambrosio, Antonino. *A Heartbeat and a Guitar: Johnny Cash and the Making of Bitter Tears*. New York: Nation Books, 2009.

"A Dance Festival Without a Single Jitterbug." *Seattle Times*, April 30, 1939, n.p.

Danelski, David. "Classic Canoe: Aging Muckleshoot Passes on Design, Technique of Dugout." *Valley Daily News*, July 13, 1989, A-1, A-4.

"Death Claims Arthur Ballard, Son of Prominent Auburn Pioneer Family." *Auburn Globe-News*, November 1962, n.p.

Deloria, Vine, Jr. "Conclusion: Anthros, Indians, and Planetary Reality," in Thomas Biolsi and Larry J. Zimmerman, eds. *Indians and Anthropologists: Vine Deloria, Jr. and the Critique of Anthropology*. Tucson: University of Arizona Press, 1997, 209-222.

"Denise Bill Earns UW Doctorate Degree." *Muckleshoot Monthly*, June 2012, 1.

Dickinson, Marke and Bill Wiggins. *A Single Acre, a Sovereign Effort: A Model for Muckleshoot Land-Use and Economic Development*. Cambridge, MA: Malcolm Wiener Center for Social Policy, John F. Kennedy School of Government, Harvard University, 1995.

"Did You Know?" *Muckleshoot News* 1:1 (May 1967), 7.

"Dr. Willard Bill Blazed a Trail for Others to Follow in the Field of Education." *Muckleshoot Monthly*, February 2008, 2.

"Doris Allen to Teach New In-Home Language Program." *Muckleshoot Monthly*, June 2001, 4.

Durham, Bill. "Canoes from Cedar Logs: A Study of Early Types and Designs." *Pacific Northwest Quarterly* 46:2 (April 1955), 33-39.

Durham, Bill. *Indian Canoes of the Northwest Coast*. Seattle: Copper Canoe Press, 1960.

"Early Childhood Education Center Celebrates Grand Opening." *Muckleshoot Monthly*, October 2010, 1.

Egan, Timothy. "New Prosperity Brings New Conflict to Indian Country." *New York Times*, March 8, 1998, A-1.

Egan, Timothy. "Debate About Tribal Rights Turns Rancorous." April 8, 1998. *New York Times*, April 8, 1998. [http://www.nytimes.com/1998/04/08/us/debate-about-tribal-rights-turns-rancorous.html]

Elmendorf, William W. *The Structure of Twana [Skokomish] Culture*. Pullman, WA: Washington State University Press, 1960.

Elmendorf, William W. *Twana Narratives: Native Historical Accounts of a Coast Salish Culture*. Seattle: UW Press/UBC Press, 1993.

Elmendorf, William W. and A.L. Kroeber. *Twana Culture, with Comparative Notes on the Structure of Yurok Culture*. Pullman, WA: WSU Press, 1992.

"Enumclaw School District Extends Agreement with Muckleshoot Tribal School." *Enumclaw Courier-Herald*, May 19, 2010.
http://www.courierherald.com/news/94273529.html]

"Enumclaw Schools Native American Program Receives Funding from Tribe." *Muckleshoot Monthly*, July 1, 2007, 1, 3.

"Even Start Grant Funded at $738,600." *Muckleshoot Monthly*, November 2000, 6.

"Explorers' Theft of Canoe to Be Made Right at Last." Associated Press in *Omaha World-Herald*, September 24, 2011, A-1, A-3.

Fabricant, Florence. "Food Stuff: A High Roller Gets a Break from a Casino." *New York Times*, August 14, 2002. [http://www.nytimes.com/2002/08/14/dining/food-stuff-a-high-roller-gets-a-break-from-a-casino.html]

"Famed Treaty Rights Attorney Walter Echo-Hawk Visits MIT." *Muckleshoot Monthly*, November 2012, 1.

"Farm Aid 2004 Heads to Seattle: Willie Nelson, Neil Young, John Mellencamp and Dave Matthews to Headline West Coast's First-Ever Farm Aid Benefit Concert." *Muckleshoot Monthly*, August 15, 2004.

Fey, Harold E., and D'Arcy McNickle. *Indians and Other Americans*. New York: Harper & Bros., 1959.

"Fire Destroys Muckleshoot Indian Hall." *Auburn Globe-News*, April 29, 1970, 1.

Flewelling, Stan, Farmlands: *The Story of Thomas, a Small Agricultural Community in King County, Washington*. Auburn, WA: Erick Sanders Historical Society, 1990.

"Florence 'Dossie' Wynne." *Muckleshoot Monthly*, February 2012, 3.

Food Sovereignty Project. Muckleshoot Indian Tribe. Accessed April 20, 2013.
[http://nwicplantsandfoods.com/muckleshoot]

Selected Bibliography

Fortier, James M., director. *Pulling Together*. Muckleshoot Indian Tribe. Turtle Island Productions, 2004. [Film]

Fortier, James M., director. *Gathering Together*. Muckleshoot Indian Tribe. Turtle Island Productions, 2007. [Film]

Foster, George. "Death's Highway: Tribe Wants Lower Speed Limit." *Seattle Post-Intelligencer*, February 14, 1991, B-1.

"Frederick 'Sonny' Woodruff: Quileute Elder Who Helped to Start Canoe Journey Dies." *Peninsula Daily News*, September 30, 2009.
[http://www.peninsuladailynews.com/apps/pbcs.dll/article?AID=2009309309983]

Garber, Andrew, and Linda V. Mapes. "GOP Sees Expanded Gambling As State Budget Solution." *Seattle Times*, December 5, 2011.
http://seattletimes.nwsource.com/html/localnews/2016943073_gambling06m.html]

"General Population and Housing Characteristics." U.S. Census, 1990. Muckleshoot Reservation. Washington State Office of Financial Management, 1991.
[http://www.ofm.wa.gov/pop/census1990/reservation/default.asp]

Gibbs, George. *Indian Nomenclature of Localities in Washington and Oregon Territories*, 1853, National Anthropological Archives Manuscript 714.

Gibbs, George. *Report on the Indian Inhabitants of Washington Territory, 1854*. Washington, D.C.: Smithsonian Institution, National Anthropological Archives. Ms# 2356.

Gibbs, George. *Indian Tribes of the Washington Territory, in United States War Department's Survey of Several Pacific Railroad Explorations*. Vol. 1. Washington, D.C.: War Dept., 1855. Reprint: Fairfield, WA: Ye Galleon Press, 1978.

Glance at a Valley: A History of the Native American in the Green River Valley. Auburn, WA: Auburn Public Schools, 1972.

Glover, H. J. "White Man, Red Making Amends: Muckleshoot Indians Await $3.5 Million Windfall from Uncle Sam." *Seattle Post-Intelligencer Pictorial Review*, August 4, 1957, 2.

Gong, E. J., Jr. "Reviving A Dying Tongue — Muckleshoots Hope Language Lessons Will Preserve Fading Culture." *Seattle Times*, August 7, 1996.
http://community.seattletimes.nwsource.com/archive/?date=19960807&slug=2343017]

Gong, Louie. "Tribal College Launches *The Muckleshoot Review*." *Muckleshoot Monthly*, July 2010, 9.

Gossett, Larry, and Janet Devlin. "Pro/Con — The Muckleshoot Amphitheatre Project." *Seattle Times*, November 13, 1997.
[http://community.seattletimes.nwsource.com/archive/?date=19971113&slug=2571967]

Green, Sara Jean. "Body Found After Muckleshoot House Fire; 3 Children Injured." *Seattle Times*, January 22, 2010.
http://seattletimes.nwsource.com/html/localnews/2008658954_webauburnfire22m.html]

"Green River Elk Augmentation – One Year Later." *Muckleshoot Monthly*, March 15, 2003, 8.

Grinde, Donald A., Jr. and Bruce E. Johansen. *Ecocide of Native America: Environmental Destruction of Indian Lands and Peoples*. Santa Fe, NM: Clear Light, 1994.

"Ground Is Blessed for New Muckleshoot Longhouse." *Muckleshoot Monthly*, March 15, 2012, 1, 10, 16.

Haeberlin, Herman, and Erna Gunther. *The Indians of Puget Sound*. Seattle: University of Washington Press, 1952.

Hancock, Samuel. *The Narrative of Samuel Hancock: 1845-1860*. New York: R.M. McBride and Co., 1927.

Harmon, Alexandra. *Indians in the Making: Ethnic Relations and Indian Identities Around Puget Sound*. Berkeley and Los Angeles: University of California Press, 1998.

Heffter, Emily. "Tribes Becoming Political Players with Casino Cash." *Seattle Times*, November 17, 2003.
http://community.seattletimes.nwsource.com/archive/?date=20031117&slug=tribes17m]

Heffter, Emily. "Willard Eugene Bill Sr., 69, Was Influential Indian Educator; Served on UW [University of Washington] Faculty." *Seattle Times*, January 2, 2008.
[http://seattletimes.nwsource.com/cgi-bin/PrintStory.pl?document_id=2004103445&zsection_id=2003925728&slug=billobit02m&date=20080102]

Hess, Thom. *Dictionary of Puget Salish*. Seattle: University of Washington Press, 1976.

Hess, Thom. "A Comparison of Marine and Riverine Orientation Vocabulary in Two Coast Salish Languages." *Anthropological Linguistics*, November 1979, 363-378.

"Hit-and-Run Driver Kills Teen; Basketball All-Star Hoped to Attend UW [University of Washington]." *Muckleshoot Monthly*, May 2001, 3.

Hogans, Mack L. "Huckleberry Exchange Was in the Public Interest." *Seattle Times*. October 7, 1998.
[http://community.seattletimes.nwsource.com/archive/?date=19981007&slug=2776188]

Hunt, Herbert and Floyd C. Kaylor. *Washington West of the Cascades*. Chicago: S.J. Clarke, 1917.

"Indian Treaty Trek Linked to Trial of 4 Muckleshoots." *Auburn Citizen*, May 18, 1966, 1.

"Indians to Form Own Housing Authority." *Auburn Globe-News*, February 12, 1971, 1.

James, Bob, John Newhauken, Frank Ross, Joe Hill, George Jack, and Walter Davis. Letter to Commissioner of Indian Affairs, May 15, 1916, in Patricia Slettvet Noel and Virginia Cross, *Muckleshoot Indian History*, Auburn, WA: Auburn Public School District No. 408, 1980, 101.

"James Fortier: The Award-Winning Filmmaker Behind 'Pulling Together.'" *Muckleshoot Monthly*, March 15, 2004, 1-2.

Jeffords, Edd. "White Man's Poverty Trap Holds Muckleshoot Indians in Misery." Tacoma *News-Tribune*, May 5, 1968, A-1, A-15, A-16.

Jeffords, Edd. "'Uncle Alex' — His Primitive Tackle Gets the Big Ones." Tacoma *News-Tribune*, May 6, 1968, n.p.

Jeffords, Edd. "Muckleshoot Preschool Prepares Tots for Burgeoning Education." Tacoma *News-Tribune*, May 12, 1968, n.p.

Jeffords, Edd. "Muckleshoots Hold All the Cards So Street in Auburn Still Unbuilt, Paleface Outfoxed." Tacoma *News-Tribune*, June 4, 1970, C-7.

"Jeannette Brown (Morrison) Miller." *Muckleshoot Monthly*, July 2010, n.p.

Johansen, Bruce and Roberto Maestas. *Wasi'chu: The Continuing Indian Wars*. New York: Monthly Review Press, 1979.

Johansen, Bruce E. and Donald A. Grinde, Jr. *The Encyclopedia of Native American Biography*. New York: Henry Holt, 1997.

Johansen, Bruce E. "The New York Oneidas: A Case Study in the Mismatch of Cultural Tradition and Economic Development." *American Indian Culture & Research Journal* 26:3 (2002), 25-46.

Johnson, Ralph W. "The States Versus Indian Off-reservation Fishing: A United States Supreme Court Error." *Washington Law Review* 47:2 (1972), 207-236.

Johnson, Robert. "Muckleshoots May Get $3,500,000 for Land 'Taken.'" *Auburn Globe-News*, Thursday, May 23, 1957, n.p.

Josephy, Alvin M., Jr. *Now That the Buffalo's Gone: A Study of Today's American Indians*. New York, Knopf, 1982.

"Julia John Siddle: Family History." Draft manuscript in Muckleshoot Preservation Program Archives, n.d.

Jung, Helen E. "Computers, 'Canoes' Pass on Traditions — Muckleshoot School Brings History to Life." *Seattle Times*, May 10, 1993. [http://community.seattletimes.nwsource.com/archive/?date=19930510&slug=1700545]

Kappler, Charles J., Comp. and Ed. I*ndian Affairs: Laws and Treaties*. Washington, D.C.: G.P.O., 1904-1941. 5 v., volume 2.

Keefe, Tom, Jr., "A Tribute to David Sohappy," *Native Nations*, June/July 1991, 4-6.

King George, Gilbert. "Journey to France: Searching for the Father I Never Knew." *Muckleshoot Monthly*, November 2011, 1.

Kluger, Richard. *The Bitter Waters of Medicine Creek: Western Washington's Indian Wars*. New York: Knopf, 2011.

LaBranche, Janet. [untitled] *New Journal Globe News*, March 14, 1984, D-1.

Lacitis, Erik. "Last Few Whulshootseed Speakers Spread the Word." *Seattle Times*, February 8, 2005. [http://seattletimes.nwsource.com/html/localnews/2002173798_muckleshoot08m.html]

LaClair, Leo. "Muckleshoot Fishing Rights Question: A Seminar Paper." Seattle: Law Library, University of Washington, 1971.

LaClair, Leo and Ralph Whitney Johnson. "Termination in Disguise." Seattle: University of Washington School of Law, 1972.

Lane, Barbara. "Memorandum: On Usual and Accustomed Fishing Places." Photocopy of manuscript in Muckleshoot Preservation Program Archives. n.d.

Lane, Barbara. "Anthropological Report on the Traditional Fisheries of the Muckleshoot Indians." October 6, 1972. Typescript in Muckleshoot Preservation Program Archives.

Lane, Barbara. "Political and Economic Aspects of Indian-White Culture Contact in Western Washington in the Mid-Nineteenth Century." May 10, 1973. Typescript in Muckleshoot Preservation Program Archives. (1973a)

Lane, Barbara. "Anthropological Report on the Identity and Treaty Status of the Muckleshoot Indians." U.S. District Court, Tacoma, WA. Plaintiff's exhibit No. USA-270, *United States v. Washington*, admitted to the record August 24, 1973. (1973b)

Lane, Barbara. "Background of Treaty Making in Western Washington." *American Indian Journal* 3/4 (1977), 2-11.

Lane, Barbara. "The Muckleshoot Indians and the White River: A Report Prepared for the Muckleshoot Indian Tribe." September 1980. In Muckleshoot Preservation Program Archives.

Lane, Bob. "Eva Mae Jerry: Focused on Saving Muckleshoot Language, Culture." *Seattle Times*, April 30, 1992. [http://community.seattletimes.nwsource.com/archive/?date=19920430&slug=1489202]

LaVatta, George P. To Commissioner of Indian Affairs, Washington, D.C. [regarding visit to Muckleshoot reservation, November 24, 1939]. December 13, 1939. Typescript in Muckleshoot Preservation Program Archives.

Lazzar, Delilah. "'Broken Chains' Shares Maori Culture." *Muckleshoot Monthly*, February 2001, 6.

"LBJ Gets Muckleshoot Land Payment Measure." *Auburn Globe*, September 18, 1968, n.p.

Leach, Leah. "Makah to Welcome 100 Canoes Today." *Peninsula Daily News*, July 19, 2010. [http://www.peninsuladailynews.com/apps/pbcs.dll/article?AID=2010307199990]

Leovy, Jill. "Louis 'Doc' Starr, 92, Chosen Chief and Master of Ancient Tribal Arts." *Seattle Times*, July 3, 1991. [http://community.seattletimes.nwsource.com/archive/?date=19910703&slug=1292515]

Selected Bibliography

"Levi Hamilton: Tribal Chairman of the Muckleshoots, Embodiment of Hope." Auburn *News-Journal*, May 4, 1975, 5.

Lewis, Peter B. "The High Costs of a Killer Road." *Seattle Times*, October 1, 2003. [http://community.seattletimes.nwsource.com/archive/?date=20031001&slug=highway01]

Lincoln, Leslie. *Coast Salish Canoes*. Seattle: Center for Wooden Boats, 1991.

Lobehan, Morris, to Edward F. Teague, July 15, 1936. Copy in files of Muckleshoot Preservation Program Archives.

Loftus, John. "A Brief History of *The Muckleshoot Monthly*, and Other Things…" *Muckleshoot Monthly*, May 15, 2008, 16.

Logelin, Michael G., DDS. "Muckleshoot Dental Clinic Opens." *Muckleshoot Messenger*, April 1976, 4.

"Logs for Carving Canoes." *Muckleshoot Monthly*, March 15, 2006, 1.

MacDonald, Patrick. "Ozzfest 2003 to Rock Muckleshoot Arena." *Seattle Times*, February 25, 2003. [http://community.seattletimes.nwsource.com/archive/?date=20030225&slug=ozzfest27]

Makah Indian Tribe v. Schoettler 192 F. 2d 224 at 226 (9th Circuit) (1951)

"Making Cedar Hats." *Muckleshoot Monthly*, February 2001, 17.

"Making the Case for Muckleshoot Treaty Rights." *Muckleshoot Monthly*, July 2012, 12.

Mapes, Lynda V. "Washington Tribes Invest Casino Proceeds by Sending Members to College." *Seattle Times*, November 3, 2002. [http://community.seattletimes.nwsource.com/archive/?date=20021103&slug=yale03m]

Mapes, Lynda V. "Tribe Buys Racetrack Property in Auburn." *Seattle Times*, November 26, 2002. [http://community.seattletimes.nwsource.com/archive/?date=20021126&slug=emerald26m]

Mapes, Lynda V. "Once Invisible, Muckleshoots Are Now an Economic Force." *Seattle Times*, November 27, 2002. [http://community.seattletimes.nwsource.com/archive/?date=20021127&slug=tribe27m]

Mapes, Lynda V. "Green Light for Muckleshoot Amphitheater." *Seattle Times*, March 25, 2003. [http://community.seattletimes.nwsource.com/archive/?date=20030325&slug=mucks25m]

Mapes, Lynda V. "Teaching the Teachers: In a New Kind of Indian Education, Lessons for Us All." *Seattle Times, Pacific Northwest Magazine* / Cover Story. November 5, 2004. [http://community.seattletimes.nwsource.com/archive/?date=20041105&slug=pacific-pindianed07]

Mapes, Lynda V. "Tribe Counting on New Facility to Lift Members' Overall Health." *Seattle Times*, October 17, 2005. [http://community.seattletimes.nwsource.com/archive/?date=20051017&slug=health17m]

Mapes, Lynda V. "Tribes Are State's New High Rollers — In Business." *Seattle Times*, February 17, 2008. [http://seattletimes.nwsource.com/html/localnews/2004186688_tribes17m.html]

Mapes, Lynda V. "Fish-Camp Raid Etched in State History." *Seattle Times*, September 6, 2010. [http://seattletimes.com/html/localnews/2012827306_fishwar07m.html]

Marino, Cesare. "History of Western Washington Since 1846," in Suttles, Wayne, Ed. *Handbook of North American Indians: Northwest Coast*. Vol. 7. In William C. Sturtevant, General Eds. *Handbook of North American Indians*. Washington, D.C.: Smithsonian Institution, 1990, 169-179.

Marr, Carolyn J. "Objects of Function and Beauty: Basketry of the Southern Coast Salish." In Barbara Brotherton, ed. *S'abadeb, the Gifts: Pacific Coast Salish Art and Artists*. Seattle: University of Washington Press, 2008, 198-225.

Martin, Joseph J. "Dear Members of the Muckleshoot Community." *Muckleshoot Monthly*, September 2009, 17.

Martin, Joseph J. "Graduations 2010: MIT Takes a Giant Step Forward." *Muckleshoot Monthly*, July 2010, 1.

Martin, Joseph J. "Graduations 2011: MIT Enjoys Another Excellent Graduation Season." *Muckleshoot Monthly*, August 2011, P-1.

Martin, Joseph J. "Joseph Martin Hired [as] Program Development Coordinator for Tribal College." *Muckleshoot Monthly*, April 15, 2002, 7.

Martinez, Regino. "Roberto Maestas Interviews: The History of El Centro de la Raza."Seattle, WA: 2004. Transcribed by Kristina Cook, 2010.

McCloud, Janet and Robert Casey. *The Last Indian War*. Seattle: Seattle Group Bulletins, No. 29 and 30, 1968. Mimeographed. In El Centro de la Raza archives.

McDermott, Terry. "The Land Is the Muckleshoots', So Get Used to It." *Seattle Times*, December 16, 1997. [http://community.seattletimes.nwsource.com/archive/?date=19971216&slug=2578369]

McIlveen, Gladys. "The Annual Report of the Muckleshoot Reservation: December 1, 1932-November 30, 1933." Mimeograph in Muckleshoot Preservation Program Archives.

McIlveen, Gladys. "Community Organization on the Muckleshoot Indian Reservation." Social Work 254a, Dr. Clara Kaiser, July 16, 1937. Institution not specified. Student paper, photocopy in files of Muckleshoot Preservation Program Archives.

McMaster, Luci. "Muckleshoot Bingo Celebrates Quarter-Century." *Muckleshoot Monthly*, May 15, 2010, 1-2.

Meany, Edmond. *Origin of Washington Geographic Names*. Seattle: University of Washington Press, 1923.

Meeker, Ezra. *Pioneer Reminiscences of Puget Sound: The Tragedy of Leschi*. New York: Lowman & Hanford Stationery and Print. Co. 1905.

Miller, Dossie. "Law Enforcement Meeting." *Muckleshoot Messenger*, September 1967, 2.

Miller, Dossie. "Cemetery." *Muckleshoot Messenger*, June 1968, 8.

Miller, Jay. *Shamanic Odyssey: The Lushootseed Salish Journey to the Land of the Dead*. Menlo Park, CA: Ballena Press, 1988.

Milne, Noreen. "My Aunty, Virginia Cross." Muckleshoot Monthly, April 15, 2002, 4.

Minard, Anne. "Food Empowerment: The Muckleshoot Tribe Reintroduces Traditional Fare." *Indian Country Today in Muckleshoot Monthly*, March 15, 2012, 8.

"MIT Gets 'Cheers' from the *South County Journal*". *Muckleshoot Monthly*, July 2000, 1.

"More News." *Muckleshoot News*, May 1967, 5.

Morgan, Murray. *Skid Road: An Informal History of Seattle*. New York: Viking Press, 1952.

"Morning Fire Destroys House, Displaces 11 on Muckleshoot Reservation." *Seattle Times*, March 16, 2010. [http://seattletimes.nwsource.com/html/localnews/2011358101_auburnfire16m.html]

"Mt. Tacoma" in *Commemorative Celebration at Sequalitchew Lake, Pierce County, Washington, July 5, 1906*. Second Ed. Pierce County Historical Association, 33–34. Copy in files of Muckleshoot Preservation Program Archives, 93–95.

"Muckleshoot Celebrates Educational Achievement," *Muckleshoot Monthly*, June 15, 2002, 1.

Muckleshoot Family Reunion, 2003. Auburn, WA: Muckleshoot Tribe, 2003.

"A Muckleshoot Gem." [Editorial] *Seattle Times*, June 14, 2005. [http://community.seattletimes.nwsource.com/archive/?date=20050614&slug=mucked1]

"Muckleshoot Honors Barbara Lane; B.C. Anthropologist's Expert Testimony Helped Persuade Judge Boldt to Rule in Favor of Tribal Treaty Rights." *Muckleshoot Monthly*, April 15, 2006, 1-2, 11.

The Muckleshoot Indian Tribe. Auburn, WA: The Muckleshoot Tribe, 1999.

"Muckleshoot Indian Tribe Gives Back to Communities." Muckleshoot Indian Tribe, April 29, 2010. [http://www.muckleshoot.nsn.us]

Muckleshoot Indian Tribe v. U.S. Forest Service and Weyerhaeuser Co, 177 F.3d 800 (1999) 99 Cal. Daily Op. Serv. 3724, 1999 Daily Journal D.A.R. 4767. Order of Ninth Circuit Court of Appeals, March 10, 1999. [http://ftp.resource.org/courts.gov/c/F3/177/177.F3d.800.98-35231.98-35043.html]

Muckleshoot Reservation and Off-Reservation Trust Land: Selected Social Characteristics. American Fact Finder. U.S. Census Bureau. 2005–2009. [www.census.gov/geo/www/tsap2010/tsap2010_tdsa.pdf]

"Muckleshoot Revenues Soar with Gambling." Portland *Oregonian*, January 21, 1996, n.p. (In LEXIS).

"Muckleshoot Theater Decried." *Seattle Times*, November 29, 1997. [http://community.seattletimes.nwsource.com/archive/?date=19971129&slug=2575144]

"Muckleshoot Treaty Trek Is Historic Indian Event: LaClair." Auburn *Globe-News*, May 18, 1966, 1, 11.

Muckleshoot Tribal Council: Annual Report for 2007. Auburn, Muckleshoot Indian Tribe, January 21, 2008.

"Muckleshoot Tribe Establishes Higher Education Scholarship Program; $175,000 Pledged to Washington Universities, Community and Technical Colleges." Muckleshoot Tribal e-Newsletter, June 2012, 1.

"Muckleshoot Tribe Gives $5,000 to St. Vincent de Paul to Help Prevent Evictions and Hunger in Seattle and King County." *Auburn Reporter*, February 3, 2011, n.p.

"Muckleshoot Tribe's Revenues Soar with Gambling." *Daily Journal of Commerce* [Seattle], January 11, 1996, n.p.

"Muckleshoots Invest Nearly $3 Million in the State." *Auburn Reporter*, April 17, 2009. [http://www.pnwlocalnews.com/south_king/aub/community/43122972.html]

Murakami, Kerry. "Opponents of Theater Counting on Corps — Hundreds Attend Hearing on Muckleshoot Project." *Seattle Times*, March 28, 1998. [http://community.seattletimes.nwsource.com/archive/?date=19980326&slug=2741699]

Nalder, Eric, Deborah Nelson, and Alex Tizon "The Muckleshoots — HUD Program Undermined, While Many Remain in Shacks." *Seattle Times*, December 1, 1996. [http://community.seattletimes.nwsource.com/archive/?date=19961201&slug=2362670]

Native American Canoes: Paddle to Seattle, 1989. Washington State Centennial, 1989.

"Native Legal Advocates Continue Fight With New Beat." Native American Rights Fund. May 8, 2007. [http://narfnews.blogspot.com/2007/05/tribal-organization-using-hip-hop-to.html]

"Native Poet from Chile Visits Tribal School; A Visit from Elicura Chihuailaf, Mapuche Poet, of Temuco, Chile." *Muckleshoot Monthly*, November 15, 2002.

"Neah Bay Packed and Prepared for Arrival of Tribal Canoe Journey." *Peninsula Daily News*, July 20, 2010. [http://www.peninsuladailynews.com/apps/pbcs.dll/article?AID=2010307209994]

Selected Bibliography

Neel, David. *The Great Canoes: Reviving a Northwest Coast Tradition.* Seattle: University of Washington Press, 1995.

"New Muckleshoot Casino II Open for Business." *Muckleshoot Monthly*, September 25, 2006, 1.

"New VISTAs Arrive." *Muckleshoot Messenger*, March/April 1968, 1.

"No Sockeye Season This Year." *Muckleshoot Monthly*, July 15, 2005, 4.

Noel, Patricia Slettvet and Virginia Cross. *Muckleshoot Indian History.* Auburn, WA: Auburn School District No. 408, 1980.

Norton, Dee. "Federal Suit Attacks Indian-Fishing Laws," *Seattle Times*, September 19, 1970, A-4.

Oliver, Emmett. "Reminiscences of a Canoe Puller," in Robin K. Wright, ed. *A Time of Gathering: Native Heritage in Washington State.* Seattle: Burke Museum/University of Washington Press, 1991, 248-253.

Ollikainen, Rob. "Makah Welcome Tribal Canoe Journey to Neah Bay." *Peninsula Daily News*, July 20, 2010. [http://www.peninsuladailynews.com/apps/pbcs.dll/article?AID=2010307209995]

"Opponents, Tribal Members Split Over Proposed Amphitheater." *Daily Journal of Commerce* [Seattle], September 24, 1999. [http://www.djc.com/news/business/10058538.html]

Our Children Are Our Future: Muckleshoot Indian Tribe. Annual Report to the Muckleshoot General Council. January 20, 1997.

"Overview: The Muckleshoot Indian Tribe." Accessed January 3, 2010. [http://www.muckleshoot.nsn.us/about-us/overview.aspx]

Parman, Donald L. *Indians and the American West in the Twentieth Century.* Bloomington: Indiana University Press, 1994.

Parriott, Breann. "Muckleshoot Project Blends Culture with Design: Philip Starr Building Reflects Tribe's Relation to Nature" *Daily Journal of Commerce* [Seattle], November 20, 2003. [http://www.djc.com/news/ae/11151123.html]

Pemberton-Butler, Lisa. "Huge Day for Muckleshoot School: Its First Two Grads." *Seattle Times*, June 19, 2001. [http://community.seattletimes.nwsource.com/archive/?date=20010619&slug=muckleshoot19m]

Perkins, Kathryn Alvord. *Hunting Stories, Indian Legends and Other Writings of Irving Thomas Alvord.* Napa, California, July 1990.

Peters, Jessica Louise. *Casinoization of Native American Cultures: Destruction or Creation of the "Authentic" Indian?* Thesis (M.A.) University of Washington, Seattle, 1997.

"Physical Yield of Washington State Salmon Fisheries, 1989-1974, " in Russel L. Barsh, *The Washington Fishing Rights Controversy: An Economic Critique.* Monograph Series, University of Washington Graduate School of Business Administration, 1977.

Ponnekanti, Rosemary. "Celebration Connects Tribes, Boats and More at Tacoma Art Museum." Tacoma *News-Tribune*, January 27, 2012. [http://www.thenewstribune.com/2012/01/27/2001039/dock-at-tam.html#storylink=misearch]

"Positive Alternatives to Gangs: 'As Warriors for Peace, We Can Change the World'" *Muckleshoot Monthly*, June 15, 2006, 3.

"Premiere Showing of New MIT Film Set for April 20: Feature-Length Documentary Tells Story of 2003 Canoe Journey." *Muckleshoot Monthly*, March 15, 2004, 1, 3.

"President Obama's Secretary of Health & Human Services Visits Muckleshoot Tribe." *Muckleshoot Monthly*, March 2011, 1-2.

"Puyallup River Indian Camp Destroyed by Bulldozers," *Seattle Times*, September 11, 1970, E-7.

Puyallup Tribe v. Department of Game 391 U.S. 392 (1968).

Rakestraw, Charles D. "The Shaker Indians of Puget Sound." *Southern Workman* 29 (December 1900), 704.

Ramon-Sauberan, Jacelle. "Inside the Muckleshoot Veterans Pow Wow." *Indian Country Today*, July 3, 2011. [http://indiancountrytodaymedianetwork.com/2011/07/inside-the-muckleshoot-veterans-pow-wow]

Ratliff, Pat. "50-Canoe Flotilla Mukilteo-Bound: I Hope This Will Give the City Some Perspective." Mukilteo [Washington] *Beacon*, July 18, 2007. (in LEXIS)

Reifert, Butch. "Tribal Schools Expand Role Preserving Native Cultures: New Designs Focus on Symbolism, Tribal Rituals and Eco-Friendly Features." *Daily Journal of Commerce* [Seattle], August 28, 2008. [http://www.djc.com/news/co/11203987.html?query=Muckleshoot&searchtype=all]

"Report on Indian Inhabitants of Washington Territory," National Anthropological Archives Manuscript 2356. Washington, D.C.: Smithsonian Institution. No date.

"Reservation Left out of First Phase of SR-164 Study; High-Accident Roadway Splits Muckleshoot Land for 4 miles from Auburn to Enumclaw." *Muckleshoot Monthly*, July 2000, 2. Reprinted from the *South County Journal.*

"Resolution." *Muckleshoot Messenger*, August 1967, 1.

Reyes, Lawney. *White Grizzly Bear's Legacy: Learning to be Indian.* Seattle: University of Washington Press, 2002.

Richards, Kent D. "Agrarianism, United States Indian Policy, and the Muckleshoot Indian Reservation." In William L. Lang, ed. *Centennial West: Essays on the Northern Tier States.* Seattle: University of Washington Press, 1991, 39-58.

Richey, Warren. "Unregulated High-Stakes Gambling Grows on American Indian Reservations." *Christian Science Monitor*, March 25, 1985, 1. (in LEXIS)

Rolph, Amy. "Willard Bill, 1938-2007: Tribal Historian Never Stopped Teaching." *Seattle Post-Intelligencer*, January 3, 2008. [http://www.seattlepi.com/local/345986_obitbill04.html]

Rommel, Bruce. "Tribe's Plan for Bingo Hall Draws Protest." Auburn *Globe*, September 18, 1984, 1.

Ruby, Robert H. and John A. Brown. *John Slocum and the Indian Shaker Church*, Norman: University of Oklahoma Press. 1996.

Rupert, Ray. "Houses Find a Home on Reservation." *Seattle Times*, n.d., A-1.

"Salish Canoes Lead Seattle Yacht Club Opening Day Boat Parade." Press Release, Seattle Yacht Club, in *Muckleshoot Monthly*, May 15, 2011, 4.

Sarvis, Will. "Deeply Embedded: Canoes As an Enduring Manifestation of Spiritualism and Communalism Among the Coast Salish." *Journal of the West* 42:4 (2003), 74-80.

Scanlon, Tom. "Flirt with the Odds or Hit the Dance Floor at Muckleshoot." *Seattle Times*, February 11, 2010. [http://seattletimes.nwsource.com/html/entertainment/2002176626_muck11.html]

Segrest, Valerie. and June Kloubec. *Feeding the People, Feeding the Spirit: Revitalizing Northwest Coastal Indian Food Culture*. Bellingham, WA: Northwest Indian College, 2009.

"Shots Fired, 60 Arrested in Indian-Fishing Showdown," *Seattle Times*, September 9, 1970, A-1.

Shreve, Bradley. *Red Power Rising: The National Indian Youth Council and the Origins of Native Activism*. Norman: University of Oklahoma Press, 2011.

Skolnik, Sam. "Tribe Targets Gaming Woes; Muckleshoots Donate to Help Problem Gamblers." *Seattle Post-Intelligencer*, June 11, 2004, B-1.

Smith, Allan H. *Takhoma: Ethnography of Mount Rainier National Park*. Pullman, WA: Washington State University Press, 2006.

Smith, Marian W. *The Puyallup-Nisqually*. (Columbia University Contributions in Anthropology, 32.) New York: Columbia University Press, 1940.

Smith, Marian W. "The Coast Salish of Puget Sound." *American Anthropologist* 43:2 (1941) [new series], 197-211.

Smith, Sherry L. *Hippies, Indians, and the Fight for Red Power*. New York: Oxford University Press, 2012.

Sneatlum, Lisa. "20th Annual Muckleshoot Easter Weekend Stickgame Event." *Muckleshoot Monthly*, May 15, 2011, 18.

Sneatlum, Shirley. "Skopabsh Committee Report." *Muckleshoot Messenger*, April 1976.

Sneddon, James O. "Out of This World: A Study of the Indian Shakers at the Muckleshoot Reservation." *Anthropology* 210, November 1960. No school indicated; probably University of Washington. Copy in files of Muckleshoot Preservation Program Archives.

Splawn, Andrew J., *Kamiakin — Last Hero of the Yakimas* [1917]; reprinted, Caldwell, Idaho: Caxton Printers, 1944, 1980.

Starr, Donna. "Whulshootseed Language Being Taught at Head Start and VCEC [Virginia Cross Education Center]" *Muckleshoot Monthly*, May 15, 2008, 8.

Starr, Marie. Letter to the *Muckleshoot Messenger*, September 1967, 3.

Starr, Marie. "Home Visitor." *Muckleshoot Messenger*, October 1967, 3.

<u>State of Washington v. Moses 1963-1967, citations:</u>
County:
No. 609180 (King Co. Super. Ct, filed Nov. 4, 1963.
Washington Supreme Court:
State v. Moses 70 Wash 2d 282,286,422 P.2d 775, 778.
U.S. Supreme Court:
Cert denied 389 U.S. 428 (1967).

State of Washington v. Satiacum 314 P.2d 400.

State [of Washington] *v. Tulee* 7 Wash. 2d 124, 109 P.2d 280 (1941) (en banc).

"Statue of Muckleshoot Elder Big John to Be Unveiled September 21 at Auburn Museum." *Muckleshoot Monthly*, September 5, 2003, 16.

Stein, Alan J. "The Echo of Distant Drums: Large Tribal Gathering Held at Juanita in 1933." 2007. Bellevue College typescript in Muckleshoot Preservation Program Archives.

Stewart, Hilary. *Indian Fishing: Early Methods on the Northwest Coast*. Seattle: University of Washington Press, 1923.

Stout, Gene. "Heart Is Ready to Rock and Roll Up the Curtain at White River." *Seattle Post-Intelligencer*, June 13, 2003, What's Happening, 7.

Strosnider, Ann. "Working to Preserve a Culture: Muckleshoot Woman Receives Award from National Indian Education Group." Auburn *Daily Globe-News*, October 29, 1985, 1.

Suckley, G, "Report Upon the Fisheries Collected on the Survey: Report Upon the Salmonidae." In *Reports of the Explorations...1854. The Pacific Railroad Report*. Washington, D.C.: Thomas H. Ford, 1860.

Suttles, Wayne. "Spirit Dancing and the Persistence of Native Culture Among the Coast Salish, " in Suttles, ed., *Coast Salish Essays*. Vancouver, B.C.: Talonbooks and Seattle: University of Washington Press, 1987, 199-208.

Suttles, Wayne. *Coast Salish Essays*. Vancouver, B.C.: Talonbooks and Seattle: University of Washington Press, 1987.

Selected Bibliography

Suttles, Wayne, Ed. *Handbook of North American Indians: Northwest Coast.* Vol. 7. Washington, D.C.: Smithsonian Institution, 1990.

Suttles, Wayne and Barbara Lane. "Southern Coast Salish," in Wayne Suttles, Ed. *Handbook of North American Indians: Northwest Coast.* Vol. 7. In William C. Sturtevant, General Ed. *Handbook of North American Indians.* Washington, D.C.: Smithsonian Institution, 1990, 485-502.

Swan, James G. *The Northwest Coast: Or, Three Years' Residence in Washington Territory.* [1857] Seattle, University of Washington Press, 1972.

"Talk by Chief Slugamus Koquilton" in Commemorative Celebration at Sequalitchew Lake, Pierce County, Washington, July 5, 1906. Second Ed. Pierce County Historical Association, 33-34. Copy in files of Muckleshoot Preservation Program Archives.

Taylor, Herbert C. "Aboriginal Populations of the Lower Northwest Coast," *Pacific Northwest Quarterly* 54:4 (October 1963), 160-163.

Taylor, Herbert C. *Aboriginal Populations of the Lower Northwest Coast in Rolls of Certain Tribes in Oregon and Washington.* Fairfield, Washington: Ye Galleon Press, 1969.

Taylor, Herbert C. "Anthropological Investigation of the Medicine Creek Tribes Relative to Identity and Aboriginal Possession of Lands, Coast Salish and Western Washington Indians." *American Indian Ethnohistory: Indians of the Northwest.* New York: Garland Press, 1974, 401-475.

Tazioli, Terry. "A Look at Salish Lodge, Snoqualmie Falls' High-end Hideaway." *Seattle Times*, May 10, 2007. http://seattletimes.com/html/outdoors/2003698889_nwwsalish100.html]

"Terann Hoptowit Killed by Hit-and-Run Driver." *Muckleshoot Monthly*, October 2010, 22.

"Things You Should Know About Clam Digging." *Muckleshoot Monthly*, May 15, 2008, 19.

Thrush, Coll. *Native Seattle: Histories from the Crossing-Over Place.* Seattle: University of Washington Press, 2007.

Tizon, Alex. "The Boldt Decision: 25 Years — The Fish Tale That Changed History." *Seattle Times*, February 7, 1999. [http://community.seattletimes.nwsource.com/archive/?date=19990207&slug=2943039]

Tollefson, Kenneth D. "Remembering the Old Ways: Louis Starr's Reflections on Traditional Indian Subsistence Living." *Columbia: The Magazine of Northwest History*, 7:3 (Fall 1993), 13-6.

Transcript of Proceedings, *U.S. v. Washington* 384 F. Supp. 312 (Western District of Washington, 1974). Civ. No. 9213.

"Treaty Between the United States, and the Dwamish [sic], Suquamish, and Other Allied and Subordinate Tribes of Indians in Washington Territory." January 22. 1855. Reproduced 1966 by the Shorey Bookstore, Seattle, WA.

"The Treaty Sesquicentennial: Treaty Wars, 150 Years Ago." *Muckleshoot Monthly*, October 15, 2005, 20. Reprinted from the *White River Journal*, newsletter of the White River Historical Museum.

"Treaty Rights Champion Barbara Lane Passes On." *Muckleshoot Monthly*, February 15, 2014, 1.

"Tribal Canoe Journey to Neah Bay Prepares to Get Underway." *Muckleshoot Monthly*, June 15, 2010, 4.

"Tribal Leaders Pave Way for Brighter Future." *Valley Daily News* (Kent, WA), January 10, 1996, n.p.

"Tribal Meeting." *Muckleshoot Messenger*, November 1967, 1.

"Tribal Meeting Held." *Muckleshoot News* 1:1 (May 1967), 10.

"Tribal School Receives Accreditation." *Muckleshoot Monthly*, June 2011, 1.

"Tribe Adds New Features to Amphitheatre Plan." *Muckleshoot Monthly*, February 2002, 2.

"Tribe Gets Approval for Sewer, Water System." *Seattle Times*, May 16, 2000. [http://community.seattletimes.nwsource.com/archive/?date=20000516&slug=4021210]

"Tribe Goes Fishing." *Muckleshoot Monthly*, July 15, 2000, 1, 12.

"Tribe Makes History with First Muckleshoot-Brand Sockeye." *Muckleshoot Monthly*, July 15, 2004, 2.

"Tribe's Request Advances." *Seattle Times*, March 24, 2000. [http://community.seattletimes.nwsource.com/archive/?date=20000324&slug=4011774]

"Tribes Win on License Plates." Associated Press in *New York Times*, July 25, 1985. [http://www.nytimes.com/1985/07/25/us/tribes-win-on-license-plates.html]

Trumbly-Lamsam, Teresa and Bruce E. Johansen. "How the Osages Kept Their Oil," in Bruce E. Johansen, ed. *Enduring Legacies: Native American Treaties and Today's Issues.* Westport, CT: Praeger, 2004, 271-282.

Tuinstra, Rachel. "Muckleshoot "Grandma Iola" Loved Life, Tribe." *Seattle Times*, October 7, 2005. [http://community.seattletimes.nwsource.com/archive/?date=20051007&slug=billobit07e]

Tulee v. Washington 315 U.S. 681 (1942).

Tyler, Ron. "Mount Rainier, Volcano Hazards, and the Osceola Mudflow." Enumclaw Plateau Historical Society, March 2002. Copy in files of Muckleshoot Preservation Program Archives.

Underhill, Ruth. *Indians of the Pacific Northwest.* Washington, D.C.: U.S. Department of the Interior/Bureau of Indian Affairs Branch of Education, 1944.

Selected Bibliography

U.S. Census 2000, Summary File 3. Muckleshoot Reservation. Washington State Office of Financial Management. September 17, 2002.
[http://www.ofm.wa.gov/pop/census1990/reservation/default.asp]

"U.S. Census: Muckleshoot Reservation and Off-reservation Trust Land."
[http://www.docstoc.com/docs/8099238/Muckleshoot-Reservation-and-Off-Reservation-Trust-Land-WA] Accessed September 1, 2010.

U.S. Commission on Civil Rights. "Fishing in Western Washington — A Treaty Right, a Clash of Cultures," 61–100 in *Indian Tribes, a Continuing Quest for Survival: A Report of the United States Commission on Civil Rights.* Washington: U.S. Government Printing Office, 1981.

United States v. Washington: 384 F. Supp. 312 (1974).

United States v. Winans 198 U.S. 371 (1905).

Vales, David. "Hunting Update: Status of Elk Herds." *Muckleshoot Monthly*, November 2000, 16.

Vancouver, George. *A Voyage of Discovery to the North Pacific and Around the World.* 3 vols. London: G.G. and J. Robinson, 1798.

Varner, Lynne K. "Culture Clash Along The White River — Rural Residents Say Lifestyle Threatened by Muckleshoots' Plans for Amphitheater." *Seattle Times*, November 9, 1997.
[http://community.seattletimes.nwsource.com/archive/?date=19971109&slug=2571252]

Varner, Lynne K. "Tribal-Immunity Issues Debated — A Hearing on Sen. Slade Gorton's Proposal to End Protection From Lawsuits Draws A Spirited Response." *Seattle Times*, April 8, 1998.
[http://community.seattletimes.nwsource.com/archive/?date=19980408&slug=2744020]

Varney, Val. "Muckleshoots Get a New Health Clinic." *Seattle Times*, November 28, 1984, n.p.,

"Veterans Are Honored." *Muckleshoot Monthly*, November 2011, 1.

"Virginia Cross Inducted into Auburn H.S. Hall of Fame." *Muckleshoot Monthly*, June 2012, 1.

Walker, Richard. "Friend of Coast Salish People Dies." *Indian Country Today*, May 30, 2005, n.p.

Walker, Richard. "John Daniels, Jr. Named to Seattle Magazine's 'Most Influential' List." *Indian Country Today*, January 30, 2006, n.p.

Wallace, James. "Muckleshoots Betting on Casino to Better Their Lot." *Seattle Post-Intelligencer*, September 9, 1995, B-1.

Ward v. *Race Horse* 163 U.S. 504 (1896)

Washington Passenger Fishing Vessel 443 U.S. 658 (1979).

Waterman, T. T. "Names of Places on the Shore of Puget Sound near Seattle." *Geographical Review* 12:2 (1922), 175–194.

Waterman, T. T. "The Geographical Names Used by the Indians of the Pacific Coast," *Geographical Review* 12 (1922), n.p.

Waterman, T. T. *Notes on the Ethnology of the Indians of Puget Sound.* (Indian Notes and Monographs, Misc. Series No. 59.) New York: Museum of the American Indian/Heye Foundation, 1973. Ms. completed in 1921, but not published until 1973.

Waterman, T. T. *Puget Sound Geography*. Original Manuscript from T. T. Waterman. Ed. with Additional Material from Vi Hilbert, Jay Miller, and Zalmai Zahir. Zahir Consulting Services, 2004. Copy in files of Muckleshoot Preservation Program Archives.

Waterman, T. T. "Puget Sound Geography." Washington DC: National Anthropological Archives, mss. [n.d.]

Waterman, T. T. and Geraldine Coffin. *Types of Canoes on Puget Sound.* (Indian Notes and Monographs, Misc. Series No. 5.) New York: Museum of the American Indian, Heye Foundation, 1920.

Waterman, T. T. and Ruth Greiner. *Indian Houses of Puget Sound.* Indian Notes and Monographs. New York: Museum of the American Indian, 1921.

Watson, Kenneth G. (Greg). *Mythology of Southern Puget Sound: Legends Shared by Tribal Elders*, reprint of the 1929 publication. Recorded, translated, and edited by Arthur C. Ballard. North Bend, WA: Snoqualmie Valley Historical Museum, 1999.

Watson, Kenneth G. (Greg). "Arthur C. Ballard: A Good Neighbor to the Muckleshoot People." White River Valley Museum in *Muckleshoot Monthly*, October 12, 2007, 8.

Welch, Craig. "U.S. to Buy Back Part of Huckleberry Mountain." *Seattle Times*, November 20, 2001.
[http://community.seattletimes.nwsource.com/archive/?date=20011121&slug=huckleberry21m]

Westneat, Danny. "Farewell to the Old Chief: Tribes Pay Respects to Muckleshoot Leader." *Valley Daily News*, July 4, 1991, A-1, A-5.

Westneat, Danny. "Muckleshoot Tribe Rises from Ashes of 1970 Fire." *Seattle Times*, July 26, 1995.
[http://community.seattletimes.nwsource.com/archive/?date=19950726&slug=2133476]

Westneat, Danny. "Tribes Target Gorton with Casino Money." *Seattle Times*, April 4, 1999.
[http://community.seattletimes.nwsource.com/archive/?date=19990404&slug=2953279]

Westneat, Danny. "Tribe Made Its Gamble Pay Off." *Seattle Times*, September 10, 2004.
[http://community.seattletimes.nwsource.com/archive/?date=20040910&slug=danny10]

Selected Bibliography

Westneat, Danny. "'Indian Pilgrimage' Reaches Beach in Triumph and Tiredness." *Seattle Times*, August 1, 2006. http://community.seattletimes.nwsource.com/archive/?date=20060801&slug=danny01m]

Westneat, Danny and Jim Simon. "Move to Tax Casino Profits Angers Native Americans." *Seattle Times*, November 19, 1995. [http://community.seattletimes.nwsource.com/archive/?date=19951119&slug=2153442]

Whale, Robert. "Tribe Opens Doors to New, Expansive School." *Auburn Reporter*, September 9, 2009. [http://www.pnwlocalnews.com/south_king/aub/news/58196072.html]

Whale, Robert. "Dream Comes to Life for Tribe: New School Officially Opens." *Auburn Reporter*, September 10, 2009. [http://www.pnwlocalnews.com/south_king/aub/news/58207197.html]

Whale, Robert. "Local Author Paul Nelson Tells of 'A Time Before Slaughter.'" *Auburn Reporter*, July 1, 2010. [http://www.pnwlocalnews.com/south_king/aub/community/97622364.html]

"White River Massacre Takes Lives of Nine Pioneers." *Kent News-Journal*, August 3, 1939, 7.

Wickersham, Hon. James. ""Is it Mount Tacoma, or Rainier?" *Proceedings of the Tacoma Academy of Sciences*. Tacoma: News Publishing Co., 1893. Copy in files of the Muckleshoot Preservation Program Archives.

Widrig, Charlotte. "Auburn's Collector of Indian Myths." *Seattle Times Sunday Magazine*, September 21, 1952, 5.

Wilkins, David E., ed. *The Hank Adams Reader: An Exemplary Native American Activist and the Unleashing of Indigenous Sovereignty*. Golden, CO: Fulcrum, 2011.

Wilkinson, Charles F. *Messages from Frank's Landing: A Story of Salmon, Treaties, and the American Way*. Seattle: University of Washington Press, 2000.

Wilkinson, Charles F. *The People Are Dancing Again: A History of the Siletz Tribe of Western Oregon*. Seattle: University of Washington Press, 2010.

"Willard Bill Jr. Appointed as Seattle School Director of Indian Education." *Muckleshoot Monthly*, September 15, 2005, 10.

Williams, John H. *The Mountain That was God*. New York: J.P. Putnam's Sons, 1911.

Wilma, David. "Tacoma Police Arrest 60 Persons at a Fish-In on September 9, 1970." HistoryLink. August 25, 2000. Accessed January 2, 2010. [http://historylink.org/index.cfm?DisplayPage=output.cfm&file_id=2625]

Woods, Fronda. "Who's in Charge of Fishing?" *Oregon Historical Quarterly* 106:3 (Fall 2005), 412–441.

Wright, Robin K., ed. *A Time of Gathering: Native Heritage in Washington State*. Seattle: Burke Museum/University of Washington Press, 1991.

Yardley, William. "A Northwest Journey by Canoe to Reconnect with the Old Ways." *New York Times*, July 25, 2011, A-9, A-12.

Ziontz, Alvin J. *A Lawyer in Indian Country: A Memoir*. Seattle: University of Washington Press, 2009.

Index

A
Adams, Hank 108, 116, 119
Addiction-recovery center .... xviii, 180
Allen, Doris, and language revival 249
Allotment Act 67
    and land loss 68
    See also: Dawes Act
Amphitheatre, White River
    construction of 161, 189, 193
    Farm Aid concert at 193-194, 201
    environmental impact statements 189-190, 193
    opening of .... xiii, 150, 193
    as sovereignty issue 187, 189
Ancestral range, Muckleshoot .... viii, 2-3, 8, 11, 39, 45, 102-103, 142
Auburn (Washington) ....
    vii, x, xii-xiii, xvii, 4, 7-8, 10, 28-29, 36, 46, 48, 50-51, 55, 63, 65, 68, 70-72, 82, 85-86, 88, 91, 93, 95-97, 110, 120, 126, 132, 152, 154-155, 157, 160, 167, 170, 172, 176, 182, 189-190, 193, 196, 205, 230, 233, 239, 247, 250
    schools .... x, 45, 89, 126, 157, 186, 219, 223, 228, 230-231, 236, 238-239, 247-248

B
Ballard, Arthur C. 48
    early life in Auburn 70-71
    Indian Claims Commission testimony 70, 73-74, 193
    interviews of Muckleshoot elders 15, 70-71, 73, 75
    myths and stories .... ix, 43, 70, 75-76
    skills as linguist 72, 245
    vocabulary of language 70
Bargala, Sonny 86, 95, 98, 183
Baskets 3, 6-7, 13, 16, 27, 29, 76, 82, 88, 96
    manufacture of 25-26, 222
    materials used for 6, 25-26
"Battle of Seattle" .... viii, 52-54
Belloni, Robert C. 117
Berry harvesting tools 7, 18
Bill, Denise .... xxi-xxii, 220-221
Bill, Willard, Jr. .... xix, xx-xxii, 212
Bill, Willard, Sr. .... xvi, xix, xx, xxii, 13, 29, 44, 55, 86, 88-89, 126, 139, 204, 206, 221, 224, 244, 249
Bingo, at Muckleshoot .... xi, xv, 149-155, 167, 170, 177, 185, 219
Boarding schools .... ix, 203, 223-228, 236-237
    assimilation and 203, 223-224, 236-237
    Chemawa Indian School .... ix, 224-227
    Native languages banned 223, 227
    St. George Indian School .... ix, 224, 227-228
    teaching methods and
        courses described 224-227

Boldt, George H. .... xi-xii, xvi, 41, 116-117, 119-123, 138
    See also: *United States v. Washington* (1974)
Brando, Marlon .... x, 107-108, 113
Brannan, William (in "Treaty War") 47, 50
Buchanan, Charles (resident farmer) 66, 79

C
Canoes
    manufacture of 7, 22-25
    revival of canoe manufacture 201, 203-205, 210
    spiritual aspects 23, 202, 206-207, 211
    trade, and 29
    types of 23-24
    See also: Tribal Canoe Journey
Casino, Muckleshoot .... xi, xvi, 45
    community contribution tax 157
    description of 155-156
    economic development and 148, 152, 160-161, 172
    education, use of proceeds (profit) for .... xii, xvii, 154, 175, 218-219, 235
    employment at 154, 161, 176
    enlargement of 155-156
    grants to community from 156-157
    poverty, alleviation of ....xii, 148, 152, 154, 157, 170, 173
    problem gambling, funds for 157-158
    taxes proposed on 159-160
    types of gaming at 156
    urban location, advantages of 148, 166
    use of proceeds ...... xvii, xiii, 133, 148-149, 153, 156, 170-171, 177, 179, 191
Cedar, uses of
    Canoes 23-24, 110, 203-204, 213
    Clothing 18-21, 204, 213, 222
    Housing 18, 27-28, 170, 222
Census statistics, re: Muckleshoot.... 39, 65, 67-68, 73, 193-194
Clark, Helen, on Shakers 79
Clothing, Muckleshoot ancestors 19-21
Community Hall
    construction of .... x, 83-84, 87-88
    destruction by fire .... x, 93-94, 171
    role as meeting place .... x, 83-84, 87-88
Coughenour, John C. 193
Courville, Chester 183
Courville, LeRoy 114, 139
Cosmology, and water's spiritual nature 9-10, 30-31, 206
Cradleboards 88, 222-223
Cross, Virginia
    in Auburn High School Hall of Fame 239

Index

canoe journey, observations 207
educational revival, role in 238
as Muckleshoot tribal chairwoman 153, 171, 230, 236, 245

D Daniels, John, Jr. ..... xvi-xvii, 75, 154, 158, 167, 219
Daniels, John, Sr. 201, 244
Dawes Act 67, 68
Deem, Peg 206
Deloria, Vine, Jr. 41, 125
Devlin, Janet 189
Dillon, Denise 235
Diseases, imported
  Measles .... vii, 38-39
  populations, reduction of .... vii-viii, 38-39, 62, 85, 245
  smallpox .... vii, 37-39, 62, 85
  See aslo: Epidemics, imported diseases
Dobyns, Henry 37
Donation Land Claims Act 40
Douglas, William O. 117, 119
Drexel, Katharine .... ix, 227
Dunn, Jennifer 190
Duwamish .... vii, 3, 26, 39, 43, 46, 68, 75-76, 96, 120-121, 132, 135, 245-246

E Early Childhood Education Center, Muckleshoot 219, 234
Echo-Hawk, Walter xix
Economic development
  alleviation of poverty 148, 152-153, 170
  fireworks stands 166
  great changes in a short time 166-168
  Muckleshoot as national example 164-166
  working with a plan 168-170
Edenshaw, Gary (Guujaaw) 202
Education, at Muckleshoot
  accreditation achieved 221-222
  Antioch University, ties with 220, 234
  as Muckleshoot priority 154, 218
  boarding schools .... ix, 203, 223-228, 236-237
  casino's role in funding .... xii, xvii, 154, 177, 218-219, 235
  contrast to boarding schools 228, 236
  cultural exchanges world-wide 234-235
  curricula in local public schools influenced 236-237
  employment in Muckleshoot schools ... 168, 231
  Evergreen State University, ties with 234
  graduation statistics 210-211
  Head Start, early start at Muckleshoot ...... x, xiii, 89, 228-230
  Inter-local agreement with Enumclaw School District 219
  Joseph Martin's role in 219, 231
  new school complex ed, 2009 .... xiii, 219, 231-234
  Northwest Indian College, ties with 178-179
  "seamless pathways" 219-221
  scholarships, college .... xviii, 235-236
  traditional educational methods ... 222-223, 228
  Virginia Cross' role 238-239
El Centro de la Raza (Seattle) ...... xv, 111, 167, 235
Elders' Senior Center, at Muckleshoot .... xiii, 179-180, 204
Elk, rebuilding of herd 140
Emerald Downs .... xii, 161, 166-167, 171-172
Epidemics, imported diseases
  measles epidemics .... vii, 38-39
  reduction of Native populations .... vii-viii, 38-39, 62, 85, 245
  smallpox, description of effects 37-38
  smallpox, spread of .... vii, 37-39, 62, 85

F Father Hylebos 227
First arrival, Muckleshoot ancestors 4-5
First Salmon Ceremony 13, 41, 136
Fish traps, design and use of 14-17, 102-103
Fishing
  Muckleshoot ancestral range .... viii, 2-3, 8, 39, 102-103
  traps: design and use 14-17, 102-103
  drying and smoking 14, 28
  First Salmon Ceremony 13, 41, 136
  fleet rebuilt after Boldt Decision 132-133
Fishing-rights protests
  Hank Adams in 108
  "fish-ins" and "sit-ins" .... x, 108
  level of intensity rises in late 1960s to 1970 106-110
  role in filing of *U.S. v. Washington*, 1970 118
Fonda, Jane .... x, 107
Food cultivation, Muckleshoot
  advocated by U.S. government 62-63
  burning of forests, pre-contact 17-18
  Food Sovereignty Project, Muckleshoot ... 178-179
  harvests of berries and herbs 18-19
  statistics, 1930s 65
Forlines, David 200
Fortier, James M. 207-208, 211
Fox Island Conference (1856) .... viii, 54-55
Frank, Billy, Jr. 109-111, 119

G Gambling, pre-contact 27
Gibbs, George 39-41, 43-44, 52, 246
Gorton, Slade
  defeat in U.S. Senate race, 2000 .... xii, 185, 189-190
  opposes fishing rights .... xi, 123, 187, 191
Gossett, Larry 189
Gregoire, Christine .... xvii, 231, 239
Gregory, Dick .... x, 107, 113
Gunther, Erna 19, 30, 82, 96, 228, 245

H Hamilton, Levi .... xix, 133

Health and Wellness Center, Muckleshoot ....xiii, xvii-xviii, 84, 176-79
Head Start
   early start at Muckleshoot ... x, xiii, 89, 228-230
   See also: Education, at Muckleshoot
Herbal remedies...........18-19, 95-98, 180, 192, 251
Hess, Thomas...246
Hillaire, Darrell..168
Homeland, Muckleshoot ancestors. described...2-4
Hoptowit, Terann...187
Housing
   conditions in past, described 173-175
   for Muckleshoot elders.....................xv, xviii, 176
   housing pledged for everyone 175-176
Huckleberry Mountain Land Exchange.......141-143
Hunting
   Muckleshoot ancestral range.....viii, 2-3, 11, 39, 102, 142
   drying of deer and elk jerky 18

I Immigration, European-American..... vii, 2, 36, 203
   to Puget Sound, 1850-1920............ vii, 29, 36-37
   railroads, role of ....viii, 42, 56, 62-63, 188
Indian Tom (Wiletchtid)................................. 48, 74

J Jack, Annie, and Shakers 79-80
Jack, Andrew ("Jerry")....................................213
Jerry, Eva...90-91, 246-248
Johnson, Marie, and language revival 249-250
Johnson, Ralph............................ 108, 119, 126, 160
Jones, Harvey and Eliza, in "Treaty War" 47, 49

K Keta Creek hatchery...............................132
King George, Gilbert (Hoagie)....xix, 111, 139, 144, 148, 166, 181-182, 248
Kinnikinnick (Indian tobacco) 19
Koquilton, Slugamus 36, 49, 66

L Lacitis, Erik 244
LaClair, Leo ....xix, 110, 126-127
Land, purchases of .... xii-xiii, 90, 169-173, 176
Lane, Barbara........................... 3, 8, 20, 125
   fishing-rights cases, role in........xi, 44, 55, 105, 115-116, 120-121, 137
   returns to Muckleshoot, 2006 124-125
Language reclamation
   canoe journeys' role in 211, 248
   cultural revival, and 201
   Donna Starr's role in 249-250
   grant to develop resources at Muckleshoot 248
   schools' role in..................................231-233
   Whulshootseed classes 250
   Whulshootseed type font 249
Leschi 43
   conviction and hanging of......................... 56-57
   exoneration..58
   "Treaty War," role in ....viii, 46-47, 50-52, 54

Longhouses
   Bedding 28
   central fire 28
   cooking spaces...28
   Interior space, uses of 27-28
Lowry, Mike 152

M Maestas, Amalia xxv
Maestas, Roberto ....xv, 112, 167, 234
Martin, Joseph..............................219-221, 231
McAllister, James.................................. 47, 51
McClellan, George B................................40
McDermott, Terry 190
McEvers, Chuck..126
McIlveen, Gladys................................ 81-83
Meeker, Ezra 19, 49, 84, 102
Miller, Dossie (Wynne) 88, 91, 97-98, 180
Minor, Edwin (Indian agent, Neah Bay) 79
Minthorn, Faith 250
Morgan, Murray..39
Moses (Ealachin), in "Treaty War"........................49
Moses family
   and fishing-rights protests .... x, 116
   and fishing litigation............................115-116
Moses, Harold 153, 245, 250
Moses, Stanley ... x, 115-116, 127, 136, 139, 161, 172
Mount Rainier (Tahoma)......xvi, 2-5, 140-141, 171, 178, 193, 219, 233
   Osceola mudflow .... vii, 4-5
"Muckleshoot" adopted as name (1860s) viii
"Muckleshoot," definition of word ..43-45, 70, 120
Muckleshoot Messenger........................ x, 88-92, 184
Muckleshoot reservation
   established and enlarged ....viii, 55-56, 63
   lands lost, after allotment...............viii-ix, 67-69
Muckleshoot Seafood Products 133-134
Muckleshoot Tribal School...............................xiii
   architecture described 233
   opening, 2009....................................219, 231-233
   size of buildings and grounds.......................219
Muckleshoots
   as a treaty tribe................. viii, 21, 44, 106, 116, 120-121, 124-125
   fishing rights, and ....viii-xii, xv-xvi, 41-42, 44, 62, 88, 90, 92-93, 97, 102-104, 107, 110-112, 114-116, 118, 121, 126
   Point Elliott Treaty, and......... viii, 41, 44-46, 55, 69, 115, 120-121
Muckleshoot v. Forest Service......................142-143
Myths and stories, by Arthur C. Ballard .... ix, 43, 75-77

N National Indian Youth Council (NIYC).......108, 126
Nelson, Louis ("Curley"), in "Treaty War" 48
Nesika Club ....x, 73
   Role in building community hall................ 81-83
Northern Pacific Railroad...................... 40, 55, 141

Index

O Oliver, Emmett 204, 215

P Pacheco, Walter 136, 212
Paisley, Gregg 154
Pasqua, Parker Maria 215
"Per capita" payments .... xvii, 90, 177
Philip Starr Building .... xiii, 154, 161, 178
Pierce, President Franklin 54-55
Place names, used by Muckleshoot
    ancestors 8-9
Population density,
    disease, role of, in reduction 37-39
    Native Americans, pre-contact 2
    reduction, 1850-1920, reasons for 37-39
Point Elliott Treaty .... viii, 41, 43-46, 50, 52,
    55-56, 68-70, 110, 115, 121, 126-127, 141
Police force, Muckleshoot .... xii, 154
Populations, reduced by imported diseases ...... vii, 37-39
Poverty, elements of, at Muckleshoot ix
    employment, lack of 85-86
    federal poverty programs, 1960s 84, 86-87
    services, lack of 84-85
    stereotypes and 85
    "War on Poverty" 90, 161
Property System, water-centric character 8-10
Puget Sound Salish (Lushootseed) 245
    Dictionaries of 246
    studies of 246
    variety of words for salmon 246
"Puyallup I" 116-117
"Puyallup II" 117

Q Quiemuth (Leschi's brother) 47, 54, 57

R Rafeedie, Edward .... xii, 138
Railroads, role in immigration .... viii, 42, 56, 62-63, 190
Rainier, Peter 3
Reid, Bill, and revival of canoe culture 202
Remains, monitoring of 144
Roegner, Bob 152, 167
Rosellini, Albert 108

S Salish Lodge 169-170
Salmon fishery
    abundance of 102
    central role in economy and diet 10, 102, 114, 223
    decline in catch following white
        immigration .... x, 105-106
    Native peoples barred from fishing 104
    role in treaties .... xi, 41, 103-104, 110, 114, 117, 119-120, 122
Sapir-Whorf hypothesis 244
Sam, Benjamin Ronald 185-186
Sarvis, Will 23, 203, 206
Satiacum, Bob 106, 108

Scholarships, for Muckleshoot
    students .... xviii, 235-236
Seasons, names for 13
Sebelius, Kathleen 180
Settlements, Muckleshoot
    ancestors .... vii, 26-27, 39
Sewer and water system, at
    Muckleshoot 170, 175
Shakers
    debate over use of the Bible 80
    government attempts to restrict 79
    healing, experiences described 79-80
    John Slocum, role in 77-78
    new Shaker church 176-177
    services, described 78-81
Shellfish, treaty rights and .... xii, 136-138
Shellfishery, Muckleshoot, on
    Vashon Island 138-139
Shreve, Bradley 108
Siddle, Julia John 96
Skopeamish 44, 52
Sla-hal games 27, 148-149
Slaughter, William Alloway
    in "Treaty War" 50-51
    town (later Auburn) named for him 51
Slocum, John, role in Shakers 77-78
Smulkamish .... viii, 44, 52, 120
Smith, Lyle 118
Smith, Marian W. 18, 27, 30, 32
Social structure, Muckleshoot ancestors ... 6, 26-27
Sockeye salmon, rise and fall of 134-136
Spearfishing 14, 17, 114
Spirituality
    drumming sticks 32
    "power," or spirits, role of 30-31
    rank and prominence in society 30
    revival, recently .... xiii, 206
    sla-hal games, and 32
    sweat lodge, role of 31, 206
Starr, Donna
    language revival role 244-245, 248-249, 251
Starr, Louis "Doc" 95, 97, 195, 205-206
Starr, Marie
    as *Muckleshoot Messenger* editor 89
    as tribal council member .... x, 89, 173, 234
Starr, Marvin ("Cubby") 95, 195, 205-206
Starr, Philip 23, 49, 97, 195
    See also: Philip Starr Building
State v. Courville 137-138
State Highway 164
    "Deadman's Corner" 184
    fatal accidents on (killer road) 184-186
    Hoptowit, Terann, death of 187
    Sam, Benjamin Ronald, death of 185-186
State v. Towessnute (1916) .... ix, 104
State of Washington v. Moses 44, 116, 120-121
Stevens, Isaac
    treaties, as negotiator .... viii, 39-40, 103, 116

"Treaty War," role in 46, 52-53
Stkamish 26, 44
Suttles, Wayne 20, 30, 77, 116
"supercitizens" 123
Survival of American Indians
  Association 97, 109

T Trade,
  and intermarriage 16, 29, 49, 75
  and Muckleshoot ancestors .... vii, 3, 11, 14, 28-29
  routes of 14, 28-30, 36
Trail of Broken Treaties (1972) 127
Treaties
  dates and places signed .... viii, 41, 45, 119
  fishing rights incorporated .... viii, ix, xi, xvi, 41, 43-45, 50, 62, 103-104, 110, 114, 117, 119-120, 122-123
  importance of 41
  Point Elliott Treaty, provisions 68
  problems with process 41-43
  provisions of 44, 46, 68
  retention of homelands, and .... viii, 2-4, 41, 102
"Treaty Trek," (1966) 109-110
"Treaty War"
  battles and ambushes described 46-54
  grievances, Point Elliott Treaty 46, 52
  Klickitats in .... viii, 47
  Leschi, role of .... viii, 46-47, 50-52, 54
  Muckleshoot ancestors in .... viii, 46, 49
  Nisquallys in .... viii, 46, 52
  Yakamas in .... viii, 46, 52
Tribal Canoe Journey
  in British Columbia 201-202
  canoe families 201
  described, on the water 209-210
  Emmett Oliver's role 204, 215
  Lower Elwha Tribe hosts, 2005 211
  "Paddle to Seattle," 1989 .... xi, xviii, 200, 204-206, 215
  Quinaults host, 2013 215
  Makahs host, 2010 214-215
  Muckleshoots host, 2006 .... xiii, 200-201, 208, 211-214
  revival of language and culture 209, 211-212
  spiritual aspects of 206-207, 210-211
Tribal College, Muckleshoot .... xvii-xviii, xx-xxii, 177, 201, 218-219, 231, 233-234, 245, 249-251
Tulee v. Washington (1941) 106, 119

U *United States v. Washington*
  ("Boldt Decision," 1974) .... viii, xi, xvi, 44, 97, 102, 105, 114, 116-125, 136-137
  appeals, affirmations 123-124
  backlash to 123-124
  precursors 117, 137
  provisions and limits of 122-123
  U.S. Supreme Court upholds ..... xi, 106, 123-124
United States v. Winans (1905) 106, 119

V Vancouver, George 3, 38
Veterans, importance of at Muckleshoot ... 182-184
VISTAs (Volunteers in Service to
  America), at Muckleshoot .... x, 86-87, 89-91

W Walterskirchen, F.A. 44, 114
*Washington v. Washington State
  Commercial Passenger Fishing
  Vessel Association* 124
Waterman, T. T. 6-8, 14, 18, 22-24, 28, 44, 72-73, 116, 245, 248
Water treatment on Muckleshoot
  reservation .... xviii, 178, 189
Webster, John (assistant farmer) 63
White, Bernice
  and Shakers 80
  as Muckleshoot leader ... 86-87, 110, 121, 125, 137
Whulshootseed (Muckleshoot language) ... 248, 250
Wickersham, James 3
Williams, Charlotte 158, 232-233
Williams, Ellen (Bena) 250
Woodruff, Frederick ("Sonny") 213-214
Woodworking
  canoes 23
  tools 3, 6, 21

Z Ziontz, Alvin 104-105, 110, 119, 121, 124

Mount Tahoma (Rainier)
Photo by John Loftus, Muckleshoot Monthly